Software Rights

Software Rights

How Patent Law Transformed Software Development in America

Gerardo Con Díaz

Yale UNIVERSITY PRESS/NEW HAVEN & LONDON

Published with assistance from the income of the Frederick John Kingsbury Memorial Fund and with assistance from the foundation established in memory of Philip Hamilton McMillan of the Class of 1894, Yale College.

Yale University Press books may be purchased in quantity for educational, business, or promotional use. For information, please e-mail sales.press@yale.edu (U.S. office) or sales@yaleup.co.uk (U.K. office).

Set in Adobe Garamond and ITC Stone Sans type by IDS Infotech.
Printed in the United States of America.

Library of Congress Control Number: 2019935201
ISBN 978-0-300-22839-7 (hardcover : alk. paper)

A catalogue record for this book is available from the British Library.

This paper meets the requirements of ANSI/NISO Z39.48-1992 (Permanence of Paper).

10 9 8 7 6 5 4 3 2 1

Para mis padres,

Gerardo Con Sanchún y Dora Díaz Castro,

con mucho amor

Contents

Acknowledgments

This book was made possible by the support of many people and institutions. First, I am grateful to my mentor, Daniel Kevles, who showed me how to be a scholar and helped me transform every aspect of my life. Naomi Lamoreaux has made an extraordinary difference in how I think and write, and Mario Biagioli has pushed me to be bold and intellectually ambitious. Nathan Ensmenger and Jeffrey Yost introduced me to the history of computing as an academic discipline, and their support and critiques have been vital to my work. Steven Usselman's incisive and generous comments were essential to this project's development. The peer reviewers that Yale University Press recruited for the proposal and manuscript prompted me to think deeply and carefully. My editor, Joe Calamia, helped this book become exactly what I hoped that it would be, and Laura Jones Dooley and Mary Pasti helped me prepare the manuscript for publication.

The STS Program at UC Davis is the perfect place to develop an interdisciplinary project like this one. The STS faculty—Mario Biagioli, Patrick Carroll, Tim Choy, Marisol de la Cadena, Joe Dumit, Jim Griesemer, Tim Lenoir, Emily Merchant, Colin Milburn, Lindsay Poirier, and Kriss Ravetto-Biagioli—inspired me to question and refine almost every aspect of this project. Nicole Kramer and Constance Suen helped me manage and organize my research budgets and professorial commitments. The ModLab, which Colin Milburn directs, is a thriving community for digital studies. There, Stephanie Boluk, Kriss Fallon, and Patrick Lemieux broadened my methodological horizons, and Ranjodh Dhaliwal and Katherine Buse showed me that the next generation of digital scholarship is in good hands. The ModLab also connected me with wonderful undergraduate interns: Chris Andoh, Andreas Godderis, Ashley Han, Kacey Huang, Karla Quezada, and Bohan Xiao. Also at UC Davis, Martin Kenney and Daniel Stolzenberg helped me find an intellectual outlet for my many interests.

This book benefited greatly from many conversations, conferences, and workshops over the years. At the Hoover Institution's IP² Working Group, Steven Haber, Naomi Lamoreaux, and Richard Sousa created a space for discussion and critique that helped me refine some of the book's most important arguments. The Center for the Protection of Intellectual Property at George Mason University, previously led by Adam Mossoff, gave me a unique opportunity to engage with IP studies more broadly conceived. The Information Society Project at Yale Law School immersed me in the legal study of digital technologies. I am grateful to the Society for the History of Technology (SHOT), the Special Interest Group in Computers, Information, and Society (SIGCIS), the Business History Conference (BHC), and the History of Science Society for years of inspiration, support, and collegiality. Janet Abbate, Bill Aspray, Michael Barany, Jonathan Barnett, Chris Beauchamp, Jonathan Coopersmith, Jim Cortada, Liesbeth De Mol, Stephanie Dick, Anne Fleming, Barbara Hahn, Tom Haigh, David Hemmendinger, Marie Hicks, Erick Hintz, Sheldon Hochheiser, Roger Horowitz, Richard John, Matt Jones, Meg Jones, Peggy Kidwell, Juliette Levy, Carol Lockman, Tom Misa, Laine Nooney, Liz Petrick, Ramesh Subramanian, Kara Swanson, Dave Walden, and Caitlyn Wylie have helped me feel at home in my academic worlds. Suzanne Moon and Andy Russell have done this as well, while also showing me how to build open and supportive scholarly communities. I am also grateful to Dennis Allison, David Brock, Martin Goetz, and to *Technology and Culture* and the *IEEE Annals of the History of Computing*.

The intellectual vitality and human warmth at the Yale Program in the History of Science and Medicine (HSHM) were crucial to this project's conception and early development. Paola Bertucci, Naomi Rogers, and John Warner welcomed me to the history of science and medicine even after my research took me far away from their own interests. Joanna Radin sparked my interest in the history of software, and William Rankin's critiques of my doctoral work always encouraged me to think broadly and deeply. Bill Summers's friendship enriched my time at Yale for more than half a decade. Sarah Bowman, Helen Curry, Angharad Davis, Jenna Healey, Barbara McKay, Kelly O'Donnell, Bernadette Peters, Rachel Rothschild, and Robin Scheffler were very kind and generous over the years. Joy Rankin inspires me every day with her research, friendship, and generosity. Before my arrival at HSHM, when I was an undergraduate studying mathematics at Harvard, Janet Browne introduced me to the history of science and helped me pursue what eventually became my greatest intellectual passion. At the University of Cambridge, James Secord, Eleanor Robson, and Richard Barnett gave me the time and guidance I needed to fall in love with historical work.

UC Davis provided the financial and logistical support that I needed to finish this book. Generous support for my research and writing was also provided by BHC, the Charles Babbage Institute (CBI), the Hagley Museum and Library, the Institute for Electrical and Electronics Engineers (IEEE), the Lemelson Center at the Smithsonian National Museum of American History (NMAH), SHOT, and SIGCIS. At the IEEE, Robert Colburn and Michael Geselowitz have been generous with their time, resources, and guidance. At CBI, I benefited from many conversations with Tom Misa and Jeff Yost and relied on the archival expertise of Arvid Nelsen and Amanda Wick. Eric Hintz helped me navigate the NMAH, where I also relied on the guidance of Peggy Kidwell and Drew Robarge. Jake Ersland at the National Archives and Records Administration and Bradley Seybold at the California State Library helped me navigate federal archival material.

Earlier versions of portions of chapters 1, 3, and 7 were published in the *IEEE Annals of the History of Computing;* an earlier version of part of chapter 6 was published in *Technology and Culture.* They are included here with permission.

My close friends and family are my world's core. Sarita Monge Conejo, Lily Zeng, and Marijo de la Fuente make a difference in my life even when we are apart. Gilberto Ruby, Rosaura Ruby, and Celeste Rubi always inspire me to be generous and openhearted. My husband, Vincent Cheng, has filled my life with joy, love, whimsy, comic books, and action figures. And my parents, Gerardo Con Sanchún and Dora Díaz Castro, to whom I dedicate this book, taught me the most important things I will ever learn.

Thank you.

Abbreviations

ACM	Association for Computing Machinery
ADAPSO	Association of Data Processing Service Organizations
ADR	Applied Data Research
AFIPS	American Federation of Information Processing Societies
AOL	America Online
ASD	Applied Sciences Division at IBM
BASIC	Beginner's All-Purpose Symbolic Instruction Code (programming language)
BEMA	Business Equipment Manufacturers Association
BTM	British Tabulating Machine Company
CBEMA	Computer and Business Equipment Manufacturers Association (formerly BEMA)
CCIA	Computer and Communications Industry Association
CCPA	Court of Customs and Patent Appeals
CD	Compact Disk
CDC	Control Data Corporation
CNC	Complex Number Calculator

COBOL	Common Business Oriented Language (programming language)
COMDEX	Computer Dealers' Exhibition
CONTU	National Commission on New Technological Uses of Copyrighted Works
CPU	Central Processing Unit
CRBE/CRJE	Control Remote Batch Entry/Control Remote Job Entry (IBM programs)
CSCA	Computer Software Copyright Act
CS&M	Cravath, Swaine & Moore (law firm)
DEC	Digital Equipment Corporation
DMCA	Digital Millennium Copyright Act
DOS	Disk Operating System
DPG	Data Processing Group at IBM
ENIAC	Electronic Numerical Integrator and Computer
FORTRAN	Formula Translation (programming language)
FSF	Free Software Foundation
FTP	File Transfer Protocol
FWA	Freeman-Walter-Abele test for patent-eligibility
GE	General Electric
GIF	Graphics Interchange Format
GPL	General Public License
GUI	Graphical User Interface
HCC	Homebrew Computer Club
HP	Hewlett-Packard Company
HTML	Hypertext Markup Language
IIA	Information Industry Association
IBM	International Business Machines
ICP	International Computer Programs
ICT	International Computers and Tabulators
IP	Intellectual property
ISP	Internet Service Provider
ITAA	Information Technology Association of America (ADAPSO's successor)
ITI	Information Technology Industry Council (CBEMA's successor)
LPF	League for Programming Freedom
LZW	Lempel-Ziv-Welch image compression algorithm (for use with the GIF format)

MAC OS	Macintosh Operating System
MITS	Micro Instrumentation and Telemetry Systems
MRG	Mathematics Research Group (Bell Labs)
NII	National Information Infrastructure
NPE	Non-Practicing Entity
OS	Operating System
PARC	Palo Alto Research Center (industrial research laboratory for Xerox)
PC	Personal computer
PCC	People's Computer Company
PMC	Personal Micro Computer (company)
PTO	United States Patent and Trademark Office (formerly, Patent Office)
RAM	Random Access Memory
RCA	Radio Corporation of America
ROM	Read-Only Memory
S/360	IBM System 360 line of computers
SCPA	Semiconductor Chip Protection Act
SDS	Scientific Data Systems
SIGGRAPH	Special Interest Group in Computer Graphics (ACM)
SJCC	Spring Joint Computer Conference
SPA	Software Publishers Association
TCB	Technical Computing Bureau at IBM
TRIPS	Trade-Related Aspects of Intellectual Property Rights (WIPO agreement)
TSO	Time Sharing Option
UCC	Universal Copyright Convention
WIPO	World Intellectual Property Organization

Software Rights

Introduction

In 1999, a young online store called Amazon.com found itself at the center of a furious controversy. Accustomed to high-stakes legal battles, it faced harsh criticism for its reliance on patent law, which grants inventors the right to exclude others from making, selling, or using their creations.[1] That September, the Patent and Trademark Office (PTO) had issued a patent over a system that enabled customers to purchase items from a store's website with a single click of their computer mouse.[2] This patent protected the 1-Click shopping feature at Amazon.com, which the firm still uses today. Within a month of its issuance, Amazon had launched an infringement lawsuit against the brick-and-mortar bookstore Barnes & Noble, and it would soon reach a licensing deal for Apple to use the 1-Click system in its online music store.[3]

Amazon had not yet seen a profitable quarter, but business commentators had spent a few years locked on to it, documenting its every move. Jeff Bezos, its founder and CEO, had become the last person in the century to be named *Time* magazine's Person of the Year.[4] The company was under perennial scrutiny for its unusual entry into the retail industry, and the issuance of the 1-Click patent underscored that its increasing power depended on both the diversity of its inventory and the proprietary software that Bezos was developing. Even Amazon's website was an implementation of one of his earlier patents, for a method of transmitting sensitive information securely through unsecure networks like the ones that everyday users often have in their homes.[5]

The problem, according to some of Amazon's harshest critics, was that the 1-Click patent shouldn't have been issued. American patent law places several restrictions on the kinds of inventions that may receive patent protection. First, an invention must be patent-eligible subject matter. That is, it must belong to the categories of invention eligible for protection under American patent law: machines, processes, manufactures, compositions of matter, or improvements thereof.[6] Second, inventions must be new, useful, and not obvious. These restrictions, codified in the Patent Act of 1952, are intended to prevent inventors from patenting things such as gravity (laws of nature) or perpetual motion machines (things that don't work).

Hundreds of concerned observers sent emails to Bezos criticizing his firm and the 1-Click patent. One critic wrote that characterizing the 1-Click system as an invention is a parody. He thought that the 1-Click patent, like many software patents before it, was "a land grab, an attempt to hoodwink a patent system that has not gotten up to speed on the state of the art in computer science."[7] The Free Software Foundation—FSF, a prominent advocacy group led by the programmer and activist Richard Stallman—called for a boycott of Amazon.com.[8] Bezos tried to defuse the situation by issuing an open letter that called for substantial reform. He explained that "software patents are fundamentally different than other kinds of patents" and called for the lifetime of patents for software and business methods to be reduced from the standard seventeen years to three to five years. At the same time, however, his firm continued to defend and amend the 1-Click patent until it expired in 2017.

Amazon's patents intensified an argument with which many lawyers and business commentators in the 1990s had become very familiar—whether the thousands of software patents that the PTO issued every year were aimed at inventions that failed to qualify as patent-eligible or otherwise did not meet patentability standards. To people such as Richard Stallman's colleagues at the FSF, the answer to this question was a definitive no. The Amazon patent, in their view, was symptomatic of how the office "issues patents on obvious and well-known ideas every day" and of how, in the process, it enables individuals and firms to control technologies essential to the everyday work of the World Wide Web.[9] To entrepreneurs like Bezos, software patents were essential rewards for the investment they made in research and development and crucial weapons to make inroads against the market dominance of industry giants. Without patent protections, Bezos argued, Barnes & Noble could simply use Amazon's proprietary research to create an online store that would drive the young firm out of business.[10]

Amazon's software patents were not the only ones under fire. By the century's end, software had become one of the most controversial technologies that the American patent system had ever faced. Disagreements over software patenting revolved around three interconnected issues. First was patent-eligibility, specifically the conditions under which inventions involving software were eligible for patent protection. A long-standing doctrinal ban on patents over abstract ideas and laws of nature was often used to argue against the patent-eligibility of software. This line of thought was especially effective because computer programs can be aimed at the performance of algorithms such as mathematical and logical operations. Second were the value and acceptable uses of patents in American innovation. Patenting software was important in industries ranging from computing and telecommunications to petrochemical processing and automobile manufacturing—anywhere wherein a computer program could provide some competitive or technological advantage. Firms of all sizes and across several industries were securing software patents as quickly as their research and development staffs could file them, and yet some companies appeared more interested in securing very broad patent rights and filing infringement suits than in producing any inventions. Third, and perhaps most important, was technological control. Many critics maintained that software patents granted an improper degree of control over fundamental technologies that anyone using a computer would need; the fiercest among them warned that software patents were unacceptable attempts to establish corporate control over the digital world.

The idea that a patent could protect a computer program has not always been this contentious. In the 1950s, when computers were big enough to fill entire rooms, the patent protection of a computer's programming was not a controversial possibility. Early programs, made before the invention of terms like "software" and "computer science," could be presented as circuits of switches using telephone relays or vacuum tubes. This physicality enabled lawyers to secure patent protection for programs developed at hardware firms and industrial research laboratories. The resulting protection was indirect, aimed at systems of circuits that worked in accordance with a given program. Scholars and practitioners today often forget about these early patent protections and their successors, even though patent law has developed jointly with the American computing industry for nearly seven decades.

This book is a history of software patenting in the United States in the twentieth century. It argues that the commercial, legal, administrative, and conceptual problems that these patent protections have generated since the 1950s have facilitated the emergence of software as a product and a technology; enabled firms to challenge one another's place in the computing industry; and expanded the range of creations for which American intellectual property (IP) law provides protection.[11] There is no single historical moment—let alone a recent one—to which we can point in order to support or oppose software patenting. This is not the story of how one court or company suddenly ruined the patent system, nor is it one of how courts systematically sided with big businesses to the detriment of users or small firms. Instead, it is the story of how competing stakeholders in rapidly changing technological and political environments negotiated what software is and what it means to own and profit from it.

ARGUMENT

The most important term in this book, "software," defies characterization. In 1958, one of the first people ever to use it, the mathematician John Tukey, understood it to encompass all the complements to the hardware: things like compilers and assemblers, which enable the computer to translate instructions from one format to another.[12] Over the next decade, this notion of software as that which is not hardware expanded to include the instructions that directed a computer's operation and the programming aids, applications, and services that a firm could obtain in connection with a computer. Even the status of computer code as software was unclear: users could consider code to be software only if they had acquired it from an outside vendor, and they could refer to it as a "program" if it was developed in-house.[13] Since then, the notion of software as the counterpart to hardware has only grown stronger, as everyday users purchase disks and digital downloads to make their machines work.

Accordingly, scholars and commentators often assume that software is an intangible invention. A pioneering historian of computing once characterized software as an "elusively intangible" thing, something that appears to acquire a tangible body only when it is stored. In this framework software gains its materiality through actions such as writing down source code on a piece of paper or loading it onto a microchip or disk.[14] More recently, drawing on historical work and on the views of several prominent computer engineers and scientists, media scholars have noted that software can appear to be a ghost in the machine, made perceptible only by its effects on the tangible devices on which it runs.[15] Scholars in software studies have repeatedly warned us not to assume that software lacks materiality, and yet that assumption continues to inform scholarly and popular discourse.[16]

The history of software patenting is rooted in computing practices that challenge these notions of the intangibility of software. In the 1950s, when the patent protection of computer programs was an unexceptional practice, lawyers and programmers protected code and programming by disclosing tangible objects in their patent applications. Computing firms and industrial research laboratories employed a patent-drafting technique that lawyers in the late 1960s would retroactively call "embodying software." It consisted of securing patent protection for a program indirectly, by patenting instead a computing system that worked in accordance with it. Not doing this risked having their applications rejected because of the mental steps doctrine—a long-standing ban on the patentability of mental steps such as mathematical calculations. As programs grew in complexity and programming languages enabled their creation through textual means, inventors and their lawyers relied on the means-plus claim structure—a claim that discloses a machine as the means to perform a given collection of functions—as a shorthand to disclose the kinds of physicality that their predecessors would have spelled out. This brought them into conflict with patent examiners, who required them to revise their claims' phrasing to identify the tangible components of the computing system that would carry out the functions at stake. The resulting patents, which domestic and foreign firms obtained, combined means-plus language with very specific descriptions of interconnected electronic components to secure patent protections for the computer programs at their core.

Software patents first became controversial in the mid-1960s because the Patent Office and IBM (International Business Machines) worked very hard to eliminate them. On the one hand, examiners at the Patent Office had noticed inventors' ability to secure patent protection for their programs by patenting specially built computers and their uses, and they worried that the office was not equipped to handle the bureaucratic burden that it would face if patent applications continued to blur the lines that distinguished hardware from software. On the other hand, IBM's long-standing entanglements with antitrust law (which precludes anticompetitive behavior) had resulted in important limitations on its ability to profit from its patents and use them to exclude competitors from a given invention. Because IBM distributed programs through bundling—free of charge with the purchase or lease of its hardware—its managers preferred to lose the ability to secure patent protections for their programs than face an industry wherein small and highly litigious firms could use software patents offensively against IBM. As smaller firms turned to IP to make inroads in the computing industry, hardware manufacturers and their trade associations joined IBM in opposing software patents in part to reduce their own licensing costs and to prevent the creation of barriers to entry controlled by small firms.

Courts' early efforts to affect software patenting from the top down, through the development of legal doctrine, hinged on the problem of determining what software is—that is, determining its nature and characteristics as an invention. Software patents first arrived at the courts in the late 1960s through industrial research laboratories such as Mobil Oil and Bell Telephone Laboratories, wherein patenting a computer program could amount to patenting new proprietary systems for the delivery and performance of their services. Facing a Patent Office that sometimes rejected applications for software-related inventions by asserting that they were ineligible for patents, these firms launched lengthy lawsuits that sometimes reached the Supreme Court. Carefully watched by the computing industry, these lawsuits became soapboxes for firms to advance their conceptions of the nature of software. This was an essential matter to settle, as the statutory grounding of American IP law requires creators to classify what it is that they have created: books, music, machines, processes, manufactures, pamphlets, and so on. Something like software, which in a second could shift from looking like a collection of numbers to looking like a machine doing its work, did not fit neatly into any category.

Software patenting became a doctrinal minefield because no conception of its nature satisfied every stakeholder. At the interface of the computing industry and patent law, software could be a machine, a text, or an algorithm. It could be some of these things at once or none of them at all, and its nature could change from one moment to the next. Each conception was designed to advance its proponents' long-term legal and commercial interests. Starting in the 1960s software firms defended the notion that software is a machine because they viewed patent protection as crucial to participation and survival in the computing industry, but in the 1970s they also started arguing that software is a text because their managers wished for stronger copyright protections. Hardware manufacturers, eager to reduce their licensing costs and retain their market share, consistently argued that software is a text because their managers viewed copyrights as an innocuous form of IP protection that they could bypass easily. Industrial research laboratories generally changed their preferred conception of software depending on the situation at hand, and they commonly argued that software has a hybrid nature. It could be machine-process (a mix between a machine and an algorithm) or a text that behaves like a machine. Even in the mid-1970s, when courts were most likely to view software as an

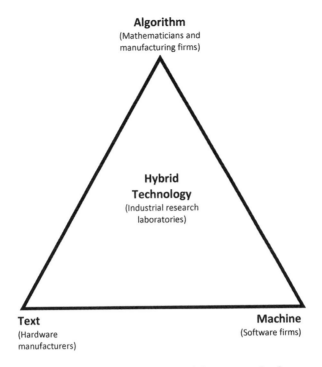

Diagram of the most prominent conceptions of the nature of software at the inter-face of the American computing industry and patent law in the 1960s and 1970s. It is a spectrum with purely textual, mechanical, or algorithmic conceptions at its vertices. Crafted by the author.

unpatentable intangible invention, legal doctrine could be bypassed in patent applications by properly transforming software's mathematical and algorithmic components into statements about a machine and its operation.

This capacity to disclose software as more than one kind of creation also made it possible for inventors to rely on patents and copyrights simultaneously. Software copyrights have been available since the 1960s, but at first they were extremely limited in scope. Unsure of how to classify software as a creative work, the Copyright Office registered all computer programs as books or pamphlets and offered them the protections normally afforded to literary works. Lawmakers in the mid-1970s considered an overhaul of the country's copyright system aimed in part to align the United States with its global counterparts, but the copyright implications of information technologies were so complicated that Congress outsourced their study to a special commission. CONTU, as the Commission on

New Technological Uses of Copyrighted Works was known, learned from IBM that the creation and development of computer networks, which could enable the transmission of data across state lines and even national borders, made software copyright a matter of primary importance. As courts at all levels grew increasingly skeptical of the doctrinal basis for software patenting, computing firms of all sizes lobbied for the recognition of software as a new category of creative work eligible for copyright protection. Their work with CONTU facilitated the passage of the Computer Software Copyright Act of 1980. It also fueled the efforts to create a hybrid IP protection for microchips to be administered by the Copyright Office, as established in the Semiconductor Chip Protection Act of 1984.

The development of the personal computer (PC) industry and the Internet generated new rationales to oppose software patenting and sparked widespread support for strong software IP rights across the federal government. As networked PCs made their way into people's homes, it became easier than ever for everyday users to share software with one another. Easier to enforce than patents, copyrights became the standard means of protection for every aspect of popular software products, from their code to their graphical user interfaces. At the same time, firms used patents to protect essential networking and data management technologies that were more likely to be duplicated by competitors or researchers than by everyday users. These legal protections caused outrage among highly skilled users, who relished the ability to interact with a computer freely, without the fear that large corporations would be able to claim ownership over the interfaces and applications that made it possible. Led by hobby computing groups and later by Richard Stallman, these users found creative ways of building the IP-free software environments that they desired. They marched to protest software IP, developed their own programs and systems, lobbied Congress, created software distribution centers, wrote scholarly articles, and delivered powerful testimony to federal agencies.

Software patenting flourished in the 1980s despite this new wave of opposition. The free-market policies of the Reagan administration, paired with a restructuring of the federal court system in 1982, allowed judges and federal agents to back broader and more generous interpretations of patent-eligibility standards. They steered away from settling on a nature for software and toward characterizing the role that software plays in creating a patent-eligible computing system. The globalization of the computing and electronics industries—which featured the development of small manufacturers of cloned computers and distributors of illegally copied software—encouraged computing firms new and old to become more vigilant than ever about their domestic and global IP rights. Customs enforcement, sting operations, and even public humiliation became important complements to the traditional patent, copyright, and trade secret proceedings that firms had been carrying out for decades.

In the 1990s, when American politicians dealt with increased pressure to align the country with global IP treaties, it became easier than ever to obtain a software patent. The Clinton administration pushed for the creation of the National Information Infrastructure (NII), a plan for a country (and later, a world) in which anyone could access the Internet with ease. Nationwide discussions of the NII provided a forum for software makers to lobby for the strongest IP protections yet. This vision of a seamlessly interconnected world worried software and media creators alike; without a strong national IP system that could work efficiently on a global scale, such a network had the potential to intensify the piracy issues that the industry had seen since the 1980s. Computing firms and Internet service providers (ISPs) lobbied for the passage of new legislation to combat online piracy that would later be known as the Digital Millennium Copyright Act. At the same time, computing, finance, and media firms turned to patent law in search of protection for the systems that would enable users to use multimedia products and the Internet in the first place. Amid this fast-paced technological and legislative change, courts and the Patent and Trademark Office started to read software patent applications as if the software in them was already embodied and part of a computing system. Acknowledging that software and patents were far too entwined for any federal agency ever to separate them, the office then braced itself for the unprecedented wave of software patenting that the new millennium would bring.

SCOPE AND STRUCTURE

Overall, the patent protections available for computer programs have changed jointly with the political economy of American computing, the country's IP infrastructure and its relations with international IP regimes, and popular and academic perceptions of computing technologies. The engineers, programmers, managers, and users on whom historians of computing usually focus are central to this book, as are federal bureaucrats, corporate lawyers, lobbyists, and judges. Each group worked at its own pace, interacting with the others in courtrooms, at hearings, and at conferences. For these reasons, this book comprises twelve short chapters with overlapping timelines that together advance a chronologically structured narrative.

Three remarks on the book's analytical scope are in order. First, this book is, above all, a work of history. It is a contribution to the histories of technology, law, and business that draws methodological inspiration from science and technology studies and legal scholarship. It is not a manifesto for or against software patenting, nor is it an institutional history of any federal agency or an analysis of the economic performance of software patents. Second, the book focuses on the United States, addressing other countries and international phenomena only as necessary to identify global forces that shaped the American story. It thus favors historical texture and contingency at the local and national levels over the broad strokes that would be required of a transnational history of software patenting without first understanding its history in the United States. Third, the book's narrative zooms in and out of organizations strategically, paying special attention to their internal politics only when an important outcome or strategy is at stake. It provides a bird's-eye view of an organization's work when research materials are unavailable (a situation noted in the text) or when the organization's internal discussions at the time are not as relevant to the analysis as the impact of its actions.

The chapters are divided among three parts. The first, "Early Patent Protections," analyzes the emergence in the late 1940s of the patent-drafting techniques that enabled hardware manufacturers and industrial research laboratories to secure patent protections for their programs starting in the 1950s. The second, "Software, Courts, and Congress," details the use of patents, copyrights, and antitrust law in the 1970s and early 1980s, analyzing how courtrooms and Congress served as battlegrounds for competing visions of the computing industry's needs and technologies. The third, "IP for PCs," shows how the emergence and development of the personal computer industry both expanded the range of protections for software afforded by patent and copyright law and encouraged everyday users to come together in protest of software IP. The narrative closes at the century's end, as firms secured software ownership rights that would allow them to deter online piracy and control profitable new media and Internet technologies. The conclusion reflects on the book's methodological grounding.

Part One   **Early Patent Protections**

Chapter 1 Code Made Tangible, 1945–1954

Shortly before the American bombing of Hiroshima and Nagasaki, a mathematician named Richard Hamming joined the Manhattan Project at the Los Alamos National Laboratory. The final preparations to test a nuclear bomb for the first time had increased the laboratory's need for people who could perform complex numerical calculations quickly and accurately, a task for which Hamming was exceptionally well suited. He was an expert on the theory of differential equations, a field of mathematics that deals with variables expressed in terms of their rates of change, and he had recently embarked on a promising academic career.[1]

Hamming joined the Theoretical Division, led by Hans Bethe, a German American physicist who would later win a Nobel Prize for his research into nuclear reactions and stellar energy production. Despite its name, the division did not perform theoretical work as a pure mathematician would have understood it. Gone were the abstract problems that Hamming had encountered during graduate school, when he was concerned with such matters as showing that an equation has solutions without having to find any of them or proving that a certain method can approximate solutions for all equations of a given type. Now he faced problems like computing chain reaction times and explosion magnitudes. He would be required to find specific solutions in rapid fashion, and a single unchecked miscalculation could be catastrophic. In designing an atomic bomb, Hamming would later remember, "no small scale experiment can be done—either you have a critical mass or you do not."[2]

Since its inception in 1943, the laboratory had steadily increased its computational capabilities. The pressures of the war and the complexity of the calculations involved made it impractical for the project's physicists to perform all their calculations themselves. Those designing uranium bombs relied on the so-called hand computers, a group of fewer than two dozen women recruited primarily from among the scientists' wives. These women had learned how to use mechanical desktop calculators after arriving at Los Alamos. Hamming's wife, Wanda Little Hamming, who held a graduate degree in English literature, counted herself among them. Her work as a hand computer will likely remain hidden inside classified folders for many years to come, but she was highly skilled. In fact, within a few months of her arrival she was reporting directly to two of the most prominent physicists at Los Alamos, Enrico Fermi and Edward Teller.[3]

Hamming himself worked with the punched card computers that the Manhattan Project had acquired from International Business Machines (IBM) and which the laboratory's scientists used to design plutonium devices.[4] These IBM machines were relay computers—electromechanical devices that processed data using hundreds of moving components called relays, which work as "on" or "off" switches. Among the computers were three copies of the IBM 601, which featured multiplication and division functions, and one IBM 402 tabulator, which could read several dozens of punched cards per minute.[5]

Hamming had no prior experience using these computers, but there was plenty of in-house knowledge on which he could draw because several physicists had developed a fascination with them. One of them was Richard Feynman, who had joined the laboratory to study experimental equipment and had spent many hours tinkering with the computers and calculators alongside another physicist, Nicholas Metropolis. By 1945, Feynman and Metropolis had gotten to know the mechanical linkages inside the computers so well that they had become their unofficial maintenance staff. This was an essential duty; it would have been impractical and time-consuming to send individual components to their factories one by one for repair, and the secrecy conditions of the laboratory precluded IBM and the calculator manufacturers from providing the full range of maintenance services that they normally offered to their clients.[6]

With IBM's user manuals and the maintenance know-how that Feynman and Metropolis had developed, Hamming became what he described as the laboratory's "computer janitor."[7] His job was to keep the computers in continual operation often late into the night, solving mathematical problems that physicists dropped off at the computer room.[8] He found computing work at Los Alamos to be exciting and fast-paced, challenging not only because of the mathematical and technical sophistication that using the IBM computers required but also because the problems he was solving could have enormous implications. By checking someone's arithmetic, for example, he could inadvertently be calculating the probability that the upcoming test of the bomb at the Trinity Site in New Mexico could ignite the atmosphere. "It was science fiction come true," he would recall many years later, "the mad scientist's laboratory."[9]

The vibrancy of the atmosphere at Los Alamos came to a swift end in August 1945, after the United States dropped atomic bombs at Hiroshima and Nagasaki. Many of Hamming's colleagues left, but he stayed behind. He had greatly enjoyed his work, but far too many personal and technical questions lingered: What had happened at Los Alamos, and why did things unfold that way? Why did the final computations work so well when the preliminary calculations often had, at best, questionable accuracy? What did the large-scale computations that he and the hand computers performed contribute to the war? And, looking forward, how could he continue to draw on the computational power that he had discovered there?[10]

Hamming spent six months pondering these difficult questions with Wanda and caring for his IBM machines. Early in 1946, perhaps not yet ready to answer all of them, the couple decided that it was time to move on. Hamming would continue to work as a sporadic consultant for the Los Alamos National Laboratory, but he and Wanda were eager to start a new life yet again, this time in New Jersey, where they remained for thirty years. Wanda stayed at home and volunteered for a range of charities while Hamming, armed with in-depth knowledge about the intricacies of electromechanical computers, worked for Bell Telephone Laboratories (Bell Labs).[11]

The industrial research laboratory for the telecommunications company AT&T (American Telephone & Telegraph), Bell Labs had spent the war years constructing computers for the Allies' use. Notable among these machines was the M9 electrical gun director, which the U.S. Army had used to control heavy antiaircraft guns and which had directed the destruction of all but two of the ninety-one missiles that Germany launched at London in 1944. This was perhaps the labs' most celebrated computer, but it was more an anomaly born of the country's wartime demand for weapon control systems than a representative of AT&T's in-house computing needs. Instead, the computers that the labs had developed since the 1930s were designed to perform basic data processing tasks in service of the Bell System, a cluster of companies owned by AT&T that together controlled most telephony services in the United States.[12]

Bell Labs' tradition of electromechanical computing was grounded on the work of George Stibitz, a mathematician who had joined the company in 1930 after completing his doctoral work on the geometry of two-dimensional membranes. Initially appointed as a "mathematical engineer," Stibitz enjoyed tinkering with the labs' machinery and finding abstract generalizations for real-world phenomena. Some of his most important contributions to the labs' work stemmed from his realization, in 1937, that he could interpret the ones and zeroes used to express numbers in binary notation as sequences of telephone relays. By representing a relay's "on" position with a 1 and "off" with a 0, he could create equivalence between binary numbers and arrangements of relays. For instance, the number 23, which in binary notation is 10111, could be expressed by setting up five relays in the following positions: on, off, on, on, on. He could then create basic circuits to perform additions on quantities represented as relay states, which enabled him to perform arithmetic operations through electrical engineering.[13]

Since then, Bell Labs had developed a line of computers based on Stibitz's work. In 1939, the mathematician had created a computer called the CNC (Complex Number Calculator).[14] Later known as the Model I, this computer could perform all the basic arithmetic operations. Thanks to the labs' telecommunications technology, it also featured remote access capability; Stibitz had installed teletypes at the labs' headquarters in New Jersey and at the New York offices of the American Mathematical Society and connected them to his machine using telephone lines. This computer's successor, Model II (placed in service in 1943), used 440 relays and five teletypes, and the Model III (developed especially for the army and put in service in 1944) used 1,400 relays and seven teletypes. The Model IV (1945) was similar in capacity to the Model III, but it was designed for use by the U.S. Navy.[15]

HAMMING'S CODE

When Hamming joined Bell Labs, the latest addition to this line of computers was the Model V.[16] With nearly ten thousand relays, this machine was so versatile and powerful that the National Advisory Committee on Aeronautics and the Ballistics Research Laboratory at Aberdeen Proving Ground, Maryland,

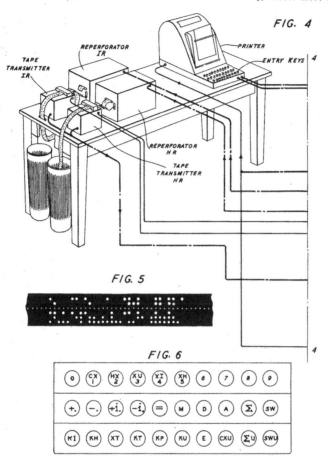

FIG. 4

FIG. 5

FIG. 6

INVENTOR
G. R. STIBITZ
BY

ATTORNEY

Third page of the patent for the Model V machine, by George Stibitz. Patents like this one were part of the tradition of electronic computer patenting on which Bell Labs' lawyers drew to secure patent protection for computer programs starting in the late 1940s. US Patent 2,666,579 (1954).

had each purchased one. One of its most useful features was alerting its users when it encountered processing errors. If a failure occurred in its operation, the computer would stop, sound an alarm, and deliver the information necessary for users to find the cause of the problem. This feature made the Model V so popular that the machine housed at Bell Labs was at times in continuous operation twenty-four hours a day, seven days a week.[17]

The Model V was popular among members of the Mathematics Research Group (MRG), to which Hamming belonged. This group was led by Hendrik Wade Bode, a physicist and engineer known for his work on feedback amplifiers, which made it possible to design vacuum-tube circuitry for precision machinery.[18] Bode had assembled a stellar team of researchers, including individuals who would later become fundamental to information and computational theory: Claude Shannon, Brockway McMillan, Donald Percy Ling, John Tukey, and, of course, Hamming himself. These men would soon be calling themselves the Young Turks, the MRG's brilliant and rebellious troublemakers. According to Hamming, their experiences living through the Depression had encouraged them to think that they "owed the world a living." Their wartime work had taught them to be "impatient with conventions" and to take on high-responsibility jobs even if they initially felt unprepared to perform them. They took pride in doing "unconventional things in an unconventional way," and their success records inspired their superiors, including Bode, to let them follow their research interests.[19]

Hamming—who was initially assigned to model the elasticity of solids, the use of traveling tubes, and call blocking—started spending so much time with the labs' computers that he soon became known as the MRG's "computer evangelist."[20] He was especially interested in the transformation of numerical data from one number system to another using the Model V, which was in such high demand that he had access to it only on weekends. This meant that he had exactly two days to test out each week's work. With so many hours of work at stake, he became frustrated with the computer's habit of aborting its operation as soon as it encountered a processing error.[21]

To correct this problem, Hamming developed an error correcting and detecting code—computer code that would allow the Model V to detect any processing errors, correct them on the spot, and continue its normal operations.[22] The computer's original error detection system ran what is known as a parity check. This meant that its components grouped the 0s and 1s they were about to transmit into blocks of a fixed length and assigned to each block an additional number: a 1 if the digits on the block added up to an odd number, and a 0 if they added up to an even number. Before processing each incoming block, the receiving component would check whether the added digits in the blocks it received were still correctly assigned. If an expanded block's additional digit was incorrect, then the entire computer would stop its operation and show its user where the incorrectly transmitted block was located. Hamming also added several parity checks to each block so that the computer would be able to determine exactly which digit in an improperly transmitted block was incorrect and change it accordingly without halting.

Eager to publish his work, Hamming wrote a paper called "Error Detecting and Error Correcting Codes" and distributed it as an interdepartmental memorandum. He then considered publishing it in the *Bell System Technical Journal*, a scientific journal with distribution outside of the labs. However, two lawyers at Bell Labs' Patent and Legal Division, M. R. Kenney and J. W. Schmied, stopped him from submitting his paper and told him that they would not allow him to publish his codes until they had obtained a patent for them. Hamming did not know much about patent law, but he suspected that he couldn't patent what he considered to be a "bunch of mathematical formulas" in his invention. Dismissing his concern, the lawyers told him, "Watch us."[23]

Kenney and Schmied's confidence was likely grounded on their knowledge of the rich patenting tradition that had developed in the American telecommunications industry since the nineteenth century. An 1854 Supreme Court opinion, *O'Reilly v. Morse*, had incorporated telegraphy into the canon of American patent law and upheld the validity of most of the patent that Samuel Morse had obtained for what would later be known as Morse Code.[24] The patent was aimed at an "apparatus for and a system of transmitting intelligence between distant points by means of electro-magnetism."[25] Its fifth claim, which the Court upheld without comment, covered the "system of signs consisting of dots and spaces, and of dots, spaces, and horizontal lines, for numerals, letters, words, or sentences, substantially as herein set forth and illustrated, for telegraphic purposes."[26] Even if these symbols were abstractions of letters and numbers, they caused the movement of electricity across telegraphy systems; according to the patent, they were electro-magnetism, "which puts in motion machinery" that the patent also covered. This made them fit neatly into developing mid-nineteenth-century conceptions of invention that favored the materiality of new machines and substances over the mathematical abstractions that enabled their creators to study and improve them.[27]

Since then, radio, telephony, and telegraphy patents had routinely covered inventions that processed and transmitted things like sound and text as electrical impulses and radio signals. Since the Second World War, Kenney and Schmied's colleagues had obtained patents for devices including signal receivers and decoders, air traffic control systems, encrypting devices, telephone pagers, and even electric wave transmission systems.[28] In these patents, processing and transmitting data was tantamount to moving waves and impulses through cables, towers, machines, and air. There was even precedent at AT&T for code-centered patents in error detection; in 1950, a subsidiary called the Teletype Corporation had submitted a patent application titled *Error Detecting Code System*, for a telegraph system that detected transmission errors automatically.[29]

At the same time, the Legal and Patent Department had been patenting Bell Labs' computers for nearly a decade. From Stibitz's CNC to the Model V, computers at Bell had all fallen under their purview. The department's staff had come to see an exchangeability between basic mathematical operations and the work of electrical circuits: basic operations in arithmetic or logic could be performed by simple circuits, with quantities represented as sequences of "on" and "off" positions. The staff had also stayed up to date on computing developments outside the labs, as it was their responsibility to demonstrate at the Patent Office that the inventions they presented were, in fact, patentable.

In this broader technological context, it was quickly becoming apparent that a machine's circuitry could be a tangible embodiment of its programming. Soon after the war's end, the University of Pennsylvania's Moore School of Engineering had inaugurated the Electronic Numerical Integrator and Computer, known as ENIAC. Unlike Bell's computers, ENIAC had no moving parts, so it could operate up to a thousand times faster than some of its best-known relay-based predecessors. Along with this speed, one of ENIAC's most celebrated features was its programmability: its programmers, a team of about two hundred women, could rewire its internal circuitry to alter the sequence of arithmetic operations that the computer would carry out. These programmers were highly trained as mathematicians and technicians, and they had arrived at their jobs through their wartime careers as human computers, often in the army's service. In their hands, programming was a distinctly physical task. It involved removing the machine's panels, unplugging its cables, and plugging them back in according to whichever arrangement was required for the computations that their superiors had selected.[30]

Kenney and Schmied planned to use this increasingly well known exchangeability between programming and circuitry to secure patent protection for Hamming's code. The main legal hurdle in their way was the mental steps doctrine, which dictated that operations that properly trained people could perform in their mind (including comparing and computing quantities) were ineligible for patent protection. In *Halliburton v. Walker* (1944) the District Court for the Southern District of California had recently ruled that processes—regardless of whether they included intangible manipulations such as mathematical computations—must always comprise manipulations of tangible matter in order to form the basis of a patentable invention.[31] The court held that an invention is not patent-eligible if its novelty resides "only in the performance of mental steps such as 'counting,' 'observing,' 'computing,' and 'comparing'" because those claims "do not involve invention" in any way.[32] Shortly before Hamming met with Kenney and Schmied, the Court of Appeals of the Ninth Circuit had affirmed and expanded this rationale. It suggested that the mere presence of these words signaled that a claim is directed at an unallowable process because the words implied that the invention consisted simply of plugging a handful of values into an equation; a "rudimentary knowledge of arithmetic" would suffice.[33]

Kenney and Schmied's experience with telecommunications patents gave them an idea to break free from the restraints of this doctrinal development. Their strategy was to secure protection for Hamming's code indirectly, by patenting a machine—an "information system," they called it—that worked in accordance with the error correction processes that he had developed.[34] Their plan was to obtain diagrams that showed the relay circuits that would allow a computer to perform Hamming's algorithms. Though much more complex than Stibitz's original binary adders, these circuits were the same in principle: electromechanical arrangements that performed basic logical and arithmetic operations. The lawyers would then file a patent application for a computer constructed in accordance with those diagrams. The application would disclose this machine in terms specific enough to describe an actual functioning computer but broad enough to cover other potential computers running Hamming's code.

The lawyers asked Bernard Holbrook, one of Bell Labs' electrical engineers, to produce these diagrams. Based at Bell's Switching Department, Holbrook had started working on Bell's computing equipment; in 1945 alone, he had submitted two patent applications for naval artillery computers.[35] He had also forged a strong friendship with Hamming during the mathematician's first few months at Bell and agreed to be listed as a coinventor in exchange for his work. He already understood how the codes worked and had no problem transforming them into what the patent application disclosed with terms like an "error correcting relay circuit."[36] This translation work likely rendered the invention unrecognizable to Hamming, but it would allow the patent application to bypass the mental steps doctrine as articulated in *Halliburton*.

The strategy of patenting a machine designed according to Hamming's codes worked perfectly. In fact, just one year after the application's submission,

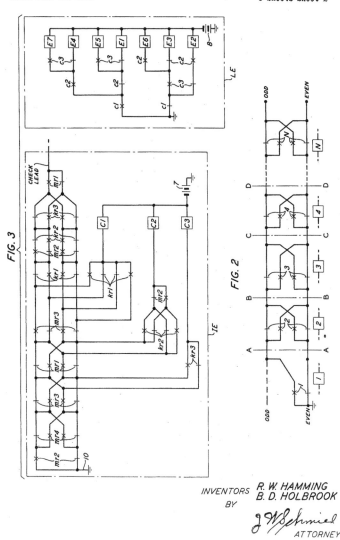

INVENTORS   *R. W. HAMMING*
                B. D. HOLBROOK
        BY

                        ATTORNEY

Second page of Richard Hamming and Bernard Holbrook's patent *Error Detecting and Correcting System*. Lawyers in the 1960s would identify this patent as an early example of what they called "embodying software"—securing patent protection for a program by patenting a machine that works in accordance with it. US Patent 2,552,629 (1951).

in 1951, the Patent Office issued their patent *Error Detecting and Correcting System.*[37] The application's surviving documentation suggests that no examiners expressed concerns with either the invention or the patent itself. On the contrary, the revisions that the office required Bell Labs to perform on the application were mostly punctuation changes and small phrasing improvements. Hamming's concern—that his invention comprised a collection of formulae—was unimportant at the Patent Office because the application had disclosed a machine.[38]

Kenney and Schmied had executed a patent-drafting strategy that many of their counterparts at other firms and industries would adopt, refine, or even develop on their own. The issued patent includes several mathematical formulas and tables, and it even refers directly to computer code. However, it identifies as the invention an "apparatus for and a method of detecting and correcting errors which impair the accuracy of the output" of a machine, not the codes themselves. It claims ownership over a particular "digital information system" comprising means that would enable it to detect and correct its own processing errors. Even Holbrook's illustrations disclose a layout of circuitry, not the internal logic of the program that Hamming developed. It is, in effect, a patent for a machine designed to protect computer code.[39]

PATENT LAW AND PATENT DRAFTING

Hamming and Holbrook submitted their patent application in an era of explosive economic development. In the late 1940s, enjoying record rates of growth and unmatched prosperity, the United States possessed more than two-fifths of the world's wealth and less than 10 percent of its population.[40] Its industries produced more than half of the planet's steel, 60 percent of its oil, and 80 percent of its automobiles. Paired with this economic prosperity were high expectations for the nation's ability to harness the power of science and technology through strong and socially meaningful partnerships among government, industry, and academia such as the ones that had enabled the creation of the bomb.[41] The war had provided a stage for new wonder drugs such as penicillin to shine, inspiring postwar funding agencies and researchers alike to believe that perhaps infectious disease had met its match.[42]

Tied to this growing faith in the power of science and technology was an impetus to perform a wholesale reform of the country's patent system. The Patent Act, on which the system was grounded, dated back to the nineteenth century, and lawmakers thought that only a new act would be able to transform into statutory law the standards of novelty, usefulness, and patent infringement that the courts had developed since then. At the Patent Office, the number of yearly applications was approaching its prewar average of seventy thousand, and examiners were working at full capacity to issue almost forty thousand patents a year.[43] This, of course, makes the quick issuance of Hamming and Holbrook's patent more remarkable: their examiner likely considered the invention just one more in a long line of electromechanical computers that Bell Labs had been patenting over the years.

It is worth noting that a patent has two major descriptive components. First is the specification, a verbal description of the invention intended to explain what it is and how it works. Second are the claims, an itemized list of the aspects of the invention over which the patent grants protection. The idea behind such a division was that the claims would identify the invention and the specification would provide essential technological context to determine the bounds of what inventors claimed as theirs. In assessing patent-eligibility, examiners could address the specification and claims simultaneously, though they often focused on the language of the claims.

In 1950 and 1951, as the passage of a new patent act drew near, the Court of Customs and Patent Appeals, or CCPA—the court to which applicants could appeal Patent Office rejections—issued several decisions on patentability standards. Two of these decisions affirmed the *Halliburton* rationales that the CCPA had handed down in 1944. Both were grounded on the CCPA judges' understanding, based on the *Halliburton* opinions, that the verb that best describes a process is the most important determinant of the process's patent-eligibility. The first decision concerned a patent application called "Improvements in Petroleum Prospecting Method," submitted in 1944 by Armand J. Abrams. Abrams was the director of the laboratory at the Magnolia Petroleum Company, a subsidiary of the Socony-Vacuum Oil Company in Dallas, Texas. Abrams's invention was a method to identify underground deposits of hydrocarbons such as natural gas and petroleum by analyzing the flow rates of gaseous emanations from the ground.[44] Using a drilling tool, users would drill holes in the ground and seal them in a way that enabled underground gases to diffuse into the hole. They would then measure the flow rate of gases into the tool and perform computations including "determining the rate of pressure rise" within the tool and "comparing the rates" at different boreholes.[45]

The examiner at the Patent Office, P. W. Shepard, rejected the patent application for several reasons. Among them, following *Halliburton*, was evidence that the processes were mental in nature: words such as "calculating," "comparing," "converting," and "determining" all referred to processes carried out by the human mind. Abrams's attorney, Sidney A. Johnson, appealed to the Patent Office's Board of Patent Appeals. The board agreed with the examiner's reasoning and decision, adding that the mental steps were "of the essence of the procedure claimed" and that the claims themselves would "lose their meaning if these steps are omitted."[46]

Johnson considered the board's rejection as an opportunity to ask the CCPA for guidance on what constitutes the mental steps doctrine. Based on his survey of the case law, he proposed to the court that this doctrine boiled down to three rules. First, if all the steps listed in a method claim "are purely mental in character," then the subject matter of the claim is not patent-eligible. Second, if a method claim involves both mental and physical steps, and if the method's novelty lies only in the former, then the claim is not patent-eligible. Third, if the novelty of a method claim that comprises both kinds of steps lies in the physical steps, and if the mental ones are "incidental parts of the process which are essential to define, qualify or limit its scope," then the claim is patent-eligible. In short, these three proposed rules meant that a method claim would be patent-eligible if, and only if, its novelty lay in its physical steps. This reasoning appealed to Judge Finis J. Garrett, a Tennessee native and former Democratic congressman who wrote the court's opinion. To Johnson's dismay, Garrett wrote that the invention fell under the second proposed category of inventions: that it was a method claim the novelty of which resides in its mental steps. This was enough for Abrams's patent to be denied.[47]

The second decision, *In re Shao Wen Yuan*, concerned a patent application in the aeronautical industry.[48] The inventor and applicant, Shao Wen Yuan, held a doctorate in aeronautical engineering and was especially interested in the aerodynamic optimization of aircrafts. During 1942 and 1943, while working for the Glenn L. Martin Company, Yuan had designed and produced a new kind of airplane wing that was well adapted for high-speed aircraft. Like Abrams, Yuan had included in his patent application claims wherein mathematical computations were central. One claim listed a method to determine the optimal shape of a plane's wing for a given performance goal. It comprised steps that Yuan's attorney had disclosed as "computing the pressure distribution," "determining the airfoil altitude," and "determining values" for certain parameters following a simple trigonometric function.[49]

Yuan's experience at the Patent Office was very similar to Abrams's: both inventors faced examiners who scrutinized the verbs used in their claims; they faced a Board of Patent Appeals that stood by the examiners; and they took their cases to the CCPA, which made the rejections final. The court's decision in *Yuan* was an affirmation and expansion of its ruling in *Abrams*. Again writing for the court, Garrett found that the patent's claims comprised no more than purely mental steps meant to be performed by a human being using paper and pencil according to the formulae that the claims themselves advanced.[50]

These two opinions remained influential even after Congress passed the Patent Act of 1952. They required patent examiners to be especially vigilant of the language that inventors used in their patent applications and provided a rough guide for the assessment of the patent-eligibility of a claim involving physical and mental steps. First, examiners should study the relations among both kinds of steps to determine if the physical steps were essential to the claim. Second, they should decide if the claim's novelty resided entirely in the mental steps. If the invention comprised only mental steps, or if its novelty lay exclusively in them, then it was ineligible for a patent. This, of course, affirmed *Halliburton's* introduction of novelty as a factor in assessing an invention's patent-eligibility. No records suggest that legal scholars or practicing lawyers considered this a problem at the time.

The CCPA's judges likely did not realize that these opinions would encourage people to adopt and refine variations of the patent-drafting technique that Kenney and Schmied had developed. Cleverly phrased applications would meet the discourse-oriented criteria for patent-eligibility that *Halliburton* had created, bypassing the mental steps doctrine and therefore yielding patent protection for computers' programming or for other automatic systems to perform computations. To illustrate how firms did this, the rest of this chapter highlights some of the most illustrative patents in this vein that the Patent Office issued over the next few years.[51] Rather than presenting an extensive list, it provides a sampling taken from three fields from which some of the legal conflicts fundamental to software patenting would later emerge: geophysical sciences, telecommunications, and computer hardware.

Patents modeled after Hamming and Holbrook's blend into the broader computer patenting landscape of the 1950s. The patents themselves did not use keywords such as "software" (which had not yet become a standard term), nor did they often announce that a computer's programming stood at their core. As a result, modern discourse-based search methods fail to generate lists of these patents without also listing scores of others aimed at electronic components and equipment. This is true even for the Bessen-Hunt technique, a keyword-based Boolean search method for the Patent and Trademark Office's patent database with which the technique's developers identified software patents issued from the 1970s onward.[52] For these reasons, what follows is not a quantitative analysis of patenting trends but a close examination of patents and their contents.

Lawyers and patent agents in the 1950s found ways of bypassing both the recent rationales and the nineteenth-century Supreme Court decision on which they were grounded, *Cochrane v. Deener* (1876). A product of the impulse to provide patent protections for the mass-manufacturing technologies of the Second Industrial Revolution, this decision deemed processes ineligible for patent protection if they do not cause a transformation in tangible substances. These tangible substances could include things like chemical substances, machine parts, and electricity itself (thanks to the earlier opinion on Samuel Morse's early telegraph).[53]

Applications for inventions in the geophysical sciences could bypass the *Abrams* and *Yuan* restrictions by specifying that any computations involved were part of a broader computerized system that involved the manipulation of minerals and gases. This was the case for *Correlation of Seismic Signals*, a patent that a Dallas firm called Geotechnical Corporation filed in 1954. It was classified as an invention in Class 367, "Communications, Electrical: Acoustic Wave Systems," subclass 40 (Received correlation). The inventor, Thomas Swafford, had developed a new way of processing seismic information. His invention allowed for the reduction of noise in seismic data, and his patent claimed a method and an apparatus. The patent's first claim follows. (Note that in this and all other patent claims in this book, any formatting has been added by the author.)

The method of detecting and presenting seismic signals including

[1] the steps of creating a local disturbance in the earth,
[2] translating vibrations therefrom into an electrical signal,
[3] *dividing* said signal into two components,
[4] *multiplying* one component by a time function and the other by a related time function but delayed in time,
[5] *squaring* the resulting products, and
[6] *summing* and continuously integrating the products to
[7] provide a composite correlogram wherein the said time functions have cancelled out.[54]

This claim comprises manipulations of tangible substances such as causing vibrations on the surface of the earth ([1] and [2]) and intangible ones such as performing arithmetic operations ([3]–[6]). It presents these manipulations as part of a single process and specifies a tangible output, namely the printout of an image (the correlogram, [7]). This strategy is likely to have made the claim less liable to facing rejection on the grounds that it covers mathematical computations or that it causes no transformations on tangible substances.

This method amounts to using a computer to perform correlations based on seismic data. The patent calls this machine a "function correlator"—a

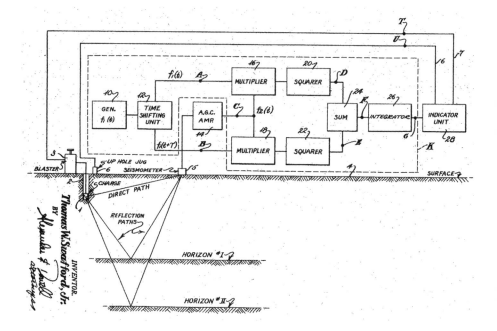

Block diagram of Thomas Swafford's function correlator. The analog computer at the system's core is embedded in a broader system to create seismic signals and process the data collected by a seismometer. US Patent 2,907,400 (1954).

device that allows for the statistical correlation between two functions—and specifies the mathematical formulae that it applies to the data.[55] Some of the machine's internal components are also covered by the patent, but nothing in the claims or specification restricts the scope of protection to a specific device; any computer that carried out Swafford's correlations could potentially be construed as infringing on this patent.

The same strategy continued to work at Bell Labs, which developed and patented several error-detection and data translation inventions for use with its increasingly computerized telephony systems.[56] Among them was *Binary Decoder*, a patent filed in 1956 for a binary-to-decimal translator.[57] This application faced no pushback at the Patent Office; it was issued about a year after its submission. Its first page notes that the translation process at hand is "an arithmetic operation which a computer can be programmed to do" and explains that the invention is not the program itself but a component that performs the same function.[58] The application's claims underscore this materiality by disclosing a device called a "translator," and its specification outlines

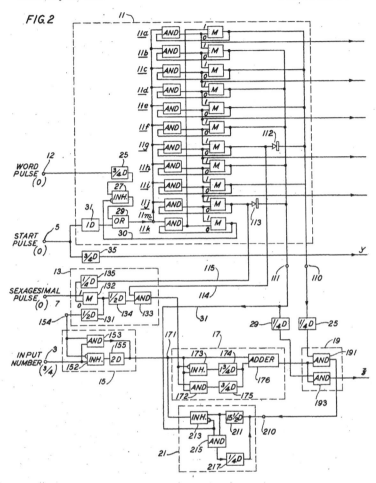

FIG. 2

INVENTOR
J. R. WOODBURY

BY

ATTORNEY

Partial logic circuit diagram for Bell Labs' *Binary Decoder*. The patent describes the data processing that this system performs in terms of the movement of electrical pulses between the machine's components. US Patent 2,814,437 (1957).

in detail the means that allow this translator to process bits and digits—a combination of specific circuits and pre-programmed components.

Binary decoders and data translating devices were especially important to AT&T, as they could be used to automate processes ranging from telephone switching to the accounting of clients' telephone bills. Especially after 1956, this was likely the main financial motivator for Bell Labs' continued patenting of electronic computing technologies. That year, the firm signed a consent decree—an agreement to change a firm's behavior in order to avoid prosecution from the Department of Justice's Antitrust Division—that precluded it from participating in the electronic computing industry (discussed in chapter 2). Bell Labs' separation from this industry was made evident by its absence from the computing market and by its reliance on a different examination department at the Patent Office. In fact, Bell Labs was likely able to win such boldly phrased patents because its applications were read by examiners in telecommunications and not by those specializing in registers and electrical engineering, as hardware manufacturers normally did.

Hardware firms' growth in the 1950s, analyzed in detail in the following chapters, left behind a trail of patents that bypassed the *Yuan* and *Abrams* rationales. By the end of the decade, IBM had filed several patents for error correction and automatic program management.[59] One of them, *Program Interrupt System* (filed in 1957 and issued in 1962), even noted in its first paragraph that the invention "relates to a program controlled data processing machine."[60] However, what mattered most at IBM was not securing as many patent protections as possible but instead developing a long-term patent strategy that would enable the firm to cope with the restrictions of business strategy that its entanglements with antitrust law generated in the mid-1950s.

The consideration of electricity as an allowable substance on which a process could act without losing its patent-eligibility even allowed hardware firms to secure patent protection for systems that translated data and computer code from one format to another. As a result, hardware manufacturers bypassed the problem of whether acting on data and code was allowed under *Cochrane*. This occurred, for instance, with the Radio Corporation of America (RCA)'s *Data Translating System* (submitted in 1953) and IBM's *Data Transfer and Translating System* (1953) and *Decimal to Binary Translator* (1959).[61] RCA's patent even describes the invention as one with the ability to "sense data encoded on perforated cards, supplement and arrange that data, verify the data, convert it to a code suitable for magnetic tape, and record the data on magnetic tape."[62]

Foreign firms entering the American market also left a trail of patents of this kind. Consider the British Tabulating Machine Company (BTM), a firm

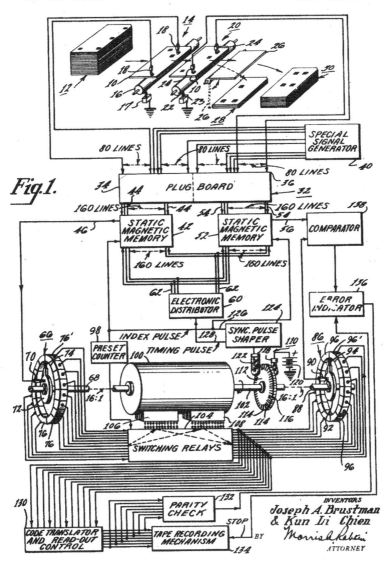

Fig.1.

Schematic diagram of the invention in RCA's patent *Data Translating System*. Note the stacks of punched cards on the top, the magnetic drum one third of the way up from the bottom, and the tape-recording mechanism blocked out on the bottom. US Patent 2,702,380 (1955).

born in the early twentieth century as a licensor of Herman Hollerith's patented tabulators from IBM's predecessor, the United States Tabulating Machine Company.[63] After BTM's licenses expired in the late 1940s, the firm faced the possibility that American manufacturers of traditional office equipment would start competing with it in the British market. Drawing on academic computer development at places such as Cambridge University and the University of London, and encouraged by Britain's National Research Development Corporation, BTM recruited promising young electrical engineers to develop a line of computers with which the firm could compete with IBM in Britain and, eventually, around the world.[64] Among these engineers was Raymond Bird, a former technical officer at the Royal Air Force who had joined BTM excited about the prospect of working on a project about what he described as "counting with valves."[65] By 1953, Bird had led the development of the Hollerith Electronic Computer (HEC), a small semiautomatic electronic computer that the company would soon develop commercially.[66]

BTM's origins as a patent licensee for an American firm are the most likely reason why its development of electronic computers was paired with an aggressive effort to secure American patents. Many of the patents for which the firm applied in the early 1950s were aimed at components such as special relays, contact devices, or impulse generators.[67] However, two of Bird's applications are aimed at inventions that perform basic data processing tasks such as adding quantities or translating a number from one number system to another.[68] Like Hamming and Holbrook's patent, these applications were directed at machines that processed and transmitted electricity. As a result, BTM used its patent applications to transform mathematical algorithms that would normally qualify as mental steps (including arithmetic operations) into statements about specific ways of storing and transmitting electrical pulses among tangible components such as shift registers and memory units.

One example is *Data Translating Apparatus*, submitted in 1953. It was aimed at an "electronic apparatus for data translation," namely a device that could translate numbers from the binary system to standard decimal notation (similar in function to Bell Labs' *Binary Translator*). The translation of a number from one system to another at the patent's core involved little more than the algorithmic application of the four basic arithmetic operations, and in fact the patent notes that the "translation may be effected by a computer itself under control of an appropriate programme."[69] However, the patent also discloses a computer specifically designed to perform only Bird's translation algorithm, and it uses its figures to disclose the computer's architecture and even the internal circuitry of some of its components.

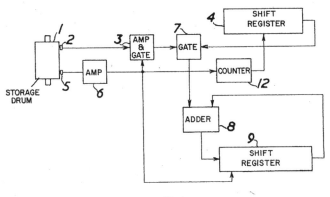

FIG. 1.

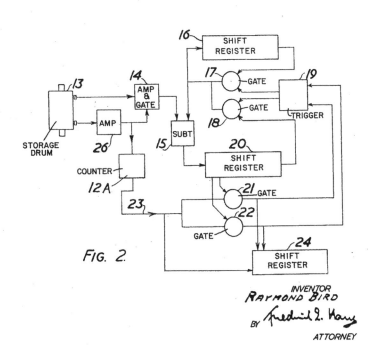

FIG. 2.

INVENTOR
RAYMOND BIRD

BY _Fredrick J. Hang_

ATTORNEY

Block diagrams of Raymond Bird's *Data Translating Apparatus.* Assigned to ICT, this patent shows how British firms were securing patent protections for their computer systems and embodied programming in the United States. US Patent 2,970,765 (1961).

While applying for this patent, the firm had responded to the examiner's complaints about the application's lack of specificity by incorporating tangible components into its claims.[70] This is the application's original first claim as Bird submitted it:

Apparatus for translating a number from a first to a second radix of notation having

[1] means for storing a limited number of equivalent values of one of the radices expressed in the other of the radices,

[2] means for reading out the stored values sequentially,

[3] *analyzing means* for determining which of the equivalent values is contained in said number and

[4] *means controlled by the analyzing means* for selecting and summing those read out values which are contained in said number.[71]

BTM's revisions to this claim transformed statements about the machine's ability to process numbers into descriptions of how electricity moved from one electronic component to the next. Chief among the changes were the firm's modifications to items [3] and [4], wherein the italicized phrases above stand in for an object that enables the claimed apparatus to perform the actual translation algorithm—an "analyzing means" that acts upon values and numbers. In the published claim, this analyzing means became the control system for a tangible circuit that processed electricity, a "control means" that moves electrical signals between objects such as memory units and arithmetic circuits.

Negotiations like these in a patent's phrasing were the norm for more than a decade. The industry had changed a lot by the mid-1960s, but the communications between patent examiners and inventors at computing firms always resembled the ones that ultimately enabled people like Bird to receive their patents. Lawyers at firms such as IBM, RCA, and Texas Instruments would become well versed in these patent-drafting techniques and in dealing with the examiners themselves.[72] Even patent-holding companies (which did not necessarily produce the inventions they patented) started drafting patents in this way, especially for computerized military technologies.[73] Judges and commentators would eventually focus on the question of *whether* programs are eligible for patents, but the question that patent lawyers and agents had started to solve in the late 1940s was *how* to draft patents to protect them.

Chapter 2 From Antitrust to Patent Law at IBM, 1950–1966

For most of the twentieth century, the Department of Justice's Antitrust Division took a keen interest in the market share and pricing strategies of IBM.[1] Tasked with precluding firms from behavior it deemed anticompetitive, the division had monitored IBM since the two had met in court in the 1930s. At the time, IBM was the world's foremost manufacturer of punched cards and tabulating equipment, and it offered its machines exclusively for lease, not for sale. The firm also required its clients to use only the patented punched cards it manufactured, effectively banning clients from turning to any alternative manufacturer that wished to offer compatible punched cards at lower prices. The Justice Department accused IBM of having created an illegal tie-in under the Clayton Act of 1914, which explicitly banned such behavior; IBM countered that the tying-in of punched cards was essential to maintaining quality-control standards.[2] The conflict eventually reached the Supreme Court, which in 1936 ruled that the firm could meet its quality-control objectives by publishing its technical standards and ordered IBM to allow customers to purchase cards from other firms.[3]

Until the 1980s, the Antitrust Division aimed to undo IBM's historically integrated approach to computing—that is, the firm's tradition of producing and marketing entire bundled systems, as opposed to individual components.[4] IBM's profits and market share increased throughout the 1940s despite the 1936 ruling. For these reasons, the Antitrust Division had kept close tabs on IBM's growth and strategies. Conversely, the firm's top management kept the division's scrutiny in mind when they were developing the IBM 701, the firm's first electronic computer. Indeed, purchasing a smaller firm to acquire expertise in electronic computing had never been an option, as top managers believed that doing so would cause further antitrust complaints.[5]

This chapter argues that IBM's encounters with antitrust law in the 1950s shaped its long-term patent strategy and framed the arguments on intellectual property that its staff would deliver at courts, federal agencies, and advisory committees over the next few decades. By the mid-1960s, IBM had become the country's most vocal opponent of software patenting in all its forms. Its managers and lawyers thought that the short- and long-term strategic and financial hurdles born from the firm's encounters with antitrust law made strong patent protections for computer programs very dangerous. Their work suggests that they preferred losing some of the patents in their portfolio over risking the possibility that other firms would use patents to create high barriers to entry into new areas of technological development. By the late 1960s, IBM's legal staff had even recommended to President Lyndon B. Johnson's administration that the Patent Act itself should be revised to ban computer programs from receiving patent protection.

A NEW CONSENT DECREE

In 1950, soon after the start of the Korean War, Thomas J. Watson Jr. sent a telegram to President Harry Truman explaining that IBM was ready to aid the war effort.[6] A bold and ambitious former U.S. Air Force pilot, Watson Jr. was IBM's executive vice president and the son of the firm's longtime CEO, Thomas J. Watson. From the IBM World Headquarters building in New York, Watson Jr. sent IBM-O-GRAMS (internal telegrams) to all company locations in the United States. He wanted everyone to know that the firm would participate in the war by offering its products and services to the government and by developing whichever new technologies were necessary. This national service was now IBM's top priority.

Watson Jr. then summoned a meeting with members of his inner circle—top managers in whom he could confide—to set out the specifics of this participation.[7] Among the attendees was James Birkenstock, his special assistant and a faithful employee who had seen the firm grow for nearly fifteen years. Despite his lack of formal legal training, Birkenstock was the senior executive in charge of managing IBM's IP rights at home and abroad.[8] Also attending was Cuthbert Hurd, the founder and director of the Applied Science Department. He knew the technical details of IBM's machines and was familiar with the needs of the firm's largest academic and government clients. He was also an accomplished engineer who had served sporadically as a consultant for the Atomic Energy Commission.[9]

During the meeting, Watson Jr. presented a strategy to identify the data processing needs of federal agencies.[10] Over the next six months, Hurd and Birkenstock spent several days at the Pentagon and at the offices of government contractors investigating what IBM could do for them. Sometimes at Birkenstock's request, especially when one of Hurd's clients was involved, the two would visit these places together. At the same time, IBM's director of military products, Charles McElwain, visited government bases and research centers to discuss military matters that fell outside of Hurd's and Birkenstock's expertise.

At the close of 1950, a few days before New Year's Eve, Watson Jr. asked Hurd and Birkenstock to find out whether any of the defense agencies would be interested in obtaining an IBM electronic computer.[11] Carrying a one-page sketch of the machine's architecture, the two men had a bold and simple pitch: they were not there to ask for any commitments but instead to show how, for just $8,000 a month, an agency could have a cutting-edge machine and access to the firm's maintenance, programming, and education services at no additional cost. Anyone interested in this possibility would simply need to sign a letter of intent—a commitment-free expression of interest that IBM could use to gauge whether there was, in fact, a market for these machines. When Hurd and Birkenstock gathered about thirty letters of intent, Watson Jr. authorized development of a general purpose computer.[12]

Almost one year later, IBM announced the Defense Calculator (IBM 701), its first commercial scientific electronic computer.[13] Like the tabulating machines that IBM and its predecessors had built for more than half a century, the 701 was available only for lease. For a flat monthly fee, users had access to both the IBM installations they had leased and all the maintenance, education, and programming services that they might need. Bundling, as this practice was known, would become the computing industry's norm in the 1950s.[14] Before computer programs started to become available for sale in the 1960s (chapter 3), these bundled programming services were often the first means for computer users to obtain the programs they needed.[15]

Soon after the 701's release, in 1952, the Antitrust Division filed a lawsuit targeting the firm's long-standing practice of offering its machines only for lease, not for sale.[16] The division accused IBM of having "unlawfully restrained and monopolized the tabulating industry" and estimated that the firm's refusal to sell its machines had enabled it to own 90 percent of all the tabulating machines in the country. It further alleged that IBM had restrained the "development and growth in the U.S. of independent service bureaus" that would otherwise have provided tabulating services to clients who did not wish to lease machines from IBM. IBM's leasing system, according to the lawsuit, carried with it "burdensome and unreasonable expectations" ranging from requiring the clients to disclose how they would use their machines to prohibiting users from creating and using their own peripherals without IBM's consent.

The targeting of IBM was the latest development in the increasingly vigorous antitrust enforcement that had characterized the Antitrust Division since the Second World War.[17] Thurman Arnold, a former Yale Law professor whom President Franklin D. Roosevelt had appointed as head of the division in 1938, believed that weak antitrust prosecution had contributed to the severity of the Great Depression, and he aimed to bring the division back to its nineteenth-century trust-busting roots.[18] The Antitrust Division had issued one or two consent decrees per year before the war, and it issued an average of three decrees between 1941 and 1945.[19] Arnold's trust-busting impetus continued after the war's end, as the Roosevelt and Truman appointees who succeeded him shared his vision for strong antitrust enforcement. The average number of decrees issued yearly rose to approximately nine in the late 1940s and dropped to seven in the early 1950s. Connecting them were assumptions that having a large market share amounted to having an unlawful monopoly and that limiting patent rights would ultimately limit a large firm's market share by reducing barriers to entry into its industry. Among the decrees' most prominent patent-related provisions in the postwar decrees was the requirement that firms would charge reasonable royalties when licensing their patents; a handful of firms even agreed to issue royalty-free licenses.

Over the next four years, the computer industry grew with bundles at its core and IBM at its helm, and the Antitrust Division kept its sights on IBM.[20] Computing firms unburdened by the division's continual scrutiny sometimes relied on mergers and acquisitions to gain the expertise required to develop electronic computers. This had happened especially frequently at the Remington Rand Corporation, which manufactured UNIVAC (a successor to ENIAC that became the 701's main competition). Remington Rand had entered the electronic computing industry after purchasing the Eckert-Mauchly Computer Corporation, and it had expanded its electronics portfolio by purchasing Engineering Research Associates in 1952. The firm underwent yet another major change in 1955, when it merged with the Sperry Gyroscope Corporation to form Sperry Rand. Similarly, National Cash Register (NCR) developed a specialized electronics division thanks to its acquisition of the Computer Research Corporation in 1952.[21] In contrast, large and well-established firms sometimes drew on proven strengths to tackle the data processing needs of industries wherein IBM machines had not yet become the norm. For instance, General Electric (GE)—one of the largest suppliers of vacuum tubes in the 1950s—manufactured a computer to automate check processing at Bank of America.[22] Called ERMA (Electronic Recording Machine Accounting) and dedicated in 1955, this special purpose computer was developed at the Stanford Research Institute for Bank of America, which had outsourced its production to GE.[23]

The growth of the industry brought with it new ways of obtaining computer programs.[24] The hardware manufacturers themselves were usually the first source; GE had hard wired its programs into ERMA, and IBM would continue to provide a mix of hard-wired programs and programming services. Sometimes, however, users could wish for a program that their manufacturer did not develop. For this reason, starting in the mid-1950s, manufacturers started to sponsor groups for users to share programs with one another at no cost.[25] Most notable among them was IBM's SHARE, a nationwide group that directors of computer centers created in 1954 to serve as an intermediary between the firm and its clients. Its volunteer members shared with one another either programs that IBM did not offer in its bundles or customized versions that the users themselves had developed.

Users generally saw bundles and user groups as the primary means for the acquisition of programs. Indeed, one former programmer at UNIVAC described the 1950s as a time when "programs were freely interchanged, since they were not viewed as property."[26] As he explained, "Free programming support, free programs, and free education became expected clauses to any hardware leasing or contractual arrangement."[27] Bundled pricing gave users "a predictable cost that they could budget against," another programmer remembered, giving them confidence that "the undefined problems that existed in data processing, in their computing world, would be covered as well."[28] These favorable views of bundling would last until the mid-1960s, but bundling as a practice started to erode in the mid-1950s, as IBM's structure and long-term strategies shifted once again in response to the Antitrust Division's pressure.

IBM's negotiations with the Justice Department intensified in the mid-1950s, but not solely because of the firm's steadily increasing power in the electronic computing industry. Across all industries, the Antitrust Division's continued frequent use of consent decrees was enabled by a series of court decisions that aligned so well with the government's demands that observers deemed the postwar years the New Sherman Era, in reference to the 1890 act on which the Antitrust Division's work was grounded.[29] In 1953, one such decision, *United States v. United Shoe Machinery*, tipped the scales further in the government's favor.[30] The United Shoe Machinery Corporation was a dominant manufacturer of shoe-making technologies. Like IBM, it offered its machines only for lease, manufactured most of the items required to operate its machines, and had an extensive patent portfolio. In response to the Antitrust Division's complaints, the district court of Massachusetts ordered United Shoe, among other things, to start offering its machines for sale, stop manufacturing the items required to operate them, and license its patents "upon a reasonable royalty basis" to anyone who wished to manufacture shoe machinery.[31] This ruling could have been even stronger, but the court declined the government's proposal to dissolve the company into three separate manufacturers.

The *United Shoe* decision showed firms that were facing similar complaints what could happen if they chose litigation. A defeat in court could generate potentially expensive licensing requirements and allow the Antitrust Division to determine how to restructure the firm and its short- and long-term strategies. Even though the *United Shoe* court had not gone this far, it had not rejected the possibility as a future measure. In this case, the court had found that enforcing a dissolution of United Shoe would be unrealistic because all the firm's manufacturing occurred at one plant that relied on a single laboratory, management, and workforce to operate. Firms generally preferred to negotiate a consent decree and appease the Antitrust Division than enter court and face the heavy precedent in the division's favor. Potentially lengthy and devastating trials were thus avoided, and firms gained the ability to foresee, and perhaps even negotiate, drastic changes in strategy and structure that would be necessary in the short and long term.

Stanley Barnes, the head of the Antitrust Division in the mid-1950s, likely thought that the two industries in which immediate intervention was most necessary after *United Shoe* were computing and telecommunications, respectively dominated by IBM and AT&T.[32] On June 24, 1956, after almost seven years of negotiation, AT&T signed a consent decree. It agreed to license its 8,600 existing patents without charging royalties and to charge "reasonable and nondiscriminatory" fees to license all future patents. Its manufacturing subsidiary Western Electric agreed not to pay patent royalties to AT&T and to refrain from manufacturing any equipment "not useful in furnishing common carrier communications services." This meant that AT&T could no longer sell electronic computers and that many of its most important patents—from those covering technologies like Richard Hamming's codes to those related to new technologies such as transistors—would remain accessible to firms of all sizes.

The very next day, Birkenstock signed a consent decree on IBM's behalf.[33] As one scholar puts it, this decree exemplified the Antitrust Division's ongoing effort to "break the bonds between providers of basic platforms and firms oriented toward tailoring those platforms to meet the varied needs of consumers."[34] The decree ordered IBM to start selling its machines and to continue providing, free of charge, the maintenance and programming services for the computers that it sold. This meant that the act of purchasing a computer would not be tantamount to foregoing the maintenance services that leasers would continue to enjoy for free.[35] It also required IBM to transform the firm's Service Bureau Division (which sold computer time and provided programming and data processing services) into the Service Bureau Corporation, a wholly owned subsidiary that would operate independently from IBM itself. The creation of the Service Bureau Corporation was a crucial step in transforming computing service firms into disseminators of technical knowledge and best practices.[36] It was, at the same time, a product of the Antitrust Division's experiments with market segmentation in the computing industry, an institutional means to accomplish what soon became one of the division's long-term goals: dissolving IBM's bundles.[37]

As it did with AT&T, the Antitrust Division precluded IBM from using its immense patent portfolio to create high barriers to entry into the computing industry. A crucial series of provisions in the decree—the section that troubled Birkenstock the most—restricted what IBM could do with its patents. Clustered in section XI of the decree, these provisions would shape IBM's legal strategies for the next two decades. They required the firm to "grant to each person" who applied in writing an "unrestricted, nonexclusive license" for any of its patents for punched cards, tabulating card machines, and any "electronic data processing machines or systems."[38] The provisions also prohibited IBM from selling or disposing of its patents in any way that could deprive the firm of the authority to grant such licenses, and they required IBM to provide "immunity from suit" to its current and future licensees.[39]

Section XI limited IBM's autonomy over the royalties it could set for its patent licenses. In order to license one of the firm's patents, a person would first need to submit a written application to IBM. The firm would then propose the royalties it would charge, and the applicant had the option of rejecting the firm's proposed royalties. If IBM failed to propose an amount that the applicant deemed acceptable over the next 120 days, then the applicant could notify the attorney general of that failure. Both parties would then turn to the District Court for the Southern District of New York, and it would be IBM's burden to demonstrate that its proposed royalties were reasonable under the decree. In the end, the court would issue a final ruling to establish the royalties that the applicant would pay.[40]

Birkenstock considered the consent decree to be a threat to IBM because it would change the firm's position in the computing industry's IP landscape.[41] Indeed, many years later he would describe the decree's signing as "the beginning of an era where IBM was no longer self-sufficient . . . under its patents as it had been in the tabulating machine era."[42] The decree had made him and other managers realize that they could easily find themselves "locked out by the patents that [other firms] held on certain key developments."[43] It would change IBM's relations with the computing industry by precluding it from using its own patents to create high barriers of entry while, at the same time, creating an opportunity for new kinds of firms to grow and set high barriers of their own.

This decree generated a serious long-term strategic challenge for Watson Jr. and his inner circle. The industry was changing rapidly following AT&T's consent decree, which had made it easier for everyone to license its patents for transistors. Manufacturers could now develop smaller transistorized devices such as the IBM 1401, a business machine for which IBM would eventually fill about a thousand orders (as opposed to a few dozen, as was the case for the 701). At the same time, even though IBM still dominated the industry, the decree had reshaped its relations with other firms. The obligation to sell had given rise to a secondary industry consisting of firms that purchased IBM machines only to lease them themselves. IBM was required to provide service to these machines, even though they no longer generated leasing income. This situation had the potential to make IBM's operating costs increase significantly; the firm could end up servicing fully paid-for machines indefinitely while competitors developed competing equipment based on patents IBM was required to license.

In the early 1960s, while overseeing at least seven lines of computers, Watson Jr. concluded that IBM needed to rethink its pricing strategy very carefully.[44] He worried that other firms were pricing their computers at the lowest price possible while IBM continued to increase its profit margins to cope with the rising operating costs borne in part from the consent decree.[45] At a meeting with his top sales staff in 1963, he explained that IBM should not aim to compete by reducing its profits because doing so risked loosening the firm's grasp on the market, lessening its prestige, and yielding even more frustration. Instead, he thought that IBM should continue "to bring machines to the market place that are low enough in price and high enough in function so as to always be competitive—machine for machine—with others who are in the market competing against us."

IBM's management hoped that the company's newest machine, the System/360 (S/360), would overcome this pricing hurdle and increase the firm's profits.[46] A system aimed for commercial and scientific tasks alike, the S/360 allowed users to customize their data processing systems by selecting whichever computers in the line best suited their needs. The firm planned to spend about $5 billion in the mid-1960s in developing and marketing the S/360, in the hopes of rendering obsolete all other computers in the market, including its own models.[47] As one writer for *Fortune* would later report, the release of this computer was akin to having General Motors scrap all its existing cars in order to offer a new line "covering the entire spectrum of demand."[48] Shortly before the system's announcement in 1964, one of IBM's vice presidents wrote that the firm's aim was to make the S/360 "economical as hell, simple to operate and the best on the market."[49] The bundled programs that IBM offered with it were crucial to this project. Indeed, according to another vice president, programming was the firm's "most critical resource," and it was necessary to "look at programming features in the cold businesslike way we look at new hardware features."[50]

Still, managers at the firm's Data Processing Division agreed that fierce price competition would remain a key concern.[51] Other hardware manufacturers were likely to compete with the S/360 by offering generous discounts, increasing their machines' performance without increasing prices, and offering special deals. They were also likely to issue so-called why wait advertisements, ads claiming that there was no need to wait for IBM's newest computers if its competitors could offer cheaper machines of comparable quality and power.[52] Still, in alignment with Watson's views, the Data Processing Division advertised no special offers or discounts. Instead, it focused on publicizing the three aspects of the System/360: its broad range of uses and compatibility features, the extensive range of applications available for it, and IBM's superior customer service and training programs.[53]

This focus on maintaining healthy profits in the face of fierce price competition made the patent-related provisions of the consent decree more dangerous than ever before. The decree had limited the amount of money that IBM could make by licensing any of its patents, but it placed no limit on how much other firms could charge if IBM needed to license any of their patents. Established firms and startups alike would develop hardware and applications for the S/360 soon after its release. If these potential competitors started to secure patents of their own for S/360-compatible technologies, then IBM would lose a lot of money in licensing royalties or else risk losing access to key technologies. This was especially problematic if small and highly litigious firms started seeking patent protection for their computer programs, as established firms were already doing. Such a development would immediately force IBM to start spending large sums of money in order to make programs that it would distribute for free through its bundles.

In 1965, Birkenstock discussed this issue with two other high-ranking executives, Burke Marshall and Eugene Fubini.[54] They told him that some kind of "ownership protection" on "selected elements of software" was possible and that there were two legal means of protection: "patents (hardware equivalent only)," and "copyrights (in combination with a restrictive clause in the sales agreement)." They also advised him that technical means were available, including the "code encrypting of programs" and the splitting of a given program into two parts, only one of which would be hard wired into the computer. In response, Birkenstock rejected any kind of protection for programs, at IBM or otherwise. According to the meeting's records, he "forcefully expressed his opinion that IBM has 'borrowed' more software technology from outsiders than it has contributed" and said that any protections "could be turned against IBM."[55] He added that IBM's market share was so high that any such protection would work to its disadvantage, especially because it could interfere with the "smooth IBM-customer interaction" that the firm had fostered over the years. After all, it would be difficult and expensive for IBM to offer programming services if the programs that service agents could install were subject to patent licensing fees. In short, Birkenstock told Marshall and Fubini, IBM "could, but very likely should not," encourage the patent protection of computer programs.

THE PRESIDENT'S COMMISSION ON THE PATENT SYSTEM

Birkenstock's first opportunity to take a stand against software patents came in 1965 thanks to Lyndon B. Johnson's interest in addressing the needs of the country's inventors.[56] Motivated by the growing geopolitical pressures of the Cold War, Johnson supported heavy investments in science and technology. The development of weapons and space technologies had already created such a consistently high demand for reliable and fast computational power that the federal government was a major source of funding for research and development in information technologies and electronics components. In fact, the Minuteman missile program and NASA's rapidly developing Apollo program were transforming the country's aerospace programs into the most important market for integrated circuits.[57]

Johnson thought that identifying and addressing the commercial needs of the country's inventors was crucial to the transformation of American ingenuity into a guarantor of continued economic prosperity. To this end, in 1965, he created a group called the President's Commission on the Patent System and appointed Birkenstock as one of its members.[58] Alongside Birkenstock were several government officials and high-ranking officers from prominent firms. One of their primary goals was the identification of any issues that could overburden the American patent system—that is, phenomena that could strain its facilities, personnel, or bureaucracy. In particular, Johnson instructed the commissioners to identify and recommend the changes necessary "to ensure that the patent system will be more effective in serving the public interest" during what he considered to be a decade of "complex and rapidly changing technology."[59] The commissioners were to focus on the extent to which patent laws served the country's needs, the aspects of the system that needed to be revised, and any new legislation necessary to meet inventors' needs.

Alongside Birkenstock at the commission were thirteen equally prominent people who represented universities, private firms, and the federal government.[60] The group was cochaired by Harry Huntt Ransom, chancellor of the University of Texas, and Simon Rifkind, a prominent federal judge and trial lawyer.[61] With them were Secretary of Commerce John T. Connor, Secretary of Defense Robert S. McNamara, Small Business Administration administrator Eugene P. Foley, and National Science Foundation director Leland J. Haworth. The remaining members of the commission represented universities, computing and biotechnology firms, and practitioners of patent law. They included a new commissioner of patents, Edward J. Brenner, the Nobel Prize–winning physicist and engineer John Bardeen, and Monsanto Research Corporation president Howard Nason.[62]

The commissioners began their work in 1966. Discussions first focused on such issues as the appropriate length of patent protection and whether patents should be granted to the first person to invent or to the first one who files an application. These deliberations were tied to their investigation of whether the American patent system would benefit from revisions that would align it with the systems of other countries. For instance, the idea that priority of invention should be given to the first person to file an application (as opposed to the first one to invent it, as was the case in American law) was becoming increasingly adopted by countries around the world.[63]

Regarding computer programs, however, the commissioners agreed that their mission was to determine how to balance the industry's needs with the Patent Office's capabilities. In June 1966, the commission gathered testimony from the Patent Office, academic programmers, patent agents, and computing firms.[64] A key witness was Malcolm A. Morrison, a head examiner for electrical engineering at the Patent Office. Since the 1950s, Morrison had overseen the issuing of hardware patents for hardware firms and industrial research laboratories such as the ones examined in chapter 1. He was currently supervising the examination of applications that would yield patents such as IBM's *Data Storage and Processing Machine* and Sylvania Electric Products' *Automated Price Computation.*[65]

Morrison submitted a paper to the commission discussing what he called "the problems involved in protection of computer programs."[66] These problems arose, in his view, from the complex and burdensome relations among the nature of computer programs, the state of patent law, and the bureaucratic needs of the Patent Office. Morrison defined a program as "a plan of procedure," or "an ordered set of instructions for the control of a general purpose data processor or computer."[67] Any program comprised a statement of a problem, an analysis of it, a procedural approach to its solution, and the development of flow charts, formatted data, memory allocations, and subroutines. Phrases such as "programming the computer," "controlling the computer," and "causing the computer to perform specified functions" all meant the same thing to him—namely, the "mental efforts, ideas, or actual operative functions" that the machine performed as instructed by the programmer.[68]

From this description, Morrison concluded that programs are not patent-eligible, but he worried that this conclusion would make little difference because firms had the habit of presenting programs "in a form which will satisfy all statutory requirements."[69] He denounced this effort to have inventions "framed and claimed" as patent-eligible as nothing but an artifice—more a rhetorical exercise than an illustration of the nature of the inventions.[70] He explained that when programs arrived at the office in this form, they posed two administrative problems. First, examiners needed a high level of experience in data processing, programming, and patent law. The people who possessed these qualities were in great demand at private firms, so the office had to compete with the industry for personnel.[71] Second, the office had to classify and search through an enormous amount of prior art in computer

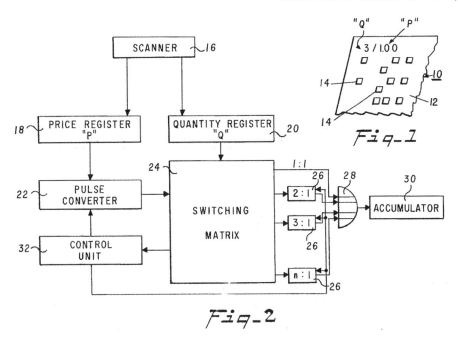

Block diagram for *Automated Price Computation,* one of the patents examined by Malcom A. Morrison. The diagram illustrates an "electronic data subsystem for computing an equitable price" for the purchase of discounted items. US Patent 3,235,713 (1966).

programming.[72] Skilled library personnel gathered and classified new advances in the field for the office's use, but few librarians had enough knowledge about mathematics and computing to solve the "extremely complex problem of classification" that programs posed.[73] Even finding a place to store prior art was a problem if this art included tapes, cords, and punched cards.

When Morrison appeared in person before the commissioners, he delivered another statement on computer program patents and warned that programmers would soon launch legal challenges to the office's practices.[74] Examiners were already facing two arguments: either that programs made general purpose machines into new single-purpose machines or that the presence of a computer in a new process does not bar eligibility.[75] Morrison suspected that these arguments had not been successful yet, but he implied that it was only a matter of time before the mental steps doctrine would fall into disarray.

Morrison also reiterated his condemnation of the use of patent-drafting strategies that disclosed programs as hardware. Applicants were obtaining protection for their programs by disclosing "that which purports to be a hardware organization of a special computer" designed to carry out the procedure of the program.[76] This had enabled them to secure several issued patents—at least a few hundred, Morrison thought, though he did not have a clear estimate. Applicants who employed this method sought broad patents in a way that covered both the machine they disclosed and a general purpose computer on which the program was loaded. This "masking of the subject" had become an intricate patent-drafting technique, and it was enabling firms and programmers to secure patent protection by mastering "different manners of the semantics of language."

Morrison's rejection of these patents was grounded both on his views of the Patent Office's needs and procedures and on his growing concern over how the British patent system was handling computer programs. In December 1965, the British Board of Trade's Industrial Property Department had issued a statement titled "Patentability of Computer Programs." This three-page document presented six ways in which inventors could present a "novel computer program" in their patent applications:

> [1] As a program, i.e. as a statement of a particular sequence of operations to be performed on data by a computer.
>
> [2] As a paper sheet, tape, or magnetic tape carrying a record of the particular program.
>
> [3] As a method of operating a computer in which the computer is caused to perform the sequence of operations.
>
> [4] As a computer arranged to perform automatically the sequence of operations.
>
> [5] As a computer when performing automatically the sequence of operations.
>
> [6] As a computing process in which a computer performs automatically the sequence of operations.

The British board found that only ways [2], [4], and [5] were allowed by the Patents Act of 1949, which required an invention to be a "manner of new manufacture" or a "new method or process of testing applicable to the improvement or control of manufacture."[77] In the United States, only way [3] was allowable. Ways [4] and [5], however, corresponded to the phenomenon that Morrison was witnessing at the American Patent Office—patenting a computer that functions in accordance with a given program. This is the technique that BTM's Raymond Bird had been applying, often successfully, on both sides of the Atlantic.[78]

In practice, the greatest difference between the American and British frameworks for the patent-eligibility of computer programs was way [2].[79] It was grounded on the assumption that a program loaded on a computer-readable storage medium can trigger physical changes on the machines into which it is loaded. According to the board, a computer program recorded on computer-readable sheets and tapes is not "theory in recorded form" but something that "physically re-operates with the computer." Such a program is akin to a machine component that can cause changes in the operation of a larger machine, not unlike the cams that open and close a combustion engine's valves. To Morrison, this reasoning posed a serious threat to the American Patent Office, which was already struggling to catch up with the backlog of inventions submitted through conventional means.

The commission's records suggest that Birkenstock remained silent throughout each session on computer programming during these early hearings. This must have been difficult, especially when witnesses hostile to IBM started to appear. Indeed, soon after Morrison spoke, a patent attorney named Alva Donald Messenheimer expressed great concern over Morrison's views. A graduate of George Washington University, Messenheimer had recently become very well known among industrial patent agents, especially at firms in the seed industry.[80] He warned that Morrison was oblivious to the needs of the computing industry because he had been inappropriately influenced by the views of hardware manufacturers.[81] A new program requires hundreds of thousands of dollars in research and development, and yet "one sale of the program and it's in the public domain unless legal precautions are taken."[82] For a hardware manufacturer, this may not represent a significant loss; selling a few computer installations may be enough to recover these development costs. However, for "the programmer who doesn't sell the machines," this could represent a devastating loss. If the law didn't provide legal protection to these programmers, the only result would be "a poor industry structure" in which only firms that could afford to underwrite development costs—that is, the computer manufacturers—would be able to develop important new programs.

Messenheimer insisted that patenting was the only way of offering programmers the IP protection they needed. Trade secrets had too many disadvantages. It was often difficult to prove that a program had been kept a secret, and secrecy would encourage the development of restrictive employment contracts that would require firms to interfere with the professional growth of young programmers at a time when their skills were in high demand.[83] Copyrights were weak forms of protection; programs could be "manifested in several forms," and merely moving a program from one medium to another or writing a new one in a different language could be enough to bypass copyright restrictions.

Messenheimer delivered passionate and thorough testimony, but the other witnesses did not share his views. Their chief opponent at this meeting was Norman Zachary, the director of the Computing Center at Harvard University.[84] Zachary was well versed in computing and programming, but he did not know much about patent law, and he was likely invited to speak because of his stellar professional record. A former mathematician, he had served as director of communications and data systems at National American Aviation, vice president at General Telephone Company in California, and staff consultant at Sylvania Electronic Products.[85]

During the two weeks before his appearance before the commission, Zachary had studied patent law on his own, hoping to find something he could apply to computer programs.[86] He contacted programmers, administrators, and organizations such as AT&T, the Department of Defense, the Association for Computing Machinery, and SHARE.[87] He had not expected to find any common themes in his research, considering programming a field in which "it was impossible to get widespread agreement on any subject."[88] After all, he explained to the commissioners, it is "unlikely that the technical interest of a corporate controller and of a nuclear physicist" would coincide.[89]

Still, Zachary was convinced that there was a surprising industry consensus. With a great sense of urgency, he stated that everyone with whom he had spoken believed that bringing patent law into programming was very dangerous. Many of them had reacted with what he construed as terror. More moderate responses included both the belief that patents cannot possibly provide effective protection for computer programs and the assumption that even though some form of IP protection for programs is desirable, patents were unlikely to be the best choice.[90] These reactions convinced him that the best thing he could do for the commissioners was to articulate the two fundamental technical matters that they needed to keep in mind. First, he argued, "the distinction between hardware and programming is not meaningful."[91] A central problem involved in the design of general purpose computers is deciding "which functions of the computer are to be wired in" and which "are to be obtained by programming," especially because programmers were trained not to think that their work was "any more or less patentable than the output of the corresponding hardware designer."[92] Second, assessing the novelty of programs was especially difficult. A program could be considered new if it was "the realization of a new theory or concept"; if it contained "a basic advance in programming technique"; or if it demonstrated "ingenuity in its implementation."[93] Only the first two of these criteria could lead to inventions that displayed what patent law called novelty. The third criterion, ingenuity of implementation, was not legally viable in his view because using "well-known computing techniques to solve problems along lines which are already well-known" should not justify a patent.

Zachary estimated that a staggering number of programs met this third criterion and that they were especially common in such areas as payroll management, word processing, textual analysis, and mathematical computation. Programmers in these fields were writing programs "in an attempt to solve a problem and not because of any particular originality which may result from the program."[94] He recognized that there may be a great ingenuity in these programs, but he insisted that there was hardly any originality involved in the programming techniques or the set of algorithms that went into them. In short, a program should be considered novel for the purposes of patent law only if it realized a new theory or concept or if it contained any advances in "computer programming technique."[95]

Zachary ended by outlining his views on what should constitute patent infringement for computer programs. The restrictions on novelty that he advocated enabled him to describe these views succinctly: once a program has received a patent, any implementation of the theory or techniques that establish its novelty should constitute patent infringement.[96] As an example he cited Hamming and Holbrook's patent for error detecting and correcting codes, which had been issued fifteen years earlier. It would not be difficult to construct a new circuit "which performs many, if not all, of the same functions of the circuit described in the patent." However, he explained that "the heart of the patent" was the theory of error detecting codes that Hamming had developed, and not any specific circuitry. In this patent, as in all others for computer programs, a "theoretical, mathematical, statistical, accounting, managerial, or programming advance" is the core of the invention; the program itself is present only "to illustrate the point rather than for its own sake."

Zachary insisted that these patents should not be granted because they would be detrimental to the computing industry. He told the commissioners that the industry had "enjoyed an exceptionally free and easy exchange of ideas, of concepts, and of actual programs" and that it now faced a "shortage of trained, well-qualified practitioners."[97] He added that the central factor in the industry's growth was programmers' ability to draw on each other's programs without restriction.[98] Patents would isolate firms and programmers from one another at a time when cooperation was essential for computing to develop. In short, Zachary concluded, allowing "patents on basic programming developments" would hinder technological development. This argument aligned with Birkenstock's understanding of how IBM had drawn from other firms' work, and it would soon become a recurring argument against the patent protection of computer programs.

Zachary's and Messenheimer's testimony made a big impact on Edward J. Brenner, who sat on the president's commission in his role as the Patent Office's new commissioner.[99] Brenner did not know much about computing; his expertise was the patenting of industrial processes and products. Until his appointment as commissioner of patents, he had directed Esso Research's Technical Information Division—a position that had placed him in charge of overseeing the firm's patents on petroleum products, processes, and engineering.[100] At the Patent Office, his goal was to expedite application processes and to help the examiners cope with the influx of applications.

Soon after hearing the testimony delivered at the commission's hearings, Brenner issued new guidelines for the examination of computer programs. Unlike Morrison, he did not wish to ban these patents altogether, but he did agree with the examiner that the office needed to acknowledge the two ways in which patent applications could disclose computer programs.[101] On the one hand, a program could be protected by claiming an apparatus—a "physical device which is associable with the machine and becomes part of that machine so as to cause the total combination to be capable of yielding the result."[102] This device-centered view would distinguish the program from "the algorithm which the machine is intended to solve as a result of its functioning," and it would allow inventors to present their program as a patent-eligible machine.[103]

On the other hand, a program could be claimed as one of two kinds of processes. The first kind, "algorithm processes," performed functions such as processing data, performing calculations, or otherwise producing alphanumerical values based on whatever the user inputs into it.[104] In contrast, the second kind consisted of the "utility processes," which "deal with tangible things and substances." The guidelines acknowledged that this categorization was not perfect, but at least it would provide a clear way of thinking about programs: a process defined as "a series of steps for the manipulation or evaluation of data" is an algorithm process; one defined as "steps for causing a series of changes in state of components of the computer" is a utility one. Only the utility process was patent-eligible, so a programmer seeking protection for his or her program as a process would need to ensure that the patent application disclosed changes in a machine, and not mathematical manipulations of data.

Brenner's distinctions among an apparatus, a utility process, and an algorithm process were grounded on an analogy between computing and weaving. In the early nineteenth century, a machine called the Jacquard loom had become a common addition to textile factories. Able to produce intricate brocades and damasks, these looms were controlled by a series of punched cards in which rows of holes dictated the lines in a design.[105] The cards could be connected to one another, so designs could become as large and intricate as their users desired. In this century-old arrangement, there was an apparatus and a program—respectively, a loom and the weaving of a design.[106] Inventors in the nineteenth century would not have been able to secure patent protection on a specific sequence of punches, but they may have been able to patent a loom or a way of operating it. In the same way, programmers in the mid-1960s could not obtain a patent for the sequence of instructions that characterized their programs, but they could attempt to patent a machine that ran in accordance with the program's instructions and a way of operating it.

Back at IBM, managers and lawyers wondered what Brenner's new guidelines would mean for the firm. Soon after their issuance, T. Vincent Learson, the firm's newest president, addressed the company's patent lawyers at a conference IBM hosted for them in New York.[107] He told them that although he had always known that they did a brilliant job he had never known just how big that job was until Birkenstock brought him printouts of IBM patents. According to Learson, these patents were so large that they were best measured by how many feet long they were. Patenting, especially with the S/360 out in the market, was vitally important to the firm, but IBM stood against the patent protection of computer programs.[108] The two thousand or so programmers that IBM employed had a big job to get done, and the firm was aiming to invest about $60 million on programming alone, but patenting programs was not in the firm's plans. Programs were part of a service, and even if the idea of patenting them was "gaining a little ground," IBM would not be pursuing any patents of that kind. Instead, it would grow its army of patent attorneys. "I believe we're in good shape," Learson explained, "because we've got both the *biggest*, and I hope the world would agree the *best* patent department around."

Birkenstock kept Learson's words to himself, but he likely felt optimistic when the commissioners concluded that IBM was the best authority to determine what to do about computer programs. This was an unsurprising development, as Birkenstock's membership in the commission had made IBM a party in the discussions, and the only substantial discussions of other firms in the industry had taken place in the context of Zachary's testimony. Even if Birkenstock had not said much throughout the commission's discussions on the matter, the commissioners likely thought that no firm could provide better guidance than IBM.

Toward the end of their term, the commissioners asked Dewey Cunningham and Alan Rose, two patent lawyers at IBM, to "develop statutory language for excluding the granting of patents on programs."[109] On their firm's behalf, the two lawyers outlined how the law should be changed in order to ensure that "programs are not patentable"; that programs "cannot be rendered patentable indirectly" by claiming them "as a process or machine"; and that no machine working in accordance with a program can be construed as an infringement on a patent for a special purpose computer. First, they handled a matter of vocabulary: they would use the term "data processing machine" instead of "computer" in order to bypass criticisms by any "purists that would argue that any machine operates according to a set of instructions." They would also refrain from defining the term "data processing machine," since they assumed that any definition for it "is going to have more questions of interpretation than no definition at all."

Second, Cunningham and Rose proposed to create a statutory exclusion of programs from patent protection. The lawyers sent the commissioners annotated and revised printouts of each section in the 35th Title of the U.S. Code (the title that serves as the backbone for patent law). To each section, they added their revisions using underlined text. First, they added the term "program" to the statute, in reference to "a set of instructions which control or condition the operation of a data processing machine."[110] Second, they proposed that section 101 of the code, which deals with the kinds of invention that are patent-eligible, should take the following form:

> Whoever invents or discovers any new and useful process, machine, manufacture, or composition of matter, or any new and useful improvement thereof, may obtain a patent therefor, subject to the conditions and requirements of this title. <u>A patent may not be obtained for-</u>
>
> (a) <u>A process which is a program; or</u>
> (b) <u>A process described in terms of operations or steps performed by a machine pursuant to a program; or</u>
> (c) <u>A machine configuration established by a program; or</u>
> (d) <u>Any new and useful improvement of (a), (b), or (c).</u>[111]

Finally, they proposed the following revision to the section defining patent infringement, section 271:

> Except as otherwise provided in this title, whoever without authority makes, uses or sells any patented invention, within the United States during the term of the patent therefor, infringes the patent; <u>provided, however, that where a machine in the form in which it is manufactured does not infringe a patented invention, the use of such machine by itself, when operated pursuant to a program, shall not be an infringement of such patented invention.</u>[112]

The commissioners did not recommend these substantial revisions of the Patent Act, likely because they weren't proposing similarly in-depth recommendations for plants or designs (the patent-eligibility of which they had also investigated). They did, however, construe Cunningham and Rose's correspondence as an indication that the patent protection of computer programs was both undesirable to the industry's firms and an undue burden at the Patent Office. This would be especially problematic given their broader recommendations, which outlined how the country's patent system was not well equipped to handle what they saw as the ongoing age of "exploding technology."[113]

The commission's *Final Report* identified several important bureaucratic and economic ailments in the patent system, and it recommended that Congress should make every effort possible to continue aligning the American patent system with those of other countries.[114] Central to this was the United States' continued participation in the Paris Convention for the Protection of Industrial Property (1883), wherein member countries agreed to such items as treating foreign inventors as they did their own and allowing applicants to use their domestic filing dates as proof of priority abroad.[115] In this spirit, the commission recommended several changes that Congress would never implement, such as the development of a first-to-file priority system in the United States.

The *Final Report* explained that recent efforts to secure patents for computer programs had placed an undue burden on the Patent Office.[116] It recommended that programs—defined as the "series of instructions which control or condition the operation of a data processing machine"—should not be considered patent-eligible. The commission added that inventors should not be permitted to present computer programs as machine components, as in the past this had only "confused the issue." They did not know that lawyers and managers at the smaller firms that they had ignored were gathering a few miles away from the Patent Office to discuss how to strengthen the patent protections that IBM sought to eliminate.

Chapter 3 The Myth of the Non-Machine, 1964–1968

The programs available through bundles and user groups in the 1960s were limited by the manufacturers' consideration of which programs were worth developing and the users' willingness to develop and share their work. This meant that any users in need of very specialized or complex programs would need to decide whether to pay someone to create the program or to develop it in-house. Because hiring a programmer was expensive, these users could turn instead to firms called software contractors, which would create custom programs on a contract-by-contract basis and provide programming services for their clients.[1]

Software contractors generally fell into three categories.[2] First, large defense contractors started taking on programming contracts in the mid-1950s. The first one to do so was the RAND Corporation, which in 1956 created a subsidiary called the System Development Corporation, or SDC. This company made the programs required to run a military air-defense project called SAGE (Semi-Automatic Ground Environment). Second, the hardware manufacturers themselves sometimes accepted custom development contracts for very large civilian projects. For instance, IBM developed a reservation system called SABRE (Semi-Automatic Business Research Environment) for American Airlines and soon did the same for other airlines in the United States and Europe. Third, younger companies started developing custom programs for small and medium-sized firms that could not afford (or simply did not want) to hire a programmer. These companies were often very small—a handful of people with no computer of their own—and they relied on getting small contracts that the larger firms would not take.

Competition among small contracting startups intensified rapidly in the late 1950s and early 1960s.[3] Programmers and engineers who once worked for hardware manufacturers realized that their skills were in high enough demand to grant them independence from these large firms. One of them described this realization as discovering that "there was more money to be made programming with an independent software firm than there was if you were in a user shop or working for a computer manufacturer."[4] If they wished to form their own company, they could arm themselves with "a coding pad and a sharp pencil" and aim to get their first government contract.[5] Otherwise, they could join one of the dozens of startup contractors. If their new employer went bankrupt, they could easily take their skills elsewhere.

In the mid-1960s, these younger firms started to adopt the patent-drafting techniques that hardware manufacturers and industrial research laboratories had been employing for more than a decade. This chapter shows how one of them, Applied Data Research (ADR), brought software patents into the spotlights of the computing industry and the legal academy. Industry periodicals in 1968 celebrated one of ADR's patents, *Sorting System*, as the first-ever software patent. This assessment was accurate in a sense: patent protections for computer programs had been available for a long time, but the industrywide recognition of software patents as strategically and commercially valuable legal objects was made possible by ADR's use of patent law to make inroads against IBM's market dominance. More important, ADR and its allies transformed software patents into a rallying call for software firms—proof that new companies could stand their ground against well-established industry giants and that they did not need to manufacture circuits in order to create patent-eligible machines.

PATENTS AND COMPETITION

Six former UNIVAC employees founded ADR in 1959.[6] The firm offered programming services for companies and government agencies with one-of-a-kind computers. One of its earliest contracts was to create a custom program to predict airline conflicts for a new computer that the firm General Librascope was developing for the Federal Aviation Agency. Since then, ADR had developed a range of assembly, sorting, and operating systems for the National Aviation Federal Experimental Center in New Jersey.

Martin Goetz, ADR's first full-time employee, was interested in both the practice of programming and the business challenges that the industry faced.[7] A graduate of the programming courses that UNIVAC offered in the mid-1950s, Goetz held an MBA and had worked at firms ranging from the gas and electric utility Consolidated Edison, to the hardware manufacturer Sperry Rand. Along the way, he had become a frequent contributor to Sperry Rand's UNIVAC Program Distribution Library—a free sharing group for programming tools and statistical programs similar to SHARE—and he had spent some spare time writing sorting programs for UNIVAC machines.

In 1964, Goetz attended the Spring Joint Computing Conference, one of the major computing conferences in the country. Organized by the American Federation of Information Processing Societies (AFIPS)—an umbrella group created in 1961 to organize professional associations in the industry—this edition of the conference had as its theme "Computers '64: Problem-Solving in a Changing World."[8] It was chaired by Herbert R. Koller, the head of information retrieval at the Patent Office, and featured introductory technical sessions on such technologies as compilers and information retrieval programs, special state-of-the-art panels on such matters as numerical analysis, and a panel on the "Social Implications of Data Processing" designed to celebrate how computing had enhanced human lives and businesses.

One of the events that Goetz attended was titled "Patents and Other Legal Problems Relating to Electronic Computers."[9] It was chaired by Morton Jacobs, a lawyer with a penchant for computer engineering.[10] With undergraduate degrees in mathematics and physics and a JD from the George Washington University, Jacobs had served in the U.S. Army Air Corps during the Second World War and worked as a physicist at the National Bureau of Standards. In the 1950s, he had become an examiner at the Patent Office, where he developed a keen interest in the computing technologies that hardware manufacturers and industrial research laboratories were patenting. More recently, he had been practicing patent law privately, working with large firms such as RCA and UNIVAC. Just as familiar with the technical details of electronic computers as he was with IP law, Jacobs did not draw a thick line to separate a computer's hardware from its programming, most likely because from his post at the Patent Office he had gotten to know computing firms' patent-drafting techniques.

The panel's abstract noted that programmers and engineers had spent fifteen years asking why patents could not be granted for new developments in programming and programming languages. It offered participants an opportunity to realize that a "variety of patent, copyright, trade-mark and other legal problems" applied to hardware, software, and their industry in general.[11] Jacobs's presentation drew from an argument that he would later publish in the *Journal of the Patent Office Society*, namely that the patent-ineligibility of mathematical computations that stemmed from the mental steps doctrine was inconsequential to the eligibility of computer programs.

Detailed records of his presentation are unavailable, but his published article suggests that he told his audience that a computer program is "a series of operations performed by a computer," that each such program can be "represented by a sequence of 'instructions' to the part of the computer," and that these instructions can be "either stored in the computer memory or 'built-in' as part of the computer controls."[12] As a result, all that programmers and their patent lawyers would need to do to bypass the preconception that programs are ineligible for protection was to direct their patent applications at "the class of circuits whose components and parameters are defined by the mathematical equations."[13]

Goetz was drawn to the prospect of securing patent protection for a computer program, and ADR could use any competitive advantage it could find.[14] Managers at the largest contractors in the industry were starting to realize that custom programming was not profitable enough to remain their only source of revenue.[15] For more than a decade, they had been able to tolerate low profit margins, normally no more than 10 percent, because developing custom programs did not require making large investments or risky decisions. By the mid-1960s, as hundreds of smaller firms like ADR entered the industry, these profit margins were starting to drop even further. In addition, the Department of Defense's increasing spending on armament (at the expense of command-and-control technologies that would require software contracting), along with computer manufacturers' growing capacity for internal software development, were reducing the demand for custom software development.

Managers at larger firms therefore started to consider other means of remaining profitable, while their counterparts at small firms sought ways to make inroads in the industry's competitive landscape. In this context, ADR was neither the first nor the only software firm to consider the potential economic benefits of treating software as a proprietary technology. Back in 1962, a mathematician named Walter Bauer had wondered what software contractors' business would look like if they could treat their products as proprietary technologies.[16] Twenty years later, Bauer remembered that there "was literally no such thing as proprietary software," as user groups such as SHARE had encouraged programmers to think that a program entered the public domain as soon as it was completed.[17] Along with three business associates, however, Bauer had founded a new software contracting firm called Informatics. Its parent company, Dataproducts, had a small patent portfolio aimed primarily at printers, motors, and transducers, but several years would pass before Informatics attempted to secure patents of its own.[18]

At ADR, however, Goetz had learned from Jacobs that securing patent protections could enable the firm to experiment with ways of profiting from software beyond custom programming. The company had just passed through a period during which, according to Goetz, it was "struggling to survive."[19] Each one of the firm's past projects had been profitable, but the instability of its upper management and low cash flow had sometimes made it difficult for the firm to meet its monthly payrolls. Goetz's expertise with sorting programs—which could sort data into a set of categories—had brought in several new contracts, and though the firm was starting to stabilize, the contracting industry remained far too competitive for anyone at ADR to declare that the firm had made it.

Curious to hear more about how he and his firm could use patents, Goetz set up a meeting with Jacobs.[20] The two men got along well, and they soon developed a shared interest in putting Jacobs's claims about the possibility of securing patent protection for computer programs to the test. Goetz told Jacobs that he had created a new sorting program that could be adapted to the newly released line of IBM S/360 machines. He had been developing the program for a few years, and his work so far had been well received among programmers. Goetz had even presented, with great success, some of this work at a conference on sorting that ADR had cohosted with the Association for Computing Machinery (ACM).

Jacobs told Goetz that the right IP protections would preclude other software contractors, and perhaps even IBM itself, from duplicating his sorting system.[21] First was the development of a leasing contract that prohibited users from the unauthorized reproduction of ADR's programs (an early form of what would later be known as a license agreement). Jacobs suggested that ADR should start listing its programs as equipment and offering contracts with three-year terms. This would enable the firm, if necessary, to sue clients for breach of contract following the standard arguments that hardware firms used themselves. Second were patents, which Jacobs proposed to obtain by employing a patent-drafting technique similar to the one that Bell Labs had used for Richard Hamming's error correcting codes the decade before. Computing technologies had changed quite a bit since Hamming and Holbrook's patent, but Jacobs could still apply the same principle to protect Goetz's sorting program: secure patent protection for a program by patenting a machine that works in accordance with it. Jacobs drafted a patent application titled *Sorting System* over the next few months, and Goetz filed it on April 9, 1965.[22] The lawyer even included snippets of the source code that Goetz had written in the patent application itself, presenting it not as the subject matter to be patented but as an example of how a general purpose computer could be programmed to perform the program's work.

Nearly three years would pass before Goetz and Jacobs heard back from the Patent Office. Jacobs's plan in the meantime was to find allies and potential clients who would be interested, at least, in talking about software patenting with him. To this end, he visited New York for the 1965 meeting of the International Federation of Information Processing (IFIP). Founded in 1960 under the auspices of UNESCO, IFIP was a worldwide umbrella organization for societies dedicated to information processing, including AFIPS. Presiding over the meeting was Isaac L. Auerbach, an engineer and physicist who had worked at Sperry Rand and Burroughs before founding his own computing consulting firm, Auerbach Associates.[23]

The IFIP meeting promised to be an exciting event.[24] It consisted of seventy-seven sessions featuring five hundred speakers, all at the New York Hilton. Also at the conference was the *Interdata* exhibit, wherein more than twelve thousand visitors marveled at the technological developments displayed in 228 booths and listened to lectures and presentations delivered by eighty-three exhibitors. Any participants seeking entertainment during the day could visit the 1964–1965 New York World's Fair, which had opened its doors a month before the conference started. At night, people could participate in a wide array of conference events, including a sold-out performance of the Broadway musical *Hello Dolly!*, featuring Carol Channing and David Burns.

Auerbach himself had sponsored a panel for which Jacobs was a speaker, "Legal Protection of Computer Software."[25] It was chaired by C. J. C. McOustra, the deputy legal adviser at the London-based computing firm International Computers and Tabulators (ICT). One of only three manufacturers of electrical computers left in England, ICT was born in 1959 from the merger of BTM and its main competitor, Power-Samas.[26] McOustra was eager to make ICT known in the American market. British machines had generally become electronic replacements of their tabulating predecessors, and even ICT's own 1901 model—intended as a replacement for IBM's S/360—was advertised as designed to perform traditional punched card applications. The success of the IBM 1401 series in Britain had caused tabulating equipment sales to collapse, and American firms were controlling 40 percent of the British computing industry.[27]

The panel's unstated goal was to discuss the need for IP protections that could travel between the two countries. At the time, the United International Bureaux for the Protection of Intellectual Property (BIRPI, the predecessor of the World Intellectual Property Organization) was receiving reports of how important it was to develop patent protections that could travel easily between national borders, and it would soon launch a formal investigation into the matter.[28] Without countries' mutual recognition of each other's patents and a unified procedure for application submission, firms would find themselves in the position that BTM had been back in the 1950s, filing brand-new applications from scratch whenever they needed patents abroad. (This situation would not change until 1970 with the signing of the Patent Cooperation Treaty in Washington, D.C.)

The panel's patent lawyers aimed to demonstrate that the British and American patent systems were highly compatible, especially regarding information technologies. They described the legal protections on which software makers could rely in the United States and United Kingdom, identified people and firms interested in these protections, and assessed future directions that firms could take.[29] Familiar with BTM's history of securing patent protections for its machines' programming, McOustra said in his opening remarks that "from the standpoint of the law, change is in the air." He explained that the lawyers and scholars who joined him on the panel were not sitting in their law offices "watching progress pass by the window." On the contrary, they were moving as quickly as the industry, and they were here on the panel to check that they were all "moving in the same direction."

In his presentation, Jacobs argued that people should "be able to use patents to protect a novel technique in programming."[30] Programmers and engineers on both sides of the Atlantic agreed that a program is "a method of operating a data-processing machine." They also recognized that a stored program is merely a part of the machine, the one that controls how it works. With these points in mind, he concluded that there should be no question that programs are patent-eligible. The problem was that the Patent Office's examiners had taken the position that a program is "not patentable because it is merely a system of mathematics," which he thought was preposterous. Certainly, mathematics was involved in all technological advances, but patents for machines or processes never covered the mathematics itself. After all, a patent for an antenna or a circuit is directed at a device, not the mathematics that underlies how it works. Similarly, a patent for a computer's logic design does not cover the underlying mathematics, and one for a program would not cover the mathematics used to develop it. Instead, these patents would merely cover the machine's operation in accordance with the program.

Next to Jacobs on the panel was a young man named John Banzhaf.[31] A law student at Columbia University, Banzhaf had received his undergraduate degree in electrical engineering from MIT, and was best known as the first person to obtain copyright registrations for computer programs. In 1964, he had submitted two short computer programs to the Copyright Office.[32] One of the programs translated Supreme Court case citations written in an old indexing format into the modern format; the other one computed automobile braking distances given the car's speed and its brakes' specifications. He had submitted his programs in two forms—the index translator program as a printout of the program's code that had been published by the *Columbia Law Review*, and the braking distance program recorded on a magnetic tape.[33] Less than one month later, the Copyright Office accepted Banzhaf's copyright registrations, not because it was certain that software was eligible for protection, but because of its "rule of doubt policy," namely the practice of resolving uncertain cases in favor of the applicant.[34] As far as the office was concerned, Banzhaf's programs were books or pamphlets.

Banzhaf was an unusual participant at an IFIP meeting. He had developed in-depth knowledge about computing and the law, but he was a student sitting on a panel with experienced attorneys and engineers. He believed that his submission to the Copyright Office was more of a legal experiment than a response to an immediate industrial need.[35] In addition, several executives and engineers at software firms had told him that although there was general interest in securing any form of intellectual property protection available, the value of copyright protection remained unclear.[36] One attorney had even told him that "there had never been any question of whether copyright could be obtained for a computer program" but that securing it would be impractical because it required full disclosure and "gives you no protection."[37]

At the panel, Banzhaf explained that copyright protection remained very limited and difficult to enforce. A program may not be protected against translation into other computer languages, and it may not be protected from duplication into formats such as punched cards and magnetic tapes. Copyright offered no protection against "a copying of the principal ideas or against the creation of a similar work" by someone working independently. Banzhaf also noted that detecting copyright infringement was a difficult problem, probably because the distinction between an idea and its expression—a fundamental matter in copyright law—might be difficult to establish in a computer program.

McOustra likely saw Banzhaf's presentation as serving two purposes. The first was to demonstrate how the United States was pioneering the affordance of copyright protections for software, even if this protection was limited by the Copyright Office's categorization of computer programs as works of literature. The second was to highlight that if the United States ever joined the Berne Convention—an international copyright treaty of which the United Kingdom was a founding member—then firms around the world would face one pressing issue: the transformation of any special regimes of software copyright that their countries developed into protections for books or pamphlets in the American market.[38]

The final speaker on the panel was Laurence I. Boonin, an attorney at Auerbach Associates who predicted that new legal concepts would need to come to existence and become relevant in order for the industry to gain solid IP protections.[39] Software would constitute a sort of "intangible machinery" that would amplify human intellect just as tangible machinery had already amplified human muscle power.[40] Humanity had entered the era of the "new intangible," and it was more important than ever to identify which of the "legal attributes and consequences" developed for tangible inventions were still applicable. By the panel's end, it was clear that patent protections for computer programs were nothing new, as long as inventors and bureaucrats were willing to stop seeing their programs as mere intangible data processing techniques.

After IFIP, Jacobs turned his attention back to ADR. His goal there was to create a stable market for a program called Autoflow, which Goetz had developed in the early 1960s to help programmers create flowcharts for their software. A user could enter the text of a computer program after adding a few special commands, and the program would automatically print a flowchart that spread over several pages and a table of contents to aid the reading of the chart. Using Autoflow would therefore help firms and programmers to create easy-to-read documentation for their programs, reduce the cost of creating this documentation, and allow programmers to focus on creating more programs instead of flowcharting the ones they had already created.[41]

First sold in 1966, Autoflow became especially popular among users of the IBM 1401 and S/360 machines. Potential customers often wrote to the company asking for a demonstration of what Autoflow could do on whichever systems they owned.[42] In response to these queries, ADR would mail out sample flowcharts, send out promotional materials, and create custom flowcharts based on

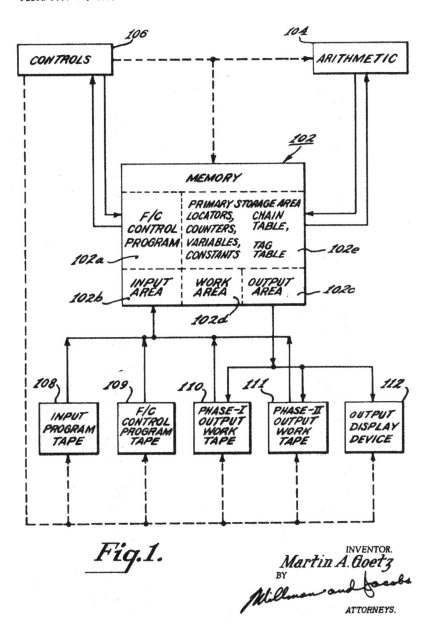

Fig.1.

INVENTOR.
Martin A. Goetz
BY
Willman and Jacobs
ATTORNEYS.

Schematic block diagram for a computer system on which *Autoflow*, ADR's proprietary program, is installed. This patent illustrates Morton Jacobs's patent-drafting strategy of embodying software. US Patent 3,533,086 (1970).

source code that the users submitted. The company advertised that this program could be "used for all flow charting requirements" and that it could produce detailed charts of programs from either assembly language or code in a programming language such as COBOL or FORTRAN.[43]

In 1968, Jacobs submitted a patent application for Autoflow.[44] Like the application for *Sorting System*, this one presented what Jacobs called a "new and improved data processing system" that would enable programmers both to produce flowcharts that met industry standards and to have a lessened burden when documenting the programs they had developed.[45] Jacobs claimed as the invention a "system for automatically controlling a computer" that includes "a sequence of instructions" that instructed the machine to "produce a visual display" of a given computer program.[46] What Jacobs described as an "embodiment of the invention" was a machine that produced flowcharts as directed by Autoflow and that would be protected by the patent.[47] The image shown here is not a flowchart of Autoflow's code, nor does it reference any programming language or algorithms. Instead, it is a visual representation of a computer's components that identifies the routes through which electrical impulses would travel. A large flowchart and a lengthy excerpt of code included in the application would eventually become part of the patent itself, but they were not exactly the inventions at which the patent was aimed.[48] Instead, they were meant to illustrate and clarify both the instructions that the patent disclosed and a way of using a computer that was already on the market (the RCA 501) as an embodiment.[49]

Jacobs construed the submission of the patent application for Autoflow as a potential weapon with which to keep IBM from releasing a free alternative to it. Soon before submitting the application, he had learned that IBM was planning to release a program called Flowchart. IBM had developed Flowchart for use with its S/360, and the firm intended to distribute it free of charge with the purchase of these machines.[50] In August 1968, Jacobs contacted Burke Marshall, one of IBM's attorneys, to request that IBM change the way it marketed and distributed Flowchart because the program was strikingly similar to Autoflow. The two programs could be used to produce flowcharts by typing in a series of textual commands; they provided a quick and easy way of documenting and mapping out a programmer's code. They also had several features that enabled users to focus more on the content and structure of the chart than on how it would look on a printed page, though Autoflow did have more automatic features than Flowchart.[51] In Jacobs's estimation, Flowchart could potentially "destroy the property value" of Autoflow as well as ADR's client base.[52] After all, it seemed difficult for a small software firm to have any sales at all if IBM could offer programs that performed the same functions and for which there was no price tag.

Jacobs's ultimate aim was to create conditions that would enable ADR's Autoflow to compete with IBM's newly released Flowchart. However, Autoflow was neither registered for copyright nor patented yet, and it had already been widely distributed among a variety of clients. This left ADR with few legal weapons if the firm were to launch a legal battle to keep IBM from driving Autoflow out of the market. Jacobs himself attempted to use two of these weapons in his letter to Marshall. First, he argued that IBM's claim that Flowchart was automatic was dishonest and that such "misleading and deceptive advertising" was meant to confuse clients into thinking that Flowchart was just as good as Autoflow.[53] Second, Jacobs tried to argue that IBM was on the verge of violating ADR's patent rights. Jacobs wrote that ADR had submitted a patent application for Autoflow, and he pointed out that once this patent was issued, IBM would be liable for infringement.[54]

IBM, however, was far too large and powerful to be concerned with these threats. In response, Marshall explained that IBM used the word "automatic" merely to reference the fact that Flowchart runs on a computer and that whatever use of the word that ADR proposed was not IBM's concern. Marshall also indicated that a patent application was worthless—that until a patent was issued, neither ADR nor IBM was in a position to assess their "respective legal rights and obligations."[55] Countering back, Jacobs turned to the one complaint against IBM's business practices that he had outlined in his original letter and that Marshall had not addressed, its bundling of hardware and software. Jacobs forwarded Marshall's letter to Goetz and asked that ADR attempt to "develop a factual picture" of the losses in Autoflow sales in light of the recent announcement of Flowchart.[56] He was looking for anything that could show the impact that IBM's bundling of Flowchart with S/360 was having on ADR's finances, its customers' questions and preferences, and the profitability of Autoflow as a proprietary program. Meanwhile, he wrote to Marshall alleging that IBM's bundling of Flowchart and S/360 was "illegal and anticompetitive" and demanding that IBM cease to distribute the program in any way other than through retail sale.[57] An antitrust battle against IBM's bundling was brewing.

Goetz and Jacobs did not think that IBM would give in to all their demands, but they did expect that the threat of an antitrust conflict would at least slow down the distribution of Flowchart.[58] Rumors that the federal government might get involved with IBM's bundling practices were circulating among software makers. In fact, Jacobs and Goetz had been in sporadic contact with the

Department of Justice, and in 1967 Assistant Attorney General Donald Turner had told them that the Antitrust Division was investigating the "pricing of computer systems."[59] Unable to rely on the threat of patent infringement to protect Autoflow, the battle was drifting away from IP and toward antitrust law, where it would continue to unfold in parallel for several years.

THE LAW OF SOFTWARE

While Goetz and Jacobs spread the word about the immense benefits that patent law could bring to small software firms, IBM's opposition to software patenting had started to spread across federal agencies. Back in 1966, Turner had told Patent Commissioner Brenner that the Antitrust Division opposed "the issuance of patents on computer programming methods."[60] Like Norman Zachary at the President's Commission on the Patent System, Turner assumed that growth in the "software portion" of the computing industry had been possible thanks to "a remarkably free and easy exchange of ideas, concepts, and programs" and that user groups had made "almost all basic ideas in computer programming" available to "all computer users." He added that small software firms, presumably software contractors, had achieved "financial and technical success" by producing more efficient versions of programs that the hardware manufacturers had developed and that these versions should remain free of patent protection so that other firms could use them to their benefit. For these reasons, he concluded that the Patent Office should proceed with the "utmost caution" when considering any measures that could upset the free exchange of programming material that had enabled the industry to thrive.

Turner's statement is an example of a phenomenon that Jacobs, Goetz, and others would often encounter: key federal agents—from examiners at the Patent Office to Congress itself—argued that they were protecting the entire industry's best interests by advancing views on software patenting most agreeable with the hardware manufacturers' needs. This became clear starting in February 1967, when the White House issued a statement celebrating the *Final Report* of the President's Commission on the Patent System. President Johnson deemed the *Final Report* a "balanced and thoughtful document" that would guide the country toward the most important changes that the patent system required.[61] The administration welcomed the reports' many proposals to simplify the patent system. As the markets for new technologies became increasingly global, firms would need both protection from their competitors and an efficient patent system that did not force them to "make their way through a complex maze of divergent patent laws and procedures."

Johnson instructed his secretary of commerce to craft a bill on behalf of the president and the attorney general.[62] The resulting bill was designed largely to streamline the country's patent system and align it with those of other industrialized nations. One recommendation encouraged the creation of a first-to-file system to preclude legal proceedings designed to establish priority of invention; another changed the term of a patent to twenty years as measured from the application's filing date, not from the patent's issuance.[63] Other provisions were designed to encourage harmony between the patent systems at home and abroad. For example, the bill would require inventions to satisfy a "world-wide novelty standard and be unobvious over all scientific and technical information available to the public, anywhere in the world."[64] It would be the inventor's burden to show that the invention met this standard. The Patent Office would also be instructed to "intensify its research and development programs," expedite classification, and search through "the world's library of patents and other scientific and technical information."[65]

Senator John Little McLellan (D-Arkansas) introduced the bill on May 17, 1967, to the Senate Subcommittee on Patents, Trademarks, and Copyrights of the Committee on the Judiciary.[66] The bill did not propose to revise sections 101 and 271 of the code, as IBM's lawyers had once suggested, but it did propose to add a new section excluding computer programs from all forms of patent protection. This proposed section, numbered 106, was titled "Computer programs not patentable." It stated that "a plan of action or set of operating instructions, in whatever form presented, to cause a controllable data processor or computer to perform selected operations shall not be patentable."[67] Section 106 would bring computer programs into the tenth chapter of U.S.C. 35, "Patentability of Inventions."

Had this bill become law, then software would have become the first technology in American history to be explicitly banned from patent protection in the Patent Act. However, more than 125 individuals and firms submitted feedback or delivered testimony declaring, for the most part, a vitriolic opposition to it. These participants included representatives from several branches of the federal government, professional associations for lawyers and patent agents, universities, and firms in such industries as aeronautics, computing, plant breeding, and nuclear energy.

A key speaker was Brenner himself, who explained that the recommendation to ban programs from patent protection aligned with the Patent Office's view and practice on the matter.[68] He celebrated the commission's recognition of the bureaucratic burden that software patenting generated and agreed that computer programming had developed satisfactorily in the absence of patent protection.[69] The Patent Office would "continue to deny applications for patents on computer programs per se," but it was premature to legislate the matter. Instead, he recommended that section 106 be deleted on the condition that the record showed that this deletion was not "intended to pass judgement on the question of the patentability of computer programs."[70]

The Department of Commerce, Bell Laboratories, and a firm called the Aerospace Group echoed Brenner's warning. Their advocates argued that programs were too new for Congress to settle on how to define them and predict their future.[71] Any legislation would probably only complicate the computing industry's relationship with the law, and the Patent Office would need to classify and search through programs even if the programs themselves were declared to be ineligible for protection. Software and hardware were technological equivalents, so this search would be necessary in order to assess novelty in hardware. In fact, declaring computer programs to be ineligible for protection could preclude patents on certain hardware, and this would be unacceptable.[72] The patent system had adapted for centuries to "embrace many complex and esoteric technologies far beyond the realm of imagination of its founders," so Congress had the responsibility of giving it the opportunity to embrace computer programming as well.[73] In agreement with these three groups, the Space Recovery Research Center (a consultant for the National Small Business Association) stated that the line that separates hardware from software was "becoming increasingly difficult to define" and that it was certainly not clear enough to form the basis for legislation.[74]

Professional legal associations generally agreed with Brenner's claim that it was too early to legislate software patents. The American Bar Association was especially opposed to section 106. Programming technologies were far too new to legislate them, and this kind of exclusion was best left for the courts to handle on a case by case basis. The language of the section was far too rigid for a technology the nature and future of which were difficult to predict. Local legal associations agreed. The State Bar of Texas explained that no one had enough experience with software to know what should be done with respect to its protection and that certainly no one knew enough to justify a statutory ban on its patentability.[75] The Philadelphia Patent Law Association shared this opinion, and it condemned "the blanket elimination of computer programs from patentability."[76]

Several trade associations also rejected section 106. The Aerospace Industry Association remarked that this section was a misguided legislative effort because "no science or technology should be excluded for patent coverage."[77] The Electronic Industries Association argued that defining what constituted programs in that section was extremely difficult to define and that any uncertainties of this kind should be resolved in the courts.[78] Even the American Chemical Association opposed section 106, though it took no position on the matter of the patentability of programs.[79] Its opposition stemmed from the possibility that such a statutory ban could end up prohibiting patents on chemical processes that were "carried out with automated equipment."[80]

Software firms and industrial research laboratories also opposed section 106. Richard Jones, ADR's president, insisted that "there is no basis for the legislation historically, theoretically, or practically."[81] He emphasized that the Patent Office was aware that there was a distinction to be made between "a computer system invention embodied in hardware and the same invention embodied in a program."[82] It was difficult for him to believe that the Patent Office would establish a policy that would "be discriminatory in favoring one segment of an industry over another," and he feared that Congress would now turn this unfair policy into law.[83] In agreement, the advocate for the Continental Oil Company warned that "big 'hardware' computer people," especially IBM and Honeywell, didn't want these patents. Their primary interest was to sell hardware, and the need to license patents for the programs they used would spike their production costs. In contrast, the "small 'software' companies" needed program patents, since they were trying to compete with the big hardware firms.

The administration withdrew the bill in 1968. No publicly available Patent Office records reveal the reasons for the withdrawal, but the Patent Reform Hearings likely revealed that the commission's suggestions were less popular than Johnson had hoped. The bill's withdrawal marked the death of section 106. According to one commentator, the discussions that preceded the section's demise showed that lawmakers and the Patent Office had realized that "if software patents were to be outlawed by statute, patents for equivalent hardware were being placed in the same jeopardy."[84]

Later that spring, in April 23, 1968, the Patent Office issued Goetz's *Sorting System* patent.[85] The published patent disclosed what Jacobs had called "an embodiment of this invention"—a machine "in which a plurality of tape memory units are utilized for serially storing data records." There was certainly a program in this machine, but the patent presented it as something that was built into the system and that, as far as the text of the patent was concerned, was as central to the functioning of the machine as a memory unit or electrical circuitry. Even the images that illustrated *Sorting System* disclosed physical artifacts. They depicted the architecture of the machine, not the design logic of the program for which they hoped to secure patent protection.

Computerworld ran a front-page story on Goetz's patent, hailing it as the "first patent for a software computer program" and the first landmark patent

Fig. 1A.

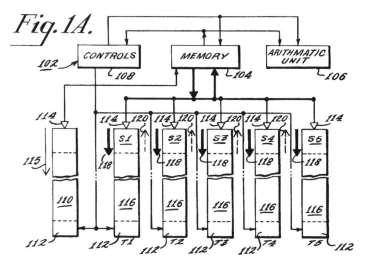

Fig. 1B.

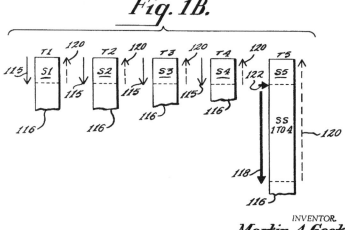

INVENTOR.

Martin A. Goetz

BY

Willman and Jacobs

ATTORNEYS.

Schematic block diagram of a tape-sorting system that embodies Martin Goetz's *Sorting System.* This patent was the first one to be widely recognized as a software patent, even though indirect patent protections for computer programs had been available since the 1950s. US Patent 3,380,029 (1968).

since the withdrawal of section 106.[86] The article noted that in the past, patents aimed at computer programs had the "involved logic design of actual hardware" that few computer programmers "could arrange to have built if the Patent Office wanted to see the system in operation." In contrast, the article implied, Goetz's patent was aimed at the software itself and had somehow bypassed the mental steps doctrine, thereby opening the floodgates for more patents of this kind to be issued.

Sorting System was indeed the first software patent, even if it was not the first patent to protect a computer program. In fact, Jacobs and some of his colleagues in the legal academy would later refer to it as a continuation of the tradition of patent drafting that dated back to Bell Laboratories.[87] It was the first of its kind in the sense that no patent before it had been identified and explicitly discussed as a "software patent" by the whole range of actors at the interface of the computing industry and the law (from programmers and lawyers to industry commentators and federal agents). However, what matters most about *Sorting System* is not its primacy but its strategic and symbolic value. ADR never sued anyone for infringement of *Sorting System*, but the patent's issuance helped managers, programmers, and lawyers at young software firms feel as if they were forming an industry of their own—one in which they were creating products that were potentially profitable and legally defensible as proprietary inventions. According to *Computerworld*'s reporter, the issuance of *Sorting System* suggested that anyone (from a lonely programmer working in an attic to one employed by a fast-growing contractor) could now fight back against hardware firms.[88] The article noted that it was now possible for programmers to get a patent "and so exclude the hardware manufacturers from using his technique without his agreement." Even if programmers now had the burden of showing novelty "and the traditional flash of genius," at least they would no longer need to rely on the "cooperation of one of the industry giants" in order to compete in the industry.

It is important to note, however, that the issuance of *Sorting System* was at once an extension of the computing industry's long-standing relations with patent law and an anomaly among software firms. Jacobs's knowledge of patent-drafting strategies for computer programs stemmed from his experience working at hardware manufacturers and the Patent Office. He was a seasoned lawyer working with a young software firm, and he was able to bring into software contracting knowledge and experience that his counterparts at ADR's competitors simply may not have had. In this sense, *Sorting System* was much more than a legal victory for Goetz and Jacobs. It was, above all, a link between the computing industry's historical patenting practices and software firms' ongoing strategic challenges.

Although ADR was the first to test how software firms could potentially rely on the patent system, it did not represent the IP strategies that its competitors employed. Rather than employing patent protection, other firms relied on a combination of contracts and trade secrecy to protect their proprietary programs.[89] Consider, for instance, the development of Mark IV—a software product that Informatics announced in 1967 and that would eventually become the first software product to generate $10 million (and later, $100 million) in sales.[90] Originally priced at $30,000 per copy, the product had been developed by John Postley, a programmer who had been developing file management programs for IBM machines (Mark I–III) since 1962.[91]

Informatics developed a combination of legal and technical means to protect Mark IV from unauthorized duplication.[92] It relied on trade secrecy as its primary means of protection for the program, and its lawyers drafted nondisclosure agreements with employees and customers. The firm also enacted a policy of distributing no source code whatsoever and marketed Mark IV as available for a perpetual license that required users not to transfer the program to other installations or third parties without the company's consent. Informatics also used specially colored punched cards and tape reels with official Informatics identification to help customers identify counterfeits. These means of protection had not been the firm's first choice; before their development, Postley had tried, and failed, to secure a patent for Mark IV.[93] Within five years, though, he and his collaborators would have obtained patents for the software product in Canada and Great Britain.[94]

Back at ADR, the issuance of *Sorting System* propelled Jacobs into the spotlight of the patent law community. It also the sparked interest of the prominent legal scholar Irving Kayton, who invited Jacobs to speak at a conference called *The Law of Software*. Like Jacobs, Kayton was a lawyer with a penchant for engineering. He had worked as a computer engineer and patent attorney for Bell Labs, GE, and the defense and space technology firm General Precision. At the George Washington University School of Law, he directed the Program on Patent Law and served as codirector of the Computers-in-Law Institute.[95]

Kayton hoped that *The Law of Software* would provide an opportunity to reflect on the host of legal issues that the computing industry was facing, especially the legal problems surrounding the efforts to develop and profit from software.[96] The conference consisted of eleven talks and discussions spread over two days. Its speakers included prominent attorneys, managers, and legal scholars representing institutions such GE, Bell Labs, and GWU's law school. Among them were John Banzhaf, who now taught law at George Washington University; Edward J. Brenner, the commissioner of patents; and ADR's Morton Jacobs.

The speakers agreed that copyrights could provide welcome relief to software makers, even if the scope of protection that they offered was hazy. Banzhaf explained that they provided a "reasonable degree of protection" if the only alternatives available were leasing contracts and the exclusive in-house use of a computer program.[97] Another speaker, Assistant Register of Copyrights George Cary, agreed with Banzhaf. He considered a computer program to be "a set of instructions which might be analogized to a 'How to Book.'"[98] That a program was useful was no issue, even though since the nineteenth century useful creations had fallen outside of the scope of copyright law. To Cary, the utility of a computer program was "similar to the situation which exists in the case of copyrighted insurance forms."[99]

Jacobs delivered a talk aimed at demonstrating that patent law was perfectly suited to protect software.[100] Titled "Patentable Machines—Systems Embodiable Either in Software or Hardware," it revolved around what Jacobs called the "myth of the non-machine," or the idea that software is not a machine for the purposes of patent law. He aimed to debunk this myth—to lay to rest the idea that "computer programs have a certain ephemeral character, a non-physical or non-machine character."[101] Jacobs did not know where and when this myth had originated, but he suspected that the characteristics of computer programming as a trade had helped to perpetuate it. Programmers "work with pencil and paper, and with symbols which we associate with mathematics."[102] Their job was to come up with solutions to problems, and they called their solutions "algorithms" without regard to whether that word reduced their work to a "mathematical or calculating process." If such a reduction did indeed take place, and especially if federal courts and the Patent Office embraced it, it would follow that computer programs "are merely mathematics and therefore non-patentable."

Jacobs argued that the myth of the non-machine collapsed under the weight of the fact that software is integral to hardware and equivalent to it, even though the two are separate products. He grounded this assertion on two observations. First, computer programs "are control mechanisms of computing machines."[103] By this, he meant that a program stored into a general purpose computer produced a new machine with a special purpose. The installation of software had a transformative power; a single program would make a computer system become a new device—perhaps a payroll accounting machine or one able to process airline reservations or typeset text. Second, a computer "has little or no practical value" if there is no computer program directing it; there is no computing system without a program to run it.

Commissioner Brenner was the keynote speaker at the conference. His stance on software patenting had changed since his appearance at the President's

Commission on the Patent System, most likely because the congressional hearings on section 106 had shown to him and everyone else in attendance that a firm stance against software patenting was benefitting only large firms.[104] This time, he used his talk to highlight that the value of software patents depended on the firm engaging with them. On the one hand, hardware manufacturers were "rather cool to protection for programs" because they feared that any protection would "impair the widespread use and availability of programs" and make their machines less useful.[105] On the other hand, software firms argued that the lack of IP protection was "a major obstacle in the development of programs" and that the "opportunity for plagiarism" caused by the lack of protection meant that the firms might be unable to recover the investment necessary to create a "marketable program."[106] The increasing costs of making software were deepening this division. Whereas in 1950 no more than 10 percent of computing research was directed toward software, Brenner estimated that by 1970 software would account for 70 percent of these costs. Moreover, as the number of software firms increased, hardware manufacturers saw the loosening of their grip over software, and the possibility of selling programs separately from the machines that ran them seemed increasingly appealing.[107]

Brenner implied that even though copyrights and patents were controversial means of protection, they were often preferable to trade secrets.[108] As the industry became more dynamic and programmers began to move from firm to firm, keeping secrets would become increasingly difficult. Moreover, trade secret law varied from state to state, so firms would potentially need to file suits in many jurisdictions. This would announce both the existence of their secret and the fact that the secrecy had been compromised. As a result, Brenner explained, many firms had become reluctant to develop programs for general dissemination, since making programs for individual clients would enable them to add a nondisclosure clause to their licensing agreement.[109]

Even if the IP protection of software was the most prominent issue at the conference, the discussions at the end of the gathering were mostly about antitrust law.[110] Participants noted that the Antitrust Division had taken an interest in the industry, especially because firms like ADR were vocal about their struggle to market programs that IBM could distribute free of charge with the purchase of its hardware. They predicted that if IBM unbundled—that is, if it started offering its software and services for a separate fee—then the computing industry would change drastically. More firms would become interested in making software or providing programming and maintenance services, competing with IBM in entirely new ways.

Part Two　**Software, Courts, and Congress**

Chapter 4 Antitrust Law and Software Sales, 1965–1971

In June 1966, an eclectic software developer named Larry Welke attended the American Banking Association's annual National Operations and Automation Conference. This three-day-long event brought together bankers interested in offering automatic data processing to clients ranging from individuals to other banks.[1] Welke, who worked at the Merchants National Bank and Trust Company, was very familiar with the software needs of financial institutions. A former systems analyst at IBM, he had created the Data Services Department at Merchants and had helped set up a computerized system for the Argentinian government to manage funds disbursed by the World Bank.[2]

Like the other participants at the Automation Conference, Welke knew that the computational needs of the country's banks were complex and diverse. One observer at the time estimated that only about five hundred of the country's more than fourteen thousand banks had either acquired or planned to acquire a computer.[3] Small banks usually outsourced their data processing to service firms such as

the Service Bureau Corporation, while larger ones tended to purchase computing equipment to handle only their more data-intensive or time-sensitive tasks.
Computerization was moving slowly but steadily even in the financial services
industry more broadly construed, wherein computation in real time was
becoming an increasingly important capability.[4]

Welke's favorite aspect of the Automation Conference was what organizers
had called the Swap Room, a space dedicated to the exchange of computer
programs.[5] On one wall of the room, attendees posted descriptions of
programs that they had developed and were eager to share, along with their
contact information. On another wall, they would post detailed descriptions
of the programs that they needed. Participants hailed from across the country,
but they often had similar needs, most likely because the regulatory environment of the banking industry generated similar data processing needs regardless of each bank's location. Like IBM's SHARE, the Swap Room allowed
users to trade custom programs with one another. The difference, however,
was that bankers were willing to pay.[6]

The astounding success of the Swap Room motivated Welke to publish a
directory listing software available for sale.[7] To this end, he created a firm
called International Computer Programs (ICP) and published a quarterly
magazine called *ICP Software Directory* starting in January 1967. The first issue
included more than a hundred program descriptions, including some for
programs Welke and his colleagues had developed at Merchants. Very quickly,
the *ICP Software Directory* expanded its listings beyond banking to include
programs developed by accounting firms, service bureaus, and even the
University of Georgia. Some vendors offered programs only as listed, while
others included customization options; prices could go as high as dozens of
thousands of dollars, if not more. As the directory's popularity increased, so
did Welke's reputation as one of the most important figures in the spread of
software products during the mainframe era.[8]

Welke's story shows that in the mid-1960s, while ADR and Informatics
developed their software products, conceptions of software as salable goods
were emerging organically and informally among computer users. The demand
for ready-made programs that manufacturers did not offer could only be
partially met by software contractors, regardless of how much expertise they
had with the industries they served. However, as this chapter documents, the
emergence of software products—that is, premade software that can be bought
or sold—into the wider computing industry triggered difficult problems in
patent and antitrust law. IBM's managers were very responsive to the increased
demand for these products. They even planned a test sale in 1966 but canceled

it in fear of its antitrust implications. While considering several alternatives to meet this demand, they revised how they conceptualized the relations among their machines, programs, and clients. The firm's unbundling of application programs, announced late in 1968, failed to appease the Justice Department's Antitrust Division and gave software firms new legal strategies that they could use in court. In particular, IBM's continued bundling of systems programs encouraged ADR to test the use of antitrust law as a means to generate temporary market exclusivity in the absence of patent protection.

IBM's UNBUNDLING

The erosion of IBM's bundles that the consent decree of 1956 had set into motion intensified in the early 1960s as other firms sought ways of competing with IBM's systems. Two of these new competitive strategies were particularly damaging to the commercial reputation and value of IBM's bundles.[9] First was the development of emulators for the IBM 1401, namely programs that enabled other manufacturers' systems to run instruction sets written for the IBM system. Honeywell announced the first such emulator in 1963, and RCA soon followed suit. Second was the emergence of minicomputers manufactured by firms such as Digital Equipment Corporation (DEC) and Scientific Data Systems (SDS), which offered a limited range of software aimed at specific market segments but cost significantly less than a full mainframe system. These two new features of the computing industry, respectively, caused users to start conceiving of IBM software as potentially separate from the manufacturer's hardware and demonstrated the value of marketing bare-bones affordable systems with a limited software offering.

At the same time, the S/360's software was proving to be expensive to develop and clients were dissatisfied with its performance, so managers at IBM started to think that justifying a separate fee for the firms' programs and programming services was difficult.[10] In 1965, a manager of sales administration at IBM, A. E. Brown, outlined this difficulty to Frank Cary, then president of the Data Processing Division.[11] Brown told Cary that unbundling would cause irreparable customer dissatisfaction. Because the firm's program libraries had been the subject of frequent customer complaints and criticisms, even a small charge for programming services would become a "major customer irritant," especially for users of large systems already receiving hefty invoices from IBM.[12] Brown also feared that the members of SHARE would either cease to contribute to IBM's program library or ask a competing manufacturer to serve as their computer distributor. Either way, users' reaction to a programming services fee likely "would be both negative and violent," and handling the resulting widespread customer irritation was just not worth it.

Another prominent obstacle to unbundling was the fear that IBM would be unable to protect itself against piracy. R. A. Reichart, one of the firm's price analysts, thought that even if charging a separate fee for programs was ultimately financially desirable, the firm's current legal environment was unfavorable.[13] Reichart and his colleagues in price analysis agreed that IBM should not consider the establishment of separate prices for its programs "until adequate means are available to control ownership and use." They knew that there were ways of achieving "controlled ownership" of programs and programming support through legal and technical means, but they seemed to have no clue as to how they would work in an unbundled industry. The firm had secured several patents protecting their computers' programming, but Reichart had difficulty conceiving how these protections would work if the firm unbundled. After all, selling a program would most likely not involve selling full electronic components or the special purpose machines that these patents could cover.

Added to these two obstacles was that IBM would need to decide which programs were to be sold before unbundling was even a possibility. Programs developed at IBM generally fell into two categories: Type I (Systems Programs) and Type II (Applications). None were treated as separate goods; all were considered part of the service bundles that the firm offered for its machines.[14] Thus, for instance, clients interested in a Type II program to process payrolls would contact IBM, and the firm would send an engineer to install it. Unbundling Type I programs was out of the question. In 1966, T. C. Papes, a director of finance for the Data Processing Group, told Cary and John Opel (a member of the firm's management committee) that it would be almost impossible to market the firm's hardware as technically superior to its competitors without offering bundled systems programming services.[15] Papes saw "no way to separate the bread and butter Type I programming" from the equipment and its price. He did, however, suspect that it might be possible and perhaps even practical to offer certain Type II programs for a special service fee. This could help the firm "contain the voracious appetite of the marketplace for more and more programming" while simultaneously articulating "a value concept" to its clients.

The increased interest in software products that would drive computer users to ADR, Informatics, and ICP carried over to IBM. Unwilling to miss out on a potentially profitable new business venture, IBM managers at all levels advocated a test run for IBM's Type II software sales. In 1966, the Data Processing Group proposed to offer for sale one program in order to "determine market response and provide a framework for solving technical, financial, legal and policy problems."[16] If the test sales revealed the potential for high profits, then the department was prepared to recommend selling all application programs. Aiming to test a program that could appeal to a large constituency without facing the intense competition that was emerging in the banking and financial services industries, the Data Processing Group chose a hospital accounting program for the System/360 called SHAS360 (Shared Hospital Accounting System). This program allowed hospitals to manage room assignments and process patients' bills—a complicated task given the number of insurance-related variables with which hospitals had to deal.[17]

The Legal Department was the strongest opponent of this project. Its staff warned that conducting test sales could "force the sale of future programs regardless of the test results."[18] After all, if IBM could sell one program, its competitors and the Department of Justice could argue that there was no reason why it wouldn't be able to sell all its programs. Moreover, other firms could follow IBM with similar tests, and a new market for the sale of computer programs could emerge—one that IBM did not mean to create and might not be able to control. In agreement, the Corporate Marketing Department issued a memorandum noting that such a market would be especially undesirable because it could weaken IBM's control over the industry while also exhibiting "low profit potential."[19] This encouraged the Data Processing Group to agree that it would not proceed with the test case unless three things were clear: that IBM could "maintain effective product control" over a sold program, that it could price it effectively, and that the program would "achieve a satisfactory market reaction."[20]

The only one of these three conditions that the department was able to meet was the first one, which boiled down to developing an IP strategy for sales. Within a few months, a task force on unbundling proposed a combination of copyrights and licenses as a potential way of moving forward. Selling a program would not entail giving users a title to the program itself. Instead, what IBM would sell was an open-ended lease. This made buying a program tantamount to buying a permanent license, and it would require clients to sign a licensing agreement that would allow them to copy the program for their own use but barred them from sharing it with others. The task force also considered what they described as physical means of protection: encrypting the programs, selling hardware components with the programs loaded onto them, and the sale only of self-destruct programs or single-machine locks and keys. However, they generally agreed that these means would discourage large clients from purchasing programs and would not be enough to deter "clever thieves."[21]

The test case failed before it began. By the end of the year, the department had abandoned it in fear that IBM would suffer losses in hardware sales and find itself in an undesirable situation under antitrust law.[22] According to the firm's sales analysts, the "sale of one program risks the sale of all."[23] After selling a program, even just once, IBM would prove that it could sell its programs. As a result, any programs distributed for free could be construed to constitute a tie-in sale, thereby making the firm vulnerable to further complaints from the Antitrust Division. This situation would force IBM to abandon its bundled business model entirely, which was undesirable because there was no guarantee that selling programs would ever be profitable.

Even though the Data Processing Group never carried out its test case, the surrounding discussions had shown IBM's managers that the inseparability between programs and machines that they had taken for granted would not remain the industry's norm for much longer. On the contrary, this inseparability would soon appear to be an artifice to their competitors and clients, and it therefore carried the risk of making IBM seem to behave in an anticompetitive fashion. For instance, the department's general counsel, H. Bartow Farr, told Cary that discussions about unbundling had forced the firm to talk about computers in ways with which he was not yet comfortable. The ongoing discussions of programming as something "separate from the machines" was inconsistent with the firm's "fundamental position that hardware and software ... are an indivisible product." This position, he noted, could now appear to be "quite illogical to begin with."[24]

Farr's concerns were well founded; software firm managers and IBM's clients had started to conceptualize programs as objects that could exist separately from the machines that ran them, concluding that bundling was unnecessary and inappropriate. Many users were seeing IBM's bundles as sources of unnecessary expense. Their logic was that if they were paying only for IBM's machines, then some portion of their bill must be going toward covering the bundle's cost. They would never need all the programs in IBM's library, so the price they were paying for their hardware included access to programs they didn't need. At the same time, software firm managers construed the bundles as evidence of unfair business practices—a dangerous situation to IBM, given its status as a perennial target for the Antitrust Division. It was clear to these managers that it would be very difficult to sell or lease a program for which IBM could distribute a free alternative.

In April 1968, a panel discussion at the Spring Joint Computing Conference turned into a forum for people to air these grievances against IBM's bundles. Chaired by *Datamation*'s editor, Robert Forest, the three-hour-long session was called "Separate Pricing for Hardware and Software?" and was attended by about a thousand people.[25] According to the meeting's program, this panel brought together "industry spokesmen, both selfish and altruistic," to discuss matters such as the viability of unbundling. Its starting premise was that while some application programs were already available for purchase, "off-the-shelf systems made up of catalog hardware and software components and subsystems remains in essence a dream which some contend would be a nightmare if ever brought about."[26]

ADR's president, Richard Jones, used his presentation to affirm that IBM's bundles were illegal under antitrust law and that they forced users to pay for low-quality programs that they didn't need.[27] He emphasized that the bundles were a key marketing tool: they enabled IBM to send representatives into people's offices for services that might not be essential, and these representatives could sell new hardware by marketing the software that would come with it. Jones also noted that ADR had a few pending patents and that until those were issued the firm would continue to protect proprietary programs through its willingness to take to court any breaches on contracts and trade secrecy.

The chief supporter of Jones's arguments on the panel was Bob Head, the president of a Los Angeles–based company called Software Resources Group.[28] Head told the audience that software was so important to users that any situation that allowed hardware manufacturers "to allocate resources between hardware and software with no accountability" was undesirable. He insisted that hardware manufacturers should be "forced to compete" with software firms and that there was no reason why users and software firms needed to accept the manufacturers' bundles. The key for this competition to happen was for IBM to unbundle; other firms were likely to unbundle if, and only if, IBM did so first. In short, software firms would need to wait for IBM to make the first move "on either a voluntary or [an] involuntary basis."

The other panelists affirmed Jones's and Head's views and demonstrated that the opposition to the bundle extended to user groups and the federal government.[29] Tom Marquez, the vice president of a Dallas-based firm called Electronic Data Systems, said that IBM had no reason to produce good software. All its engineers needed to do was to provide enough software for the firm to market the hardware. Then Herb Grosch, from the National Bureau of Standards, added that even though the federal government would be slow to incorporate unbundled systems into its purchasing and contracting models, he would continue to advocate for them over the coming years. Even the president of SHARE, Phil Cramer, stood in opposition. He explained that IBM's unbundling would cause computer prices to drop, and he predicted that bundles were doomed to be dissolved in three to five years.

To the IBM representatives in attendance, none of whom were on the panel, the entire event appeared to be an industrywide condemnation of their firm.[30] This became obvious when Forest opened the floor to questions and comments from the audience. One after the other, attendees spoke up against bundling. They represented consulting and computer leasing firms, time-sharing companies, banks, and even large government agencies such as the Los Alamos National Laboratory. By the end of the session, according to one IBM employee, it was clear that everyone had reached the same two conclusions: "separate pricing isn't worth the effort," and "better software is worth the money right now anyway."[31]

The panel caused a flurry of activity among IBM's managers, who exchanged reports about it with one another for a month.[32] The last memorandum available for research, dated May 13, 1968, was addressed to Frank Cary and several other high-ranking managers. It outlined three trends that the panel had highlighted. First, software firms, federal agencies, and leasing firms would continue to "seek avenues for improving their positions vis-à-vis IBM." Second, the Antitrust Division was likely to continue exerting pressure for the separation of hardware and software for several years. Third, unbundling was unavoidable, but there was no reason for it to occur all at once. It would "come about in stages but stop somewhere 'close to the machine,'" namely at systems programs.

Customer satisfaction was an important issue, but the most pressing matter was legal in nature. At IBM's request, the law firm of Cravath, Swaine & Moore (CS&M, which handled most of IBM's legal challenges in court) analyzed several actions other than unbundling that the firm could take in response to these pressures.[33] CS&M concluded that IBM couldn't just ignore the problem and fight software firms' antitrust lawsuits as they came, especially because one ill-fated suit could place IBM's corporate structure in the Justice Department's hands, and a court-ordered reorganization could force IBM to change beyond anyone's control. In the worst-case scenario, if IBM suddenly found itself facing intense legal pressure as a result of its bundles, then it could simply reorganize on its own. The law firm even suggested that IBM could "throw sand in the eyes" of the Antitrust Division by breaking up the Data Processing Group into regional branches and selling each one off on a franchise agreement. Perhaps by giving the appearance of a reduction in size, the firm could continue to market bundled products without raising red flags.

CS&M's report on unbundling circulated among some of IBM's top executives, from Hilary Faw (the firm's director of business practices) to Birkenstock and Watson Jr. It implied that unbundling was the only viable course of action, but it did not specify a timeline or procedure for the process. The law firm identified more than a dozen alternative courses of action, dismissing several as ineffective and unworthy of consideration. For instance, the firm could continue to bundle its existing accounts but offer newcomers the option not to take the bundle in exchange for a discount. This "looks good at the first glance," CS&M reported, but "it does not change the tie-in." IBM could also unbundle all but the low end of its hardware lines, but chances were that competitors would attack whatever lingering bundles IBM had left, especially given the sentiments they had expressed at the Spring Joint Computing Conference. The lawyers also advised against any reference to the firm's software as products. This was becoming especially common among the marketing and sales staff, who were now referring to applications as free products that the firm offered. One sales newsletter, for example, instructed that since IBM's programs are products, their specifications are "carefully reviewed to ensure that they meet significant customer needs." Even if programs are included in written hardware system proposals and promotional materials, and even if they don't carry a price tag of their own, the advertisement emphasized, "Type II programs are IBM products."[34]

In June 1968, an IBM staff lawyer responded to this situation by sending out a memorandum to various departments to emphasize that referring to IBM system or applications programs as products was "potentially dangerous."[35] He explained that programs "should be considered part of IBM's service and support" and that no official document for use outside of IBM should refer to programs as products unless it contained a detailed disclaimer specifying the many ways in which they were not, in fact, products. This disclaimer would also need to highlight things such as the lack of a warranty for any programs, the fact that program specifications are never part of hardware contracts, and that the firm charged no money for them.

By then, all the incentives for IBM to retain its bundles were gone. The computer conference panel had suggested that if IBM and the Antitrust Division came head to head, the Justice Department would have no problem finding managers for small firms and government agencies who would be willing to condemn IBM's bundles and describe their dissolution as the only way for the software industry to thrive. In addition, ADR's increasing sales of Autoflow had demonstrated that software products were already gaining momentum, and there was every reason to believe that small firms would not hesitate to file an antitrust complaint against IBM. The recent patenting of Sorting System and the high praise that ADR had received in industry periodicals suggested that IBM's ability to draw on other firms' programs freely would be either limited or a potential legal liability. By November, Faw realized that IBM would probably need to unbundle unless a "new answer to the tie-in problem" suddenly became apparent.[36]

On December 6, 1968, IBM announced that in the coming year it would change how it charged for its data processing equipment and its support. The firm would unbundle, but the details of how that would occur were forthcoming. Until then, IBM's legal and marketing departments had ordered the firm's staff always to advance the same narrative on why the firm had finally made this decision. This narrative presented unbundling as the firm's response to a fast-changing market, the needs of the leasing companies, and the customer's desires for "more comprehensive systems support."[37] No one was to mention that there were crucial legal issues behind the decision. In fact, IBM would never admit that its unbundling decision and its antitrust concerns were somehow related.[38]

The Department of Justice's filing of a complaint against IBM on January 17, 1969, increased the pressure for a rapid plan of action.[39] The complaint alleged two interrelated offenses. First was the monopolization of interstate commerce in digital computers, a complaint similar in tone and spirit to the ones that had led to the consent decree of 1956. It was grounded on the fact that IBM manufactured its computers from its plants in Poughkeepsie and Endicott, New York, and then shipped them to clients located across the United States. Second was IBM's development of manufacturing and marketing policies in furtherance of the first alleged offense. These policies included its bundles and its use of IBM software to appeal to potential hardware customers. According to the Antitrust Division, these policies limited the "development and scope of activities of an independent software and computer support industry."

The government's complaint prompted IBM's executives to discuss how to conceive of the relation between hardware and software in preparation for unbundling. The complaint's scope was limited by its implicit conception of software as the opposite of hardware. The document noted that hardware includes "all the physical components used in a computer" and that software is "the programming know-how and materials necessary to make the computer hardware operative." However, according to one of IBM's vice presidents, Jacques Maisonrouge, the relative value between hardware and software at hardware firms was very different from the one at their clients' offices. To the hardware firms, software was just "another product" with development and maintenance costs.[40] To clients, it was "an essential matter, because nothing works without it." This meant that software is "a product with an n-fold discrepancy between its manufacturing value and its utility value."[41] To illustrate this point in an internal memorandum, he represented a computer as a collection of 10,000 points. IBM's staff saw in that collection 9,800 hardware points and 200 software points, but customers tended to see at least 5,000 software points. This disparity in value meant IBM could unbundle a little bit of its software while appearing to be unbundling a lot of it.

Maisonrouge also predicted that unbundling would "mark the end of an era."[42] IBM would enter unfamiliar territory, as hardware manufacturers would start "entering the software-company market." As a result, IBM would no longer be able to "set the rules of the game," as it had normally done, and software firms would start to grow and multiply. IBM's own programmers might start their own companies or join a small firm where they could climb up the ranks quickly. If these firms started to offer good services and demonstrated their ability to develop operating systems, IBM would be in a market wherein customers hoped to pay low prices for hardware with minimal software. In other words, the more software was provided for a fee, the more IBM would find it difficult to justify high hardware prices. "The hardware will lose its glamour," Maisonrouge explained, so "prices will fall and profits will follow" even though the computing industry would no doubt be stimulated.[43]

Maisonrouge proposed two ways of moving forward. The two courses of action corresponded to what he identified as the two contrasting notions of software. First, if the firm were to adhere to the manufacturers' view of software, it could implement a 2 percent reduction in hardware price and start charging for all its programs and services. This would amount to a token gesture from IBM to the market that might just be enough to convince the Department of Justice that IBM was willing to forego some of its market dominance. Of course, IBM could reduce its hardware prices by more than 2 percent, but Maisonrouge suspected that the additional loss in profits would not be worth it. The second, far more appealing option, was for IBM not to change its hardware prices but, at the same time, to start charging for its software. This was equivalent to increasing IBM's prices, as clients would need to pay more money to obtain a functional system. He hoped that the government would be somewhat satisfied, as IBM would "lose its market position" by allowing competition in the market for computer programs to increase. Even IBM could benefit from this move, because it would remain competitive without appearing to be engaging in a "typical monopolistic move."[44]

While a secret task force with over a hundred members considered all the possible ways in which IBM could unbundle, the firm's legal and marketing teams launched an internal campaign aimed at educating the firm's staff on how to discuss unbundling with their clients. The teams' main lesson, which they printed using all capital letters in a handout, was "WHAT WE SAY CAN HAVE A DIRECT BEARING ON WHAT WE MAY BE REQUIRED TO PAY!"[45] At a presentation delivered in April 1969, they warned that the immediate issue was not whether there could be a successful monopoly suit against the firm but whether the firm could be accused of having an illegal tie.[46] Additional problems could stem from contract law, especially since prior purchase contracts had required IBM to provide "services necessary to install the applications contained in or reasonably contemplated" by both parties.[47]

The handout stated that unbundling would force the firm to grapple with very difficult strategic and legal problems. IBM's old application programs would be left in the public domain, and requiring users to sign licensing agreements for them would diminish IBM's image at a time when the firm's reputation was already suffering.[48] Relinquishing IP rights over these past programs would not generate a significant financial loss, but it did mean that small firms would be able to draw as much as they wanted from them in order to create their own products. More important, firms in every sector of the industry (from IBM's competitors to the trade presses that followed computing technologies) could react adversely to unbundling. In particular, software firms could join forces with more established competitors and argue that IBM had done either too little or too much. On the one hand, they could complain that unbundling would do nothing to foster competition—that IBM could "continue to impede the independent development of improved basic software and related subroutines."[49] After all, by keeping systems software bundled, IBM remained in a position to "trade off its hardware profits against heavy investments in leading edge software" that would enhance its overall market dominance. On the other hand, they could argue that "IBM had gone too far in its program unbundling." By issuing a blanket statement for all application programs, IBM could appear to be creating a division of computer programs into two commercial categories that should not exist. Other firms would complain that they "must now follow IBM with an illogical and unnecessary separation," and as a result IBM would eventually have to unbundle its systems programs.

Finally, on June 23, 1969, IBM announced the details of its unbundling.[50] Systems engineering services would now be offered at a price, as would courses that the firm offered to educate clients on how to use the machines. More importantly, all new programs would now belong to one of two categories. First, "systems control programming" encompassed programs that "provide functions that are fundamental to the operation and maintenance of a system." These were the programs that Cary would have considered to be "close to the machine," and they would still be available in a bundle.[51] Second, "program products" were those "related to the application of a system to user tasks." They would be offered at a separate price under a "License Agreement for IBM Program Products," which resembled the one that the 1966 task force had proposed.

IBM's unbundling is perhaps the best-known development in the early history of the software industry. Generally agreed to be the industry's "crucial inflection point," it prompted firms of all sizes to transform their own software into salable goods.[52] Software firms' profits started to grow, and other hardware manufacturers quickly established task forces to unbundle their own programs and maintenance services from their hardware.[53] In the words of one of IBM's marketing directors, this was a "new world," one in which firms would compete with one another through the development and sale of software products.[54] At the same time, however, the unbundling decision gave firms the legal arguments necessary to use antitrust law as a complement to patent law in their effort to make inroads against IBM's dominance.

SELLING SOFTWARE AT ADR

The Patent Office finally issued the Autoflow patent in 1970.[55] By then, Autoflow had become ADR's best-selling program, but it had also been the most expensive one to develop. In 1969, as ADR was starting to reach foreign clients, Autoflow had generated over $2.25 million in domestic sales and $500,000 abroad. At the same time, the program's development costs had nearly doubled. No records suggest that Jacobs ever followed through on his threat to sue IBM for patent infringement, most likely because IBM eventually licensed the product for its own use, but the Autoflow patent allowed ADR to solidify its roles as both one of IBM's competitors in the software market and one of its software providers.[56]

Unlike application programs, however, systems programs continued to be part of IBM's bundles. This meant that there was still an entire segment of the software market in which IBM could distribute free alternatives to the programs that small firms developed. The impact of this continued bundling was most evident to ADR's sales staff. Consider, for example, the experience of Robert Caughey, an ADR project manager who visited the Gulf Oil Company in January 1970. Caughey hoped to sell Roscoe (an ADR systems program that enabled time-sharing) to the firm's Houston office.[57] One of Gulf Oil's

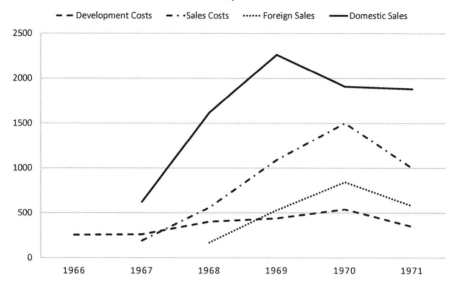

Autoflow Costs and Sales, in Thousands of Dollars

Costs and sales for Autoflow, in thousands of dollars. Note that its sales in 1969 were more than three times as much as those in 1967, and that its yearly development costs doubled from 1966 to 1970. Crafted by the author based on data collected by ADR. Box 1, folder 14, Applied Data Research, Software Products Division Records (CBI 154), Charles Babbage Institute, University of Minnesota Libraries, Minneapolis.

executives, a man of last name Claighorn, seemed very impressed by Roscoe, but he was especially interested in understanding the differences and similarities between Roscoe and a similar program called CRBE (Conventional Remote Batch Entry), which IBM distributed for free. In fact, Claighorn asked Caughey, "Can you tell me what Roscoe has that CRBE doesn't that would justify my paying $1000/month?" Caughey did his best to convince Claighorn about the technical superiority of Roscoe over CRBE, but Claighorn remained unimpressed, and the sale was lost.

Caughey's experience was not atypical. Clients of all sizes were dropping ADR as their provider for time-sharing programs. Firms such as Eastman Kodak, the Union Pacific Railroad, and the Chalmers Manufacturing Company (many of which had been Autoflow clients) were backing out of potential purchases on the grounds that there was no reason to buy any systems programs for which IBM distributed free alternatives.[58] Even NASA had withdrawn on the grounds that Roscoe was not technically superior enough to CRBE to merit the price tag.[59] Some firms were willing to delay purchasing any new computer programs at all until they made sure that IBM would not release free alternatives in the near future. One Kansas-based potential customer went as far as writing to an ADR salesman to say that he would "do nothing until we find out what IBM has for *free*."[60]

ADR was just introducing Roscoe into the market. The firm had already invested over $400,000 in research and development, and it was expecting to double that investment in 1970 alone. Roscoe was already in direct competition with CRBE, and it would soon compete with two more IBM programs, CRJE (Conventional Remote Job Entry) and TSO (Time Sharing Operation), which IBM was scheduled to release later that year. By 1971, ADR's sales representatives realized that their efforts had generated just over $95,000 in sales, even though the firm's investment in Roscoe was approaching the million-dollar mark. These sales seemed negligible, given that ADR's flagship program, Autoflow, had generated more than $2 million in sales in 1969 alone.[61] In fact, Roscoe was ultimately a disappointment for ADR's otherwise profitable Software Products Division.

With no patents for Roscoe, ADR had turned to antitrust law in an effort to keep IBM's alternatives off the market. Soon after IBM's unbundling announcement, ADR had filed an antitrust lawsuit against IBM in the District Court for the Southern District of New York.[62] ADR's antitrust attorney was Michael Hoffman, a prominent New York lawyer who sought more than $900 million in treble damages from IBM.[63] His brief complained that IBM was illegally tying "the sale of its programs to the sale of its computer," so that consumers felt that programs were being given away without charge even though the price for the programs "was subsumed in the price charged for the computer."[64] He presented IBM's unbundling decision as merely a policy that "segregates programs into two classes": those for which IBM was willing to compete with software-making firms, and those for which it desired to preclude the growth of potential competitors.[65]

ADR's suit was part of an extraordinary wave of litigation that IBM faced in the early 1970s. By June 1970, when IBM and ADR appeared before Judge Philip Neville in Saint Paul, Minnesota, a multidistrict judicial panel had ordered the suit to be merged with similar lawsuits filed by Control Data Corporation, the Data Processing Financial and General Corporation, and Programmatics Incorporated.[66] Hoffman stood with five additional attorneys representing his client and its allies; opposing them were five attorneys representing IBM, led by Thomas Barr.[67] Overwhelmed by the volume of the cases involved, Neville was completely unprepared. He had just arrived from trying unrelated jury cases in Duluth, Minnesota, and no one had sent him any documents related to the case, so he was not familiar with any of the parties' arguments.[68] For this reason, he asked the lawyers to summarize the key arguments that their clients had submitted.

Hoffman opened by explaining that the stakes of seeking relief from IBM's free distribution of time-sharing programs were so high that ADR's staff had been "burning the midnight oil" for several days preparing for the trial.[69] He claimed that if IBM started distributing CRJE, then within a month ADR would probably have to "fold up Roscoe"; it would be "pointless to maintain a salesforce [to] sell against a give-away competition."[70] ADR and its allies at the court, in Hoffman's opinion, had the right to compete with any program they had developed, but IBM's continued bundling of systems programs was standing in their way. He even alleged that IBM was putting firms "out of the program business" instead of allowing the programs' merits and the firms' service to determine who got to participate in the market.[71]

The problem, Hoffman implied, was that IBM was playing a trick on the market and its regulators. He told Neville that IBM's talk about bundling and unbundling was just a way of disguising what was actually happening—the illegal tying together of two products that could be sold separately. A climactic point of his explanation is worth quoting at length to illustrate both the aggressive nature of his argument and the unusual gendered metaphors with which he delivered it. Hoffman told Neville,

> IBM, it is true, wouldn't use such as mischievous word as "tying," and to my great admiration, I found they came up with this word "bundle." . . . [This word] has got the pleasant associations that suggests a young man and a nubile young woman in the Revolutionary days in New England on a cold night with a small board that separates them. That's bundling; the same thing as tying, your Honor. . . . There is no defense, there is no explanation, it seems to me, that can be afforded to selling as part of one deal, your Honor, the Programming and the machinery.[72]

Underlying these metaphors was Hoffman's understanding of software as a "separate, tangible product."[73] The programming of a computer, in his view, was a physical object—a magnetic disk, a tape on a reel, or some punched paper, and not "some mysterious element that lurks in the bowel of the computer."[74] Following Goetz's arguments on the separation of hardware and software, Hoffman argued that since the mid-1960s, IBM had acknowledged that the two were separate from each other.[75] He also claimed that IBM had unbundled only after its executives agreed that tying application programs to the hardware would no longer give them the market advantage that it had given them up until the mid-1960s.[76] From this, Hoffman concluded that believing that IBM was not engaging in illegal tying amounted to "ignoring the reality of this industry."[77] At the very least, in his opinion, the court should grant an injunction to stop IBM from releasing CRJE and TSO. Otherwise, the court would be doing nothing to stop "the blight which the IBM tying practice has thrown over the software industry."[78]

In opposition, IBM's lead attorney in the case, Thomas Barr, aimed to convince Neville that the case had no merit.[79] He contended that there was no time to "deal with all of the misstatements" in the affidavits submitted to the court and that ADR's quick actions were merely a "maneuver to abort the discovery process."[80] Hoffman's motion for an injunction was no more than a sham, and it was not unlike Jacobs's previous claims that IBM had tried to keep Autoflow off the market.[81] Indeed, Barr explained, although IBM had already released Flowchart, ADR had continued to profit from Autoflow's healthy sales. If Roscoe was not profitable, perhaps it was just because the program was not ready for the market.[82] This suit was merely the most recent version of the same argument that IBM had been fighting program by program and court by court—that "the bundle, so-called, is an unlawful tie per se."[83]

Barr also contended that ADR had not fully complied with IBM's right to demand ADR's clarification, under oath, of the terms and claims in its complaint against IBM.[84] In June, IBM had sent ADR a series of questions meant to clarify both what ADR identified was the relation between programs and the computers that ran them and the laws that IBM had allegedly broken.[85] In particular, IBM demanded that ADR define the term "computer-program"; that it specify how a computer program "acts as a control mechanism for the hardware"; that it describe how computer programs could be "attached to" hardware; and that it describe any ways in which a program can "control hardware" without being "attached to" it.[86] The surviving archival materials suggest that ADR addressed none of these questions in its reply and that instead its lawyers confined their answers to delineating the ways in which IBM had allegedly violated the Sherman and Clayton Acts.[87]

Barr's argument did not convince Neville that ADR's suit should be dismissed. On July 7, 1970, the judge issued a temporary restraining order that forbid IBM from releasing CRJE and TSO.[88] There would be a hearing in August to review this decision, but ADR's management and attorneys saw Neville's ruling as undeniable proof that software houses could stand their ground against the hardware giant. ADR's new president, John Bennett, released an open letter describing this victory as a small step in ADR's struggle to create "an open and competitive marketplace for all computer software programs."[89] In his view, ADR had set an important precedent, because other software houses could follow its footsteps if IBM threatened to release a free alternative to their system operation programs.[90]

Hoffman then negotiated a settlement with IBM. ADR and Programmatics (one of its subsidiaries, suing concurrently) agreed to dismiss their suits in exchange for IBM paying $1.4 million.[91] As part of this settlement, ADR also leveraged the patent it had obtained over Autoflow to obtain a licensing deal for IBM's use of the program. The exact details of this settlement are unavailable for research, but a commentator at the time estimated that IBM would be paying at least $600,000 in licensing revenue over the coming years.[92]

Released of liability, IBM started distributing CRJE and TSO later in 1970. ADR had prepared for this release by advertising the technical superiority of Roscoe over IBM's alternatives. For instance, one staff writer at *Computerworld* reported ADR's own findings about Roscoe's benefits over the counterparts produced by IBM; Roscoe required less disk space, had more flexible direct access storage, and had significantly lower operating costs.[93] Still, ADR did not seem intent on investing a lot in selling Roscoe. Their yearly sales costs for Roscoe had increased sevenfold from 1970 to 1971, but only from $3,000 to $21,000.[94] This was minuscule in comparison to Autoflow, for which in 1970 ADR had invested nearly $1.5 million in sales and marketing alone. In the end, despite Hoffman's apocalyptic warnings, Roscoe's sales did not drop after IBM released its free alternatives. The program's sales increased from just over $10,000 in 1970 to nearly $100,000 in 1971, but these amounts were now minuscule, as the firm was approaching the $7 million mark in yearly sales.[95]

However, ADR's David-and-Goliath suit had generated much more than just profits and publicity. It taught the firm's managers that competing with IBM would require them to develop both a reputation as makers of superior products and a long-term legal strategy. After all, the settlement had demonstrated that software patents, even if obtained with defensive aims, could generate significant licensing revenue. This encouraged them to spend a lot of time and money in an effort to strengthen the patent protections available to software, beginning with countering IBM's notion that it is ineligible for patent protection. To this end, Goetz, Jacobs, and their allies started spreading the word among other software firms and their clients that software has a certain materiality—that it is not disembodied information but a tangible invention separate from, and loadable into, computers.

The firm's marketing staff incorporated these ideas about the materiality of software into their corporate image by giving ADR the moniker of "the software builders." In 1971, as Roscoe's sales increased slowly and Autoflow continued to enjoy seemingly unstoppable popularity, ADR's executives approved an advertising campaign aimed at users of IBM machines.[96] The idea was to show potential customers that ADR was "hard at work building new software products" and that these products would make clients' machines more efficient, their in-house programmers more productive, and their in-house documentation, debugging, and maintenance more effective.[97] The campaign was meant to sell the three programs that formed the core of ADR's sales, Autoflow, MetaCOBOL, and the Librarian. If the programs' technical specifications and low prices did not convince potential clients to write to ADR asking for more information, then perhaps the company's customer service would; ADR highlighted that they "smother our customers with loving support," and that more than two thousand customers could testify that making clients happy made ADR happy.[98]

ADR's executives hoped that customers would realize that "software, like most computer hardware," requires services that ADR was happy to provide—installation, training, maintenance, and upgrading.[99] The resulting advertising series, called "Did You Know?," depicted the materiality of software in a lighthearted way. The campaign consisted of a series of cartoons designed to tell customers how ADR was always "making IBM installations work better."[100] Although the cartoons were produced in a format and size appropriate for periodicals, it appears that they were distributed primarily as loose leaflets, perhaps at conferences, fairs, and private meetings.[101]

ADR did not produce these cartoons for Roscoe, but it did make some for each of its other products. For instance, the cartoons for Autoflow show how the program's flowcharts could provide "hardcopy communication medium for all projects and personnel" and assist in any company's "management in educating and training junior personnel."[102] The cartoons showed how investing in Autoflow amounted to acquiring the tools necessary to facilitate internal communications, keep track of how a program works and how programmers change it, and diagnose any errors and identify the portions of the program that were responsible for them. They also implied that Autoflow was an essential tool that would "help bring management control into your computer scene," from the programmer's desk to the manager's office.

This campaign depicted software as a tangible good. In its carefree universe, computer programs were machine components or raw materials, ADR's personnel were diligent mechanics, and a client's personnel were potential

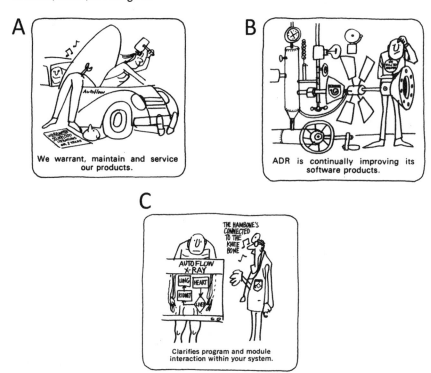

Excerpts from ADR's "Did You Know?" advertisements, depicting software as tangible machinery: a car (A), a humorous contraption (B), and an X-ray machine (C). Images courtesy of the Charles Babbage Institute, University of Minnesota Libraries, Minneapolis.

users of the devices that ADR was creating. Consider the samples reproduced here. Image A depicts Autoflow as an automobile, ADR's maintenance personnel as mechanics, and a client as the satisfied owner of the car who is whistling on the front seat. On the ground is ADR's warranty—maintenance for fifty million iterations or two years, whichever comes first. Image B portrays an ADR programmer as someone (perhaps a mechanic or an inventor) working on a complicated device that includes a fan, a pressure valve, a lightbulb, and an alarm. Finally, image C depicts Autoflow as an X-ray machine that allows a doctor to see a flowchart of his patient's internal organs. These cartoons were humorous, but the materiality of software that they depicted was much more than an advertising gimmick. They were, in fact, the basis of a legal argument that ADR would make repeatedly over the coming years, as patent applications filed in the early 1960s began to arrive at the courts.

Chapter 5 Software Patents at the Courts, 1961–1973

Computer science coalesced as an academic discipline between the mid-1950s and the mid-1970s.[1] A core tension that computing professionals had to resolve, especially in the 1960s, was whether computer science would deal primarily with mathematics or with electrical engineering. Led by academics such as Donald Knuth, advocates of more theoretical approaches distanced the young field from its origins in electric engineering and electromechanical computation, favoring instead the abstraction and formalization that a focus on algorithms and information enabled. In doing so, they aligned themselves better with university academic departments than with computing firms and industrial research laboratories, which faced labor shortages that would be best met by people who could deal with abstractions and circuitry at the same time. Indeed, computing professionals outside of academia generally favored a more engineering-oriented approach to computer science, one that would feature design and applications over algorithmic formalities. Richard Hamming himself criticized the academic approach to computer science in 1968 by complaining that recent graduates in the field were more interested in "playing" with computers than in obtaining results because they had been "taught by people who have the instincts of a pure mathematician."[2]

While computing professionals debated the proper agenda and scope of computer science, judges and lawyers in the patent system developed their own ways of conceptualizing computing as a practice and as an object of study. Like their counterparts in academia and industry, these legal professionals were concerned with the relations between algorithms and circuitry and the importance of mathematical abstractions in the operation of a computer. Legal conflicts on the patent-eligibility of software could hinge on whether the Patent Office and the courts deemed software to be machines, texts, or algorithms. Academic programmers played an indirect role in informing this debate, as Knuth's efforts to establish the algorithm as the primary object of study for computer scientists reached examiners at the Patent Office. At the same time, hardware manufacturers continued to argue that software is a text and that it is best protected by copyrights, not patents. Software firms continued to advance the notion that software is a machine, while industrial research laboratories advanced the notion that software is best understood as a hybrid technology. This situation forced the judges at the Court of Customs and Patent Appeals to develop their own conceptions of the nature of software and to use them as conceptual underpinnings for IP law. In the process, they infused patent law with an intense conceptual dissonance that would continue until the 1980s.

Software patents arrived at the courts in the late 1960s through patent-eligibility suits filed by firms in industries wherein control of a computer program could yield a competitive advantage. Each suit was the culmination of a longer process that had begun with the submission of a patent application at the start of the decade, as it could take more than five years for the Patent Office to issue final rejections that applicants could appeal to the courts. The two most prominent early suits of this kind, one launched by the Socony Mobil Oil Company and another by Bell Telephone Laboratories, are the subjects of this chapter. Their parallel histories reveal two characteristics that legal battles over software patenting would continue to exhibit for the rest of the century. First, the legal frameworks governing software patents failed to crystallize early on because no conception of what software is could satisfy the legal and commercial needs of software firms, hardware makers, and industrial research laboratories. Second, judges and bureaucrats infused their own qualitative understanding of software into the doctrines and policies that they developed. In the process, the courts of the patent system started to become grounds for firms to contest not only the outcomes of specific applications and suits but also the conceptual grounding that would govern software ownership in the computing industry and beyond.

FROM MOBIL OIL TO THE CCPA

In the 1960s, the Socony Mobil Oil Company was one of the largest sellers of oil and gasoline in the country. This firm had a very active research and development department, and it possessed a portfolio of more than thirty brands of gas and lubricants that it sold around the world. Its product lines had changed rapidly after a new generation of cars that used high-compression engines created a demand for gasolines with higher octane ratings. As Mobil's research efforts intensified throughout the 1950s, the firm's scientists had become especially interested in problems stemming from the high volume of computations that even the simplest field tasks could involve.[3]

Prominent among these problems was to determine the concentrations of the substances contained in a given mixture. This was especially important in the study of petroleum and natural gas, because their naturally occurring deposits often differed, not in the substances mixed together, but in their concentrations. Two of Mobil Oil's scientists, Charles Prater and James Wei, solved this problem by automating a technique called mass spectrometry, which measures the concentration of different atomic masses in a given sample to produce a two-dimensional graph called a spectrogram.[4]

Mass spectrometry involved an extraordinary number of elementary calculations. For each peak in the graph, there was a linear equation that expressed its height in terms of the concentrations of the mixture's constituents. This generated a system of linear equations relating the heights of the spectrogram's peaks to the concentrations the user wanted to find out. However, the number of peaks in a spectrogram was usually higher than the number of constituents in the mixture, so there were often many more equations than there were constituents. To determine the concentration of each constituent, it was necessary to select the collection of equations that would yield the most accurate estimations.[5] Choosing this collection could be extremely labor intensive. For instance, if thirty peaks formed in the spectrogram for a mixture with ten components, the number of possible collections surpassed thirty million.[6] It was at this step of the process that Prater and Wei intervened. It would create a list of all the equations associated with the spectrogram, perform very lengthy arithmetic computations on the equations themselves, and select the final subset based on the results of these computations.[7]

In October 1961, Mobil had filed an application entitled "Multicomponent Reaction Analysis and Control" for this invention. The primary examiner in charge of the application was Malcolm A. Morrison, the supervising examiner who would later testify against patent applications such as Prater and Wei's

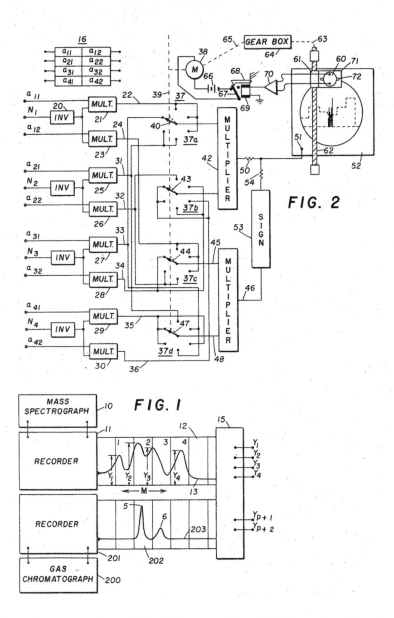

FIG. 2

FIG. 1

Schematic representations of Charles Prater and James Wei's invention. Note the spectrograms on the bottom image and the cathode ray oscilloscope (a circle in a square on the right-hand side of the top image). US Patent 3,551,658 (1970).

before the President's Commission on the Patent System. Morrison had rejected the fourteen claims in Prater and Wei's application on two grounds.[8] First, the application did not disclose the "best mode of invention" and did not "point out and distinctly claim the invention." These grounds for rejection pointed at what legal scholars at the time described as the problem of "insufficient disclosure." This term referred to the requirement of disclosing what the inventor considered the best form of the invention in a way that would enable a person skilled in the art to make and use the invention. Second, and more pressing, was his belief that the invention was not eligible for patent protection.[9] Grounded on *Halliburton* and *Abrams*, he wrote that a mental step "constitutes the very substance of the alleged invention" and that Prater and Wei were "merely measuring a property inherent in any rate reaction."[10]

Morrison divided the application's claims into two groups. The first comprised the application's method claims. Consider Claim 17, for a method of "determining with minimum error" the concentration of the components of a mixture that included steps such as "generating physical representations" (namely, graphs) for a collection of magnitudes and "comparing said representations" to one another in order to select the greatest magnitude. According to Morrison, these claims were problematic because they lacked a machine; they merely recited "a mathematical operation divorced from any structure."[11] Even if they could be rephrased to include an allowable apparatus claim, they would continue to be improper method claims.[12] The second group was the application's single machine claim. It disclosed a computer that comprised both "means for generating" a series of mathematical functions and a means for "determining that one" function that would yield the most accurate computations. Morrison thought that this machine was fictional. The claim may "appear to be drawn to structure," but it actually refers to "a program prepared for a general purpose digital computer."[13] This meant that the claim was merely a rhetorical exercise designed to make programs appear to be hardware.

In response, Mobil's attorney, D. Carl Richards, argued that the *Abrams*, *Yuan*, and *Halliburton* cases were inapplicable. His argument revolved around the fact that Prater and Wei's application mentioned that a machine was involved in the process. Whereas *Abrams* concerned inventions that were "purely mental in character," Prater and Wei's claims involved "instrumentalities completely independent of any mental operation."[14] Richards explained that the Patent Office should recognize the existence of processes "which *can* be carried out through mental gymnastics" but which can also be "carried out completely independent of mental operations and solely by physical instrumentalities."[15] In short, if a process could be performed by a machine from start to finish, it couldn't possibly be purely mental. To stress this point, he requested that the application be revised to add the word "automatically" before each of the computations recited in the claims.[16]

Richards told Morrison that the rejection of the claims in the first group was grounded on a misunderstanding of what Prater and Wei had invented.[17] The claims in this group were "drawn to method steps which are performed by physical instrumentality."[18] This physical quality was evidenced by two aspects of the application. First was the use of the computer disclosed in the application, regardless of whether this computer was analog or digital. Second was the ability to use phrases such as "generating physical representations of determinants" and "generating physical representations of the concentration of each component" in a mixture.[19] These claims were "of a class for a method of analysis of physical functions," which meant that they fell outside of the doctrine on methods of doing business that the examiner had cited.[20] To Richards, the application's claims were directed, not toward computer programs, but to "combinations of method steps involving generation of physical representations of physical conditions."[21]

Unconvinced, Morrison issued a final rejection, and Mobil appealed to the Patent Office Board of Appeals on July 13, 1965. The firm repeated the same arguments it had used in its dealings with Morrison.[22] In response, Morrison argued that the method claims comprised only mental steps and that the sole limitation on them was that they would occasionally generate "physical representations."[23] He continued to apply the *Abrams* rationale, which had banned processes "having only mental novelty."[24] Moreover, he wrote,

> It should be noted that *if such method claims as these are allowed, the following state of law will exist:*
>
> 1. New and unobvious equations will be unpatentable.
> 2. The process of working new and unobvious equations by hand, with pencil and paper only, will be allowable.
> 3. *Claims to a process of working new and unobvious equations by hand, with pencil and paper only, will be allowable.*[25]

Morrison insisted that the invention's essence was a mathematical principle, so it was not eligible for a patent even if it "may be utilized through the art of mathematics or through a general purpose digital machine."[26] Since Prater and Wei "did not invent mathematics," they had "not invented an art" with which to use their discovery.[27] The only physical steps involved in the invention were generating physical representations such as images and printouts—something that "is done by every school child with pencil and paper, in addition to being done on computers."[28]

He added that the inventors would have been "entitled to an apparatus claim" if they had "invented a machine to utilize their discovery and if their claim were directed to that machine."[29] The subject matter in any claim of this kind "must have been invented, discovered, or devised" in three steps: inventing the general purpose computer, discovering the mathematical principle, and programming the general purpose computer to use the new principle.[30] Prater and Wei had not invented the general purpose computer, and anything they had discovered in the second step was ineligible for patent protection. This meant that if they had invented anything, it must have been in the third step. However, the presence of mathematics made this step "a simple and obvious programming job"—a mere adaptation of mathematics in a digital computer that would be "obvious to any programmer."[31]

The Board of Appeals did not doubt that Prater and Wei's invention was new, useful, and nonobvious, but it ruled that the patent-eligibility of the method claims was precluded by the *Yuan* opinion of 1951.[32] The board considered it "beside the point that the solution of the mathematical problem can be done by machine."[33] The problem was that "the claims have set forth nothing which cannot be performed purely as a mental exercise," and they had not transformed or reduced any material to a different state or thing. On the one hand, the method claims did not constitute a patent-eligible process. The board based this ruling on *Cochrane*, which had defined processes as modes of treating materials to produce a result. The claims presented nothing that could not be "performed purely as a mental exercise" using the mathematical relations that Prater and Wei had discovered. On the other hand, the single machine claim was ineligible for protection because it was "nothing more than a general purpose programmed computer to perform the required mathematical operations." According to the board, this programming would be obvious to anyone skilled in the art, and the claim itself was just "an apparatus counterpart" of the process claim. After all, arithmetic operations such as the ones Prater and Wei proposed could be done "by a pencil making marks."

In 1966, Mobil hired Virgil Woodcock, from the law firm Woodcock, Phelan & Washburn, to file an appeal at the CCPA, which handled appeals to final rejections from the Patent Office.[34] There, Woodcock identified two primary issues. First was the problem of whether the processes described in the application were eligible for patent protection. These processes described the operation of a "machine invented by the appellants" that could operate "without human intervention," but the board had denied them because the claims were "broad enough to cover the operation of a digital computer programmed to carry out the steps of the process."[35] Second was whether a claim for the machine itself was eligible for patent protection. The main argument that Woodcock opposed was that the claim was nonstatutory because it was too broad—that is, that it would cover the operation of any general purpose computers programmed to perform Prater and Wei's process.[36]

Joseph Schimmel was the Patent Office's solicitor.[37] He insisted that "there can be no mistaking the essential mathematical character of their claims."[38] After repeating many of the arguments that the Patent Office had used to reject the application, he added that the appellants had conceded that "though not practical for most of the needed applications, [the] method, theoretically, can be practiced by hand."[39] This claim, Schimmel insisted, "was an understatement." For simple mixtures, it would be easy for a person with basic mathematical knowledge to perform all the required computations. This person could do this with paper and pencil or a desk calculator, and then move on to identifying the collection of equations with the highest determinant. This person could record all the calculations in a log book, thus producing "physical representations" only as "memory aids to impart information to others."[40] This made computers "merely ancillary to the basic mental steps involved."[41]

The court was a captive audience for Woodcock's arguments. Its judges tended to favor expansive conceptions of patent-eligibility, most likely because of the influence of one of its judges, Giles Rich. Back in the early 1950s, Rich had joined forces with Pasquale Federico, a high-ranking official at the Patent Office, to draft the bill that would become the Patent Act of 1952. While discussing their bill with a subcommittee at the House of Representatives, the two men had expressed their intent of having the scope of patent-eligible inventions to encompass what Federico had described as "anything under the sun that is made by man."[42] No records suggest that Rich used this phrase exactly in the court's assessment of Prater and Wei's application, but the court's record over the coming years suggests that his expansive view of patent-eligibility often informed his colleagues' views on the matter.

In 1968, the CCPA handed down a 3–2 decision in favor of Mobil Oil, but the case was far from over. Writing the opinion was Arthur Smith, a judge eager to keep working despite his doctor's orders to reduce his workload. Aligned with Rich's views, Smith wrote that a process in which a sequence of steps can be performed "without human intervention" is not necessarily ineligible for patent protection just because the process can "alternatively be carried out by mental steps."[43] The presence of a digital computer in Prater and Wei's invention was central to his ruling. It distinguished this invention from the one in *Abrams*, wherein there was no computer whatsoever.[44] Smith also explained that allowing the process claims made reversing the rejection of

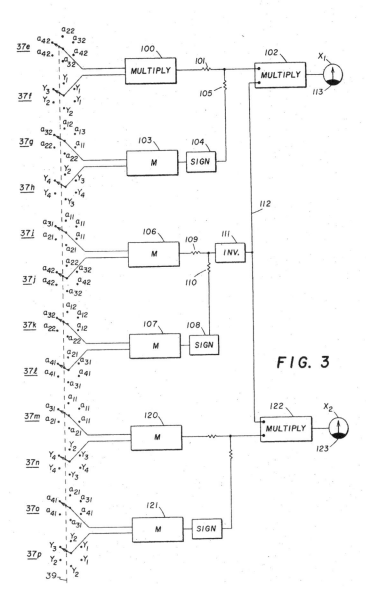

FIG. 3

Another schematic representation of Prater and Wei's invention. The values on the left-hand side are the quantities being manipulated, stored in a computer's memory. In mathematical terms, the operation being performed is finding the inverse of a matrix. US Patent 3,551,658 (1970).

the machine claim simple; it would be "an anomaly" to allow a patent on the former without allowing one on the latter.[45]

Smith died in his sleep on November 20, 1968, on the very day that the court handed down its decision. In mourning, the judges thought that the shock of his passing had prevented them from "becoming as conversant with the details and issues," even if their vote had yielded a decision in Mobil's favor.[46] This gave Schimmel an opportunity to contest the opinion without having to appeal to the Supreme Court because a legal technicality related to Smith's death enabled him to petition for a rehearing.[47]

The CCPA reopened the case in 1969. By then, IBM's unbundling and the issuing of *Sorting System* had sparked industrywide discussions on the value of patent and antitrust law to the industry. Jacobs and Goetz were starting to become patent prophets to firms across the industry, and hardware manufacturers were following IBM's lead in opposing software patenting in all its forms. Goetz and Jacobs construed the CCPA's 1968 decision as demonstrating that their patents were as valid as those for any machine. This could now change overnight, especially given that the court's judges were now equally divided on the matter. In contrast, IBM's entrance into the software products industry was intensifying the firm's opposition to software patenting. Still restrained by the 1956 consent decree, IBM's managers now feared that a single software patent could cause reductions in hardware profits and preclude any new software products and service offerings from being as profitable as they could be.

This situation made Prater and Wei's case the first major software patenting battleground between hardware and software firms. On behalf of ADR and other software firms, Jacobs filed an amicus brief opposing the rehearing of Prater and Wei's application.[48] He explained that ADR, like all other software firms, had "for many years been a victim of the Patent Office's policy of discrimination and violation of substantive due process in the administration of patent law with respect to computer technology." The court had finally cleared away these obstacles, and a rehearing would only threaten their continued existence. Jacobs also argued that overturning Smith's ruling would mean failing to see how hardware and software are "different sides of the same coin."[49] They are "so equivalent in their capabilities" that system developers are "free to choose between them" in whichever way is most convenient. Hardware and software "are premised upon the same principles," and they are each other's engineering equivalents. For this reason, "any categorization of one as an embodiment of a mental process necessarily categorizes the other." In any case, using the word "mental" is not applicable to either one, since the computing systems "eliminate the participation of the human mind."

The core of this case, according to Jacobs, was not whether the "so-called mental processes are patentable subject matter," because *Abrams* and *Yuan* had been left unchanged by Smith's decision.[50] Nor was the issue "whether computer machines and machine processes are patentable"; they had been "patentable for years under Patent Office practice and decisions so long as they are presented in the 'hardware' form of technology." Instead, the issues were "the false legal obstacles erected by the Patent Office which have denied equal patent protection for 'software' or computer programs." With Smith's opinion, the court had eliminated "the unequal treatment of equivalent forms of technology," and yet the Patent Office was requesting a rehearing.

Jacobs warned that a rehearing would enable the Patent Office to continue its oppressive and inappropriate treatment of computer programs. He wrote, "This Court's opinion has unclothed the Emperor and the Patent Office stands exposed as the creator of a legal fiction that does not stand up under the keen and brilliant analysis it has been subjected to by the distinguished jurist who spoke for this Court. No wonder that the Petition for Rehearing so desperately employs scare tactics as it seeks to create an atmosphere of fear and apprehension."[51] To Jacobs, the Patent Office's general treatment of "software embodiments of computer systems" as unpatentable was erroneous. The office had recently taken the position that these embodiments were merely mental steps, even if a process was being performed by a machine and was not something that a human being could do. Moreover, the 1966 guidelines had transformed software into a strange form of hybrid technology as far as patent law was concerned. Programs were not "patentable subject matter" if they were defined as a process, since they would constitute mental processes as shown in *Abrams* and *Yuan*.[52] At the same time, they were patent-eligible "when defined as a machine or apparatus." This had left programmers with the need to phrase their applications in ways that created "computer-program embodiments" featuring novel machine configuration.

Jacobs also told the judges that IBM would try to trick them into rejecting software patents. This was a response to IBM's petition to submit an amicus brief of its own, which Mobil's lawyers construed as IBM's effort to assert its market dominance.[53] In agreement with Mobil, Jacobs insisted that IBM was approaching the court "with unclean hands."[54] The firm was seeking to participate just because it wanted both to "maintain its effectively complete monopoly for the sale of software" for IBM machines and to "utilize with impunity any concept in computer programming developed by others."[55] Jacobs portrayed IBM as a deceitful firm willing to manipulate law and policy for its own benefit. He told the court that IBM had secured software patents of its own "based on the stratagem of converting the software programming to equivalent hardware programming." The firm had even secured patents for inventions the novelty of which "consisted of the computer programming there disclosed."[56] Jacobs added that IBM was aware of the equivalence of hardware and software but simply did not wish to recognize it. The firm had asserted publicly, at the Patent Office and the President's Commission, that software programming was "unpatentable subject matter." At the same time, however, it "disclosed the equivalent hardware programming" of its programs in order to secure software patents.[57] This meant, in Jacobs's estimation, that IBM was willing to confuse courts and legislations in order to retain its dominance over software firms. What IBM called its "point of view" and "expertise" were tainted by its history of antitrust violations and its patenting record.

Later that year, the CCPA reheard Mobil Oil's case. The lawyer, D. D. Allegretti of the firm Bair, Freeman & Molinare, submitted a brief on behalf of Honeywell. He argued that the court should restrict itself to ruling on Prater and Wei's invention, and not on the patent-eligibility of software. The court had not been correctly advised on the nature of computer programming, nor did it have a proper understanding of the legal, economic, and business implications of any holding that approved of software patenting.[58] Allegretti told the judges that they should not consider it their burden to determine whether it should "'force-fit' computer programs into the existing patent statutes."[59]

He argued that a ruling in favor of software patenting would add an undue burden to the Patent Office. The court's 1968 decision had provided "an open invitation to a flooding of the Patent Office with applications which were never intended to be covered by the present patent statutes."[60] The Patent Office was unprepared to cope with this increased number of applications, and there seemed to be no impulse from software firms to stop submitting them. On the contrary, Allegretti told the court that he had even seen announcements for schools and seminars aimed exclusively at teaching patent professionals how to write applications so that computer programs could be "'squeezed' into the patent system."[61] Kayton's *Law of Software* conference stood out to him as the most dangerous one. These were places that, in his view, "would appropriately be characterized more as schools for inventing patents, rather than schools for patenting patentable inventions."

Allegretti then proposed to the court that computer programs are more like texts than like machines. He argued that they are "created in essentially the same manner in which written works are authored, and musical compositions are composed."[62] The best way of understanding the relations between a program and the machine that runs it was to think about how automatic piano players work. These pianos had programs of their own, namely the punched rolls that conducted their operation. The creation of these programs began with musical composition, which amounted to having a "human composer writing out in general or specific form" a score. The notes of the composition would then be "placed or coded in a storage medium," a punched roll.

Piano rolls did not fundamentally change the pianos that ran them. The encoded music is "a new method of operation or 'program.'"[63] However, the piano's hardware (its mechanical parts) operate "in exactly the same way that they were designed and intended to perform," regardless of the specific program that directed their operation.[64] Thus, the playing of a new roll did not constitute the making of a new piano, and a new "musical program" did not become patent-eligible just because it could be played on an existing player piano. Certainly, there was creativity involved in the making of piano rolls, but this form of creativity was to be protected by copyrights, not patents. The same was true for software.[65]

On behalf of IBM, the lawyer W. Brown Morton submitted a brief arguing that the presence of a general purpose digital computer in an invention is irrelevant to its patent-eligibility. In his estimation, "[The] fact that the computer is a machine no more makes mathematical innovation or improved library organization or musical composition or drawing a patentable process than the same innovation or organization or composition or drawing would have been had the general purpose digital computer never been invented."[66] The firm also presented what it called a "Brief History of Computer Development" to the court.[67] It defined a computer as "a performer of calculations"—a person or a machine able to take information, perform operations, and "put out answers."[68] A computer's defining trait was "that it (or he) handles information reasonably," and not the presence of machinery. Human beings with paper and pencils could be computers; the presence of devices to aid computations did not make them any less of a computer. In fact, IBM explained, "the history of machine aids to human computation is almost as long as the history of mathematics itself."[69] In recent decades, machines had become especially popular among people interested in solving the mathematical calculations required for scientific and engineering work. However, a machine "is not a thinking being," regardless of how complex or powerful it may be. Instead, it is "simply an automaton which acts according to the laws imposed upon it."[70]

Software, in IBM's account, was nothing more than "the programs written for telling a machine what to do."[71] In the past twenty years it had become "a major task for the manufacturers and users of large scale systems," but it was actually nothing new. Ultimately, a program was no different from the punched cards that directed the work of a Jacquard loom, the nineteenth-century punched card–operated looms that had inspired the creation of punched card computers. A loom would weave a pattern in accordance with "the step-by-step instructions given it from a particular deck of its cards," but it "always performs the same basic job," namely looming.[72] Each deck of cards may produce a different pattern, but the only differences among the decks were the locations of the holes, and none of the decks constituted a patent-eligible invention. In the same way, general purpose digital computers act to determine ballistic missile trajectories, evaluate mathematical functions, or keep inventories "in accordance with the instructions given it from a deck of cards or other program source."[73] The computer "always performs the same basic job." It may be useful to link computers in an "*overall* process that displays patentable invention," but the program "is certainly not patentable," since the only difference between it and its predecessors is "the location of the holes (or other information bits) it contains."[74]

IBM advanced Edward J. Brenner's analogies on programming and looming. Its brief identified the first programmer in history as whoever was the first apprentice punching out cards for a Jacquard loom.[75] The firm acknowledged that the British mathematician Ada Lovelace may have been the first programmer in the modern sense, but it insisted that Jacquard's unknown apprentice was doing the same work well before the first computers ever became a reality. A fabric designer can "express copyrightable designs in a series of Jacquard cards" in the same way that a "gifted mathematician" will express "highly original computational methods in a series of digital computer program cards." Therefore, it is an "inescapable corollary" that neither the design nor the program are patentable inventions.

IBM also submitted one of its in-house pamphlets, "Programming: Words That Move Machines," to the court. The idea that computer programs are texts was central to this pamphlet. Just as writers can use the letters of the alphabet to produce all the words they need, programmers "can combine basic computer operations into a limitless number of programs."[76] For this reason, "the essence of programming" is "translating concepts and commands" into languages that the machine can understand.[77] This pamphlet advertised the S/360 as the culmination of decades of progress in the programming arts—decades during which business and scientific applications, computer systems, and even programming languages had grown increasingly complex and more flexible. As devices became faster, smaller, and more popular, programming would continue to be a hybrid between science and art. On the one hand, the science of programming would require programmers to analyze problems and reduce them to sequences of small steps that a computer can follow. On the other hand, the art would require them to select, connect, and use these steps using words that machines could understand.[78]

While all these parties awaited a decision from the CCPA, a new acting commissioner of patents, William E. Schuyler, replaced Brenner.[79] Schuyler had received his J.D. from George Washington University, and in the early 1960s he had served as the president of the American Bar Association's patent section. Like Brenner, he hoped to reduce the office's backlog, which now stood at 233,000 applications, including 15,000 patents approved but not yet issued.[80] He knew that the previous software patent guidelines were easy to bypass through properly phrased claims and that they had done little to reduce the burden that computer programs placed on the office.[81] He therefore aimed to impose an important restriction on software patents: regardless of how inventors claimed their software, a patent would not be issued unless the software was part of an invention that produced a tangible result. In other words, software aimed at producing numbers, statistics, or some "other informational result" would not be patent-eligible. Only software that was "combined in an unobvious manner with physical steps" would not necessarily be barred from protection. This meant, for instance, that a control system for a chemical processing plant would be eligible for protection if inventors could show that the system itself caused chemicals to change.

The CCPA's decision, issued that August, reinforced Schuyler's guidelines. Delivered by Judge Phillip Baldwin, it explained that a step is considered "purely mental" if it "may only be performed in, or with the aid of, the human mind."[82] These steps stood in contrast to "purely physical steps," which can only be performed "by physical means, machinery, or apparatus." These two kinds of steps formed the ends of a spectrum, and in between there was "an infinite variety of steps that may be either machine-implemented or performed in, or with the aid of, the human mind. In order to determine whether a step is mental or physical, it was necessary to consider the entire application and determine which end of the spectrum is closest to the step under review.

What Baldwin called the "disclosure of apparatus for performing the process without human intervention" could constitute prime evidence of the fact that it is not mental in nature.[83] Moreover, he thought that there was no reason to believe that claims that encompass the operation of a general purpose digital computer are necessarily ineligible for a patent. Such a computer may constitute nothing more than "a storeroom of parts and/or electrical components," but introducing a program into it made it into something else—a special purpose digital computer, namely a "specific electrical circuit" that may be eligible for patent protection.[84] In short, Baldwin's decision implied that the Patent Office had been right in issuing Goetz's *Sorting System* patent and allowed the issuance of Prater and Wei's.

FROM BELL LABS TO THE SUPREME COURT

Three years after the CCPA issued its second *Prater and Wei* decision, in 1972, the Supreme Court of the United States handed down *Gottschalk v. Benson*, its first-ever decision on software patenting.[85] It concerned the work of two engineers at Bell Telephone Laboratories, Gary Benson and Arthur Tabbot, who worked on the computerization of a telephone switching system called a private branch exchange. A PBX, as this system was called, enabled the creation of a private network of telephones within a building and the connection of these networks to one another and to standard telephone lines. It would receive a signal from a telephone, identify the telephone being called, and connect the caller to his or her target. Benson and Tabbot's PBX performed these connections by directing the signals with the use of a computer, and not with the permanent wiring together of every pair of telephones in the network.[86] In particular, they had written a computer program that converted the signals that the PBX received into signals that the computer could process. This program translated numbers written in one number system into another one—from their so-called binary coded decimal form to their binary counterparts.[87]

Like Mobil Oil's patent battle for Prater and Wei, the one for Benson and Tabbot lasted through most of the 1960s. In the process, one of Bell Labs' chief attorneys, Robert O. Nimtz, developed a reputation as one of the country's authorities on software patenting. Nimtz knew that the issue was not whether Benson and Tabbot's invention was patent-eligible. After all, since the 1950s the labs' patent and legal department had continued to secure patent protections for its computer programs. To him, Bell Labs' decade-long battle was instead a test case to determine whether it would be possible to secure such protections without disclosing the electronic components that would otherwise be required for the patent application to succeed. This would lead to a patent with a broader scope of protection; it would not be restricted to any specific computer architecture, which meant that any computer running the program could potentially infringe it.

Nimtz and his colleagues filed a patent application for Benson and Tabbot's invention in 1963.[88] Their application included descriptions and illustrations for a machine that would perform the translations, but it was not intended to patent any apparatus. The two claims that would prove most controversial were Claims 8 and 13, which described a "data processing method" of "converting signals from binary coded decimal form into binary."[89] Each disclosed data manipulations such as storing a binary coded decimal number in a shift register, adding a digit to the start of a specific number, and identifying each number one digit at a time.[90]

The patent examiner, Daryl W. Cook, rejected these claims and noted that the invention was no more than a software implementation of a series of mathematical computations that a person could perform on his or her own.[91] Indeed, Cook explained that a mathematician would be able to accomplish the same task by "carrying out a set of rules," and that, like the software, this mathematician would perform "no physical act on a physical thing."[92] To Cook, a programmable computer was just like paper and pencil in that a person could use it in order to grasp algorithms such as the one that Benson and Tabbot had encoded into a program.[93] This led him to conclude that storing data into a shift register amounted to writing; that transforming data from one form to another amounted to manipulating "meanings and representations made by signals"; and that no manipulation of tangible subject matter occurred at any step in the translation. From this, he had concluded that granting patent protection to Benson and Tabbot's method amounted to creating "a restriction on mental processes" that would in no way help to "promote science or the useful arts."

In 1967, the Board of Patent Appeals affirmed Cook's rejection based in part on the views on the nature of algorithms of the academic programmer Donald Knuth. Earlier that year, in an article for *Datamation*, Knuth had written that no one should ever expect to understand how an algorithm works by just reading it, and that everyone "should always take pencil and paper" and work through an example for each algorithm they encounter in a text.[94] This "simple and painless" way of engaging with an algorithm was in Knuth's view the only way of grasping it.[95] His essay was a promotional excerpt from the first volume of his work, *The Art of Computer Programming*, but in the board's hands it had an important legal consequence: it justified the view that engaging with an algorithm required the use of tools. The board quoted Knuth's article at length to justify its finding that the application's claims would deny mathematicians access to the tool needed to make sense of Benson and Tabbot's algorithm, a programmable computer. As a result, granting the patent would restrict both the computerization of the algorithm and the very ability to understand it fully.

Nimtz appealed to the CCPA with a patent-eligibility argument of his own.[96] It revolved around the notion that software has a dual nature. On the one hand, there was what he called the "explicative program," which he identified as "merely a list of instructions"—the program's "purely descriptive aspect." These programs were "closely analogous to the schematic diagram of an electrical circuit" and no more eligible for patent protection than "the schematic diagram of an electrical circuit." On the other hand, there was the "actual process, procedure, or method" that is carried out when the program's instructions are executed. When executed, these processes "correspond to actual embodiments of a circuit which are merely represented by the schematic diagram." These processes were what Nimtz called the "extant program," and their relation to the explicative program resembled that of an electrical circuit and its schematic diagram. Whereas explicative programs were best understood as writings eligible for copyright protection, extant programs were just "methods of processing signals." In Nimtz's view, extant programs had been the subject matter of patents ever since the Supreme Court issued the so-called Telephone Cases in the nineteenth century, wherein the original patents for telephony had been assigned.[97]

Nimtz argued that the coexistence of explicative and extant programs explained software's complicated relation with IP law.[98] He noted that the Patent Office's rejections confused the extant and explicative components of Benson and Tabbot's invention. Nimtz highlighted these moments of confusion by annotating Cook's text with bracketed words of his own. For instance, he contested Cook's observation that one of Benson and Tabbot's claims "is merely a program which is a set of instructions [explicative] to control the operation of a computer [extant]."[99] To Nimtz, this confusion was analogous to a rejection on a claim for an electrical circuit on the grounds that the circuit's schematic diagram is printed matter.[100] Explicative programs were texts and illustrations, and as such they may be the object of copyright protection. However, this did not mean that the extant programs that they described were necessarily banned from patent protection.[101]

In 1971, the CCPA embraced Nimtz's argument for the patent-eligibility of Benson and Tabbot's invention.[102] Following the reasoning for Prater and Wei's invention, Giles Rich wrote an opinion noting that the presence of electrical signals and shift registers in the claims was sufficient to demonstrate that Benson and Tabbot's claims were not directed to mental steps. The idea that the invention was mental in character because it dealt with numbers was also inadmissible in his view, especially because inventions such as cash registers were eligible for protection even though they, too, dealt with numbers.[103] In his account, the translation process that Benson and Tabbot had invented could be performed with "any kind of writing implement and any kind of recording medium."[104] However, this did not render the invention ineligible for protection because the hardware made the algorithm fast enough to be useful; it was improbable that any human being would ever be able to perform the data translations in the "milli- or even micro-seconds" required to operate the PBX.[105] In Nimtz's terminology, this amounted to ruling that the claims for the extant program were sufficient to issue a patent that did not cover its explicative counterpart.

A new commissioner of patents, Robert Gottschalk, appealed the CCPA's decision to the Supreme Court. His team reiterated the arguments that Cook and the Board of Appeals had made, emphasizing that the invention was ineligible for patent protection because it was no more than mental steps.[106] Representing Bell Labs was Hugh B. Cox, who had taken over for Nimtz likely because Nimtz did not normally handle cases at the Supreme Court. Rather than advancing Nimtz's arguments on the dual nature of software, which focused on what software is and how it works, Cox blackboxed the term "software" and focused on finding a description for it using the language of patent law.

Cox argued that Benson and Tabbot's creation was a type of patent-eligible invention best understood as a machine-process—a way of arranging a data processing machine in order to elicit operations such as the transfer and modification of electrical signals.[107] This shifted the focus from the nature of software toward that of the data it processed. Cox added that numbers, text, and any other information would be stored in the data processing machine in the form of electrical signals. Like flour, metal, or glycerin, these signals were the "proper work stuff for a process patent."[108] Otherwise the telegraphy, telephony, and radio patents that the Patent Office had been issuing since the nineteenth century would not exist.[109]

The Supreme Court case prompted several attorneys to submit amicus briefs on behalf of firms and trade associations.[110] Hardware manufacturers opposed granting Benson and Tabbot's patent, in part because they continued to predict that the production and marketing costs for their own software could rise if they had to pay licensing fees to the software firms and to one another.[111] In contrast, software firms argued that denying Benson and Tabbot's patent would make the patent system even more ill prepared to encourage the growth of their young industry.[112] In their collective wisdom, the hardware manufacturers' support of the Patent Office's position illustrated how giants such as IBM attacked any "hope of innovation and competition" and attempted to terminate "the very existence of an independent software sub-industry."[113]

Leading the software firms once again was ADR's Morton Jacobs, who wrote one brief for each of his main clients in the software industry—the software firm Applied Data Research, and the Association of Data Processing Service Organizations (ADAPSO).[114] Founded in 1961 as a trade group for service bureaus, ADAPSO had become the primary trade association for the nascent software industry. Its primary function in this capacity was to provide a forum for the discussion of the factors that could stand in the way of the creation and development of a software products industry.[115] Central to these factors was the patent-eligibility of software. Leading ADAPSO on this matter was Martin Goetz, who had become the chairman of the group's Software Protection Committee. Together with Jacobs, Goetz had brought many of ADR's views into ADAPSO's official positions on the relations between software and IP law.[116] For this reason, Jacobs's brief argued that "software programming is a machine device" and that the office was as well equipped to handle the search and classification of "inventions embodied in software" as it was for inventions "embodied in hardware."[117]

Jacobs's views stood in stark opposition to the position advanced by the Business Equipment Manufacturers Association (BEMA)—the primary trade association for firms including IBM, Honeywell, and Burroughs.[118] BEMA's attorney, John S. Voorhees, explained that software was akin to text or music in that it merited protection by copyrights, not patents. He insisted that a computer program "is nothing more than a set of instructions to a computer as to how it should manipulate information and data," and he rehashed the analogies with player pianos that IBM and BEMA had used in the past.[119] Creating a program was akin to writing a book or composing a song; inscribing the program in some storage medium was analogous to punching holes on a piano roll; and running a programmed machine was like listening to a music player.[120]

IBM and Honeywell were keen supporters of this argument.[121] The Burroughs Corporation, however, took BEMA's argument one step further by claiming that the presence of hardware descriptions in a claim for a computer program was improper. According to this firm's lead attorneys, James Clabault and Edward Fiorito, Benson and Tabbot had attempted to mask their invention, which was in essence an algorithm or mathematical expression, by "garbing their claims" using "digital computer operations or well-known hardware."[122] Their claims' description of hardware was unnecessary, which meant that patent protection over them would grant "a monopoly as broad as the algorithm."[123] This echoed Cook's original rejection back at the Patent Office. The wording of the patent application could "sound like a hardware component," but a countless number of hardware arrangements other than the ones that they proposed could perform the same function equally well.[124] Their claimed invention did not enhance or change the algorithm in any way; it was merely a transparent "façade of computer hardware" written with unnecessarily broad language that would read "equally well on any form of general-purpose computer."[125]

Those were the arguments that emerged victorious. On November 20, 1972, the Supreme Court issued its ruling in *Gottschalk v. Benson*, holding that programs such as Benson and Tabbot's were ineligible for protection. In the Court's view, there was no duality between extant and explicative programs. Instead, software was merely a "sequence of coded instructions," a vehicle for an algorithm that was no more patent-eligible than a formula or an electrical current.[126] This sent a discouraging decision for any programmers who would be interested in securing a software patent. At least for a few years, they would have a very difficult time trying to secure a patent for software that was not embodied.

Following the *Benson* decision, newspapers across the country declared that software was not patentable. A staff reporter at the *Wall Street Journal* wrote that the Court had "ruled that computer programming isn't patentable" and that Congress should be the one to make that determination.[127] The battle raging around Benson and Tabbot's invention was, in his view, one between "computer users" such as Bell Telephone Laboratories, which sought to secure their investments in computing, and "computer makers" who believed that "patents would hinder development of programming."[128] Similarly, *Time* magazine reported that the Supreme Court, in ruling that software "does not fall into any patentable category," had rightfully stopped Benson and Tabbot in their effort "to have the US Patent Office register an idea."[129]

In contrast, authors in the trade literature for the electronics and software industries were much more restrained in their reading of *Benson*. For example, the journal *Electronic News* wrote in its headline, "U.S. Supreme Court Rules Bell Labs Program 'Idea'; Therefore Not Patentable."[130] In addition, *Computerworld* wrote, "Supreme Court Rules against Program Patent." Among the more hopeful commentators were those representing the software industry. One sentence in the Court's *Benson* decision—"We do not so hold"—gave Morton Jacobs hope.[131] Groups such as BEMA had requested the Court to declare that all software is unpatentable, but the justices had refused to do so. In fact, as Jacobs explained in an article for the *Journal of the Patent Office Society*, *Benson* "left intact" many of the CCPA decisions that had approved the granting of software patents. Most important, in his view, was *In re Prater and Wei*. Unlike the Supreme Court Justices, the CCPA judges in the 1960s understood something that computer scientists had long known—that "computer programs provide an engineering technique" for the construction of special purpose computers.[132]

Perhaps instead of talking about hardware and software, Jacobs thought, courts should talk about "softwiring," or the use of a computer program to achieve in a computer the effect that would result from manually wiring a computer to achieve a certain result.[133] Unlike the Supreme Court, the Patent

Office, and the hardware manufacturers, the CCPA had displayed an implicit embrace of softwiring—its decisions suggested that the judges had come to understand that "computers are built by software." This suggested to Jacobs that the conflicts over the patent-eligibility of software were just starting. However, he wondered if Congress was a more appropriate venue for these conflicts to unfold. Perhaps there, opponents of software patenting would have better luck convincing people that "software companies do not need and deserve the same incentives of the patent system" for their products as the hardware makers enjoyed for their own.[134]

In agreement with Jacobs, as usual, Marty Goetz emphasized that ADR construed *Benson* very narrowly. In an article for the Association for Computing Machinery, he wrote that ADR had sought to "patent a machine process and not a program," even if it happened to be the case that the processes of interest could be "implemented in software or hardware."[135] Patents such as *Sorting System* and the one for Autoflow were "essentially apparatus claims which are best implemented in software, though they need not necessarily be so." Goetz added that the Supreme Court had answered the wrong question. Instead of thinking about algorithms, the Court should have asked if "a *machine process*, when implemented in software," is patentable subject matter. No one—not even ADAPSO or ADR—ever sought to advocate for software patents. Instead, they merely aimed not to have the patentability of an "inventive machine process" denied just because its inventor "chose to embody that machine process in software."[136]

At the ACM, wherein software patenting had been a recurring but never especially prominent issue, the *Benson* decision generated more questions than answers.[137] Since the mid-1960s, when the Patent Office first issued guidelines for the examination of computer programs, the ACM had hosted a Committee on Copyrights, Patents, and Trademarks. Norman Zachary, the director of the Harvard Computing Center, who had testified before President Johnson's Commission on the Patent System, had served as the committee's first director. Zachary personally opposed software patenting, but his committee never took that official stance.

In response to the *Benson* decision, Michael A. Duggan, Zachary's successor, published an opinion piece in a prominent legal journal, *Jurimetrics*. A professor of business law and computer science at the University of Texas, Austin, Duggan thought that the Supreme Court had made matters more complicated than ever. He believed that hardware and software were interchangeable but that *Benson* had rendered algorithms to be unpatentable.[138] Since "algorithms may be represented in hardware as well as in software," does it follow that "a computer program infringes an otherwise valid hardware patent"? Conversely, if something could be accomplished by hardware or software, does its "duality in and of itself preclude patenting the hardware"? Perhaps these questions were just the consequence of the courts' "unfortunate language" in their decisions, but the industry needed answers.[139]

Over the next few years, the CCPA attempted to provide some answers by developing what it called the "point of novelty" test for patent-eligibility.[140] This test was simultaneously a synthesis of decisions dating back at least to the 1950s and an endorsement of a method of examination that the court had advanced in its *Yuan* decision.[141] Standing by Rich's broad conception of patent-eligibility, the court continued to reverse the Patent Office's rejections, articulating what its judges considered to be the limitations of the *Benson* decision. The so-called point of novelty test, which it developed through these cases, consisted of determining whether what made a claimed process novel was a mathematical algorithm or a formula.[142] If this novel feature was the algorithm itself, then the invention was ineligible for protection; if it wasn't, then the claim was eligible. This test was not new—Zachary himself had proposed something similar when he had visited the President's Commission on the Patent System—but it now formed part of the country's common law. As a result, patent-eligibility was now formally tied to the complicated bureaucratic problems that assessing the novelty of a computer program could generate at the Patent Office.

However, even if the point of novelty test provided applicants with a way of appealing the Patent Office's decisions, the *Benson* opinion made software patents appear to be fickle legal protections. Defendants in infringement cases could draw on the Supreme Court's opinions in their effort to invalidate the patent that they had allegedly infringed. This meant that patent holders' best-case scenario was to engage in potentially lengthy and expensive legal battles. In the worst-case scenario, they would have their patents invalidated. This encouraged programmers and managers to start turning to other forms of protection, especially copyrights, in a search for a more reliable and less risky source of IP rights. As a result, two simultaneous long-term efforts unfolded over the 1970s: one aimed at negotiating the conditions under which software could be considered patent-eligible and another focused on delineating the protections that copyright law afforded to software.

Chapter 6 Remaking Software Copyright, 1974–1981

The 1970s were a turbulent period in the history of American copyright. Lawmakers had been attempting to overhaul the nation's copyright system since the 1950s, but a series of disagreements had prevented the passage of a new copyright act for nearly two decades.[1] Still not a member of the Berne Convention, the United States had continued to base its copyright system on the 1909 Copyright Act. The primary international treatise to which the country belonged was the Universal Copyright Convention (UCC), an alternative to the Berne Convention that UNESCO had developed in the early 1950s.[2]

Many American lawmakers had worked to strengthen the copyright protections afforded to objects like music records and television shows, which were becoming cheaper and easier to reproduce and transmit than ever before.[3] This interest intensified thanks to a 1971 revision of the UCC that spelled the minimal reproduction, public performance, and broadcasting rights that signatories had to recognize for foreign copyrights. It intensified further three years later, when the United States became a member of another international agreement colloquially known as the "record piracy treaty," most likely in an effort to protect the booming American music industry during a period of global expansion. However, determining the place of software in the country's copyright system required lawmakers to do more than just pay attention to the demands of international treatises and the needs of traditionally well represented copyright owners such as musicians or filmmakers.

This chapter analyzes how computer programs became a new category of copyright-eligible work on their own terms after more than a decade of being treated as books or pamphlets. By the mid-1970s, lawmakers were starting to hope that they were finally approaching the passage of a new copyright act, but one final hurdle stood in their way: the fear that computers would soon enable users to unleash a wave of paperless copyright infringement. With this in mind, Congress created the Commission on New Technological Uses of Copyrighted Works in 1974. CONTU, as this commission was known, spent four years discussing the relations between the copyright system and the development of information technologies. Introduced to computing technologies by IBM's staff, the commissioners proposed important revisions to copyright law that included the passage of what would later be known as the Computer Software Copyright Act of 1980. In the process, CONTU became a forum for hardware and software firms to advance textual conceptions of the nature of software and for semiconductor chip manufacturers to destabilize these conceptions by emphasizing that microchips could serve as material embodiments of software.

CONTU

Computers in the 1970s were becoming cheaper and smaller than ever. Integrated circuits, which allowed manufacturers to place hundreds of circuits inside a small chip, had slashed the cost of computer power.[4] Nearly a decade had passed since Gordon Moore, the cofounder of Intel and Fairchild Semiconductor, had posited Moore's law—that the number of components in a microchip would double every year—and there was no reason yet to suspect that he was wrong.[5] Manufacturers such as the Digital Equipment Corporation were producing minicomputers, small machines that cost up to a hundred thousand dollars and for which there was often a very limited line of peripherals and software. DEC's model PDP-8 fit in a portable box, cost just $18,000, and was popular among users with computational needs for science and engineering. Minicomputers were becoming common sights at industrial research laboratories, manufacturing firms, and universities. The industry was growing quickly, with new entrants including smaller firms such as Data

General and Prime and large ones such as Hewlett-Packard (HP), Honeywell, and IBM itself.

Like their larger and better-established counterparts, smaller minicomputing firms routinely secured patent and copyright protection for their programs. For instance, at Data General, patents protected much of the firm's systems software, from the computer's memory management to its error detection and correction.[6] Data General and other relatively new firms rarely got involved in any significant litigation, but their machines' lower cost and rapid dissemination gave lawmakers and commentators the impression that computers were starting to become more popular, powerful, and affordable than ever.

At the same time, computer networks were demonstrating that individual computers and workstations could be connected with one another across vast landscapes.[7] Time-sharing networks allowed many users to take control of a mainframe computer simultaneously from independent terminals; a single computer would divide its processing power among the terminals to give users the illusion that they were controlling the entire machine. These networks had been spreading around the country since the mid-1960s, giving users an opportunity to experience computing as a distinctly personal activity. Connected to one another on campus and across the country, students could share information with their peers, make and distribute their own programs, and perhaps even share someone else's texts without the appropriate copyright clearances.

No prominent corporate or federal agents believed that users were already committing computer-assisted copyright infringement, but lawmakers and the heads of the Copyright Office agreed that it was only a matter of time before computers became the new machine of choice for the copyright pirate.[8] Reformers and scholars alike predicted that computer-enabled data transmission would create a sequel to the paper-based piracy that had accompanied the spread of photocopying machines since the 1960s.[9] This was an ominous prediction, because the use of photocopiers had wreaked havoc on the publishing industry. Academic journals had perished because users were canceling their subscriptions in favor of photocopying the articles that interested them; publishing firms had become especially litigious against public libraries that provided photocopying services; and libraries and individual users continued to photocopy millions of pages every year.[10] However, photocopiers had ceased to be the only popular machines that could reproduce information at the touch of a button. The new generations of minicomputers could do the same, even though their reproductions did not necessarily leave behind a paper trail.[11]

In 1974, Congress created CONTU. Lawmakers acknowledged that the spread of computers and photocopiers created important problems in

CONTU commissioners and administrative staff. John Hersey Papers, Yale
Collection of American Literature, Beinecke Rare Book and Manuscript Library.

copyright law, but they did not want to delay further their efforts to pass a
copyright reform act. CONTU would enable them to exclude from the
upcoming Copyright Act what lawmakers called "some of the knotty problems" created by these two technologies.[12] President Gerald Ford approved of
this mission statement, and in 1975 he appointed CONTU's twelve commissioners, who were selected among copyright owners, copyright users, and the
general public. The author John Hersey and three publishing executives represented the owners.[13] The commissioners representing copyright users included
the Harvard Law professor and intellectual property scholar Arthur Miller and
three representatives from the professional community of librarians.[14] Those
selected on behalf of the public included Melville Nimmer, a prominent copyright scholar; George Cary, a former register of copyrights; Stanley Fuld, a
former federal judge; and Rhoda Karpatkin, the executive director of the
Consumers Union. Chairing the commission was Arthur Levine, a prominent
intellectual property scholar.

The commissioners' collective expertise covered all matters relevant to
CONTU's mission except one: computing. Instead, they brought to the table
decades of experience studying copyright law on an academic level, navigating
its implications for different kinds of institutions, and protecting the needs and
rights of copyright owners and users. Their exposure to the relations between

computing and copyright law began on December 18, 1975, when a copyright attorney for IBM named Joseph Taphorn took them on a tour of his company's facilities.[15] Several months earlier, Taphorn's colleagues had written to CONTU offering the commissioners an opportunity to learn the basic components of a computer and to become familiar with software programming.[16] Although some commissioners doubted that such education was necessary, Levine and Karpatkin eventually convinced their colleagues that understanding the point of view of a firm as important as IBM would be valuable both to CONTU and to the computing industry as a whole.

At IBM's Data Processing Headquarters in White Plains, New York, Taphorn and his colleagues introduced the commissioners to the history and technical details of hardware and software. The IBM staff presented the company and its machines as the culmination of centuries of data processing, which they defined as "recording and handling of information by means of mechanical or electronic equipment."[17] In their view, the history of data processing was a teleological narrative of isolated technological advances that began with adding machines in the seventeenth century, passed through Charles Babbage's designs in the nineteenth century, accelerated with the development of ENIAC and transistors, and culminated with IBM's current devices.[18] There were no corporate interests, regulatory frameworks, or industrial conflicts in this narrative, nor was there a history of usage, programs, or programming. Instead, the history of data processing appeared to the commissioners as the history of how a series of isolated and benevolent inventors created groundbreaking devices for the benefit of humanity. The endpoint of this history was the modern computer—a device that operated with punched cards, magnetic tapes, or disks and which the IBM staff defined as a machine that can accept, organize, and manipulate input to produce "an output that does not look like any other product."[19]

The records of this meeting suggest that IBM did not refer to software as an entity that could exist separately from any hardware. Instead, hosts such as Taphorn used the terms "software development" and "programming of a machine" in reference to the "instructions sets" that directed the operation of a computer and which were "intimately related" to the design of the machines they controlled.[20] In other words, the collective wisdom of the IBM staff suggested that if there was such a thing as "software," it was inseparable from the hardware. A set of instructions did not become a computer program until it became the programming of a machine after being loaded onto a tape, disk, punched card, or computer. This meant that everything that a programmer did before this loading—the brainstorming, flowcharting, and even the writing of the instructions in a particular language such as COBOL and FORTRAN—constituted writing. The IBM staff did not explicitly articulate the legal implications of this observation, but this view of programming meant that the human-readable code that programmers produced was nothing but a text similar to the ones that copyright law had protected for centuries.

After this discussion on the nature of software and a brief, informal chat with a few executives, the commissioners examined a handful of printers, card readers, and terminals. The IBM staff took them from room to room, showing them a collection of devices that were probably unfamiliar to some of the commissioners. As the visitors marveled at some of the devices they encountered, Ralph Gomery, IBM's vice president and director of research, casually explained his vision of what the future could bring to the computing industry. Devices would surely get cheaper and smaller, and there was no doubt that the ability to copy and transmit data would soon become very affordable, even to casual users sitting in their homes. Processors were becoming more powerful, so the computer's ability to copy and transmit information was bound to improve considerably, diminishing "the clumsiness of copying."[21] As computer networks became wider and denser and machines became more widely available, transmitting any material at all from one computer to another would become a pedestrian task regardless of the copyright status of the material being transmitted. In short, Gomery presented the commissioners with a view of the future in which poems, books, and maybe even images and computer programs could be transmitted from one machine to another as easily as television sets received their signals through broadcasting or cable.[22]

IBM's presentation gave the commissioners a knowledge base (grounded on the firm's own legal strategies) with which they could dive deeper into computing technologies. Nearly a year after their visit, on November 1976, the commissioners heard testimony from Daniel McCracken, an independent consultant.[23] McCracken was the vice president of the ACM, where he had previously served as chairman of the Committee on Computers and Public Policy. Bright and persuasive, he had written at least fifteen books on computer programming and the social implications of computing. Most recently, while working as a consultant for the Intel Corporation, he had developed an appreciation for a form of software embodiment that Taphorn had likely left out of IBM's presentations: through microchips.

Intel and other manufacturers had mostly secured patents for their chips and their associated technologies, since chips had no clearly defined place in the American copyright system.[24] The thousands of electrical circuits in these chips were another way of embodying a computer program. However, unlike the embodiments of the 1950s and 1960s, which involved components large enough to fill an office, these were small enough to sit on a person's thumb. They were also the drivers of computing technologies' steadily decreasing price and size. While working for Intel McCracken himself had learned that there were even groups of computing enthusiasts—hobbyists, they called themselves—who used microchips to build their own low-cost computers.[25] However, these hobbyists' market for computers (discussed further in chapter 8) was so small that McCracken and the commissioners were not concerned by it.

What did concern them was that the chips in small computers appeared to be technologies constructed through images. Microchips blurred the lines between patents and copyrights because they involved the layering of images akin to photographs to create a useful product that appeared to be better protected by patents.[26] Each chip could involve several thousand transistors, all contained in a silicon wafer with a surface area of a quarter square inch or less. Firms could make each of these chips by layering three-dimensional patterns called mask works on the surface of the wafer. This was done by covering the surface of the wafer in a thin layer of oxide, covering the oxide with a layer of a photoresistive material called the resist, and etching a pattern called a mask on the resist itself by exposing it to light. The light caused the photosensitive material to wear off, thus revealing the portions of the oxide that would be carved out by dipping the wafer in an acid bath. This process was a form of photolithography that had to be repeated several times in order to create a three-dimensional circuit on the surface of the wafer.

Firms often considered every aspect of this process—from the engineers' blueprints to the masks used to develop the photoresistive material—to be trade secrets.[27] However, a firm aiming to replicate a competitor's chip did not necessarily have to secure these masks and blueprints. The reverse engineering process was relatively simple: a person could take a photograph of the top of the chip, draw it on paper or on a computer graphics program, remove the top layer of the chip's surface, and repeat the process to re-create all the masks. This information would make it possible to replicate the mask work without the need to develop the chip from scratch.

McCracken believed that this ease of duplication raised a crucial problem that the commissioners had not considered—determining whether copyrights granted over a program's source code extended to the chip that embodied it. To correct this situation, he visited the commissioners with an ambitious goal: to show them a program's journey from a programmer's mind to an end user's computer. This task was so time-consuming that he was the sole speaker for the day during one of CONTU's meetings, but he considered the effort necessary to ensure that commissioners understood "what constitutes copying and what it is some of us at least are trying to protect in the software business."[28]

McCracken gave the commissioners a printout of the source code for an Intel product called Text Editor. Perhaps anticipating the question of whether Intel would want to secure a patent for the program instead of worrying about copyrights, he noted that the program might be useful, but it was "rather rudimentary," definitely "not a new idea."[29] The source code in front of the commissioners was written in PL/M, a programming language developed at Intel three years earlier. This was a so-called higher-level language, he told the commissioners, meaning that it operated "in an intermediate stage between the kinds of ways the people want to talk and the ways the computers want to talk."[30]

McCracken asked the commissioners to focus on specific pages of the printout, sometimes asking them to consider individual lines of code. While pointing at the printout's first line, he said that a "program consists of statements and explanatory text." Not every word in the source code instructed the computer to do anything. On the contrary, a lot of the words that the commissioners saw were just explanations that programmers had written to aid future programmers interested in understanding the source code. Comment sections in a program could even include copyright notices; Intel and most other firms included these, even if they did not register their programs at the Copyright Office.[31]

After explaining the meaning of some of the instructions, McCracken noted that the process of having a computer run this program required the use of a compiler (another program able to translate from source code to object code). This object code, in his view, is "what people steal." This raised the problem of assessing the extent to which automatically produced object code could be protected by the copyrights that a programmer had secured over the source code. What the industry wanted, according to McCracken, was to protect the object code, even if it "is a mechanical, simply mechanical, derivation" of something that human beings wrote.[32]

McCracken's testimony engaged CONTU in the most sophisticated conversation about software of the two years' collaboration. The commissioners asked questions about the compilers' work on source code, the machine-independence of different programming languages, and even the ability to translate between different machine codes. Propelling their discussion was a collection of analogies: Is translating a program akin to translating *Moby-Dick*? Or is it perhaps best understood as the process of translating a film into VHS format? The former implied no loss of information and a new copyrightable text, whereas the latter resulted in reduced resolution and no new copyrightable work.

As the commissioners debated the merits of various analogies and discussed the qualitative features of machine translation, McCracken interrupted to "make things even more complicated" by introducing the commissioners to how microchips work.[33] Pointing at a second printout, for a systems program called Intellec/MDS Monitor, he noted that a program may be so essential to the operation of a computer that it "has to be there before you know how to load anything else." This means that it couldn't possibly be distributed on a tape; it "has to be sitting there all the time." The solution to this problem was to put the program into a microchip similar to the ones he had distributed among the commissioners.

Pointing at the chips, McCracken emphasized their materiality by saying, "This would all be hardware in ordinary terminology. They are connected together by copper wires. They have been painted green. They look like copper. But all the lines on here are wired. There is solder on here. This is visible equipment. You can kick it, it is hardware in that sense."[34] The program "sits" on the chip as 0s and 1s, up to sixteen thousand digits stored in silicon bridges, metallic connections, and apparently "solid hardware." Perhaps that wasn't so much hardware, McCracken went on to say, as it was a materialization of a program. He added that there wasn't any difference between a program expressed as ink on paper and one as pieces of silicon. The printout of Intellec/MDS Monitor and the chip were, in fact, the "same program." Even if the chip itself was not a materialization of a given program, it could serve as memory onto which the program itself could be stored.

Michael Keplinger, CONTU's senior attorney, summarized McCracken's explanations on microchip technology as a classification into two types: a chip that can be erased and rewritten on the one hand and a special purpose chip "that embodied in hardware the equivalent of a program" on the other.[35] McCracken agreed and added that the chips themselves were designed automatically, by inputting object code onto yet another machine that would translate it into the appropriate mask works. This prompted Commissioner Alice Wilcox, the head librarian at the University of Minnesota, to wonder whether these chips should be copyrightable at all. Certainly, she told McCracken, there were images involved in the creation of mask works, but if a machine was the one producing them, what kind of human-made image would be the one receiving copyright protection?[36] McCracken retreated, noting that his job was not to make legal arguments but simply to show them the many ways in which a program could exist.

McCracken's lengthy testimony generated among the commissioners much more doubt than consensus. It was unclear, still, whether microchips were at all relevant to the question of software copyright. Regardless of what McCracken had said, an object with soldering and copper wires was very different from what Taphorn and his colleagues at IBM had described as the programming of a computer. Perhaps for this reason, the commissioners had slowly started to gravitate away from microchips in their discussions of software copyright, favoring instead an effort to agree upon some of the features that defined software. This, too, proved to be very difficult. Their efforts to determine what "computer programs are more or less like" had only enabled them to determine the categories of things to which software did not belong.[37] They had decided that programs "are 'like' little else" and that they might not be "like" books, paintings, or many machines. This had swayed them toward IBM's views on the matter, and in fact they decided to adopt a preliminary definition of software as "a fixation of a series of statements or instructions to be used in conjunction with a computer in order to bring about a certain result."

To test the viability of this definition, they invited Internet pioneer Joseph C. Licklider to testify. Licklider's reputation in government circles had skyrocketed in the 1960s, when he served as the director of ARPA, the organization that would later become DARPA—the Department of Defense Advanced Research Projects Agency—which would subsequently fund the networking precursor to the modern Internet.[38] Since then he had become especially interested in widespread time-sharing networks that connected several workstations to a central processing terminal and gave users the impression of having full control over their machines.[39] Licklider was now a professor at MIT, and he remained very interested in networking and resource sharing.

Licklider described how computer networks worked and how they could change over time, but his primary goal was to discuss what software was. He told the commissioners that their definition of software bothered and distressed him, but he fell short of telling them that they were entirely wrong. Certainly, text in a programming language could be transmitted from one computer in a network to the next, but according to Licklider, programs should not be reduced to the texts that programmers used to construct them. To him, a program was, ultimately, "something that gets slipped into a computer."[40] A program might have instructions written in a specific language, but for these instructions to become useful, they required a computer; unlike a poem or a novel, a program was worthless without this connection to a device. For this reason, Licklider held that it was a mistake to think about a computer program as a description of a process or as a set of instructions, regardless of the medium in which a programmer submitted it to the Copyright Office. To press this point further, Licklider added that the commissioners' question of whether a program "is more like ink on paper or like magnetics in a magnetic medium, or holes in electrons in a semiconductor" would become irrelevant if CONTU accepted that software was an object that transcended any medium used to transmit it.

Licklider insisted that the commissioners' decision to focus on copyright was inappropriate.[41] His argument that a program was a thing to be inserted in a computer was central to his more ambitious goal of arguing that patent law provided more appropriate protection for software. To him, a computer program was "very much like a machine"—that is, that software is "something which, when activated, when energized, behaves and produces process." Thus, the problem of securing intellectual property protection for software amounted to recognizing that protecting the code that a programmer wrote did nothing to protect the program itself. "All people want is the effect of the action of the program," he said in a climactic point of his oral testimony, "they don't care a thing for the particulars of the expression."

CONTU'S FINAL REPORT AND JOHN HERSEY'S DISSENT

Licklider's passionate testimony did not ultimately sway the commissioners to accept that software was ineligible for copyright protection, but it did put a quick end to the possibility of debating whether software was such a novel form of technology that it required the development of an entirely new form of intellectual property protection. Commissioner Hersey had become the most avid advocate of this argument.[42] Before joining CONTU, Hersey had become a central creative and political figure in American fiction, nonfiction, and journalism.[43] His first novel, *A Bell for Adano*, had won a Pulitzer Prize in 1945. By the start of his tenure at CONTU, Hersey was preparing to publish his twentieth book while serving as master of a college at Yale and as president of the Authors' League of America. It was in the latter capacity that he had been appointed as commissioner; his presence in CONTU was meant to ensure that the commission would take into consideration the best interests of the country's authors.

At CONTU, Hersey had become especially interested in computer programs. What intrigued him most were not the technical details but that programs included text. He explained that these texts were not of the same kind as those he already knew. Instead, they seemed to be a blend between text and machine—a hybrid object that replaced human creativity with the potential for mechanical and electronic efficiency. It was on this point that Licklider's testimony resonated most with Hersey's views. Indeed, the two men came to agree that computer programs were devices that triggered specific processes—that is, that they belonged to a category of objects that fell under the purview of patent law. These devices had a textual component, but they were not what Hersey identified as works of authorship.[44]

Prominent attorneys at industrial research laboratories joined Licklider and Hersey in their belief that copyright was an inappropriate form of protection for computer programs. Among them was Robert O. Nimtz. As a staff member at Bell Telephone Laboratories' intellectual property division, Nimtz had become well known in his field for his advocacy of software patenting. His ideas on the nature and patent-eligibility of software had risen to prominence in the 1960s thanks to his central role in the *Benson* case. Writing on behalf of Bell Labs, Nimtz submitted a detailed critique of CONTU's work. He warned that Congress and the commission had failed to realize that a legal mechanism such as copyright would ultimately "hinder the further development" of software.[45] He provided two justifications for this reasoning. First, he argued that secrecy was the "main avenue of protection" that had enabled the widespread use of computer programming, and from this he concluded that the widespread adoption of copyright would strip companies of their preferred method of protection. Second, he insisted that software was "radically different from any other subject matter" ever to fall under the purview of copyright. In his view, this was because computer programs were simultaneously machine control elements and writings. Regardless of how firmly copyright law could restrict the use, reproduction, and distribution of the text of a computer program, it would fail to protect what was actually the "valuable subject matter" of a program—its uses.

At the heart of this critique was Nimtz's understanding of software as an object with an unstable nature.[46] He explained that software could be found in two forms. First, there was text: flowcharts, verbal descriptions of algorithms, and even written statements of the program steps in a programming language. In this form, software was a writing akin to books, poems, and hand-drawn illustrations, and so it was eligible for copyright protection. This is where Nimtz's understanding of the nature of software was most distinct from Licklider's: unlike Licklider, who saw software as an entity with a dual nature, Nimtz conceptualized the nature of a computer program as a function of the relation between its history and its medium. As long as the program took the form of texts or diagrams, it merely conveyed information to a reader. However, Nimtz insisted, the journey of a computer program from a programmer's mind to the work of a computer involved more than just the typing of text. At some point, the program would need to be fixed in a machine-readable medium such as a magnetic tape; otherwise no computer would be able to run it. Once this fixation occurred, not "for the purpose of recording or storing the information in the writings," but for "the sole purpose of controlling a machine," the program ceased to be merely a text. At this point, the program became a "machine element," thus making patents, not copyright, the appropriate legal protection for it.

The views of Nimtz, Hersey, and Licklider stood in stark opposition to those advanced by the people representing hardware and software firms. The firms' advocates appeared before the commission with the apparent aim of securing any form of protection they could. For instance, Martin Goetz, on behalf of Applied Data Research, claimed that copyrights would give his company additional protections that would complement software patenting and trade secrecy. He appeared to have no qualms with the assertion that computer programs were writings, or even literary works.[47] ADR had secured copyright protection for all its major products; high-demand programs such as Autoflow were protected by both patents and copyrights; and users were required to sign an agreement that precluded them from distributing or reproducing any programs or their components.[48] Goetz insisted that the view of programs as machine components was inaccurate and that programs were essentially texts that could be translated from a programming language into machine language.[49] That they could embody a machine process was irrelevant to the question of software copyright, even though it remained crucial to software patenting.[50]

The computing industry appeared to form a single school of thought on software copyright. Indeed, Goetz stood alongside the Information Industry Association (IIA) and the Computer and Business Equipment Manufacturers Association (CBEMA)—the professional association for firms such as Honeywell and IBM. Representatives from CBEMA and the IIA agreed that extending copyright protection to computer programs was a desirable development. Like Goetz, they did not protest the treatment of software as a form of literary work that had sparked deep concern in Hersey, Licklider, or Nimtz. On the contrary, the industry representatives argued that the working definition of software as a literary work comprising a set of instructions should be further amended to protect any programs that were automatically generated by a computer in the course of executing another program.[51]

As CONTU's term came to an end, the commissioners received the results of a survey that they had commissioned to the Boston-based consulting firm Harbridge House.[52] This survey was designed to identify the financial and legal needs of the software industry based on a study of 116 firms affiliated with ADAPSO, the main trade organization for the software industry. Harbridge House reported that the limited monopolies afforded by patents and copyrights were "a matter of monumental insignificance to the industry," even though firms seeking such protection seemed to be an anomaly. It also found that a few firms were more willing to seek intellectual property protection for their programs than others. One important characteristic that determined whether a company would be interested in seeking such protection was the kind of programs it produced. Firms that sold custom-made programs for engineering or other technical fields were the least likely to seek copyright or patent protection, and firms that created off-the-shelf applications or systems programs were the most likely to seek it. A more important characteristic was firm size; large firms that produced operating systems and business software often sought IP protection.

ADAPSO's leaders insisted that the Harbridge House survey clearly demonstrated one crucial point: the IP protection of software, which could be partially achieved through copyright, was immensely important to the industry.[53] In their formal statement to CONTU, they explained that all the companies that had answered the questionnaire agreed that it was important to protect the programs that had become their primary assets. Some had relied on patents, and for more than a decade others had relied on copyrights. Most even relied on several forms of protection simultaneously, since there were no clearly defined legal mechanisms to provide what ADAPSO called "the degree of protection deemed necessary by the industry."[54] The organization wholeheartedly rejected the idea that software could be considered "mechanical devices," and it insisted instead that programs were written by professional programmers and that they were merely writings for highly technical areas. Unlike IBM, which had defined programs as objects that came into being once the instructions written by a programmer were loaded onto a computer, ADAPSO insisted that everything—from the flowcharts to the machine code that directed a machine—was a text and that all of it was therefore eligible for copyright protection.[55]

The needs of the industry as portrayed by ADAPSO and Harbridge House motivated the commissioners to favor software copyright. CONTU's *Final Report* shows that the commissioners' work to identify the nature of computer programs relied on the computing industry's argument that computer programs were, ultimately, text. It proposed that copyright law should be amended to declare that "computer programs, to the extent that they embody an author's original creation," are eligible for copyright protection.[56] This was grounded on the assumption—opposite to the views of Nimtz, Licklider, and especially

Hersey—that a computer program is merely a form of writing that consists of sets of instructions. The *Final Report* stated that software was "prepared by the careful fixation of words, phrases, numbers, and other symbols in other media."[57] It also presented a new analogy that paired computers with music systems.[58] A computer's circuit boxes were analogous to music boxes, punched cards to piano rolls, and magnetic disks to music tapes. This analogy advanced the view that programs loaded onto a computer, like recorded music in a music player, were just "sets of information in a form which, when passed over a magnetized head, caused minute currents to flow in such a way that desired physical work is accomplished."[59]

John Hersey wrote a fiery dissent against his colleagues' stance on the ontology and copyright-eligibility of software. He thought that CONTU's decision was inappropriate and unnecessary, and in his private drafts he condemned the commission's misunderstanding of what he understood as "the duality" of software.[60] By this, he meant that at "a certain point in its development," a computer program transforms from a writing to "a machine control element, a mechanical device," which "ought not to be copyrighted." In his dissent, Hersey transformed his ideas on the duality of software into a framework to understand the nature of software that took into consideration each program's own history. Following Nimtz's arguments, he noted that the development of a program proceeded through several stages. A program would first be born out of programmer's effort to define a task. It would then be outlined through flowcharts, translated into code using languages such as FORTRAN or COBOL, and then retranslated, this time into machine language that was illegible to human beings.

After this final translation, the program entered maturity—a "mechanical phase" in which it "becomes physically embodied" in punched cards, disks, tape, or chips.[61] Programs only became valuable in this mature stage, for only then did they become able to perform their unique function, namely the control of the electrical impulses within a computer that enable the completion of the prescribed task. By this point, the program did not merely describe or direct mechanical work. On the contrary, the program was what actually did the work. For this reason, Hersey warned that CONTU was committing a grave mistake by failing to realize that the instructions (which they equated with the program) eventually became "an essential part of the machinery to produce desired results." In his view, the commissioners did not understand that software is merely a "device capable of commanding a series of impulses which open and close the electronic gates of the computer."

Hersey's views on the nature and copyright-eligibility of software were also motivated by his personal understanding of the value of human creativity.[62] In a commission that often seemed to focus too much on what Hersey described as "excessively lawyerish fine points," he felt responsible for taking his colleagues on long "excursions into emotion."[63] He had insisted throughout the hearings that the decision to extend copyright protection to computer programs was a misguided legislative maneuver and an attack on the cultural well-being of the nation. More important, he repeatedly reminded commissioners that the equation of software with writings was an affront to human nature. In his view, copyright protection was intended for categories of media made by and for human beings, including "written words by the human eye," "music by the ear," and "paintings by the eye."[64] He complained that the commissioners were polluting both human creativity and the notion of a writing and causing a dangerous "blurring and merging of human and mechanical communication."[65] This negation of the qualities that separated human beings from machines would equate the work of a computer with literary expressions of human emotion. The great danger was that a culture that accepts the equivalence of people and machines would eventually become unable to experience, bring to life, or even communicate "the bundle of qualities" that comprise humanity— emotions such as courage, fear, desire, and hope.[66]

Hersey lost this battle, however, and CONTU's *Final Report* made evident the high premium that the testimony of the computing industry's representatives carried. His colleagues proceeded as if they had chosen to ignore most of the testimony delivered by the opponents of software copyright, and they explicitly rejected Hersey's opinions. They viewed his attempts to plea for human emotions as a prompt to legislate in a way that would give the government the right to "assess the merits of a work and choose only those works which in its view are 'good enough' for copyright."[67] This in turn would create an unfair distinction between works of "great and small aesthetic value" that determined eligibility for copyright. They therefore concluded that extending protection to computer programs was essential to ensuring that copyright law "applied to all forms of expression." Indeed, they explained that this was the only way to ensure that the country would have a copyright law broad enough "to shelter the works of Nobel Laureates and computer programmers without causing any confusion about which is which."

These recommendations on software copyright faced no opposition in Congress. In 1980, lawmakers passed the Computer Software Copyright Act, an amendment to the Copyright Act of 1976 designed almost exclusively to incorporate CONTU's recommendations into copyright law. With widespread industry support, the act defined computer programs as software firms and hardware manufacturers understood them, namely as "a set of statements or instructions to be used directly or indirectly in a computer in order to bring about a certain result."[68] It also amended the Copyright Act's 117th section to allow the owner of a copy of a computer program to make copies of it as needed to use the program or archive it.

The act single-handedly established computer programs as a new class of copyright-eligible works, and users gained the right to make backup copies of programs they purchased themselves. No longer classed as literary works, as they had been since John Banzhaf obtained his registrations in the 1960s, programs could now be registered by submitting a collection of materials—the texts written in any programming language, any verbal or graphic descriptions of the program, and any supporting documentation—as a single bundle for the purposes of copyright registration.[69] These two changes sparked an exponential increase in the number of registered computer programs; by the mid-1980s the Copyright Office was accepting over five thousand yearly registrations for computer programs—a thousand more than the total number of registrations accepted from 1964 to 1980.[70]

Before this happened, however, the legal battles over software patenting would intensify, as examiners at the Patent Office, along with several legal commentators and judges, started to interpret the *Benson* decision as having precluded software patenting altogether. In fact, behind the unprecedented alliance between software and hardware makers that the CONTU commissioners witnessed was an ongoing and extraordinary series of conflicts through which managers, lawyers, academics, programmers, and judges slowly negotiated the place of software in the country's patent system.

Chapter 7 Making Sense of *Benson*, 1976–1982

While the CONTU commissioners were considering the nuances of software copyright, the Court of Customs and Patent Appeals was handling a series of appeals through which the Patent and Trademark Office (the Patent Office's successor after 1975) sought guidance on the *Benson* decision's legal impact. Tension grew between the CCPA and the Supreme Court as the Court continued to side with the Patent and Trademark Office and adopted views on the nature of software that agreed with those advanced by hardware firms since the 1960s. These appeals allowed the CCPA to delineate the conditions under which an invention involving a computer program is eligible for patent protection. However, the lower court's attempts to shape software patenting on a doctrinal level were far better equipped to generate broad categorizations of software-related inventions than to manage the patent-drafting techniques that inventors could use to disclose their creations.

Three patent appeals that culminated in landmark Supreme Court opinions, *Dann v. Johnston* (1975), *Parker v. Flook* (1978), and *Diamond v. Diehr* (1981), are the subject of this chapter. Their stories demonstrate the differences in how appeals courts and the Supreme Court understood patent-eligibility. The CCPA, grounded on the broad conceptions of eligibility that had informed the drafting of the Patent Act of 1952, was particularly amenable to machine-based conceptions of software that rendered it patent-eligible. The Supreme Court, which originally conceived of software primarily in algorithmic terms, ultimately adopted a similarly broad conception of patent-eligibility and allowed for the patent protection of a system of manufacturing controlled by a computer program. Far from a radical doctrinal break, however, this allowance was compatible with the arguments for patent-eligibility that software firms, industrial research laboratories, and the CCPA had been using throughout the 1970s. It also aligned the law of software patents with the free-market views advanced by the administration of President Ronald Reagan.

AFFIRMING *BENSON*

In 1967, an Iowa-based independent inventor named Thomas R. Johnston hired Morton Jacobs to serve as his patent agent and attorney.[1] Johnston had created a computerized financial record-keeping system. It enabled the automatic processing of deposit slips and made unnecessary "much or all of the tedious book-keeping and accounting" that customers would have to perform to balance their checkbooks.[2] The invention required the formation of machine-readable records based on checks and deposit slips; the use of magnetic readers to enter these records into a computer system and process the relevant data; and the creation of a summary record that could be distributed to the customer. Jacobs drafted the application as one for embodied software, covering an "automatic record-keeping machine system . . . suitable for record keeping and bank checks and deposits."[3]

This was an application for what scholars in recent years have been calling a business method patent, namely a patent for a method of conducting and coordinating business transactions, broadly conceived.[4] The computerization of financial transactions at large organizations such as banks and insurance companies was encouraging inventors like Johnston to turn to patent law. Because their computerized finance-related inventions involved both software and high volumes of mathematical computations, they were likely to run into the patent-eligibility obstacles created by the mental steps doctrine. Since the 1960s, this situation had pushed them toward their own versions of software embodiment.[5] Their variation of the technique involved disclosing a special purpose computer or a full computing system and indicating in the specification that a particular embodiment of the invention was a computer that could perform certain financial transactions under the control of a computer program.

By the late 1960s, business method patents covered systems that enabled the coordination of several bank teller machines, generating and printing account statements, and updating balances. For instance, just a few months after Johnston filed his application, an inventor named Gerhard Dirks (of the Dirks Electronics Corporation) secured a patent inconspicuously called *Data Handling System*.[6] First filed in 1963, this patent listed as the invention a low-cost means of processing data in large capacity memory computers. Aimed at a special purpose computer and its uses, as embodied software patents normally were, the patent explained that a possible implementation of the invention was a financial record system that keeps track of the expenses of an organization's individual departments and generates expense reports at both the departmental and organization-wide level.[7]

Jacobs drafted Johnston's patent application in the same style as the *Sorting System* application. He even included flowcharts and a block diagram showing "a computing machine system for automatic handling of banking transactions and record-keeping in accordance with this invention."[8] The examiner raised no issues with the invention's patent-eligibility—a success for Jacobs's drafting method—but he did reject the application on the grounds that it was obvious over the prior art and not sufficiently disclosed in the patent application.[9] Jacobs appealed, and the Board of Patent Appeals rejected it on the same grounds, adding that the invention was ineligible for patent protection. This ruling on ineligibility rested on the board's assumption that banking was not a technological art and that a patent over the invention would improperly "allow the intrusion of the patent system into the social sciences."[10]

Jacobs appealed once again, this time to the CCPA. This court's opinion, written by Judge Phillip Baldwin, embraced Jacobs's usual arguments for the patent-eligibility of software and dismissed all of the board's arguments, but it was not unanimous. Howard Markey, the chief judge, wrote in a dissent that Johnston's invention was obvious and that once an invention is found to be obvious, considerations of disclosure and patent-eligibility become moot. Giles Rich also wrote a dissent contending that Johnston's invention should be rejected as being patent-ineligible. Most troubling to Rich was Johnston's admission that his invention was a computer program and that it was being sold as such to banks and other large organizations.[11] He wrote,

> My problem is that, knowing the invention to be a new program, I must decide whether it is patentable in any claimed form in view of *Benson*, whether claimed as a machine, a "machine system," or otherwise. I am probably as much—if not

more—confused by the wording of the Benson opinion as many others. . . . Benson et al. had a program invention too and they could have cast their claims in machine system form just as appellant did. Every competent patent draftsman knows how to do that.[12]

To Rich, then, Johnston's application highlighted two key problems. First, it asked judges to decide whether a machine implementation of a program was just as ineligible for a patent as a process implementation was under *Benson*. Second, and perhaps most important, it highlighted the fact that the lower courts needed a systematic way of addressing a key ambiguity in the *Benson* decision—the fact that the Supreme Court had denied the patent-eligibility of a computer program while simultaneously stating, with no explanation, that its intent was not to ban software patents altogether. Concluding his dissent, Rich wrote, "I deem it to be the Supreme Court's prerogative to set the limits on Benson, which was broadly based. I hope it will do so."[13]

Under a new commissioner of patents, C. Marshall Dann, the Patent and Trademark Office appealed Baldwin's decision. A distinguished scholar and practitioner of patent law, he was best known for his work as a litigator for infringement trials.[14] He was also the first commissioner of the newly minted PTO. At the Supreme Court, his lawyer, Howard Shapiro, presented the office's long-standing arguments against the patent-eligibility of software, and he further contended that computers were so common in the banking industry that Johnston's invention was obvious. In contrast, Morton Jacobs— making his first and only appearance before the Court—focused his energy on arguing for the patent-eligibility of Johnston's invention. "This is not a method of bookkeeping that is inside the machine," he told the justices, "it is not an accounting algorithm that is inside the machine." Instead, Johnston had invented "a machine that adapts to any body's method of bookkeeping, adapts to any ledger format," and "does whatever is required."[15]

In 1976, Justice Thurgood Marshall delivered the unanimous opinion of the Court, affirming the PTO's rejection of Johnston's invention. However, instead of addressing patent-eligibility, Marshall affirmed that Johnston's invention was obvious. The Court did provide one significant snippet of guidance on the meaning of *Benson*, by noting that the prior decision's "limited holding" was that Benson and Tabbot's "method was not a patentable 'process'" as defined in the patent statutes.[16] This would encourage the judges at the CCPA to continue pondering whether there was any reason to believe that a similar situation applied when inventions were disclosed as machines, and not as processes.

Giles Rich's greatest ally at the CCPA on this matter was Edward Lane, a Richard Nixon appointee who was approaching a full decade of service at the court. Lane and Rich were particularly interested in thinking about how to deal with claims that, in Lane's words, "cover programming, albeit disguised in apparatus format."[17] They agreed that *Benson* represented a "general proscription on the patenting of computer programs," regardless of whether an inventor had included in the claims "apparatus limitations" such as the internal structures of a computer programmed to carry out a particular program.[18] Rich in particular held that if an invention is "in essence a new program," then any competent patent writer "can readily define the invention as either a process or a machine, or both."[19] Indeed, the two men agreed that it made no sense to restrict the scope of *Benson* to method claims, because this would enable inventors to circumvent that decision "by the facile drafting device of claiming in apparatus form an idea for programming computers."[20]

The Supreme Court would intervene directly again in 1978, in *Parker v. Flook*. This case concerned a patent application that Dale R. Flook, an employee at the Atlantic Richfield Company (ARCO), had submitted in 1971. Formerly a part of the Standard Oil Company, ARCO was an American oil company with a global reach best known for its gas stations and for its discovery of oil at Prudhoe Bay, Alaska, in 1968. Since then, the company had been involved in the construction of the Trans-Alaska Oil Pipeline, and a merger with the Sinclair Oil Corporation had brought it into the refining business.[21]

Flook's application disclosed a method to update periodically a numerical threshold for a system that would ring an alarm when a hydrocarbon conversion reached a certain point.[22] This invention was particularly useful in industries such as petroleum refining, where hydrocarbons would need to be broken down at rapidly changing rates. Flook's invention would allow for the monitoring of a large collection of variables—from heat input to the internal pressure within which the reaction was taking place. Central to the industrial uses for these reactions was the problem of determining how much longer the reaction needed to finish. This was a problem that firms usually solved by having an alarm go off after a set time, but Flook was interested in being able to adjust the alarm in response to the rapidly changing conditions that his system monitored. In particular, his invention automatically adjusted the alarm limits with the use of a personal computer that kept track of whichever variables the user desired to specify.[23]

One of his claims covered a sequence of calculations that could be performed manually or with the use of a computer.[24] It read,

1. A method for updating the value of at least one alarm limit on at least one process variable involved in a process comprising the catalytic chemical conversion of hydrocarbons wherein said alarm limit has a current value of Bo+K wherein Bo is the current alarm base and K is a predetermined alarm offset which comprises:

(1) *Determining the present value* of said process variable, said present value being defined as PVL;

(2) *Determining a new alarm base* B[1], using the following equation: B[1] = Bo(1.0−F) + PVL(F) where F is a predetermined number greater than zero and less than 1.0;

(3) *Determining an updated alarm limit* which is defined as B[1] + K; and thereafter

(4) *Adjusting said alarm limit* to said updated alarm limit value.

In 1974, the examiner, Eugene G. Botz, rejected this claim on the grounds that it was drawn to an algorithm and that a patent containing this claim would therefore be a patent on the algorithm itself. Another grounds for rejection, which Botz later abandoned, stated that the application did not provide an adequate disclosure of the invention. The claim was "unsupported by structure or method steps," because it could just as well be performed by an operator using pencil and paper to make the calculations and manually adjust the controls. In his opinion, the only difference between Flook's invention and "that which is conventional" was the computation of the alarm limit. In response, Flook's attorneys insisted that the claim's requirement to adjust alarm limits to their updated value did not amount to performing a mathematical algorithm and that *Benson* should not be construed as a ban on the patent-eligibility of all claims that involve algorithms.[25]

On May 19, 1976, both parties repeated their arguments on patent-eligibility before the Board of Patent Appeals, which sided with Botz.[26] Citing one of the CCPA's most recent decisions, *In re Christensen*, the board found that *Benson* required the office to consider patent-ineligible any claim in which a mathematical equation was the only novel component. Regardless of what additional content a claim may have, there was no way of converting "an unpatentable method" such as solving a mathematical equation into "patentable subject matter."[27]

Flook's attorneys appealed to the CCPA on March 21, 1977. They argued that the board's reliance on *Christensen* was erroneous because the final step in the claims did not involve a mathematical relation.[28] The claims at stake in *Christensen*, they contended, ended with a computation; those in Flook's application ended with the adjustment of an alarm limit. Moreover, the attorneys argued, another recent court decision, *In re Chatfield*, established that claims for a method in which an algorithm was used to carry out intermediate steps were patent-eligible.[29] Once again, Judge Baldwin reversed the rejections.[30] His decision explained that the primary question under consideration was whether "a claim to a process which *uses* an algorithm to modify a conventional manufacturing system is statutory subject matter."[31] This question, in his opinion, required him to decide whether the claim at issue included any step "which materially limits the claim to a scope less than the mere act of solving an algorithm."[32] These limits could not possibly arise from any data-gathering steps in preparation for the algorithm's execution, but they could in fact arise from actions taken with the algorithm's output.[33] This meant that Flook's requirement to set an alarm limit after performing the mathematical computation made his claim eligible for patent protection. Such a patent, Baldwin implied, would cover only a particular use of the algorithm—the use in association with this particular alarm—and not the algorithm as a whole.

The materiality to which Baldwin pointed in his *Flook* decision was becoming a central component in how he and his colleagues were making sense of *Benson*. For instance, Howard Markey, the CCPA's chief judge, attempted to distinguish between mathematical algorithms and their nonmathematical counterparts while reversing a rejection of a patent application by Richard D. Freeman, from Bell Telephone Laboratories.[34] Filed in 1970 and entitled *Computer Typesetting*, Freeman's application claimed a method and apparatus to define and control "the relative positioning of symbols in a computer-based imaging system."[35] The application's claims described two interrelated inventions, first a "computer display system" comprising a display device, a data processor, and means for the storage, retrieval, and display of information about the symbols that the user wanted. The second invention was the method controlling this system that enabled users to control the size and spacing of the symbols on the screen. This invention, then, included tangible machinery and computer programs. More important, its ultimate outputs were neatly arranged mathematical symbols displayed on a computer monitor.

As usual, the Board of Patent Appeals had rejected the claims for the control system for this computer display on the grounds that it was not subject matter. Markey critiqued the board's lack of concern for how Freeman's invention worked. He thought that their ruling was grounded, not on "the nature of the algorithm involved," but merely on the assumption that a patent over it "in practical effect would be a patent on the algorithm itself."[36] This suggested, according to Markey, that the board seemed to construe "every implementation with a programmed computer" as an algorithm as *Benson* had defined it—that is, as a "procedure for solving a given type of mathematical problem." Should this line of thought become law, then every claimed method that could be implemented using a computer would constitute nonstatutory subject matter. In Markey's opinion, this reasoning "sweeps too wide and is without basis in law."[37] After all, the Supreme Court had included in the *Benson* decision the caveat that its ruling should not be construed as one that "precludes a patent for any program servicing a computer."[38]

Markey proposed that not all algorithms were algorithms in the *Benson* sense. This criterion took the form of a two-part test for patent-eligibility. First, an examiner must determine whether a potentially problematic claim recites, directly or indirectly, an algorithm in the *Benson* sense. This algorithm could take many forms, such as a series of mathematical formulas or prose that describes the mathematical procedure at hand. If such an algorithm was present, then the examiner could take the second step: analyzing the claim to determine "whether in its entirety it wholly preempts that algorithm."[39] If no algorithm in the *Benson* sense was present in the claim, as far as Markey was concerned, then there was no reason to judge it as ineligible for a patent under *Benson*.

Over the next few years, the CCPA would expand this procedure into a test of patent-eligibility called the Freeman-Walter-Abele (FWA) test. This process began in 1978, when Lutrelle F. Parker, a new interim commissioner of patents, brought Flook's case to the Supreme Court, using the same arguments that his office had delivered at the CCPA. Several firms and trade associations now submitted amicus briefs. In particular, John S. Voorhees and Kenneth Krosin submitted an amicus brief on behalf of the Computer and Business Equipment Manufacturers Association (CBEMA). The question, as they saw it, was whether a process in which "the sole point of novelty is a mathematical algorithm" can be patent-eligible. They warned that Flook's attempt to patent his process "flies in the face of the long-standing rule that the discoverer of a scientific or mathematical principle has no claim to a monopoly of it."[40] By this, they did not mean that all inventions "embodying a novel mathematical algorithm should be patentable." On the contrary, they contended that patent-eligibility should remain possible when there was "co-action among the steps of the process, or the elements of an apparatus," wherein there is a mathematical principle at work. This could occur, in their view, when the combination of the algorithm and its counterparts is not obvious even if every individual component happens to be obvious.[41]

Voorhees and Krosin also presented a policy argument against software patenting. They argued that patents for programs were unnecessary and detrimental because the computing industry had "developed and grown rapidly in an atmosphere of free interchange of computer programs."[42] Since the late 1940s, the group argued, the "tremendous growth of the computer software industry" and the "vast number of breakthroughs in the field of programming" had taken place within a legal framework "conducive to the free interchange of ideas and information about computer users.[43] New algorithms, programming procedures, and even programs had been widely disseminated in an "atmosphere of intellectual freedom" that facilitated the growth of the industry.[44] This intellectual freedom allowed journals to publish algorithms and mathematical discoveries in order to advance the state of the art in programming. Seminars and symposia on computer programming featured public discussions on new formulas and algorithms that enabled participants to "build upon and improve the overall level of knowledge" in the field.[45]

Voorhees and Krosin suggested that perhaps the best way to proceed was to leave computer programs to copyright law. However, there was no certainty that copyright protection could be effectively extended to them. Even if this protection did become available, it was difficult to predict whether it would cover anything beyond the texts that programmers wrote, and there was no reason for the Supreme Court to intervene. Indeed, the lawyers wrote, "if increased protection for computer programs is considered necessary, it will be accomplished through legislation and not through distortion of the patent laws."[46]

On behalf of ADR, Carol Cohen submitted a brief. Unlike Jacobs, who had retired from ADR, Cohen was not an IP attorney, but she was a talented and multifaceted corporate lawyer. She dealt with all other aspects of the firm's operations, and in recent years she had started to advocate for software patenting using Jacobs's materials.[47] Regarding Flook's case, she argued that "the real issues involved in this case are machines and machine systems, not 'mathematical algorithms.'"[48] CBEMA, in her view, was simply attempting to perpetuate the myth of the non-machine—advancing legal arguments that run against the manufacturers' long history of advertising "superior machine construction and operation due to the software."[49] Citing the story of ADR's struggle to sell Autoflow, she argued that the software industry needed patents. "Without the reasonable prospects of obtaining a patent," she wrote, "IBM could use the concepts of the Autoflow system" and produce a similar program that the firm could give away for free. The Autoflow patent, however, had enabled the software firm to keep the manufacturing giant at bay, generating gross sales of about $15 million.[50]

Most recently, ADR had obtained a patent for its so-called STAR system, which monitored telephone lines.[51] This patent disclosed an invention that used software to control the system of telephone monitoring operations at the core of this product line. The STAR software, according to Cohen, was "comparable to the use of software controls for the automation of an oil refinery" at the core of Flook's case. A ruling against Flook could be devastating, especially given that STAR generated profits only because the firm issued licenses for others to make and sell versions of it. Arguments such as the PTO's, directed at the notion that software patents were unallowable grants over ideas, algorithms, and methods of doing business, had the potential of interfering with the firm's livelihood.

Cohen implied that the PTO's arguments were grounded on the misconception that software patents were newfangled protections that had emerged with the growth of the software industry. She explained that hardware manufacturers had long been obtaining software patents by "presenting the invention as though implemented by hardware programming, not by software."[52] For instance, the brief mentioned, IBM had obtained one such patent in 1967, *Optimum Result Computer*.[53] Patents like this and the PTO's recognition of this patent-drafting strategy suggested that software patents had not come into existence with the birth of the software industry. On the contrary, patents such as IBM's were manifestations of "the common understanding of the engineering equivalence of the software and hardware technologies."[54] This suggested that software patents were best defined as "patents on special-purpose machine systems that, because of technological and economic reasons, are constructed by means of stored programs (i.e. software) and a general-purpose computer."[55]

The justices did not adopt Cohen's arguments. In 1978, they ruled that even though Flook's claims did not actually "cover every conceivable application of the formula," they did cover "a broad range of potential uses of the method."[56] This broad scope, however, was not the reason for the claim's rejection. Instead, according to the Court, "The process itself, not merely the mathematical algorithm, must be new and useful. Indeed, the novelty of the mathematical algorithm is not a determining factor at all. Whether the algorithm was in fact known or unknown at the time of the claimed invention, as one of the 'basic tools of scientific or technological work,' it is treated as though it were a familiar part of the prior art."[57]

Back at the CCPA, Rich responded to this reasoning by revising Markey's patent-eligibility test. The abstraction that Flook attributed to mathematical principles signaled to Rich that tangibility was an important matter in the examination of the patent-eligibility of claims that involved mathematical algorithms. For this reason, while reversing a rejection for an applicant named William Walter, he suggested a revision to the second step of the test that it had articulated in Freeman. Now, to assess whether the recitation of an algorithm in a claim was improper, examiners could turn to the relations between the algorithm and the tangible components that the claim recited.[58] Rich's opinion, *In re Walter*, stated that a claim could be patent-eligible if its mathematical algorithm "is implemented in a specific manner to define structural relationships between the physical elements of the claim" or "to refine or limit claim steps."[59] This meant that the presence of an algorithm was not a bar on patent-eligibility if the algorithm either directed the operation of the physical components recited in the claim or limited the scope of the process as a whole.

ANYTHING UNDER THE SUN

As all these applications made their way through the patent system, engineers at a manufacturer called Federal Mogul developed their own interest in software patents. An Ohio-based firm that specialized in rubber products such as the rings used to seal oil inside motor vehicle engines, Federal Mogul had launched an investigation into the efficiency of its manufacturing processes. Of greatest concern was curing, the process by which rubber can be transformed from a malleable substance into a hard yet elastic material with the help of heat and a chemical agent such as sulfur.[60]

Back in 1970, one of the firm's engineers, James Diehr, had discovered a crucial flaw in the firm's procedures. Federal Mogul's Materials Group manufactured all the rubber products together, regardless of size. This meant that the people overlooking the presses where the objects cured often needed to open the ovens. With each opening, the presses lost heat, delaying the curing process. Diehr reasoned that the firm could reduce manufacturing costs by separating the objects by size and shape, determining the curing time required for each class of object, and automating the ovens' operation. After some original research, he found that the process was governed by the so-called Arrhenius equation—a formulation, discovered in 1889, that would enable him to determine the rate of a curing reaction in terms of the temperature of the environment in which the reaction took place and the thickness of the rubber.[61]

Along with another engineer, Theodore Lutton, Diehr invented a system controlled by a computer to open the rubber curing presses automatically.[62] This system would come into operation as soon as a human operator loaded a rubber molding press and closed its door. At this point, a timer would start running, and an internal thermometer would continually measure the press's temperature. A computer would process the thermometer's data as soon as it was received. Its programming enabled it both to compute how long the curing was supposed to take from start to finish and to update its results with each communication from

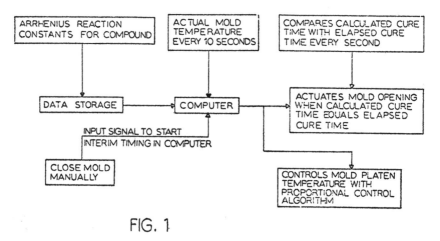

FIG. 1

Schematic diagram of James Diehr and Theodore Lutton's computerized rubber curing press. Transcript of Record, *Diamond v. Diehr.*

the thermometer. The computer would then open the doors of the press automatically when the length of curing time that it calculated equaled the time that had elapsed since the operator first closed the press's doors.

In August 1975, Federal Mogul's lawyers submitted a patent application for Diehr and Lutton's invention. In the claimed invention, the computer received its inputs from three sources: its own internal memory, the timer that started running upon manual closure of the press doors, and the thermometer that took temperature every ten seconds. The application's first claim spelled out the entirety of the process, and it made a digital computer essential to what the application claimed as the invention. It read,

> 1. A method of operating a rubber-molding press for precision molded compounds with the aid of a digital computer,
> comprising:
>
> [1] *providing said computer with a data base* for said press . . .
> [2] *initiating an interval timer* in said computer upon the closure of the press for
> [3] *monitoring the elapsed time* of said closure,
> . . .
> [4] constantly providing the computer with the temperature (Z),
> [5] *repetitively calculating* in the computer, at frequent intervals during each cure, the Arrhenius equation for reaction time during the cure . . .
> . . .
> [6] *opening the press* automatically when a said comparison indicates equivalence.

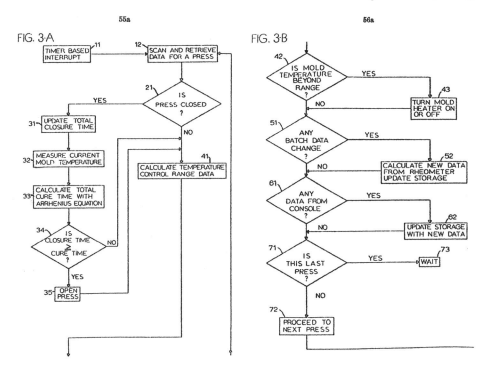

Flowchart of the program that controlled James Diehr and Theodore Lutton's rubber curing system. Transcript of Record, *Diamond v. Diehr*.

The application also included a hand-drafted flowchart, spread over two pages, for the simple program that controlled the computer's operation. The flowchart depicted the actual program controlling the systems that Diehr had installed in more than fifty of Federal Mogul's presses. This simple program, in Federal Mogul's estimation, had increased productivity by 20 percent and generated savings of at least $25 million.[63]

The PTO rejected the application on the grounds that the invention was ineligible for patent protection, and Federal Mogul appealed to the CCPA in 1979. The court had recently acquired a new member, Helen Wilson Nies, the first woman ever to serve as a judge at the CCPA. Named by President Jimmy Carter, Nies had started working at the Justice Department in 1948, and more recently she had been practicing patent law at law firms in Chicago and Washington, D.C.[64] At the CCPA, following the court's usual line of thought, Nies reversed the PTO's rejection, basing her argument on the two-step test that Markey had developed in the typesetting case *In re Freeman*. The first step was to determine whether the claim at hand recited a mathematical equation. This one certainly did: the invention relied on the Arrhenius equation in order to control the rubber molding presses. Second was to determine whether the claim was directed at the mathematical algorithm itself or to a specific application of it. Nies found the latter to be true: the claims were directed toward a rubber molding process. These kinds of claims, in her view, "involve the employment of a scientific truth to a new and useful end without attempting to control the use of the truth itself."[65] For this reason, Nies reversed the board's decision.

When Nies wrote this opinion, a series of applications in biotechnology were prompting her court to assess the limits of patent-eligibility. In the late 1970s, two major cases regarding the patent-eligibility of living things were making their way up to the Supreme Court. The first case concerned a bacterial culture that an engineer named Ananda Chakrabarty had developed at General Electric. The PTO had denied GE's patent claim on the grounds that the bacteria were alive, but the CCPA, in a 3–2 decision, had reversed this ruling.[66] The second case involved a bacterial culture capable of producing the antibiotic lincomycin, which a scientist named Malcolm E. Bergy, at the Upjohn Company, had developed in the early 1970s. This case, too, also divided the CCPA judges into a 3–2 decision in favor of patent-eligibility.[67]

The CCPA judges generally avoided imposing limits on the scope of article 35, section 101, of the U.S. Code that Congress may not have envisioned, by which they meant not imposing limits that Rich and Federico had not foreseen. For instance, in his decision for *Bergy* (1977), Rich had noted that nothing in the statutes excluded patents for living organisms.[68] In his view, it was illogical to assume that "the existence of life in a manufacture or composition of matter" precluded patent-eligibility, especially because the existence of life in a process or the use of an organism's life functions did not have the same effect.[69] This alone was, in his view, grounds to reverse the rejection of Bergy's patent. After all, the patent statutes made "no distinction between manufactures and compositions of matter on the one hand and processes on the other," and it was beyond the CCPA's duties to start distinguishing between the two.[70] Using this same rationale, Rich would allow the patent on Chakrabarty's bacteria a few months later, and Nies would adopt a similar one to allow Diehr and Lutton's claims.

In 1978, the Supreme Court ordered the CCPA to vacate its decision in *Bergy* and instructed the lower court to reconsider its judgment in light of *Parker v. Flook*.[71] Later that year, the CCPA vacated its ruling in *Chakrabarty* on similar grounds. The judges decided to rehear both cases and issue a single decision for both, which Rich took on the task of writing. Issued in 1979, this unanimous opinion highlighted that nothing in *Flook* changed the judges' views on *Bergy* and *Chakrabarty*. "Life is largely chemistry," Rich had written in the *Bergy* decision, so microorganisms "should be treated under 101 no differently from chemical compounds."[72] The PTO appealed once again, and the Supreme Court ruled that Chakrabarty's bacteria were eligible for a patent. The 5–4 decision, written by Justice Warren Burger, echoed a lot of Rich's rationale at the CCPA.[73] Burger found that the language of the patent statutes was broad enough to accommodate categories of inventions that Congress could not have foreseen in the 1950s.[74] He noted that Federico had testified in Congress that "under section 101, a person may have invented a machine or a manufacture, which may include anything under the sun that is made by man."[75] Burger explained that Congress "plainly contemplated that the patent laws would be given wide scope."[76] This is not to say that section 101 has unlimited scope, or that it embraces every discovery; laws of nature, physical phenomena, and abstract ideas remained unpatentable under *Chakrabarty*. However, the requirement that something be "made by man" appeared to the Court to be the primary limit on section 101, and in fact Chakrabarty's bacteria—which the Court found not to be naturally occurring—were patent-eligible subject matter.[77]

The commissioner of patents, Sidney A. Diamond, having just stood on the losing side of the landmark *Chakrabarty* decision, appealed the CCPA's decision to allow Diehr and Lutton's patent.[78] He feared that if the Supreme Court didn't issue a clear ruling on the patent-eligibility this time, the PTO would find itself in an "untenable position."[79] Given his office's recurring disagreements with the CCPA and the Supreme Court's lack of clear guidance, he felt that his choices were limited. On the one hand, he could align himself with the CCPA, thus enforcing a rule that he considered an affront to the Supreme Court. On the other hand, continuing to uphold the PTO's stance would result in "the gloomy prospect" of years of costly and unsuccessful litigation at the CCPA.[80]

At the Supreme Court, Diamond's lawyers presented what the PTO considered to be the question at stake: "whether a computer program that regulates the curing time of rubber products in a mold is patentable subject matter under 35 USC 101."[81] They argued that this case is not "meaningfully distinguishable" from *Flook*, in that both involve "process claims that recite unpatentable subject matter."[82] In their view, the main difference between the two cases was the way in which the claims had been drafted. In *Flook*'s case, the claims "focused on the algorithm and recited only minor post-solution activity."[83] Federal Mogul was reciting a comparable invention, but it had done so by reciting "the entire conventional rubber molding process." Granting a patent over Diehr and Lutton's invention was improper, in the PTO's opinion, because *Flook* was "a guide to the drafting of claims" and not "an interpretation of the scope of Section 101."

By far the most striking feature of Federal Mogul's case was its oral argument, which a patent attorney named Robert E. Wickersham delivered in October 1980.[84] Wickersham said that he did not want to talk about mathematics, the intricacies of programming, or even computers. "We don't care if it's printed in the newspapers," Wickersham told the Court about the computer program that controlled the rubber molds, "we don't care if it's distributed to everybody in our business."[85] His goal, as every onlooker must have noticed, was to convince the justices that the eligibility of computer programs for patent protection was irrelevant to Federal Mogul's case. He even told the justices that he had never "given it much thought whether a computer program is patentable" and that in fact he couldn't conceive of why anybody would hope to secure a patent for one.[86] To press his point, Wickersham directed the justices' attention to a small round blob of uncured rubber and a smooth rubber ring bonded to a piece of metal. He insisted that what Federal Mogul was attempting to protect was just the process of changing the "floppy, rather useless material" that he held in one hand into the perfectly shaped ring that he held in the other—a ring similar to those that the justices must have encountered when dealing with oil leaks in their automobiles.[87]

This line of argumentation—that software patenting was not the issue at hand—was a significant departure from arguments the Supreme Court had heard in the past. Indeed, ADR had filed its usual amicus brief arguing for the patent-eligibility of computer programs along the lines that Morton Jacobs had developed in the 1960s, but Federal Mogul's line of attack had made this argument obsolete. Instead, the firms standing with Federal Mogul insisted that the issue at hand had nothing to do with software patenting. For example, the Chevron Corporation (also a successor to Standard Oil) reinforced Wickersham's point by explaining in its amicus brief that "one must be particularly careful to distinguish between a 'computer program' and what the computer does."[88] Chevron defined a program as no more than "a series of instructions" that tells a computer how to operate, and it insisted that the Court should make a sharp distinction between a "computer program" and a "programmed computer." This distinction was the crux of the matter, in Chevron's opinion, for a computer program is "something akin to a writing," while the programmed computer is a "machine having a mode of operation."[89]

The Supreme Court did not embrace Chevron's line of thought, but five justices were swayed by Wickersham's unusual and forcefully delivered argument. In a decision delivered by Justice William Rehnquist, the Court ruled in 1981 that the method of programming a computer was patent-eligible if the computer directed a process that elicited physical or chemical transformations such as the one that Wickersham had described.[90] The resulting decision, *Diamond v. Diehr*, soon entered the canon of intellectual property law as a harbinger of hope for a generation of inventors and business people who had worked to protect their products for nearly twenty years.[91]

By then, software patents comprised at least 1 percent of the country's yearly issued patents. One study published nearly two decades later suggests that the number of issued patents rose from 765 in 1976 (1.1 percent of the total number of issued patents) to 1,275 in 1981 (1.9 percent of the total).[92] This steady rise in the number of issued software patents, paired with the Supreme Court's opinion in *Diamond v. Diehr*, prompted the PTO to issue new guidelines on the patent-eligibility of computer programs for the first time since the 1960s, and later that year it incorporated them into its Manual of Patent Examining Procedure.[93] According to the guidelines, whether a claim recites how "a computer performs certain calculation steps" is entirely irrelevant to its patent-eligibility.[94] Similarly, an application's disclosure that "a mathematical formula is implemented solely by computer programming" is immaterial when it comes to section 101. Following Markey's line of reasoning from the late 1970s, the guidelines instructed examiners to recognize that processes implemented through a computer could be as patent-eligible as those implemented by machines.[95]

Following the issuance of the PTO's new guidelines, programmers and their lawyers could rely on the simplest patent-drafting strategy yet. Instead of disclosing computer programs as circuitry arrangements, inventors could now secure a patent merely by including a physical element or step in their claims. These could include the opening of a door, the movement of an electrical charge, or even a flash of light or burst of sound. The requirement for tangibility—which in the 1960s rested on the embodied software—now became external to the computer program: as long as the application disclosed a tangible component, patent-eligibility was possible. Never again would software need to be embodied.

This loosening of patent-drafting standards aligned very well with the vision that Ronald Reagan's administration had for the country's IP. By the time Reagan took office in 1981, the consequences of the United States' transformation into a postindustrial society—one more dependent on services than on manufacturing—had become very apparent.[96] Economic indicators for national productivity had declined steadily, suggesting that the stagflation of the 1970s would continue to unfold into the new decade. Growing competition from foreign industries, most notably Japan and West Germany, had caused important losses in the American automobile industry, and many electronics firms were outsourcing their manufacturing to countries wherein labor costs were cheaper. The federal minimum wage had not increased enough to keep up with prices, and the automation that computerized systems enabled across industries reduced employment rates in manual labor.

Committed to free-market economics from the get-go, the Reagan administration built on the extraordinary deregulatory momentum that had preceded it.[97] Jimmy Carter's administration had responded to the country's economic ailments by embracing deregulation in air travel, banking, gas, electricity, railroads, trucking, and telecommunications. These efforts were having mixed results, but they aligned very well with Reagan's market-oriented campaign rhetoric. More important, they also aligned with his advisers' and appointees' desire to reduce government oversight, increase corporate autonomy, and strengthen the country's economic output at home and abroad by enabling and fostering competition.

The Reagan administration also inherited from Carter's the interrelated projects of strengthening the country's intellectual property system and restructuring the nation's courts. A few days before leaving office, in December 1980, Carter had signed the Bayh-Dole Patent and Trademark Amendments Act into law.[98] A turning point in the country's patent history, this act ended the long-standing practice of requiring inventors who used federal funds or contracts to assign ownership of their inventions to the federal government. This meant that all inventors, whether corporate or academic, could file for patents on their research and assign those patent rights as they wished. The act's passage signaled the executive and legislative branches' desire to strengthen academic-industrial linkages through patent rights and encourage the commercialization of federally funded technologies.

Like Carter, Reagan favored strong IP rights. Soon after taking office, with extraordinary support from several industries, he signed into law the Federal Courts Improvement Act.[99] The act merged the CCPA with the U.S. Court of Claims to form the Court of Appeals for the Federal Circuit. The court's patent jurisdiction included appeals from the PTO and from the district courts scattered around the country.[100] By funneling all patent appeals into a single court, Congress had intended to reduce forum shopping and make the outcome of patent infringement and validity cases less contingent on the idiosyncratic views on patenting held by judges at the various federal appeals courts. The result was the formation of a court that was far less sensitive to the regional variability of how judges assessed the value and validity of patents and more directly influenced by the broader economic ideals and technological forces that shaped the country during the 1980s.

The centralization of patent appeals in a single court, the strong deregulatory impulse that swept across the country, and Reagan's free-market policies fueled a pro-patent ethos that continued for the rest of the century. Stronger IP protections were especially important to the computing, electronics, and telecommunications industries, wherein American companies new and old needed new and stronger protections against piracy.[101] Foreign firms, especially from Japan, were making significant inroads in the global electronics industry, producing both original devices and low-cost alternatives compatible with their American counterparts. Unbundled since 1977, Japanese computing firms in particular were even developing a robust domestic software industry even though they had significantly weaker software IP protections and lower venture capital investments than their American counterparts.[102]

Even as American firms and lawmakers called for additional protections for the country's inventors to compete globally, the Federal Circuit fully embraced the broad standards for the patent-eligibility of software that many of the CCPA's long-standing judges had been favoring for more than a decade. One of their most important early opinions in this vein is *In re Abele and Marshall*.[103] In this 1982 decision, Nies spelled out the final step of the FWA test for patent-eligibility. This test consisted of two parts. First, an examiner would need to determine whether a claim recited an algorithm in the *Benson* test. Second, the examiner should determine whether the algorithm is "applied in any manner to physical elements or process steps."[104] If so, then the invention was to be considered patent-eligible. Behind the test stood an impetus that remains with us today. As Nies explained it, "If the claimed invention is a mathematical algorithm, it is improper subject matter for patent protection, whereas if the claimed invention is an application of the algorithm, 101 will not bar the grant of a patent."[105] In other words, the presence of algorithms in an invention—as far as the Federal Circuit was concerned—did not automatically preclude its patent-eligibility.

Passing muster under the FWA test was much easier than disclosing specific electronic circuits and components as firms had done back in the 1950s and 1960s. In fact, throughout the 1980s mainframe firms would routinely secure software patents clearly drafted to leap over the FWA standards, especially after the rapid growth of online service providers increased the pressure to develop new industry standards. By then, however, an industry for personal computers (PCs)—microprocessor-based machines that could cost just a few hundred dollars—had displaced mainframes from the spotlight of computing IP battles. IBM would soon become this new industry's leading firm, but the managers at new PC firms had entered the computing industry in the late 1970s, when a quick glance at the state of patent law would have made any casual onlooker guess that the future of software patenting was bleak, at best. Paired with the fact that many PC users had never construed the making of a program as equivalent to the creation of a circuit, this would result in a shift away from patents and toward copyrights and trade secrets as the primary means of IP protection for early PC software.

Part Three   **IP for PCs**

Chapter 8 Hobbyists and Intellectual Property from Altair to Apple, 1975–1981

In 1975, a small New Mexico firm called Micro Instrumentation and Telemetry Systems (MITS) released a machine called the Altair 8800.[1] Unlike giant mainframes, which only large organizations could afford, or minicomputers, which could cost over $10,000, this was a personal computer: a microcomputer small and cheap enough for casual users to purchase. Sold by mail order, unassembled computers cost less than $500. The firm's founders, Edward Roberts and Forrest Mims, had purposely aimed the machine at the hobby electronics market, wherein build-your-own radio and calculator kits could be especially profitable. In fact, the Altair 8800 marked the firm's effort to expand its own line of electronics kits, which featured mostly clocks and calculators.[2]

This computer became very popular because of its low price point and the challenges that its usage posed. A cover story of *Popular Electronics* called it "Project Breakthrough! World's First Minicomputer Kit to Rival Commercial Models."[3] Advertisements flaunted that assembling the computer would be both difficult and rewarding— an opportunity to build a "real, full-blown computer," not

Top view of the Altair 8800 with a wooden keyboard. This computer connected hobbyists with one another and sparked the PC revolution. Image courtesy of the Charles Babbage Institute, University of Minnesota Libraries, Minneapolis.

a demonstration kit.[4] After building the machine, users could program it themselves by entering their programs in pure binary using a series of switches in the front. With no screen, the computer would then blink the red lights on its front panel in accordance with the program; that was its only built-in output means.

Like MITS's other products, the Altair 8800 relied on microchip technology to deliver small and affordable processing power. It was powered by the Intel 8080 chip, which MITS purchased for $75 apiece.[5] Unlike the integrated circuits of minicomputers like the PDP-8, the 8080 was a microprocessor—a chip that contained all the basic components of a general purpose, stored-program, electronic computer. It could run programs stored on other chips, and its processing capacities were strikingly close to those of minicomputers already on the market. Intel had originally priced the 8080 at $360, but its pricing strategy was experimental at best, able to accommodate a tremendous amount of flexibility in the bulk discounts Intel could offer. This meant that MITS was able to offer its computers for an unusually low price.[6]

Purchase of an Altair 8800 included membership in the Altair Users' Group, a MITS-sponsored community through which users could access a software library. Each program cost $2 and could range in length from a few dozen lines of code to dozens of pages of it.[7] In order to keep a steady supply of programs, MITS sponsored a monthly software contest. All users were free to submit programs into one of two categories: subroutines or major programs. MITS would screen and test the programs, and it would make all acceptable programs available for purchase through its software library. No portion of the retail price would reach the program's creator because programmers gave MITS the right to distribute their work when they submitted the program for consideration. In exchange, they received a $10 credit they could apply when they purchased software from MITS. Monthly winners received credits ranging from $15 to $50. At the end of each year, MITS selected the authors of the best subroutine and major program and awarded them credits, respectively, for $250 and $1,000.

The PCs of the 1980s were born from the computing cultures that developed around machines such as the Altair 8800.[8] At the same time, as this chapter argues, hobby computer users developed their own idiosyncratic views on what it meant to own a computer program. Far from united on this matter, hobbyists often disagreed on the proper balance between corporate control and user autonomy that should inform their communities' engagement with their machines and the markets through which they circulated. While now-famous hobbyists like Bill Gates and Steve Jobs eventually came to cherish IP protections, many of their peers agreed that software is best understood as a communally produced and jointly owned good and that acknowledging authorship and respecting the intent of a program's creators are far more important than establishing commercial control through legal means.

THE PEOPLE'S COMPUTER COMPANY

At first, MITS relied mostly on user licenses to prevent the unauthorized distribution of its software. Buying a program from its library required signing a license agreement. The licensed program that users obtained encompassed tapes and listings in machine readable or printed form, as well as any updates or portions thereof. Any users who wished to distribute the program to authorized parties such as their employees or subsidiaries would need to include the following proprietary rights legend: "This software is the property of MITS, Inc., . . . and has been supplied by MITS, Inc. to [Licensee] pursuant to a Program License Agreement. This software is furnished subject to the following restrictions: it shall not be reproduced, copied, or used in whole or in part on equipment other than the Designated Equipment with which it was furnished without the express written permission of MITS, Inc."[9]

However, Altair 8800 users did not normally resort to these formalities when acquiring software from one another, preferring instead to collaborate and exchange their work freely. This was the case for Robert Albrecht, a former engineer for Control Data Corporation and Honeywell who had taught computing at public schools for more than a decade.[10] Albrecht's experience as an educator had shaped his vision of computers as tools that people could use to enhance how they lived and learned, and his published work showcased his effort to transform computers into everyday objects with which anyone could engage.[11] In the 1960s, he had published a book called *Computer Methods in Mathematics*, on using a programming language called BASIC—which allowed users with little training to use time-sharing systems—as an instructional tool in high school mathematics. Since then, he had published *Teach Yourself BASIC*, a how-to guide for amateur programmers, and *My Computer Likes Me When I Speak BASIC*, a book written with what Albrecht described as an "easy going, conversational style" that "introduces BASIC to young or old."[12]

Albrecht was a founding member of a newsletter called the *People's Computer Company (PCC)* and a storefront called the People's Computer Center. By the mid-1970s, the distribution list for the newsletter had several thousand subscribers, and it had become a central source of information for computer hobbyists and anyone else who wished to personalize their experience with computers. It printed articles on programming, reviews of hardware and software, and even simple programs in BASIC. *PCC* cost a dollar an issue for people who ordered fewer than ten issues at a time and thirty cents per issue for orders of a hundred or more issues.[13]

Alongside Albrecht at *PCC* was Dennis Allison, who worked at the Stanford Research Institute (SRI) handling radio equipment that tracked the flight of military rockets.[14] While at SRI, Allison had started writing software compilers and other programming tools for his own use. He had even developed a version of BASIC for mainframes called Interaccess BASIC, which a group of SRI alumni had commissioned in an effort to establish a time-sharing firm called Interaccess. Allison also became president of the local chapter of the ACM, and he had met Albrecht during an ACM conference in San Francisco.

Since the start of the decade, Allison and Albrecht had shared a vision of computers as machines that could be transformed into tools meant to enhance people's lives. Drawn to the countercultural spirit of the 1960s, they conceived of the People's Computer Center as a force to liberate computers from the grasp of the military-industrial-academic complex. Languages such as FORTRAN and COBOL were antithetical to this group—these were the languages of the computer centers from which they sought liberation. To this end, they had transformed the People's Computer Center into a community center, and they hoped that enthusiasts would gather to play with computers, learn how to use them, and experiment with time-sharing and calculators.

The center became a hub for the so-called computer hobbyists, electronics enthusiasts who gathered to discuss microcomputers, trade parts and programs, and generally have a good time sharing their love for tinkering with machines like the Altair 8800.[15] It was well connected with other hobbyist organizations in California, especially the Homebrew Computer Club, from which Apple Computer would develop later in the decade. These communities' hobbyists relished the challenges involved in building microcomputers and developing programs for them, often relying on nothing but the Altair's blinking red lights to determine whether their program had been properly loaded.

Allison and Albrecht hoped that their fellow tinkerers would gravitate toward one of the first major challenges that using the Altair 8800 posed: enabling the computer to process programming languages. In 1975, they published a series of three articles in the *People's Computer Company* to sketch a framework for the creation of a language for the Altair 8800 to be called Tiny BASIC. Soon they started receiving letters with different versions of the language's compiler that other hobbyists had written based on their sketch. Allison and Albrecht were so pleased with this response that they started publishing a newsletter dedicated to programming in Tiny BASIC, and over four hundred people expressed their interest in subscribing to a publication of

Cartoon protesters from the first issue of the *People's Computer Company*. The PCC advocated the widespread use of computers and considered programming languages such as BASIC to be key to computer liberation. Image courtesy of Dennis Allison and the People's Computer Company.

this kind. The magazine had a peculiar name, *Dr. Dobb's Journal of BASIC Calisthenics and Orthodontia*. The first part of the name, Dr. Dobb's, was a contraction of the names "Dennis" and "Bob"; the second part was a tongue-in-cheek rephrasing of their mission to publish programs that would run quickly and without consuming too much memory, or "overbyte."

Dr. Dobb's was dedicated to the study and dissemination of programs written in Tiny BASIC, but Albrecht was interested in exploring other programming languages for hobbyists. In this spirit, he wrote to a programmer named Calvin N. Mooers. By the 1970s, Mooers had achieved some financial success as founder and president of Rockford Research, a Massachusetts-based software company. He had also secured several patents for a punched-card-based information retrieval system called Zatocoding, which he had developed in the late 1940s.[16] More recently, he had become especially involved with the development of a new programming language called TRAC (Text Reckoning and Compiling Language), which he had conceived and financed on his own.[17] In an effort to secure control over the language and its name, he had secured a trademark over the name "TRAC" and copyrights over several key texts involved in its creation. In the process, he had even developed the habit of sending infringement notices to any firm that advertised programs or computers under that name.[18]

Mooers was an avid amateur commentator on IP law, and he had taught himself enough about copyrights to correspond with some of the best-known IP lawyers in the nation. He personally requested materials from prominent scholars and practitioners, offering his own views on their works whenever he felt moved to do so. His requests and commentary were formal, detailed, and very well informed; he wrote his letters with great care, and he expected the same from his correspondents. He had even written to the CONTU commissioners explaining that their reduction of computer programs to lists of instructions was unnecessary and detrimental to the industry.[19] He also told them that he "deplore[d] the awe, reverence, and mystery" that they had attached to computers and that this reverence had made computers and their programs appear to be different from the kinds of inventions and creative works that were unproblematically eligible, respectively, for patents and copyrights.[20] It didn't take much technical or legal training, in his view, to know that this was wrong.

Albrecht's short, handwritten note was the opposite of what Mooers valued in a letter.[21] Using informal prose with a few typos and prominently displaying a cartoon question mark, the letter asked Mooers to outline what the readers of the *PCC* should know about TRAC. Mooers, who already knew that hobbyists did not share his preoccupation with software IP, responded with a lengthy letter that included several attachments describing both TRAC and the legal protections that he had arranged for it.[22] He had developed the language using his own time and money, and he continued to support its development using his own funds. Recently, he had started to market processors for it through time-sharing outlets under license agreements, but he and Rockford Research continued to be "a very small operation."[23]

Mooers told Albrecht that the hobby market posed him a serious, and perhaps insurmountable, challenge. The cost of CPUs, or central processing units, was "going asymptotically to zero," and more people than ever were using computers.[24] This meant that software was becoming increasingly important but, at the same time, it meant that he would have to "do what [he had] to do to make a living in this business." This included being careful not to disclose too much information without a good reason, securing trademarks and copyrights for promising languages such as TRAC, and being willing to take people to federal courts for committing "what could best be described as piracy." Should he fail to take those measures or to explain clearly the legal rights he had obtained, an "uncontrolled widespread unauthorized building of processors" among the hobbyists could destroy TRAC's future.

Overwhelmed by Mooers's response, Albrecht set aside the lengthy letter and decided to address it later. He suspected that Mooers's fear of engaging with him was symptomatic of a bigger problem that characterized the relation-ships between many hobbyists and their business-minded peers. Indeed, two programmers—William Gates and Paul Allen—had recently found themselves in the situation that Mooers had been so careful to avoid.[25] Based at a small Albuquerque firm called Micro-Soft (later renamed Microsoft), Allen and Gates had developed a version of BASIC for the Altair, named Altair BASIC. Copies of it were meant to sell for about $500 each, and Gates and Allen had worked out a deal with MITS to receive between $30 and $60 for each copy of the program sold.[26]

In April 1975, MITS sent Gates's program on a West Coast tour in the "MITS-mobile," a camper van that MITS had launched in April 1975. The van carried an Altair 8800, copies of Altair BASIC, a teletype, and a printer. It had made its way from Texas to California, enabling MITS to set up computer seminars at hotels and motels around the country. These seminars usually attracted two hundred or more people and featured lectures, discus-sions, and hands-on demonstrations. Each seminar cost just $9.75, and the participants who arrived first would receive a three-ring binder of information on MITS products. From July to August 1975, the MITS-mobile was sched-uled to travel across the South, from Tulsa and Little Rock to Orlando and Raleigh. From there it would move to the Northeast and the Midwest, and hobbyists were welcomed to nominate their town for addition into the van's tour schedule. In fact, MITS vowed to add any town where a hobbyist had enlisted at least seventy-five people to attend a computer seminar.[27]

When the van reached Palo Alto, one of the tapes containing Gates's program was missing, and it did not reappear until several weeks later, in the hands of Dan Sokol, from the Homebrew Computer Club. That same day, a box containing fifty copies of the tape appeared at the club, only to be ambushed by hobbyists who left it empty within a few seconds.[28] Enraged, Gates sent a letter in January 1976 to hobbyist journals such as *Computer News, Radio Electronics*, and the *People's Computer Company*. At the letter's core was Gates's condemna-tion of the hobbyists' sharing of Altair BASIC and, more generally, computer programs altogether. He explained that he, Allen, and another programmer named Monte Davidoff had been working on Altair BASIC for almost a year and that the "value of the computer time" they had spent surpassed $40,000.[29] However, the feedback he had received from hundreds of people who now used the program had made him realize that less than 10 percent of these users bought Altair BASIC. In fact, the royalties he and his colleagues had received were so scarce that they amounted to less than $2 per hour of work. The prob-lem, Gates wrote, was that "most of you steal your software." In his view, hobbyists assumed that "hardware must be paid for, but software is something to share," and they didn't care whether the people who worked on the software got paid. "Most directly," he told the hobbyists, "the thing you do is theft."

Gates's letter was entitled "An Open Letter to Hobbyists," and it has become a key document in the history of computing—evidence that software makers in the 1970s faced the challenge of creating a market for their products by selling to a group of potential users who shared, free of charge, any programs they acquired or developed.[30] The editors at hobby magazines did not hesitate to publish it. The *Homebrew Computer Club Newsletter*'s editor, Robert Reiling, reproduced Gates's letter in its entirety, adding that it should be "should be read by every computer hobbyist" and that the *Newsletter* was interested in publishing readers' replies.[31] The varied responses to Gates's letter underscored the different ways in which hobbyists understood the ownership and sale of software. Dozens of them were prompted to articulate their views on the nature of computer programs as a proprietary technology, and editors were encouraged to publish pieces on the relations among software as a commodity, hobby users, and legal mechanisms including copyrights and patents.

Hobbyists freely distributed and reproduced programs at their meetings, but this sharing should not be construed as their universal embrace of the idea that the market should be bypassed altogether. On the contrary, some hobbyists regretted that this unauthorized reproduction was taking place, and others viewed their sharing practices as one of the factors that determined the value of a program in the free market for computing. Among the latter was Michael Hayes, an employee at a firm called MNH Electronics. In a letter published in the February 1976 edition of the *Newsletter*, he chastised Gates for failing to realize that the value of a software product is determined not just by its technical specifications or functionalities but also by its qualities as a commodity.[32]

Hayes told Gates that he should not blame the hobbyists for his "own inadequate marketing" of Altair BASIC, because a program's value is determined by the market, not by its makers. Moreover, Hayes wrote,

> You *gave* it away; none stole it from you. Now you're asking for software welfare so you can give more away. If $2/hr is all you got for your efforts, then $2/hr is what they're worth on the free market. You should either change your product or change your way of selling it, if you feel it'll bring more money. . . . It's too bad you didn't get the profit from your efforts that [MITS] did from theirs, but that's *your* fault, not theirs or the hobbyists. You underpriced your product.[33]

Perhaps Hayes misunderstood the conditions under which Gates's program first circulated, but his point was that selling and marketing were as important as coding. He thanked Gates for creating Altair BASIC, and he explained that MITS should be equally grateful. After all, without the "marvelous software," the Altair 8800 was just a computer that "none would have touched, except as a frustrating novelty item."[34] Still, Hayes concluded that Gates was blaming everyone but himself for his own lack of business savvy. To increase future profits, Hayes told Gates, "you had better stop writing code for a minute and think a little harder about your market and how you are going to sell it."

In contrast, some hobbyists thought that their community should work on the honor system to protect software makers when the intellectual property system couldn't. A programmer and accountant named Charles Pack, for example, wrote an open letter of his own, taking pride in the fact that he was one of the few users who actually paid for the Altair BASIC for professional use.[35] Pack "deplore[d] the flagrant abuse of copyright software" that professionals and hobbyists committed repeatedly, and he believed that stealing software, like stealing equipment, was just common theft. The problem was that even though copyright protections could potentially stand up in court, they were so limited that "computer programs are very easy to copy and steal." In fact, one of his great concerns as a professional programmer was that the hobbyists would once again end up forgetting that "we programmers have to eat, too!"

Back at the PCC, the letter prompted Albrecht finally to make public his experiences dealing with Mooers. In charge of reporting this was the new editor of the newsletter, a teacher and programmer named Jim Warren.[36] After moving through several teaching jobs and countercultural scenes, Warren had taken a job as a computer programmer at the Stanford Medical Center, where he learned how to use the PDP-8 machines. He had taken a class at San Francisco State University taught by Albrecht, with whom he shared a vision of computers as machines that could teach and entertain anyone interested in them. Since then, Warren had become a key member of the *Dr. Dobb's* editorial team.

Warren's note was titled "Copyright Mania: It's Mine; It's Mine, and You Can't Play with It!"[37] It mocked Mooers's views on proprietary software to protest the "blanket indictment" that Gates had issued—that most of them stole their software.[38] Instead of providing any information whatsoever, Mooers had embedded his communications in dense legal prose, and he had sent along a price list for his software and documentation; an appendix disclosing TRAC's copyright protection and the name's trademark registration; a copy of his policy on licensing; a description of his willingness to go to court; and an assortment of articles about his own views on the legal protections for software. Even the price list bore the copyright sign, ©.

Jokingly, Warren explained that if Mooers's package of materials was any indication, TRAC must have been, "at the least, a registered trademark, and probably patented, copyrighted, and marked with infra-red dye to boot."[39] Just to be safe, Warren jested, it would perhaps be best not to include in *Dr. Dobb's* the titles of the articles that Mooers had written on intellectual property. Otherwise the programmer might decide to sue the journal for printing the titles without permission. Or perhaps Mooers's desire to rely on intellectual property did not apply to magazines. After all, the materials that he had sent included what appeared to be unauthorized photocopies of *Computerworld* articles.[40]

Warren did not object to copyright altogether.[41] What he did object to, however, was what he called the "incredible teapot tempest" that revolved around whether hobbyists were misappropriating proprietary programs. He thought that people such as Mooers and Gates were giving a bad name to all hobbyists just because some of them happened to be thieves and that firms such as Rockford and Micro-Soft seemed to overlook that the reproduction of a copyrighted program was as easy and cheap as that of a newspaper article. Talented programmers were dedicating too much time to this "proprietary preoccupation," concerning themselves more with what people did with their programs than with the programs themselves. In any case, hobby software was not expensive enough to be an important source of profits. In contrast, businesses and industrial research laboratories could make hundreds of thousands of dollars in financial gains by doing essentially the same thing, and yet Gates and Mooers seemed unconcerned with them.

According to Warren, the relation between hardware and software in the hobbyists' minds was similar to that between a photocopier and a book as envisioned by a photocopy machine user.[42] He proposed the following mental exercise: Imagine that a publisher decides to sell a reference book to users of photocopiers and that its sales tactic is to place copies of it next to a manufacturer's machines under a sign that says, "If you want a copy of this book, you must send us $350." In that case, regardless of how "excellent and useful" the reference book may be, no one is likely to pay that much money for something they could do on their own for a small fraction of the asking price. In this situation there were only two ways of getting people to pay: either to reduce the price of the book to something so low that spending money made more sense than spending time making photocopies, or to sell the book for a high price, but only to the photocopier manufacturer, and not to the machine users. The same was true of software. If people such as Mooers and Gates wanted to make any money out of software, Warren insisted, they should either charge very little and depend on volume sales, or sell their programs for a high price to the only market within which they could keep unauthorized reproduction in check: hardware manufacturers.

In the end, Warren argued, software should be like *Dr. Dobb's*. An annual subscription to this magazine cost only $10.[43] This meant that with a healthy enough readership of "non-profit-making hobbyists," *Dr. Dobb's* would not run into financial trouble. In contrast, journals such as *Microcomputer Digest* charged at least the same amount in monthly fees alone, and some charged up to four times as much for a single copy of a slender report. According to Warren, this made sense for these publications because they were being marketed to "the highly profitable business and industrial computer communities." If software makers for microcomputers could adopt this pricing strategy, then *Dr. Dobb's* would be happy to publicize them free of charge.

The programs that most approached Warren's vision for software were written in Tiny BASIC, the language to which Albrecht and Allison had dedicated *Dr. Dobb's*. Surrounding the language were a collection of examples of the kinds of software making and distribution practices that would be known as free software one decade later. In his own announcement of Tiny BASIC in the PCC's newsletter, Allison had noted that he and his collaborators at the PCC hoped that the development of the language would be "a participatory design project" and that it would lead to a language that was "open-ended—a toy for software tinkerers."[44] He asked readers to submit corrections and suggestions for improvement, and he explained that he had planned out the development of the program to make it "easy for people to change without access to specialized tools" such as parsing programs. Now that more people than ever before owned computers, Allison hoped that Tiny BASIC would one day enable anybody to operate their machines without having to know much about software and without having to program in machine language.

Allison envisioned the relation between hardware and Tiny BASIC software as a series of mediations best understood as the layers of an onion.[45] The onion's outside layer was the application program written in Tiny BASIC; its core was the machine that would run the program. The middle layers of the onion were a sequence of programs called interpreters—programs that execute other programs without requiring a full translation of the program to be executed into machine language. In other words, a given program in Tiny BASIC (the outermost layer of the onion) had its own interpreter (the second outmost layer, in charge of executing the first layer). However, this interpreter was in itself a program, so it, too, had an interpreter (the third outmost layer of the onion). This process would continue until a final interpreter connected its predecessor to the machine itself, which stood at the core of the onion.[46]

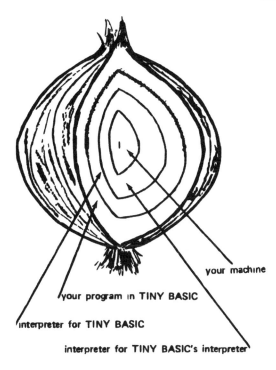

your machine

your program in TINY BASIC

interpreter for TINY BASIC

interpreter for TINY BASIC's interpreter

Jim Warren's illustration of the relations among a program in Tiny BASIC, its interpreters, and the machine that runs them. The use of an onion matches the *People's Computer Company's* informal and lighthearted style, but the notion that layers of interpreters connect a given program with a machine was common among hobbyists in the 1970s. Image courtesy of Dennis Allison and the People's Computer Company.

The onion metaphor was meant to simplify the repetitive layering of interpretations that connected a program with the machine that ran it.[47] It was a complement to Allison's own intentionally verbose and confusing description of the same process, which read, "The machine which is interpreting the interpreter interpreting the interpreter interpreting BASIC is in fact interpreted."[48] The onion was especially apt as a symbol not only because of its layered structure but also because each layer has a smaller diameter than the one that covers it. This decreasing size mimicked the decreasing memory space occupied by the interpreters that connected the program to the machine. This illustrated Tiny BASIC's small memory requirements, which stemmed from the fact that a program's interpreter was usually smaller and simpler to write than the program itself. The layering of software that this entailed made the program slower than it could be, but it also meant that it could be tiny enough to run in a microcomputer.[49]

Warren could not have been more pleased with hobbyists' adoption of Tiny BASIC. In a publication of the ACM's SIGPLAN (the Special Interest Group on Programming Languages), he celebrated that, finally, there was a "viable alternative to the problems raised by Bill Gates, in his irate letter to computer hobbyists concerning 'ripping off' software."[50] People were creating all sorts of simple programs—games, calculators, and many other applications—using the language, and these, too, were being distributed for a very low cost and published in hobby journals. Moreover, there were at least five versions of Tiny BASIC, and most of them had been published, including the necessary source code, in journals such as *Dr. Dobb's*.

Among the new versions was one developed by a programmer in Palo Alto named Li-Chen Wang, whose source code included the following new and unusual disclaimer: "TINY BASIC FOR INTEL 8080; VERSION 1.0; BY LI-CHEN WANG; 10 JUNE 1976; @COPYLEFT; ALL WRONGS RESERVED."[51] In hopes of encouraging people to modify his work, Wang wrote in the source code itself, "You may need this space to patch up the I/O routines. To fix up bugs, or to add more commands and functions. Sky (Space) is the limit. Good luck and Good Bye. Lichen Wang, 10 June '76."[52] Wang did not explain what he meant by the term "copyleft," but it was clear that he expected people to modify and distribute his code and that, in the spirit of *Dr. Dobb's*, he certainly had no intention to restrict the future spread of any modifications. Other hobbyists copied Wang's source code, modified it, and published the resulting code in other periodicals.[53] In one of the earliest iterations of this cycle, a programmer named Roger Rauskolb made it a point to retain the copyleft disclaimer that Wang had included and to publish it in *Interface Age* as part of his own modified code.[54]

Wang himself, like the editorial staff at *Dr. Dobb's*, encouraged people to modify and distribute his language, and people like Rauskolb respected and acknowledged that Wang was the creator of the language. The program was freely available, but an acknowledgment to Wang's status as the author remained attached to it. This mode of making and distributing software troubled the more business-minded hobbyists. Gates construed the spread of source code and programs in journals such as *Dr. Dobb's* as evidence that the hobbyists were doing valuable work but that their community's attitude toward software ownership needed to be reformed.[55] In his "Second and Final" open letter, he acknowledged that there were some "intelligent and honest" hobbyists who shared his concern for the future of software development.[56] Some of them were upset because theft was taking place, but they remained in the minority. This was problematic, according to Gates, because the rapid expansion of the hobby market would only increase the demand for high-quality software, especially now that the commercial applications of micro-computers were becoming clear. Without a new attitude toward the programs that other people developed, hobbyists would just leave themselves out of the excitement because firms would become reluctant to give them any programs at all.[57]

Mooers was one of these reluctant potential developers. By 1977, he had grown so concerned that he believed it was his responsibility to warn others about the hobbyists' willingness to steal software from those who made what he called "serious software."[58] By this he meant the "new and powerful software" that took several months of work to develop and was directed toward businesses and industries, not hobby and home computers. All hobbyists did—if they happened to be creating a program instead of stealing it—was to make "'Chouly-In-A-Cave' games in BASIC" and to remain "too dangerous to deal with." In short, people like him were doing the real programming work; hobbyists were just stealing for fun.

In contrast, Warren believed that software had never had a more exciting present or a more promising future. The spread of programs and code among hobbyists had shown him that "when software is free," or at least so cheap that it is easier to pay for it than to duplicate it, then "it won't be stolen."[59] He thought that hobbyists would continue to make "free and inexpensive software" widely available, thus succeeding where businesses and industrial communities had failed—the "SHAREing" of programs. He counted four reasons why this success had been possible. First, hobbyists developed "home-grown hardware and software" because it was fun. It was easier to give something away if it was made for fun, and not for work. Second, hobbyists knew that the only people who could pay high prices for software were the hardware manufacturers. This is where Gates had failed, since he assumed that hobbyists were willing to invest large sums of money in programs just for their amusement. Third was the hobbyists' skill level; many were experienced programmers and engineers with the skills needed to design and implement excellent software. This is where Mooers had failed, since he seemed unaware that hobbyists could make their own programs and languages even if he chose not to share his work with them.

Last, and most important, was the approach to project management that users of Tiny BASIC sometimes adopted—a fast-paced hierarchical division of labor in which people with different skill levels shared everything through periodicals. Warren called this management form the "Chief Programmer Team approach."[60] It consisted of having an "experienced pro" craft the overall design and outline an implementation strategy through widely distributed journals such as *Dr. Dobb's*. Then the "more experienced amateurs" would complete the "necessary hack-work," which they found exciting and which the experienced pro would have found tedious anyway. The journal-mediated communication between the pro and the amateurs would create a "symbiotic effort," and it would disclose the knowledge that everyone else would need to design their own program and perform bug tests. In return for this knowledge, readers would find a way to disclose any applications they created, perhaps by publishing their work in the same issues wherein the professionals and the amateurs were still disseminating their thoughts. This process made programming labor a form of playing, not working, and it ensured that everyone would share in the "amazing [amount of] 'good stuff'" that they produced together.

This was not to say that Warren would object to paying a few dollars for a computer program.[61] On the contrary, for five dollars, hobbyists could obtain a tape containing a version of Tiny BASIC along with documentation and implementation details. The point was that if the maker had included a profit margin on that price, it was minuscule. Any hobbyists who did not want to pay would be able to find the source code and documentation in the community's periodicals, but they would have to invest their own time to inscribe the source code onto their storage device. In other words, any payments made to acquire software should cover only the costs of paper, storage media, and convenience—not the programmers' labor, which would be, in any case, a community effort.

Warren knew that publishing a program in *Dr. Dobb's* usually led to many requests for copies of the program in tape form. For this reason, he celebrated the fact that an allied hobby group, the Community Computer Center (CCC) in Menlo Park, California, had created a small business called the Program Repository & Tape Duplication Facility.[62] Any programmer who wished to contribute programs to the public domain could do so by forwarding paper tapes to the CCC. The facility would distribute the programs, so that makers could publish any important documentation in *Dr. Dobb's* and direct potential users to the CCC. No membership fees were required to request materials from the facility, and the nominal prices included nothing more than duplication and mailing costs.[63]

The facility's low prices and appealing selection made it an overnight success and a common advertiser in *Dr. Dobb's*. Software was priced by weight at $1 per ounce, and its final price was computed after the program had been punched into it. This ensured that customers were paying only for the tape they were receiving, and not for the little paper disks that had been removed during the punching. Postage was 50¢ for any orders that totaled less than $5, and $1 for all other orders. This pricing scheme allowed hobbyists to access the facility's fifty different programs. About half were games; number-guessing games, word scrambles, board games, and simple adventure games were especially numerous. The rest of the programs included applications designed for simple business functions such as computing taxes or studying stocks. The cheapest programs cost $2 each; they included pattern-matching and word-guessing games. The most expensive ones were up to $22 apiece, and they were primarily business applications and simple statistical tools.[64]

For the rest of the 1970s, Warren, Albrecht, *Dr. Dobb's*, and the hobbyists who followed them embraced Warren's vision of cheap software. This is what Warren considered to be the magazine's primary purpose—to fill the "information vacuum" on how to make and obtain "free and very inexpensive software."[65] Warren promised that low-cost systems software, interpreters, compilers, assemblers, games, and other programs would always be welcome at *Dr. Dobb's*. The journal would always encourage users to test out the programs printed in its pages or made available through the facility. It would also hold an unwavering stance against firms that hired people such as Mooers and Gates, who would "peddle [software] to unsuspecting customers for a healthy profit." Thus, at least for a few years, Warren had turned *Dr. Dobb's* into what he hoped software would become—a low-cost and high-volume publication made by and for computing enthusiasts.

APPLE COMPUTER

Like Gates, two hobbyists at the Homebrew Computer Club, Stephen Wozniak and Steve Jobs, soon developed an appreciation for software IP incompatible with Warren's vision.[66] In the HCC Wozniak had found a group of like-minded hobbyists with whom he could tinker with computers. Soon after his first visit, he had built a computer based on the MOS Technology 6502 chip—a microprocessor priced at $35, for which the firm MOS Technology had just filed a patent.[67] In contrast, Jobs saw the club as an opportunity to create a market aimed at people such as Wozniak and his new community of computer tinkerers. He also thought that Wozniak's makeshift computer could serve as a test machine for selling to hobbyists across the country. Jobs persuaded Wozniak to develop his new computer into a stand-alone machine, the Apple I. This was a naked circuit board onto which users could solder their own chips, featuring no case, screen, power supply, or keyboard of its own.[68]

Throughout their first few months working together, Jobs and Wozniak didn't worry too much about IP or its financial implications.[69] Wozniak would later remember that the two of them "didn't see any dollars at the end of the rainbow" and that they "didn't pay much attention to patents."[70] Instead, the development of the Apple I felt to him like "doing things for the fun of it" without having to think about IP or any of the other legal matters that could affect their company.[71] He "was in a very hobbyist realm," not "designing a product, just something that would work at home in my own TV."[72] They knew that there was something new and useful about the Apple I and Wozniak's software for it, but their aim was exclusively to make and sell machines, not to patent them. This is not to say that Jobs and Wozniak had no conception that they could assert some sort of legal claim over the Apple I.[73] HP had its own line of minicomputers, and the HP 9830 calculator, released in 1972 and priced at $10,000, could run BASIC. Jobs and Wozniak even worried that HP might be interested in claiming rights over the Apple I because Wozniak had developed it while in the firm's employment.

When they realized that HP had no intention of asserting legal claims over the computer, Jobs and Wozniak became interested in selling the manufacturing rights to it. With no patents to assert his ownership over the Apple I, Wozniak explained to his managers that he and Jobs had created a small machine that could run BASIC and connect to a home TV.[74] Certainly, the lack of patent protection over the Apple I would have made it unappealing to a large firm such as HP, but Wozniak's managers declined his offer on other grounds: HP would pass, not because of issues with its technical capabilities or lack of legal protections, but simply because their firm "couldn't do a hobby product." Even if Wozniak had shown them a patent, the market for hobby computers was too young and unpredictable for HP's comfort, and its products were far too inexpensive.

Soon after HP granted Wozniak a legal release, he and Jobs realized that selling copies of the Apple I directly to users would be difficult.[75] In 1976, they demonstrated a prototype of the Apple I at a meeting of the Homebrew Computer Club. They showcased its ability to run BASIC and even went to people's homes to "build and test the computers out."[76] Firms such as MITS had created profitable businesses by visiting hobbyists and promoting their products directly, but Jobs and Wozniak did not have the direct-to-consumer sales experience and strategy that MITS had developed before marketing the Altair.

Aiming for a more effective way of selling the computer, Jobs approached Paul Terrell, a club member who owned a microcomputer store in Mountain View called Byte Shop.[77] Jobs wanted to sell him a kit that included the Apple I's printed circuit board and all the components necessary for users to assemble the device, but Terrell was unimpressed. Thinking back about this initial meeting, Terrell recalled, "The problem was I had computer kits coming at me from everywhere, and my partner and I had a sales rep company that represented MITS with their Altair 8800—so I didn't need another kit."[78] Instead, what his store needed was "an assembled and tested microcomputer that I could sell to all the programmers who were storming my stores for a taste of the hobby computer."[79]

While Wozniak and his friends at the HCC thought about how to deliver assembled machines, Jobs sought out to establish a supply chain of components. Terrell and Jobs agreed to try an initial order of fifty units priced at $666 each, to be paid for upon delivery in thirty days.[80] In need of electronic components worth between $15,000 and $20,000, Jobs struck a deal with a store called Kramer Electronics. Kramer would supply the components necessary for Wozniak to complete the Byte Shop order, and Kramer would be paid upon the Byte Shop's receipt of the machines. Within a month, Jobs and Wozniak delivered the fifty machines to Terrell, and the Apple I became a regular machine at HCC meetings. "It was the most incredible thing we had ever done in our lives," Wozniak would later say. "We were just having fun and getting known."[81]

Jobs and Wozniak soon noticed an opportunity for further development and sales: computers featuring interactive color displays.[82] Microcomputers with color graphics capability were becoming regular display pieces at the HCC's meetings. The club's members marveled at computers such as Cromemco's Color Dazzler, which their proud owners showed off by displaying images such as clocks and colored text. Wozniak had plenty of experience working with color screens; while working at Atari several years earlier he had designed the systems necessary to display color in television screens. He and Jobs therefore set their sights on developing a computer in which a part of the main memory could be used as its video memory. This would enable users to modify the contents of the color screen without needing to switch back and forth between the color display and their work screens.

The success of the Apple I had enabled Jobs and Wozniak to move out of their original garage workspace, and their company started to develop its own legal protections. Wozniak remembered that he and Jobs had decided to make Apple "a real company," one that would reach beyond the hobby market.[83] This involved hiring people such as patent attorneys, who "sat down and kind of explained to us some of the rules that we had to follow."[84] Among these rules was the patenting of Apple's core products, including Wozniak's color display computer, the Apple II. In April 1977, they debuted their computer at the West Coast Computer Faire and reached out to Blakely, Sokoloff, Taylor

& Zafman, a two-year-old law firm that specialized in patent and trademark litigation.[85] The firm's lawyers assisted Wozniak with filing a patent application entitled *Microcomputer for Use with Video Display*, directed at a "microcomputer including a video generator and timing means which provides color and high resolution graphics on a standard, raster canned, cathode ray tube."[86]

Jobs's aim to transform Apple into a far-reaching manufacturer made the legal protection of the firm's programs crucial to its long-term needs. However, the company's origins in the hobby community and recent developments in patent law limited their options. On the one hand, the transparency and community-oriented software development practices that characterized hobby clubs made their members averse to trade secrecy. On the other hand, the future of software patenting appeared to be bleak at best. Many lawyers were interpreting the Supreme Court's opinion in *Gottschalk v. Benson* as a significant blow to the strategic value of software patents, and it appeared likely that the Court would soon affirm it. This left them with one tool at their disposal: copyrights.

In 1977, Wozniak filed several copyright registrations for three interrelated components of his BASIC interpreter—three registrations for an interpreter to be stored on a computer's read-only memory, Applesoft, and one each for two disk-based versions of it, Apple Integer BASIC and Floating Point BASIC.[87] He also filed a registration for Autostart ROM (the program that initializes the system) and for programs that managed the system's random access memory, enabled the copying of programs from one disk to another, and controlled disk operating systems.[88] By the end of 1980, he had secured at least fourteen copyright registrations for his programs, including one for the DOS 3.3 operating system.[89] Copyrights were not perfect, especially if programs were loaded onto inventions like microchips, but the passage of the Computer Software Copyright Act earlier in 1980 made them appear more reliable than patents.

Unlike systems programs—which Apple produced and copyrighted and for which the source code was built into the machines—applications for the Apple II were often third-party programs available through floppy disks. This made applications easy to replicate using a new kind of program called a bit copier, which made it possible for users to create identical clones of programs stored without ever running the program on their computers. The most prominent among them was called Locksmith. Created in 1980 by a programmer who forever remained anonymous and distributed by a firm called Omega Software, Locksmith allowed users of the Apple II to make bit-by-bit copies of a disk's tracks.[90]

The Computer Software Copyright Act's allowance for the creation of personal backup copies enabled the makers of bit copiers to claim that their programs broke no laws. It was in fact common for representatives of the firms that distributed these programs to quote the act to justify the legality of their endeavor; they claimed that it would not be their firm's fault if users asked their friends to keep one of the backup copies allowed by law, only to find out later that these friends were using the copies as their own programs. A published interview with one such representative even featured the full text of the portion of the U.S. Code that contained the act's provision allowing the creation of backups.[91]

Apple II computer users' craving for duplication software did not escape the editors of user magazines. This was most evident in *Softalk*, an opinion and news magazine that everyone on Apple Computer's mailing list started to receive in September 1980. *Softalk* was created by Margot Comstock and Allan Tommervik, a couple who had used Comstock's winnings in the television game *Password* to purchase their first Apple II+ in 1979.[92] Unlike such periodicals as *Apple Orchard, Call Apple,* and *Micro,* this magazine was concerned less with programming tutorials than with news about the industry's software. *Softalk* featured advertisements from software firms dedicated to making Apple-compatible software, interviews with managers and programmers at those firms, and a monthly ranking of the industry's most popular applications.

Comstock herself had no desire to focus on business issues affecting the industry, but her magazine's advertisers and interviewees had a keen interest in condemning the impact that software piracy could have on the industry. In response, she and Tommervik published a feature story titled "Pirate, Thief. Who Dares to Catch Him?" in *Softalk*'s second issue. The accompanying cover image featured a joyful pirate standing by a treasure chest full of shrink-wrapped computer tapes and disks. In the article itself, Comstock and Tommervik explained, "The pirates of today sail no ships, fly no flags, and don't engage in swordplay or murder; but plunder they do. Their thievery is still theft; but their booty is not diamonds and doubloons, it's plastic—in the form of floppy disks and cassette tapes loaded with popular computer programs."[93] Comstock and Tommervik's condemnation of piracy had four interrelated components. First, a user making one or two copies for friends or relatives could set off a chain reaction of undesired copies. After all, no one knew what people would do with the copies they received. Second, hobby groups could be divided into "honest user group[s]" and "bootleggers."[94] The former comprised primarily groups under the sponsorship of International Apple Core, Apple Computers' official user group association. The latter included all groups wherein "members meet to swap information," where it would not be unlikely to find "common perpetrators" and people willing to "exchange secrets of the trade."[95] Third, software piracy could drive firms out of business or force companies to raise their prices to make up for lost profits. This would ultimately harm the consumer, and (according to one manager they interviewed) it would cause the industry to "revert to the weekend programmer who operates out of his garage and come out with more pong-type games."[96] Finally, pirates were guilty of "making waves in the market-place" and of bringing "the software industry face to face with a new copyright conundrum."[97]

In response to people such as Comstock and Tommervik, two other Apple users, Charles and Beverly Haight, created a magazine dedicated to the dupli-cation of copy-protected disks. Soon after purchasing their own Apple II+ in 1979, the couple had heard about bit copiers and Charles was eager to dupli-cate the disks for some of the programs he had purchased.[98] He was disap-pointed to find that no magazine ran advertisements for programs such as Locksmith and that mainstream user magazines would not help him attain his real goal, which he would later describe as "to get into the 'core' of the Apple and all its peripherals." The Haights therefore created a magazine called *Hard-core Computing* in 1981. Their publication's tagline summarized its mission: "HOW TO BACK UP YOUR COPY-PROTECTED DISKS." He would serve as the magazine's publisher; she would serve as its editor.

The first issue's central theme was censorship, by which the Haights meant that mainstream publishers such as *Softalk* would not print advertisements or in-depth articles on how to use duplication software. In his opening letter to the readers, Charles wrote that there is "a raging, silent battle between Apple-users and the magazines."[99] On the one hand, magazines would accuse users of "being pirates and thieves" for duplicating software they had purchased. On the other hand, users would accuse the magazines of hypocritical censorship— proclaiming that they aimed to help users when they were merely "peddling software." Perhaps this happened, he explained, because the magazines them-selves were fronts for software houses or because they depended on software firms for advertising revenue. Either way, it would be "suicide for them to stand up for Apple-users," from whom it was "a need and a right to back-up copies of protected disks." In response, *Hardcore Computing* would welcome "computerists who dislike being manipulated by the software industry."

The Haights saw their mission as giving users all the information necessary to make backup copies of their programs.[100] Central to this mission was their effort to counter software firms' notion of a pirate as one that applied to all users, and not only to people committing "commercial piracy" (the practice of selling copies for profit).[101] The first issue of *Hardcore Computing* included in-depth reviews of duplication software, narratives and tables meant to help users choose which duplication program would meet their needs, and step-by-step guides on how to duplicate popular programs such as *Alakabeth, World of Doom* (a game for the Apple II). They would keep the magazine running by filling a need that *Softalk* and its peer publications had created: selling advertisement space to firms that made duplication software.

In her article, Beverly argued that the industrywide calls against piracy that she saw in magazines like *Softalk* were an affront to what she called "info-x rights" (the users' rights to exchange information with one another).[102] At the core of her argument was a simple scenario:

> You just finished typing in a program published in a well-known computer magazine. A friend comes over and you make your friend a copy. . . . Well, at that moment of generosity, you have just become a software pirate, legally and ethically and if that idea makes you guilty or angry then read on. You had no right to give that copy to anyone. You had no right to copy it for a friend; you had no copyrights at all![103]

She added that people completing these innocent transactions were the pirates about whom software firms complained so often. The industry was not using the word "pirate" in reference to some fictional professional making a living out of copying and selling software. Instead, she wrote in boldface type, "We are the pirates! We are the 'threat to the entire software market.'" By this logic, "it would not be too erroneous to say that we, the software consumers, are all pirates!"[104]

Readers of subsequent issues would have likely concluded that no IP protections could make disks safe from bit copiers, nor would any patents or copyrights deter users from duplicating floppy disks in the privacy of their home. This situation was not restricted to Apple, especially because Locksmith and some of its competitors would eventually launch bit copiers for use with IBM PCs.[105] It was impossible to police individual users to ensure that they did not perform any unauthorized duplications, so firms of all sizes sometimes relied on print technologies to discourage piracy.[106] This usually involved leaving something essential out of the software and distributing the missing piece separately. For instance, a game maker could leave a crucial dungeon map off a floppy disk, offering a free printout of it (on a photocopy-resistant sheet) with purchase of the game. Similarly, makers of office or educational software could distribute physical templates that users would need to install over the screens to make sense of their data, as home video game users in the 1970s often did.[107]

Still, duplicating software could be so easy that home users even started setting up mail-order shops to distribute unauthorized copies of PC firms' software to users around the world. Aware that such distribution constituted copyright infringement, some of these tiny shops required their clients to sign something akin to a license agreement. One Canadian shop called Avant Garde64 Software & BBS (the logo of which was a pirate skull) required users to do two things.[108] First, users had to agree that any fees they paid—$5 per disk on top of a $15 yearly membership fee—were intended for "administration and handling only." This was likely an effort to bypass the statutory damages that a copyright holder could claim if a person sold their creation for a profit without permission. Second, users agreed to use the software they acquired only for evaluation purposes and to destroy it as soon as their evaluation was complete. This was, of course, a symbolic agreement; no one was policing the users themselves. Ironically, the agreement also noted that some of the software available could be copyrighted by AvantGarde 64.

These stories illustrate how the spread of PCs was enabled not just by the widespread availability of cheap, off-the-shelf technologies but also by unauthorized software that could travel from place to place, even across national borders, on easily duplicated storage media and electronic components. In this context, microchips were especially problematic: duplicating them was very easy, and doing so could yield clones of an entire system. Many PC firms soon felt pressured to renegotiate the scope of protection that copyright law afforded their programs and to pair traditional IP suits with international customs enforcement and undercover operations.

Chapter 9 Cloned Computers and Microchip Protection, 1981–1984

The computing industry's struggles with piracy in the early 1980s encompassed much more than the unauthorized duplication of individual applications. Major PC firms were especially concerned by the birth and rapid growth of small firms dedicated to producing low-cost alternatives to their flagship computers. These alternatives, known as clones, could run most software and peripherals designed for their expensive counterparts. From storefronts in Hong Kong to American periodicals, advertisements for these cloned computers announced that users could obtain the computing power of a brand-name PC without having to pay thousands of dollars. Their reduced prices were made possible by some combination of the lower cost of labor and generic electronic components outside of the United States, reverse engineering and some PC firms' disclosure of their machines' technical standards, reduced profit margins intended to generate economies of scale, and the ease of duplicating microprocessors.

Focused on Apple and IBM, this chapter examines the great lengths to which computing firms went to protect the American market for their products from unauthorized cloning. Intellectual property protections alone were simply not enough for this task. IBM's struggles to protect proprietary information about its upcoming products in the 1980s involved undercover operations at home and abroad and even lawsuits against some of its employees. Apple Computer's effort to curb the proliferation of compatible devices forced federal courts to assess the extent to which the Computer Software Copyright Act afforded protection to copyrighted software embodied in a chip. In the mid-1980s, as it became clearer than ever that proprietary microchips were relatively easy and cheap to duplicate, computing and semiconductor firms successfully lobbied for the creation of a new hybrid form of IP protection that blended patents and copyrights to protect microchips from piracy.

CLONING THE IBM PC

IBM entered the PC industry after the increasing popularity of spreadsheet and word processing software suggested to its managers that the personal computer could be, in fact, a business machine.[1] At the firm's helm was John Opel, who became CEO in early 1980 and who believed that leasing computers was unlikely to be in the company's best interest. Opel worried that if customers could obtain low-cost computers, then they might feel the urge to cancel their leasing contracts. This would not only reduce the firm's profits but also quickly make its existing inventory obsolete and force it to develop devices at a much faster pace than usual. Opel thus changed IBM's pricing policy, abandoning the leasing model altogether for new clients and offering lessees the option to buy their machines at low prices. IBM's business model began to shift from the account management practices that it had perfected over several decades and toward the direct sale of computers.

To enter the PC industry as quickly as possible, Opel allowed the PC team to abandon the firm's standard vertically integrated approach to computer development. This meant that IBM would start selling assemblages of components that had been almost entirely outsourced.[2] One such component was software, which IBM outsourced to Microsoft.[3] This small firm adapted a program purchased from the Seattle Computer Corporation to create the MS-DOS (Microsoft Disk Operating System), which IBM bundled with its personal computers.[4] In addition, IBM agreed to purchase its microprocessors, disk drives, and printers from Intel, Tandem, and Epson, respectively—a mix of American and Japanese firms that could produce their components as quickly as possible. Even sales efforts were outsourced: IBM teamed up with the Sears Company and ComputerLand in order to bring their computers to consumers, incorporating them into well-known catalogs for office products.[5]

IBM's outsourcing of software shifted the burden of software IP onto small firms such as Microsoft, but IBM did make an aggressive effort to protect the IBM PC itself. In the month and a half before announcing the PC in August 1981, the firm filed several patent applications designed to create a dense cluster of protections around PC components such as memory access, motherboard, keyboard interface, and screen display.[6] Together, these patents covered many of the PC's peripherals and some of the internal processes that coordinated the operation of the off-the-shelf components that made up the PC.

IBM's patenting effort was parallel to one in copyright law. The passage of the Computer Software Copyright Act had encouraged the firm's lawyers to pursue an aggressive copyrighting effort. In 1980 alone, they obtained 191 copyright registrations for their computer programs—all primarily for the systems programs they incorporated into their mainframe computer.[7] The Copyright Office's records do not make it possible to estimate how many program registrations IBM obtained for PC software alone, but they do show that in 1981 the firm obtained a total of 221 software copyright registrations in total, and that at least 3 of them corresponded to systems and application software that Microsoft completed and assigned to IBM.[8] These included, for instance, the PC's DOS and BASIC programs.[9]

IBM's entry into the PC industry occurred at a time of rapid change in the country's antitrust landscape. In 1982, the Antitrust Division's long-standing suit against IBM, the one that precipitated its unbundling, came to a swift end after a judge ruled that it had no merit.[10] After nearly fourteen years of litigation, the commercial, technological, and political landscapes of American computing had simply changed far too much for the original complaints to hold weight. Software development firms of all sizes were making significant inroads in the computing industry at home and abroad, and minicomputing firms remained profitable even despite IBM's entry into this market for smaller and cheaper machines. At the same time, the Reagan administration—which aimed to eliminate or at least substantially reduce government regulation—had placed adherents of the Chicago School of economics as heads of the Antitrust Division and the Federal Trade Commission. This meant that the people in charge of antitrust prosecution believed that reliance on market forces would generate more economic growth and create more wealth than the use of government regulations.[11]

Of course, this is not to say that government regulations were entirely absent. For one, IBM was still bound by the consent decree of 1956 (the Antitrust Division would not start to phase it out until the mid-1990s).[12] More importantly, Reagan's Antitrust Division intervened very aggressively in the telecommunications industry. In 1982, AT&T signed a new consent decree in exchange for the division's agreement to rescind the one issued in 1956.[13] This development stemmed from an investigation initiated in 1974 by the Federal Communications Commission targeting AT&T's monopoly over American telephony and its vertically integrated structure, which covered everything from the production and delivery of telephones to the provision of long-distance services. The firm agreed to divest its twenty-two local telephone companies, which in turn were reorganized into seven regional holding companies. In what scholars recognize as the most complex restructuring in the history of American business, AT&T retained only Western Electric, Bell Laboratories, and its long-distance networks, and it agreed that any firms interested in competing in the market for long-distance telephony would have equal access to its network and local operators.[14]

Intellectual property rights were especially valuable in this free-market-driven business environment, and the developments of the early 1980s were making them stronger than ever. The passage of the CSCA had made copyright protection significantly more robust for software, and the FWA test and the broad reading of patent-eligibility that the Supreme Court had articulated in *Diamond v. Diehr* had made patent protections very accessible. In the years from 1976 to 1985, the number of software patents issued each year increased steadily from at least 765 (1.1 percent of all issued patents) to more than 2,400 (3.5 percent).[15] The FWA test allowed firms to patent software inventions such as spelling correctors for word processors and automatic programming tools without needing to spell out machine embodiments as their predecessors would have done.[16] By the mid-1980s, even Microsoft—which had traditionally relied on copyrights and licenses for software protection—was filing software patent applications.[17]

At the same time, however, IBM made the PC's technical specifications of its hardware and software freely available. This enabled the growth of firms dedicated to making peripherals, enhancements, and fully compatible machines.[18] In 1982, for example, a Maryland-based company called Columbia Data Products released the Multi-Personal Computer (MPC), a PC that the firm advertised as able to "use software and hardware originally intended for the IBM Personal Computer."[19] Loaded with MS-DOS, the MPC was just as powerful as its IBM counterpart. It also included a BASIC compiler and a host of applications such as *Space Commanders*, Home Accountant Plus, and Fast Graphs.[20]

Columbia Data Products, like other manufacturers of IBM-compatible PCs (called clones), would drop out of the industry within a few years, as PC prices dropped far too low for small firms to remain profitable.[21] A notable

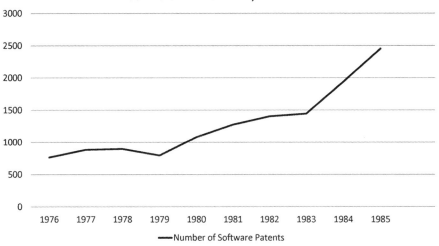

Software patents issued each year from 1976 to 1985. Data collected by James Bessen and Robert Hunt. Bessen and Hunt, "An Empirical Look at Software Patents." This graph and all others showing number of software patents issued depict minimum numbers, because the methods used to obtain them do not account for the possibility of software embodiment.

exception to this trend was Compaq, a firm founded in 1982 that remained afloat in part because its first product, the Compaq Portable Computer, offered something that the original IBM PC didn't: portability.[22] Weighing just twenty-eight pounds, the computer fit into a plastic carrying case, and it arrived loaded with licensed copies of MS-DOS and BASIC.[23] Within a few years, as IBM prepared to issue a portable PC of its own, Compaq's upper management (which included several former IBM employees) remained confident that their firm's reputation and existing client base would remain strong. "IBM is good, very good," one such manager told *InfoWorld*, "but if you're going to be the best, you've got to compete with one of the best."[24]

The proliferation of IBM clones created a demand in the industry for engineers with intimate familiarity of the IBM PC. These engineers could carry with them privileged information on upcoming IBM products that could allow a compatible-PC manufacturer to release cutting-edge products before its competitors. This information may not have qualified as a trade secret in any legally meaningful way, but it was the source of the most dramatic legal battles in the early history of the PC. After all, engineers leaving the firm could take with them knowledge that could allow rapidly growing firms such as Compaq to commercialize IBM-related technologies before IBM itself had a chance to do so.[25]

The most notable example of the legal issues surrounding the mobility of IBM employees involved Bridge Technologies. This was a company that an engineer from the PC team named Lewis Eggebrecht founded alongside two other IBM employees, William Erdman (product line manager) and Peter Stearns (another senior engineer).[26] Early in 1982, soon after leaving IBM, the three men started approaching smaller companies and offering designs for devices that would either enhance the performance of the PC or connect it to IBM's mainframe computers.[27] Among these firms was Tecmar, to which Bridge offered product designs that would enable the firm to compete with some of IBM's upcoming (and still secret) PC-related technologies.[28]

Later that year, Tecmar's president, Michael Alpert, accused Bridge Technologies of having disclosed potential trade secrets, and he agreed to cooperate with IBM's investigation into the situation by secretly recording his next conversations with Bridge.[29] The recording did not confirm that Bridge was explicitly revealing IBM's secrets, but it did show that Erdman leveraged both his status within IBM and the knowledge that employees such as himself had gained in order to promote his company.[30] According to Alpert, Erdman had guaranteed that Bridge knew more than anyone else about the design of IBM machines because when engineers like himself left the firm, "a good deal of knowledge leaves with them."[31]

Alpert also reported that Bridge had offered him at least forty products, each one priced starting at $100,000 in advance royalties.[32] Based on this testimony, IBM's lawyers filed suit against Bridge.[33] IBM sought damages, the restitution of the salaries of any engineers who carried out business with Bridge while still employed with IBM, and an injunction against the further disclosure and unauthorized use of IBM's secrets. The records of the court case are no longer available for investigation, and the parties are legally bound not to discuss its details.[34] Within a few months, however, IBM agreed to settlements with Erdman, Eggebrecht, and Stearns, and the court awarded IBM a permanent injunction prohibiting the three men from designing, making, or marketing computer products related to the case.[35] Media coverage of the case suggests that IBM's top management considered the lawsuit to be an opportunity for IBM to affirm its commitment to protecting its intellectual property at all costs. Indeed, later that year, Opel told the *New York Times*: "As we have said many times in the past, we will do whatever we must to protect our company's assets."[36]

Eggebrecht's actions shook IBM's PC operations to its core. The firm's staff construed the suit as a warning that IBM would not shy away from aggressive legal action against any engineer who divulged company secrets (including product development information). The announcement of Eggebrecht's actions at an auditorium in Boca Raton, Florida, had moved several staff members to weep openly, and it became public knowledge that the firm's conditions for the settlement required Eggebrecht to refrain from working on a wide range of PC-related projects. In effect, Eggebrecht would never again work as an on-staff PC engineer.[37]

Despite this restriction, Eggebrecht became a well-known figure among PC hobbyists, software makers, and clone manufacturers. After leaving IBM, he wrote and published a book titled *Interfacing to the IBM PC*—a guide to the key features of the IBM PC that would enable hobbyists to attach their computer accessories to the computer.[38] He also worked briefly as an industry consultant for a word processing firm called CPT and then for Franklin Computer, a firm that manufactured clones of Apple-brand computers. From there, he would witness some of the important legal battles ever to face software IP, though he would never again be in the legal spotlight.

The success of the investigation encouraged IBM to continue handling potential breaches of company trust and trade secrecy through undercover investigations. The explosive growth of Japanese industries in the late 1970s motivated American computing firms, IBM above all, to become vigilant of their foreign IP rights.[39] For nearly thirty years, the Japanese government had nurtured its domestic computing industry through a range of programs including financial assistance, protectionist trade policies, aggressive exporting programs, and state-sponsored research and development. By the early 1980s, Japanese companies were emerging as strong global competitors in computing, electronics, and telecommunications. Unbundled since 1977, many of these firms naturally gravitated toward the IBM PC: its technical specifications were becoming open industry standards, and the availability of low-cost electronics components in Japan made it possible to produce cheap IBM-compatible PCs and export them around the globe.

In this fast-moving global market, undercover operations such as the one that IBM used to catch Eggebrecht provided quick-acting protection. IBM's managers suspected that major Japanese firms including Mitsubishi, Hitachi, and Fujitsu were stealing proprietary information in order to release cloned PCs quickly enough to replace IBM's own machines. IBM and the FBI therefore collaborated in a series of undercover operations in 1982 and 1983, generating what Japanese business leaders termed the "IBM Industrial Spy Incident."[40] Undercover FBI agents videotaped high-ranking managers from these firms offering to pay over $500,000 for trade secrets. Once the operation became public knowledge, Fujitsu's chairman revealed that his firm was receiving proprietary information from its American partner, Amdahl, and subsequent investigations revealed that the firms had copied IBM's software so hastily that they had even copied its bugs.

No detailed English-language records of these investigations are available for research, but it is clear that the suits concluded quickly in a flurry of settlements and public apologies.[41] Hitachi signed an agreement allowing IBM to inspect its upcoming products to determine whether they contained any unauthorized IBM technologies. It also agreed to pay more than $45 million for legal costs and its past uses of IBM software and to pay annual licensing fees of more than $35 million. Mitsubishi's settlement details are not known, but Fujitsu paid more than $25 million annually—more than 5 percent of its annual profits—for the rest of the decade. The more important consequence of these investigations, however, is that they demonstrated just how aggressively IBM was willing to protect its intellectual property: the firm would go after anyone, from one of its own employees to global firms across the Pacific.

CHIPS AND CLONES

The Eggebrecht and Japanese spying incidents show just how difficult it was for a firm to restrict the flow of sensitive technical information. This was especially problematic for computer programs—even a snippet of code could reveal the algorithms at the core of an upcoming product. The ease with which floppy disks could be duplicated, paired with a general sense that software was contained *in* the disk, and not in some form of embodiment such as the ones for which mainframe software makers had once advocated, generally encouraged firms to turn to copyright law, not patents. Since the passage of the CSCA, these firms had been able to submit a bundle of materials, from printouts of source code to floppy disks and flowcharts, for registration.

Despite this expansion of what the Copyright Office considered to be software for registration purposes, there remained a crucial ambiguity in software copyright law. The CSCA said nothing about microchips, and CONTU had steered clear of the copyright-related problems that they generated. However, the miniaturization that had enabled the PC revolution had been made possible by the widespread availability of affordable chips, many of which could contain a computer's entire proprietary CPU. Even a small firm could develop clones of brand-name computers simply by reproducing the chips' mask works, and no clear copyright infringement standard would apply to them.

This was happening at several firms in East Asian countries and territories. Often incentivized by some combination of government investments in the computing industry, official licenses for software production, and trade associations, firms in places like Taiwan, Japan, and China were developing computers of their own.[42] Their developers' technical skills were often tied to the movement of engineers and programmers across national borders.[43] Leading this movement were either talented students who left their home countries to study at American universities and spent some time at an American firm before returning home or first-generation Americans who leveraged a combination of technical, linguistic, and cultural skills to mediate between two or more national industries. These groups' work could be very profitable, especially because American firms (IBM included) were strengthening their foreign branches, adapting technical and managerial know-how developed in the United States to foreign cultures of research, development, and management.

Consider Hong Kong, which by 1980 had become a trade hub for the entire region and a popular center for the production and sale of Apple and Tandy computers. The markets in Kowloon, on the northern side of the city, were known for their fresh fruits, their proximity to the living spaces of Thai immigrants, and the ease with which anyone could find Apple II clones.[44] One American visitor reported to *Computerworld* in 1982 that the machines were in full display on the streets, operating in more than a dozen storefronts. As a result, what maps labeled as Kowloon Street was known among locals and visitors alike as Apple Street—a name befitting the prominence with which store owners displayed the Apple logo. The price of an Apple II clone varied by its national origin. At the higher end of the spectrum, Japanese versions cost about $370; at the lower end were Taiwanese machines, which cost $260. Peripherals were also available for sale. Disk drives and printers were similarly priced to the American originals, but several microprocessors and memories could be up to 80 percent cheaper.

Aggressive enforcers of their firm's IP, lawyers at Apple eventually developed, sometimes on the fly, alliances with the federal government to keep these foreign clones out of the American market. The U.S. Customs Service (predecessor to the U.S. Customs and Border Patrol) was on alert to confiscate any Apple clones its officers found.[45] Spotting these clones was expensive and time consuming, especially because it was unlikely that a customs agent would be able to identify a computer as a clone simply by looking at it. For this reason, Apple's lawyers recruited the FBI, customs agents, and state police forces to conduct undercover operations similar to the ones that IBM had performed to verify Hitachi's and Fujitsu's breaches of trade secrecy. Extensive records of these operations are not available for research, but media reports suggest that Apple clones were usually found not at the country's ports of entry but at places like apartment buildings, where their importer stored them.[46]

Sometimes, however, these cloned machines could enter the country legally to join the product lines of well-known local distributors. One of the American firms affected by this phenomenon was Tandy, which by 1980 was struggling to preclude the sale of TRS-80 clones worldwide.[47] A few years earlier, a Hong Kong–based company called EACA Limited had created a computer equivalent to the TRS-80 and intended to compete with Tandy in the United States, Australia, England, and several European countries. A California electronics company called Recortec had purchased from EACA the distribution rights to this machine for the entire Western hemisphere, and early in 1980 it had created a subsidiary called Personal Micro Computer (PMC) to manage this international distribution program from the heart of Silicon Valley.

PMC's director of product management for the United States, Ron Troxell, launched a marketing campaign for EACA's machine, which he called the PMC-80.[48] He began by reaching out to organizations that owned more than one TRS-80 to explain how the PMC-80 would offer them the same functionality at a lower cost that could appeal to schools and universities. Troxell then reached out to dealers in several countries in an effort to create a network of distributors who could handle large volumes of machines, and he soon started to draw attention from Tandy and several other electronics manufacturers. After all, one of EACA's secrets to reduce the price of the PMC-80 was its use of a clone of the Z80 microprocessor, a commonly used and Intel-compatible CPU for personal computers.

To Tandy and its users, it was soon apparent that the two machines were essentially interchangeable even though they were not visually similar.[49] The PMC-80 cost $595, about $200 less than the TRS-80. PMC's machine did not include a monitor, but it had a port that would enable users to connect a color television to it. The two machines' hardware design did have some significant differences; most notably, EACA machines lacked the ports required to connect to the peripherals normally used with Tandy machines. However, PMC also produced a $35 adapter that would enable users to connect Radio Shack peripherals to it. In this way, *Infoworld* reported, "the PMC machine can form the core of a system with TRS-80 peripherals."[50]

The Tandy Corporation had protected its computers, electronic components, and peripherals through a few utility and design patents.[51] Yet the firm didn't develop a robust patent portfolio, suggesting that Tandy's managers considered that what made their computers competitive and distinctive was not so much their hardware but their in-house programs. After all, the firm's computers were initially aimed at gamers and hobbyists, for whom assembling or modifying a computer's internal components may have constituted a fun challenge. In any case, even if Tandy had sought strong patent protection for its hardware, the difference in appearance and overall internal architecture between its own machines and PMC's would have made it difficult for the firm to win a patent infringement suit.

Tandy did, however, develop a strong portfolio of copyright registrations to protect its systems and applications programs. Perhaps because users were very likely to share games among themselves, the firm had first registered copyrights for two of its 1978 games, *Blackjack: Backgammon* and *Quick, Watson!*[52] When the firm prepared to enter the market for business applications, it had registered programs that enabled the analysis and processing of things such as real estate information and financial data.[53] At the same time, perhaps to test whether Tandy clients would want educational applications, it registered a few computerized tutorials in mathematics and computer programming.[54] Along the way, it registered copyrights for a handful of its systems programs; no more than seven of the thirty-one copyright registrations for computer programs that Tandy received from 1978 to 1981 protected systems software.[55]

To the surprise of Tandy's lawyers, one of these systems' software registrations became their primary defense against PMC's clones. The registration protected Input/out, an interpreter for the Radio Shack BASIC that Tandy had developed in 1978.[56] Like many software registrations for programs developed before passage of the CSCA, this one carried with it a printout of the program and nothing else—no storage media, accompanying flowcharts, or anything of the sort. However, rather than storing the program in a hard disk drive or requiring users to load it using a floppy disk, Tandy imprinted the program into a microchip.

In 1981, soon after the Copyright Office issued the registration for Input/out, Tandy sued PMC for copyright infringement. At the West Coast Computer Faire then taking place, PMC's president, Lester Lee, responded that Tandy's suit was entirely without merit. He proclaimed that his firm "will not be intimidated by the giant" and that it would "continue selling and supporting the PMC-80 while vigorously defending [its] right to manufacture it."[57] Lee considered the suit to be not only unwarranted but also a breach of professional courtesy because Tandy had never notified PMC that a suit was forthcoming. He concluded that this lawsuit was just a means to discourage current PMC-80 dealers to continue their relations with PMC and to "scare off potential dealers" who might otherwise choose to sell it.

Tandy sought an injunction that would preclude PMC from manufacturing and selling its computer, and the two firms appeared before the District Court for the Northern District of Illinois in 1981. Tandy's chief complaint was that PMC had infringed its copyright over Input/out, and PMC claimed that the duplication of a chip did not constitute the reproduction of a copyrighted program stored in it.[58] The court disagreed with PMC, holding that a chip is a "tangible medium of expression" and that the point of the fixation requirement in the Copyright Act of 1976 was to protect "copyrighted material inputted into a computer," not to "provide a loophole by which someone could duplicate a program fixed on a silicon chip."[59] Moreover, the court found that PMC had likely duplicated the chip by reproducing (perhaps with a photograph) its visual layout, making a copy of this reproduction, and imprinting the image onto a new chip. As a result, this reproduction of a "visually displayed copy of the program" fell within the reach of copyright law, so the court denied PMC's motion to dismiss the case.[60]

At the core of the *Tandy* decision is the reasoning that a microchip is at once an electromechanical device (as the decision's predecessors had sometimes held) and an acceptable medium wherein to fix a computer program, one in which programs became visual displays protected by the copyrights over the programs themselves. This reasoning was especially valuable to game-making companies: it meant that they could now rely on the copyrights that they had obtained for the broad range of media and devices that a video game could comprise—from character designs and in-screen text to the chips included in consoles or cartridges.[61] To PC makers, however, the *Tandy* reasoning would soon become a major weapon against foreign clones; it could allow them to keep full machines off the market by arguing that the chips at their core infringed on their copyrights.

Tandy's struggles stemmed from the introduction of foreign clones into the American market, but clones could also enter the industry from domestic manufacturers. Consider the work of Russ Bower and Joel Schusterman, two enterprising engineers who used to work together at the Burroughs Corporation.[62] Eager to own a company of their own, they had left Burroughs in the mid-1970s to create BAI Data Products, a manufacturer of paper tape equipment. As the demand for paper tape products dropped in the late 1970s, the two men decided to try their luck in the nascent microcomputer industry. Perhaps inspired by the success of stores such as the Byte Shop, they opened a microcomputer store called Computer Emporium and remained in business until loan interest rates in 1980 started to make it difficult for their clients get funding for their machines. Bower and Schusterman sold the store to a movie theater chain and fast-food franchise, and soon they found themselves looking for another way of entering the industry.

In 1981, they partnered with R. Barry Borden, who had founded a computer terminal manufacturer called Delta Data. Shusterman would later remember that the three of them realized that "Apple was unique because there was a whole industry built around it."[63] Purchasing a CPU from Apple was but the clients' first step, as they would then buy "all the peripherals and boards from hundreds of other companies." This meant that an entire industry revolved around a single CPU for which there was no serious competition. "We feel that the market of Apple users is very large," Shusterman said in an interview with *Infoworld*, "and we want to be in that marketplace."[64]

The three men called their company the Franklin Computer Corporation and set up shop in Cherry Hill, New Jersey. Shusterman, who would serve as Franklin's CEO, aimed to market a computer to compete directly with the Apple II.[65] The three entrepreneurs sought legal counsel. They decided not to use the word "apple" or the name of any other fruit in their products, and they searched through the Patent Office's records to determine which aspects of the machine's hardware they should not replicate. They also agreed not to replicate things such as the wording of Apple Computer's manuals, but they concluded that it would be acceptable to duplicate operating systems, which Apple had protected through copyrights rather than patents. Shusterman would later explain that this duplication was allowable because "you may not copyright processes, functions or systems. They may be patented if they're patentable, but you may not copyright them."[66] Indeed, their legal counsels advised them that operating systems were integral parts of the Apple II that had "no protectable expression" under copyright law.[67]

Early in 1982, Franklin released its new computer, the Ace 100, for a price of $1,695.[68] Its advertisements featured the tag line, "What Is Sweeter than an Apple?" They were aimed exclusively at showing how the Ace 100 was a superior alternative to the Apple II. One of the ads described the Ace 100 as being "hardware and software compatible with the Apple II." It stated that the Ace "is sweeter than an Apple": it was more versatile, it had more RAM (random access memory), and it cost less. Any program or peripheral that would work on an Apple would also work on a Franklin, and in fact the Ace 100's keyboard included keys for VisiCalc—a spreadsheet application for the Apple II that had fueled the machine's popularity.

In May 1982, Apple sued Franklin for infringement of the fourteen copyrights that it had registered since Wozniak had started working on the Apple II, and the two firms went to trial at the District Court for the Eastern District of Pennsylvania. Over two and a half days in the early summer, both parties brought to the court expert witnesses to discuss each of the programs involved; they even introduced as exhibits one machine each for the Apple II and the Ace 100.[69] Apple grounded its case on three points: that an operating system is a form of expression and not an idea or a process; that object code is a form of expression and a work of authorship regardless of the medium in which it is contained (be it a printout, a disk, or a ROM chip); and that a chip is not a mechanical device but a medium of expression.[70] Franklin countered by arguing that the ROM chips are in fact just tangible objects in a computerized system aimed at running copyrighted source code. In this sense, they are more akin to the control systems of videotape recorders and record players than to the videos and records that those machines play.[71]

During the trial, one of Franklin's engineers admitted that his company incorporated Apple's object code into its systems programs, but the court still sided with the clone manufacturer. Judge Clarence Newcomer wrote,

> If the concept of "language" means anything, it means an ability to create human interaction. It is the fixed expression of this that the copyright law protects, and only this. To go beyond the bounds of this protection would be ultimately to provide copyright protection to the programs created by a computer to run other computers. With that, we step into the world of Gulliver where horses are "human" because they speak a language that sounds remarkably like the one humans use. It is an intriguing analogy but false.[72]

In Newcomer's opinion, decisions like *Tandy* demonstrated that there was no clear-cut way of analyzing object code, its authorship, or ROM chips under copyright law. For this reason, he grounded his decision on his notion that duplicating ROM chips does not constitute infringement not because the chips themselves are mechanical in nature but because they convey nothing to human beings. To him, this course of action aligned with the purpose of copyright law of protecting only materials with an "underlying expressive or communicative purpose."[73]

Bower, Schusterman, and Borden were thrilled. Their company was preparing to launch two more computer clones, the Ace 1000 and Ace 1200. Both machines were meant to be clones of the Apple II+, the successors to the Apple II with a few inbuilt peripherals such as floppy drives (which the Ace 1200 included).[74] They intended to rewrite some of the programs they had drawn from Apple's chips, but that was a choice rather than a necessity. In their view, however, the fight was far from over. As their lawyers started gathering depositions and preparing arguments in expectation that Apple would appeal, they were hopeful that the increased media attention that the case had generated would reassure customers that their firm could reliably meet their Apple II–related computing needs.[75]

The Ace 1000's manual of operation was a parody of standard computer manuals, and it was infused with an attack on corporate software practices. It included funny cartoons of Benjamin Franklin engaging with computers and quirky titles such as "The Territorial Imperatives of the Trumpeter Swan." However, the humorous manual carried with it a poignant critique of how to reproduce proprietary programs in the face of corporate greed. It explained, "Believe it or not, however, there are programs out there that are expressly designed to PREVENT you from backing them up. They can't be copied unless you're a teenage computer genius with plenty of free time in your hands. This may be a user's manual, but when it comes to some programs that you buy off the shelf, you're more in a position of being used than you are of being a user."[76] The manual went on to encourage users to use programs such as Locksmith and Nibble Away to copy the "downright diabolical" programs that resist reproduction. Software makers—the "natural paranoids" of the industry— would regard any and all users as "potential thieves" likely to "hand out copies of the program like candy to everyone [they] meet" and therefore deprive the firms of their profits. In contrast, at Franklin Computer, the pamphlet stated, "We are not crooks."[77]

Apple filed an appeal in 1983 at the Court of Appeals for the Third Circuit, sparking one of the most closely watched legal battles in the industry. The arguments that each firm delivered at the court were essentially enrichments of their arguments at the lower courts, and firms and trade associations submitted amicus briefs. Together, these briefs suggested that the conflict was no longer just about the copyright status of object code or ROM chips but about the role that cloning would play in the microcomputing industry at home and abroad.

Microsoft submitted an amicus brief written in a tone reminiscent of Gates's original "Open Letter to Hobbyists." It warned that the "software pirate has a considerable advantage" over legitimate software makers because his only costs are what he pays for machines and storage media; he doesn't pay for "the time and expertise required to create the program he steals."[78] Pirates "need not even understand or be able to understand" the programs they copy, and they can make profits that should be reaching the technically capable people who actually create things. In order to prevent this situation from causing the death of the industry as a whole, the brief concluded, the court must realize that a program is a program regardless of where and how it is stored and that it is counterproductive to differentiate ROM chips from printouts and applications from system software.

Another PC software firm, Digital Research, expanded Microsoft's point by arguing that conceptions of program authorship developed for the mainframe era were ill suited to serve the needs of the PC industry.[79] Its brief explained that the advent of the microcomputer in the past three years had caused a sudden rise in the number of clients that a firm could serve, thereby making impractical traditional means of distributing software. Microcomputer software was certainly first written in source code, but it had become standard practice to distribute only object code to the end user. This amounted to changing the relationships between authors and users in the computing industry: while users of mainframe computers could often get source code directly from the authors of the programs they used, users of microcomputers rarely did the same.

According to Digital Research, it was now impractical to distribute source code. Indeed, the brief read, "There is absolutely no reasonable way of restricting improper use of the source code, were it to be mass distributed. Nor is there any way of protecting it under trade secrecy principles without a direct contractual arrangement when there are hundreds of thousands of users."[80] The microcomputer industry revolved around "mass distributed object code" that is "physically embodied" either in magnetic media (floppy disks) or silicon chips (ROMs).[81] Object code had, in fact, become the "media of distribution of computer programs," in the same way that a novel's medium is a printed book and that of a motion picture is the videodisk. In this context, Franklin's arguments in the district court were sure to "destroy the copyright system for computer software"; they amounted to holding that only a novel's handwritten manuscript is copyrightable on the grounds that a machine needs to intervene in order to produce a typewritten form.

While Digital Research's brief implied that that mainframe-era notions of program authorship were inapplicable to microcomputing, ADAPSO's own brief argued that siding with Apple was the proper next step given the computing industry's long and complex relations with IP law.[82] Morton Jacobs had retired from ADAPSO, taking with him his unwavering stance in favor of patents over copyrights. The trade association's membership was also changing, as young PC firms created by people who favored copyrights had joined its ranks. With a new team of lawyers who also favored reliance on copyrights, ADAPSO argued that strengthening the copyright protection of computer programs was essential to strengthen America's software industry at home and abroad. Certainly "no form of protection is a panacea," but the microcomputer software industry was in dire need of a stronger weapon.[83] Even technical solutions such as protecting microcomputers through encryption had backfired by enabling the popularization of Nibble Away and Locksmith. No program seemed safe from piracy anymore, and secrecy was no longer a feasible option, given the high number of clients that firms handled.

Because the upcoming trial would revolve around software copyright, it was in ADAPSO's best interest not to celebrate the Supreme Court's *Diehr* decision as a victory for software patenting. The main issue with software patenting, the brief explained, was that most programs in the market would fail the "kind of novelty and nonobvious required to sustain a patent." Even the *Diehr* decision had not guaranteed the patent-eligibility of software in the first place; it had only held that "a patentable invention was not rendered nonpatentable merely because it used a computer program."[84] Moreover, ADAPSO argued that interpreting the lower decision as a reason to consider programs to be patentable would be detrimental to the industry, as "a patent on most computer programs would be impossible to defend or ineffective in protecting the author's investment."[85]

ADAPSO criticized the patent system on two grounds. First, it was far "too rigid to allow effective protection" of items such as computer programs, which were in "a continual state of flux." Programs often underwent debugging and refinements, and they were from time to time "completely recompile[d]" to incorporate improvements and new features. This meant that a brand-new patent could be required after every major recompiling, and perhaps even after debugging sessions that improved a program's productivity. Second, the slow pace of the patent system was detrimental to firms' profits. It would take several years for the Patent Office to grant a patent, and infringement suits could move so slowly that by the time they concluded, the programs at their core could be obsolete.

To component manufacturers that supplied parts to major firms and clone manufacturers, the legal conditions that would enable a competitive market were the opposites of those that ADAPSO had identified. One such company, the Pro-Log Corporation, submitted a brief supporting Franklin's case.[86] It predicted that allowing object code and ROM chips to receive copyright protection would "stifle the software and related computer industries." After clarifying that Pro-Log had no interest in endorsing piracy, the brief noted that the firm stood by the notion that "copyright law should not be extended to protect operating system computer programs embodied in a computer which together form a machine."[87]

Pro-Log's brief cautioned that Apple's argument would accomplish something that Congress never intended: enabling the use of copyright law to "foster 75-year monopolies for machines."[88] This argument hinged on Pro-Log's conception of the dual nature of computer programs:

> A computer program involves two discrete conceptions: what it is and what it accomplishes. What it is (the expression alone) is copyrightable. What it accomplishes may not be. If what it accomplishes is a fixation of a work from which a copyrightable work of authorship—either the program itself or another work—can be retrieved, reproduced, or perceived, the reach of copyright protection continues. If what is accomplished by the program is the formation of an electrical circuit, copyright protection is ended.[89]

Pro-Log was likely mimicking the style of argumentation that mainframe firms had used in their software patenting battles the decade before—grounding their argument on legal precedent and on whichever conceptualization of the nature of software best suited their needs. This time, rather than arguing that software is a machine, Pro-Log argued that object code existed in a "continuum of embodiments" that ended the moment it became "embodied in a machine."[90] At the "narrower part of the spectrum," the object code became "merely a part of an electrical circuit" embodied either in a ROM chip or in a "disk the sole function of which is to transfer that part of the circuit contained in the program into a RAM."[91] These embodiments, Pro-Log argued, should never be protected by copyright. It was best left to patents or to whichever form of protection Congress would develop later on.[92]

The court sided with Apple—and, therefore, with PC firms—by delivering three interrelated rulings. First, a computer program expressed in object code is copyrightable. Specifically, a program "whether in object code or source code is a 'literary work' and is protected" from unauthorized reproduction. The court grounded this reasoning on the precedent of the copyrightability of answer sheets and code books, which had allowed for numbers and numerical symbols to be copyrightable.[93] Second, a program embedded in a ROM chip is copyright eligible. The court reasoned that Tandy's allowance of the copyrightability of an "audiovisual display of video game 'fixed' in ROM" implied that fixation in a ROM was allowable.[94] Third, operating systems are copyrightable. Neither CONTU's majority nor Congress had distinguished operating programs from applications in their discussions, and the Computer Software Copyright Act of 1980 illustrated both Congress's "receptivity to new technology" and its desire to use copyright law to encourage "continued imagination and creativity in computer programming."[95]

Few documents were as influential to the court's reasoning as CONTU's *Final Report*.[96] The judges considered the report to be an accurate sketch of congressional intent because Congress had enacted CONTU's recommendations almost verbatim in the CSCA. Though likely unaware of IBM's influence on that group, the court assumed that the CONTU majority's understanding of the relations between programs and computer media was superior to those advanced by any individual firm. This included CONTU's provision that "programs should no more be considered machine parts than videotapes should be considered parts of projectors or phonorecords parts of sound reproduction equipment," as well as the fact that a program's words "are used ultimately in the implementation of a process should in no way affect their copyrightability."[97]

Apple's victory at the courts did not drive Franklin out of the industry. For about a year before the appeals court handed down its decision, the clone manufacturer had considered the possibility of filing an antitrust suit.[98] Franklin sought at least $150 million in damages and a way of stopping Apple from its continued trend of "harassment to intimidate potential manufacturers and marketers of Apple-compatible personal computers."[99] No records suggest that Franklin pursued this course of action; perhaps the possibility of a lengthy trial discouraged them from doing so. Instead, its attorneys filed an appeal to the Supreme Court, which proved unsuccessful in 1984.[100] At this point, Franklin paid $2.5 million to Apple Computers and continued producing successful Apple II clones such as the Ace 500 using internally developed operating systems.[101]

MICROCHIP PROTECTION

Apple's suit showed how, even with clear guidelines for software copyright, the IP protection of programs built into microchips was uncharted territory. The ability to replicate mask works by photographing existing chips meant that firms dedicated to replicating chips had significantly lower costs than their counterparts.[102] This was especially problematic, according to the Semiconductor Industry Association, because of the industry's high capital expenses and research and development costs. The association estimated that these costs would only grow as chips became more complex and their demand increased in tandem with the PC revolution.

Until the early 1980s, the association repeatedly argued that piracy—which they often called photographic copying—generated two major economic disincentives.[103] First, it reduced revenues that the association's members would normally funnel into R&D. Any corporation facing such losses would necessarily lose its competitive edge, and competitiveness in the semiconductor

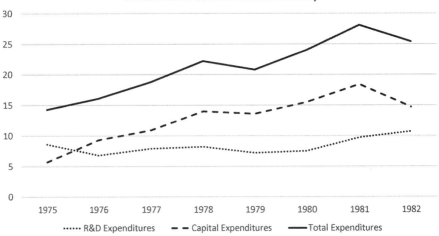

Expenditures as a Percent of Sales
United States Semiconductor Industry

...... R&D Expenditures   – – Capital Expenditures   ——Total Expenditures

Yearly expenditures of the semiconductor industry as a percentage of its annual sales. Crafted by the author, based on data collected by Technecon and submitted by the Semiconductor Industry Association to the House of Representatives in 1983. Copyright Protection for Semiconductor Chips, Hearings before the Subcommittee on Courts, Civil Liberties, and the Administration of Justice of the Committee on the Judiciary, House of Representatives, 98th Cong., 1st Sess., H.R. 1028, August 3 and December 1, 1983, 187.

industry depended on the ability to innovate. Second, piracy forced companies to account for the possibility that their work might be stolen whenever they planned new products. This made firms less willing to invest in new products, because a single pirate firm could preclude any such product from generating an adequate return on investment.

The Copyright Office's standing policy on semiconductor chips was grounded on its policy for technical drawings. It was an uncontested principle that technical drawings of electrical circuits could constitute original works of authorship and were eligible for copyright protection as what the Copyright Act called "pictorial, graphic, or sculptural works."[104] When Congress was working on the Copyright Act of 1976, Register of Copyrights Barbara Ringer had taken care to distinguish between those drawings and any useful objects that could be produced based on them. In her report to the House of Representatives, she had noted that "copyright in pictorial, graphic, or sculptural work, portraying a useful article as such, does not extend to the manufacture of the useful article itself."[105] Based on this distinction, the Copyright Office considered semiconductor chips to be useful embodiments or publications of technical drawings, and it therefore refused to register copyrights for their layouts.[106]

Lawsuits involving the copyright protection of the chips themselves often ended in settlements.[107] Most notable among them is the lawsuit filed in 1983 by the Zilog Corporation (a subsidiary of Exxon) against a Japanese firm called the Nippon Electric Corporation.[108] Zilog had traditionally secured patents to protect its Z80 line of 32-bit microprocessors, and it had also secured copyright protection for them by registering technical drawings on paper blueprint. In 1983, Zilog granted Nippon a license to manufacture its upcoming Z80,000 model.[109] Nippon allegedly copied the Z80 chips and imported them into the United States as part of its own line of microprocessors. Zilog sued Nippon for copyright infringement in the United States and sought $40 million in damages at the Northern District of California, and the two firms also asked the U.S. International Trade Commission to investigate the matter.[110] Within a year, the two companies had settled for an undisclosed amount.

Congress had been considering the possibility of granting explicit copyright protection to microchips since the late 1970s, but a lack of support from industry representatives had kept both the House and Senate from moving forward. Bills introduced from 1978 to 1982 proposed adding semiconductor chips as a new category of copyright-eligible work.[111] A ten-line-long bill introduced by Representative William Edwards (D-California) in 1978, for example, aimed to expand the Copyright Act's definition of "pictorial, graphical, and sculptural works." It proposed to include "the photographic masks used to imprint patterns on integrated circuit chips and include the imprinted patterns themselves even though they are used in connection with the manufacture of, or incorporated in a useful article."[112]

In April 1979, managers and lawyers for prominent semiconductor chip companies attended hearings in San Jose, California, to discuss Edwards's bill.[113] On behalf of the American Electronics Association, Intel president Andrew Grove delivered testimony in its support of the bill on the grounds that the robust IP protection of microchips, which copyrights would be able to provide, was essential to grant firms the incentive to remain innovative.[114] This protection was essential in order to deter firms in Russia and Japan—wherein the copying of Intel's chips was becoming especially prominent—from exporting their goods into the United States. Given that semiconductor chips were becoming increasingly complex and therefore more expensive to produce, the lack of stronger intellectual property protection was creating a risk far too high for companies to consider their R&D expenses to be sound investments. According to Grove, the semiconductor industry in the United States would continue to thrive only if it had "the assurance that its gigantic investment in research and development will have a chance to pay off: it needs protection from pirating!"[115]

No other speaker shared Grove's enthusiasm for the bill. On the contrary, most firms submitted testimony noting their concern that the declaration of chips to be a new kind of copyright-eligible work would have a chilling effect on the American semiconductor industry. John Finch, a vice president and general manager at the National Semiconductor Corporation, argued, for example, that the bill would have no impact on a foreign firm's ability to repli-cate American chips in their home countries. In addition, the fact that copy-rights were granted for at least seventy-five years meant that the designer of any chip could potentially gain "exclusivity for a copyrighted design beyond the dreams of any patentee."[116] More important, it would be impossible to forecast how much of a firm's chip "may be emulated without rising to the level of copyright infringement," which in turn might leave the industry in "a position where reverse engineering is unavailable and illegal."[117]

Lacking industry support, Edwards's bill was unsuccessful, as were other Senate and House bills introduced over the next three years. In 1983, the Senate considered S. 1201, the last bill to propose the creation of a new cate-gory of copyright-eligible work for microchips.[118] The hearings for this bill revealed how Intel's view of the semiconductor industry differed from the smaller firms that aimed to compete with it or use its products. Speakers at a semiconductor industry panel convened to discuss the bill's merits concluded that it offered the protections that chip makers needed most sorely. Thomas Dunlap Jr., Intel's corporate counsel and secretary, drew an analogy between engineering and writing to articulate his firm's lack of concern over reverse engineering. He noted that current copyright law "does not prevent a second writer from writing a biography of the same person," though it does require this second writer to "use different words in the expression of the second biog-raphy."[119] This meant that even though the second biography "cannot look like the first," it could still convey the same information.[120] Dunlap explained that the bill would preclude piracy while allowing for what he called "fair reverse engineering." By this he meant "the reproduction of the pattern from the semiconductor chip" for purposes such as "teaching, analysis of the chip, or evaluation of the circuit concepts or techniques imbodied in the chip."[121] Indeed, fair practices of reverse engineering would enable firms to "fabricate a version of the semiconductor chip which is functionally equivalent to the original chip but has different visual patterns on it."[122] Another speaker, Christopher Layton, echoed Dunlap's testimony in his capacity as spokesperson for the Semiconductor Industry Association.[123]

In contrast, speakers at a panel comprising computing and publishing trade associations were hesitant to endorse the bill as keenly as Intel did. First, Jack Biddle, president of the Computer and Communications Industry Association, hailed the bill as a valuable effort against piracy but worried that the bill might have more serious implications on reverse engineering than Dunlap had acknowledged. He explained that the bill could "inadvertently impair the existing rights of third parties to produce functionally equivalent chips through the design of alternative masks of their own creation."[124] Second, Ronald Palenski, ADAPSO's general counsel, worried about the conceptual issues that the bill would raise. Likely aiming to avoid entanglements similar to those that ADAPSO had faced in defining "software" for the purpose of assessing its patent-eligibility, Palenski warned that defining a chip as a "writing" or as a "discovery" could work "to the benefit of no one, except perhaps the misappropriators of semiconductor chips."[125]

As the House considered a similar bill, Commissioner of Patents Gerald Mossinghof testified that patent law could not give chip manufacturers the protections they needed. Certainly, patents are "available for the process of making the chip, for the electronic circuit embodied in the chip, or for the chip itself as an article of manufacture."[126] However, the circuits in chips were usually well known, so chip makers could rarely patent them. As a result, most firms had the option of patenting either the process of making the chip or the "chip itself as an article of manufacture."[127] This left them vulnerable to pirates who aimed at "the taking of the design."[128] Because trade secrets were only available until a maker's first disclosure or unrestricted sale, copyrights became the remaining form of protection.

As Congress approached yet another failure in its effort to develop microchip protection, Dorothy Schrader, the associate register of copyrights, provided a concrete and effective way of moving forward. A Harvard Law graduate who had taken a brief break from her career as a copyright examiner to sing opera in Germany, Schrader had been an adjunct professor of law at George Washington University, where she had likely gotten to know Irving Kayton's software law working group. She had also been a keen advocate of the country's inclusion in international copyright treaties.[129] These treaties included the Berne Convention, which the United States had not yet joined. Member countries agreed that the protection of designs and models would be a matter for each country to determine individually through its legislative process and that countries with no such protections would grant foreign designs the same protections it afforded to artistic works.[130] Aligning the country with this reasoning likely appeared to Schrader a good step to take were the United States ever to join the convention.

Late in 1983, Schrader visited the Senate and the House to present what she called the "design approach."[131] By this, she meant that semiconductor chips would be best protected by reviving and adapting a defunct bill that would have established a "Design Protection Act." Introduced by Representative Carlos Moorhead (R-California) earlier that year, this bill would have amended copyright law to protect "ornamental designs of useful articles," or designs that would make useful articles "attractive or distinct in appearance to the purchasing or using public."[132] It would do so, not by deeming the design of useful items to be a new category of copyright-eligible work, but instead by adding a wholly new chapter to the first section of 17 U.S.C. that created a new form of protection—similar to copyright but restricted in term to ten years and reliant on a different symbol, Ⓓ. The bill required the designs to be original, but it did not deem them to be discoveries or inventions of any kind, thus avoiding conflict with patent law.[133]

Schrader submitted to Congress an annotated version of Moorhead's bill in which she had crossed out some of the original text and written new passages on microchips. The text below reproduces her annotations on the bill's table of contents (with Schrader's text in italics):

FOR ORIGINAL DESIGNS
CHAPTER 9—PROTECTION ~~OF ORNAMENTAL~~
OF SEMICONDUCTOR CHIP PRODUCTS
~~DESIGNS OF USEFUL ARTICLES~~

Sec.

901. ~~Designs protected~~ *Chip designs protected*

902. ~~Designs not subject to protection~~ *Chip designs not subject to protection*

903. Revisions, adaptations, and rearrangements

904. Commencement of Protection

905. Term of Protection

906. ~~The design notice~~ *Notice of chip design*[134]

At the core of Schrader's proposal were both the notion that layouts of microchips are another kind of industrial design and the assumption that the casual usage of such terms as "mask work" in any legislation on the matter could generate unsolvable discursive puzzles.[135] Instead, the design approach would "specifically protect the features of shape, pattern or configuration of the surface of the layers of semiconductor chip products," thereby leaving "no question of protecting the electrical components as such."[136]

The House and Senate embraced Schrader's proposal, and in November 1984 they passed the Semiconductor Chip Protection Act (SCPA). It offered ten years of protection to "a mask work fixed in a semiconductor chip product, by or under the authority of the owner of a mask work."[137] This protection was subject to a set of restrictions on the owner's nationality that favored work by American firms or foreign firms aiming to develop an American market for their products. The act also created two intertwined standards that mask works had to meet for their fixtures to be eligible for protection: originality and novelty. Without defining either term, the act noted that the mask work could not consist of designs that "are staple, commonplace, or familiar in the semiconductor industry, or variations of such designs, combined in a way that, considered as a whole, is not original."[138] A blend of copyright and patent protections, the SCPA thus established what scholars and commentators were quick to call a "chip design right."[139]

One month later, the Copyright Office issued official guidelines on the SCPA.[140] The circular noted that protection under the act encompassed the mask works themselves and the "topographies" of the chip—the "three-dimensional images or patterns formed on or in the layers of metallic, insulating, or semiconductor material and fixed in a semiconductor chip product."[141] Unlike the images protected by copyright law, each of these three-dimensional images was "purely functional," and each was protected under the SCPA as long as it was "neither directed by a particular electronic function" nor "one of the few available design choices that will accomplish that function."[142] According to the circular, "no protection is available for any procedure, process, system, method of operation, concept, principle or discovery associated with a mask work, regardless of the form in which it is described, explained, illustrated, or embodied in a mask work."[143]

During the next two decades, however, only two published court cases relied on the Semiconductor Chip Protection Act.[144] Economic and legal scholars have provided several reasons for this. Some have suggested that semiconductor technologies became far too complex for the kinds of duplication that motivated the SCPA's passage and that the SCPA itself may have passed under the mistaken assumption that reverse engineering constitutes chip piracy.[145] Others have proposed that the combination of the market structure for microchips and the availability of technical means against unauthorized duplication made the SCPA unnecessary in the first place.[146] Yet even if the SCPA never became the subject of substantial litigation, its passage demonstrates just how quickly Congress could respond to a practice that threatened the country's computing and semiconductor industries at home and abroad.

Chapter 10 Look, Feel, and Programming Freedom, 1984–1995

During its early years, the PC revolution had been largely text-based.[1] MS-DOS had propelled Bill Gates to great success, and Microsoft would continue to release updated versions of it for decades even though more than two dozen operating systems were competing with it in the mid-1980s. Preloaded into IBM and IBM-compatible PCs, MS-DOS required users to study thick manuals and to type their instructions very carefully; a single letter out of place would invalidate any instruction. Avid programmers often enjoyed the intricate work that this involved, but casual users at home and at small firms were less likely to have fun reading through manuals and examining their syntax. Early versions of MS-DOS also had an important technical limitation: a lack of multitasking capabilities. For instance, a payroll department needed to use several applications, one at a time, to view the time logs of a firm's employees, compute the weekly payments owed to each worker, generate a chart with the data, and incorporate the chart into a word processor.

Apple broke from this tradition of single-task, text-based interfaces in the mid-1980s by popularizing the Macintosh computer.[2] Its operating system, MAC OS, featured a graphical user interface (GUI) wherein users' interaction with the machine was modeled after what they would normally do at an office. The screen depicted a desk with a set of nested folders, each one containing some of the files stored on the hard drive. This enabled a more intuitive and engaging mode of human-machine interaction for casual home users. Instead of having to type in a command to change a file's address, they could use their mouse to "grab" a file, scroll across the screen, and "drop" it into its new location. A collection of menus at the top left of the screen provided shortcuts to commonly used functions, including a command line prompt in case users needed to perform more advanced functions.

GUIs like MAC OS made computers more accessible than ever. They were easier and more intuitive to use than text-based operating systems, and their visual layout allowed users to multitask with great ease, simply by switching from one application's window to another's without needing to close either program. By the mid-1980s, at least five developers had introduced GUIs for IBM PCs, ranging in price from $95 to $495.[3] Users around the country started to conceive of GUIs as the ultimate interface between humans and PCs—the primary means into the computer's file structures and processing capabilities.

GUIs were mostly subject to copyright protection. There was no controversy in classifying elements such as icon designs, menu layouts, and computer sounds as creative works; they constituted what users and commentators called the GUI's "look and feel." However, copyrighting a GUI could amount to controlling a standard and potentially profitable interface between computers and their users. The struggle to assert ownership over GUIs, documented in this chapter, generated some of the highest-stakes legal conflicts in the first two decades of the PC industry and encouraged everyday users to unite in protest of corporate control over user interfaces. Opponents of look and feel copyrights, led by the programmer and advocate Richard Stallman, soon gained national prominence as fierce critics of software IP protection in all its forms.

GUI LICENSING

Apple was not the first firm to develop a GUI for a personal computer, though the Macintosh was certainly the first popular personal computer to feature one. In the mid-1970s, the Xerox Palo Alto Research Center (PARC) in Silicon Valley developed a pioneering mouse-controlled user interface called Smalltalk. Led by Robert Taylor (the former head of ARPA's Information Processing Technique's Office), PARC was dedicated to developing products for the office of the future.[4] Smalltalk, allegedly the first-ever mouse-controlled

GUI, allowed users to select menu options instead of having to type them in.[5] Later in the decade, Apple's Steve Jobs and Bill Atkinson (the chief developer for a new business PC called the Apple Lisa) had visited PARC for a demonstration of Smalltalk.[6] The system made such a big impression on them that Jobs visited PARC a second time, this time bringing the entire Lisa development team with him. Bruce Daniels, the Lisa's software manager, would later remember that the trip inspired him turn to a "new paradigm" for the Lisa wherein users would interact with the machine using the tiled windows like the ones that Xerox had built into its own systems.[7]

Xerox never secured a copyright registration or patent for Smalltalk, most likely because the program was meant to be a test run for the use of a mouse in human-computer interfaces.[8] Still, Jobs's great interest in Smalltalk prompted Xerox to license Smalltalk to Apple so that the two firms could collaborate in its development. In formal terms, the license granted Apple permission to "participate in a project with the Learning Research Group at PARC/Xerox for the purpose of implementing the Smalltalk-80 language and system on a hardware system" that Apple would develop.[9] No records suggest that Xerox granted Apple permission to commercialize whatever system they developed based on Smalltalk.

While Apple worked on this project, the staff at PARC created a follow-up GUI called the Star, which featured the same mouse control as Smalltalk, as well as on-screen icons, folders, email capability, and pop-up menus. Given the commercial intention behind this GUI, Xerox filed a copyright registration just in time to release a PC of the same name in 1981.[10] Xerox's weak marketing and its $40,000 price tag for the Star made its ground-breaking computer a financial disappointment, but the idea of a desktop-based GUI lived on at Apple Computers.[11] To develop software similar to Smalltalk and the Star, Jobs hired Larry Tesler (the engineer who had demonstrated Smalltalk to Apple's staff) and assigned him to work on the Lisa, which Apple launched in 1983 and priced at $16,995.[12] Like the Star, the Lisa did not sell very well either, most likely because it was still far too expensive for the personal computer market. Although these computers were not commercially viable, they did demonstrate that mouse-controlled GUIs with icons and folders featured things that users desired—from easy-to-use and intuitive file management to the ability to work in more than one application at once. These were, in fact, two of the features that Apple most celebrated in the Lisa's $2,500 successor, the Macintosh (released in 1984).

Unlike Xerox, Apple secured many IP protections for its computers and GUIs. Its patents covered objects such as the mouse and the designs of the two computers' casing, while a series of interrelated copyright registrations protected the machines' GUIs and applications.[13] In 1983, soon after the release of the Lisa, Apple submitted a copyright registration for its Xerox-inspired GUI (the Lisa Desktop) and its associated graphics applications.[14] The Macintosh GUI was also subject to several copyright registrations, though they were directed primarily at its so-called Finder. This was the main folder on the GUI's desktop, in which users could find icons representing the system's control panel and the hard drive's file directory. To register this program, Apple submitted a collection of images (most likely icons and screenshots), the Finder's source code, and the program loaded onto a cassette.[15] The firm also submitted registrations for the Macintosh ROM (in the form of a printout of its source code) and for applications such as MacPaint and MacWrite.[16]

By then, Apple had become an aggressive enforcer of its copyrights as its primary means for software IP protection. Its clash with Franklin Computer in 1983 had cost the clone manufacturer $2.5 million, and a more recent suit had forced a firm called DRI to change some of the icons in its own GUI, Graphics Environment Manager Interface.[17] Apple had also developed close relationships with Microsoft, which in 1982 licensed the copyrights for Apple's applications for graphics, database management, and word and spreadsheet processing. These licenses had been crucial to programs such as Excel and Word, which Microsoft would soon be developing for Macintosh, Atari, and Unix machines.[18]

In October 1985, Microsoft released Windows 1.0, its own window-based desktop GUI. Apple's counsel Al Eisenstat worried that Microsoft was using the Macintosh's copyrighted visual elements without the proper license.[19] After all, Bill Gates had seen a prototype of the Macintosh during a visit to Apple in 1981, and the Windows system's reliance on the mouse as a mediator between user and computer was very similar to Macintosh.[20] Eisenstat called Microsoft's legal team, accused the firm of copyright infringement, and threatened to file a lawsuit if Microsoft did not change the features of Windows that resembled the Macintosh's.[21] In response, Gates picked up the phone to call John Sculley, Apple's CEO, and requested to speak face-to-face with him.

Gates and Sculley met to discuss the situation, along with Eisenstat and Gates's private counsel, William Neukom.[22] Gates insisted that Microsoft had not infringed on Apple's copyrights, and he and Sculley agreed to develop an amicable resolution. For his part, Sculley saw this conflict as increased leverage for Apple. Microsoft's versions of Word and Excel for the Macintosh had made the machine more appealing to business consumers, which Apple was struggling to reach. It therefore made sense to grant Microsoft a license in exchange for the firm's agreement to focus its application development on Apple's products. Eisenstat, who negotiated on Sculley's behalf, requested that Microsoft delay the release of Excel for the IBM PC, issue an enhanced version of Macintosh Word, and commit to continuing its Macintosh software development. Gates informally agreed to this arrangement in exchange for Apple's relinquishing of its claims to the visual displays in Windows 1.0.

Eisenstat asked one of Apple's in-house lawyers, Irvin Rappaport, to draft the agreement.[23] Rappaport's draft shocked Gates, for it would have licensed entire products (instead of visual displays) and required Microsoft's future Windows versions to have the same visual elements as Windows 1.0.[24] Gates's team then drafted their own version of the agreement, which he and Sculley would sign on November 22, 1985. In this agreement, Gates acknowledged that the visual displays in Windows and many of its applications were derivative of the Apple Lisa and Macintosh GUIs. In exchange for this acknowledgment and for permission to use Microsoft's own visual elements, Apple granted Microsoft both a license for its patented mouse and a "non-exclusive, worldwide, royalty-free, perpetual, non-transferable license" for those visual elements, and it waived any other rights it might have over Windows 1.0.

Microsoft's marketing staff hoped that Windows would become the standard for multitasking and windows-based GUIs in the market.[25] In addition to the Macintosh GUI, its competing products included IBM's TopView and Digital Research's Graphics Environment Manager (GEM). Priced at $99, Windows appealed to office managers both because it was less whimsically designed than the Macintosh (which office staff considered to look too unprofessional) and because it had multitasking capabilities that TopView didn't.[26]

More than a million people would eventually buy Windows 1.0, but for the most part this system did not become Microsoft's stellar product.[27] As Microsoft prepared to release Windows 2.0 in 1987, its relationships with IBM and Apple started to change. On the one hand, Microsoft and IBM were collaborating to develop OS/2, IBM's own GUI for the PC and a potential competitor for the Windows family. Microsoft had already spent two years developing IBM's operating systems, but Gates's effort to market Windows as a stand-alone product independent from the IBM brand was starting to position Microsoft as a rival to IBM in the market for systems software.[28] On the other hand, Gates envisioned greater independence from Apple's registered copyrights, especially regarding the visual elements of the Macintosh GUI. His lawyers agreed that the 1985 agreement gave Microsoft the leeway to continue drawing on Apple's GUI, and so they neglected to renew the firm's license for the icons, windowing, and overall appearance.

This time, lacking permission from Apple, Gates's legal team licensed Windows to other firms interested in creating their own graphical user interfaces. Among them was Hewlett-Packard, which was developing its own networked desktop environment, New Wave. The firm would market this GUI as a tool that would allow users to transform Windows into a system "similar to the Macintosh, but with more features."[29] HP's license ran against Sculley's vision for Apple's GUI copyright management. The 1985 agreement contained no language that expressly excluded systems such as Windows 2.0 from the scope of Microsoft's license, but Apple's lawyers never intended to allow Microsoft to draw from the Macintosh GUI indefinitely, let alone to license out its own Macintosh derivatives and allow third parties such as HP to develop competing software.[30]

Early in 1988, soon after announcing the Macintosh II, Apple sued Microsoft and HP for infringing what Apple called the "look and feel" of the Macintosh and the Apple Lisa.[31] This term refers both to visual elements such as icons, colors, and fonts (the look) and to dynamic ones such as how the interface displays menus and the effect that a click of mouse has on a button displayed on the screen (the feel). Apple was not the first firm to launch a copyright infringement suit of this kind. A few months earlier, Broderbund Software had launched a suit against Unison World, claiming that Unison had infringed its copyrights over a profitable desktop publishing program called The Print Shop.[32] A federal judge had ruled that copyright law protects both the program's code and its "overall structure, sequencing, and arrangement of screens," and it soon became apparent that other firms would follow Broderbund's lead.[33]

In turn, these suits prompted the Xerox Corporation to sue Apple and seek $150 million in royalties and damages.[34] In its conflict with Microsoft, Apple's lawyers had claimed that the Lisa and Macintosh Finder applications "consist of material wholly original to Apple."[35] Xerox's lawyers disagreed with this statement, accusing Apple of infringing its copyrights over the Star and of wrongfully claiming that it created and owned portions of the Star and Smalltalk GUIs.[36] They also claimed that Apple's GUI copyrights had precluded their firm from licensing Star to other companies, because potential licensees worried that doing business with Xerox would leave them vulnerable to a lawsuit from Apple. According to David T. Kearns, Xerox's chairman and CEO, "Xerox is not a litigious company . . . but we have no other recourse than to seek relief from the court for actions we believe to be unfair and unlawful."[37]

The conflicts among Apple, Microsoft, and Xerox would end abruptly within a few years, largely through settlements, but their development had three important consequences. First, Apple's arguments against Microsoft revealed to judges and industry observers that firms were willing to rely on their copyrights to obtain patent-like protections for their GUIs. A few years into their conflict, a judge presiding over one aspect of the cases wrote, "The elements of such an arrangement [the GUI] serve a purely functional purpose in the same way that the visual displays and user commands of the dashboard, steering wheel, gear shift, brakes, clutch, and accelerator serve as the user interface of an automobile."[38] He considered the images in a GUI to be no different from the controls necessary to operate any kind of machinery, akin to the wheel of a car to the dialing wheels of a telephone. His ruling explained that these elements "are wholly beyond the realm of copyright," for they are no different from other "common examples of user interfaces" such as those found in dials, remote control devices, or the buttons on an oven.[39] Later on, another judge in the case would add that Apple "cannot get patent-like protection for the idea of a graphical user interface, or the idea of a desktop metaphor which concededly came from Xerox."[40]

Second, the suits revealed that commercial GUI development involved a lot of knowledge-sharing among programmers from competing firms. Jobs himself acknowledged that the invention at the core of his firm's copyrighted GUIs was not entirely of Apple's own making. Shortly after Apple filed its suit, he noted in an interview, "When we were developing the Macintosh, we kept in mind a famous quote from Picasso, 'Good artists copy, great artists steal,' and we believed that after seeing the user interface technology at Xerox in 1979, that our mission was to get this out to the world."[41] Third, and perhaps most important, the suits became closely watched representatives of what one industry commentator called the lawsuits that "are splitting the software industry."[42] The battles over look and feel copyright had highlighted exactly the same issues that John Hersey had described in his CONTU dissent, most notably those relating to how difficult it is to distinguish creativity from utility in a computer program and the relative merits of copyrights over patents when seeking protection for software. These issues would continue to inform discussions on software copyright for decades, but back in the 1980s they sparked much more than dialogue. Indeed, to many everyday users, these lawsuits were a prompt to protest corporate greed.

FROM ADVOCACY TO ENFORCEMENT

By the mid-1980s, two things had become clear to software makers and publishers. First, GUIs would enable users to interact with their machines in ways more intuitive and engaging than ever before. Coupled with the continually increasing processing power of microchips, this made the market for microcomputer software very promising. Second, as computers became cheaper and more accessible than ever, firms' power to control what users did with their machines and programs was likely to erode unless their industry achieved some degree of piracy protection through a combination of technical and legal means. The outcome of *Diamond v. Diehr* in 1982 had been favorable to software makers, as had passage of the Computer Software Copyright Act, but enforcing IP rights could become an impossible task as computers made their way into everyone's homes and daily lives.

Technical developments in computer networking were enabling the networked distribution of software that had troubled CONTU's commissioners. Since the late 1970s, users in separate locations had been able to communicate with one another using a dial-up computer server called a bulletin board system (BBS). By connecting a computer to a telephone line, users could connect with a larger community, sometimes anonymously, to discuss anything they wished: politics, sex, humor, gaming, and the latest technological trends.[43] Generally unregulated spaces, BBSs also allowed users to share more reprehensible interests, from child molesting to white supremacy, so by the mid-1980s it was not unusual for newspapers and magazines to report arrests and FBI raids in connection with BBSs.[44]

BBSs allowed users to distribute any files they wished, including computer programs. One industry periodical estimated that by 1983, nearly half of the BBSs distributed pirated software. Unauthorized software duplicators such as AvantGarde 64 (discussed in chapter 8) used BBSs to identify potential clients and distribute their software, but a lot of the distribution occurred casually, as technically skilled hackers bypassed any antipiracy protections built into disks and software and shared the fruits of their efforts on a BBS.[45] Entire software libraries were available online, often through hidden paths within a BBS that not everyone could access.[46] By phreaking—breaking into telephone networks illegally to make free calls—hackers, often in their teens, could download popular software almost as soon as it was released.[47] The financial losses that this generated are nearly impossible to estimate, given that much of this distribution took place in secret, but one market research firm at the time estimated that losses through piracy (through BBSs or otherwise) cost the computer industry at least $1 billion between 1981 and 1985.[48]

Some hackers saw themselves doing to the software industry what Robin Hood, the heroic outlaw, did to the English nobility.[49] Speaking to a *New York Times* reporter, a fifteen-year-old hacker who went by "Chaz" explained that although he knew that his distribution of pirated software was technically illegal, he considered himself a "pirate with morals."[50] In his view, sticking to pirating was a safer way of being a hacker than breaking into federal agencies' computer systems, as some of his online friends had done. Refusing to reveal his identity, he told the reporter that he didn't sell the software; he would simply take software from wealthy corporations and distribute it among everyday people. Chaz estimated that he was among the top twenty pirates in the country, by which he meant that he could get and post all the newest games before anyone else did. "I know it's wrong," he explained, "but, you know, it's no biggie."

Trade association leaders knew that spunky teenagers were not the only ones to blame for piracy. Late in 1984, ADAPSO launched an ambitious direct mail antipiracy campaign titled "Thou Shalt Not Dupe."[51] The campaign, titled to evoke the Bible's Ten Commandments, centered around a collection of pamphlets shaped like floppy disks explaining that software piracy is "just as wrong" as shoplifting.[52] ADAPSO mailed them to corporations, government agencies, and educational institutions, sometimes along with a handful of bright yellow stickers with the campaign's slogan in bold letters. Software piracy, or "softlifting," as the pamphlets called it, was a violation of copyright law punishable by large fines and even imprisonment. With no mention that the CSCA allowed users to make backup copies, the pamphlets explained that "software developers *do not* condone unauthorized copying," not even to "gain market penetration."

The Lotus Corporation, which made a popular spreadsheet program called Lotus 1-2-3, connected ADAPSO with the advertising firm Ogilvy & Mather to prepare a follow-up campaign. The ad firm recommended the creation of a series of posters aimed at CEOs, students, corporate employees, and the public. Half of each poster was a photograph of a person wearing a pirate eye patch. This person sometimes had tears in their eyes or their hands cupped around their face. Underneath the photograph was an explanation of the person's crime and its repercussions. At the posters' footer were the ADAPSO logo and the words, "Software piracy is a federal crime." In the poster shown here, the explanation of the photograph reads, "I got in big trouble with my company. I thought I was saving us money by copying software. I didn't know it was a Federal crime. Now I'm trying to save my job."[53] Another poster, showing a worried teenager, read, "No one told me it was wrong. I thought I was helping my friends. I never really thought that copying computer programs was stealing. If only someone had told me."[54] Nothing was an excuse for piracy: not an employee's desire to help a company, and definitely not ignorance.

Aggressive campaigns like these were especially well received among software publishers because copy protection through technical means was not

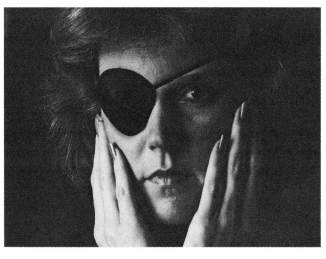

I got in big trouble with my company

I thought I was saving us money by copying software. I didn't know it was a Federal crime. Now I'm trying to save my job.

Some people think they're saving their companies a few dollars by knocking off copies of software and giving them to fellow employees. However, that's a Federal crime. And lawsuits and negative publicity can cost companies far more than any savings. That's why companies everywhere are cracking down on pirates.

At ADAPSO, the computer software and services industry association, we're working to keep you informed. Before you do your company any "favors," do yourself one. Return the coupon for a free brochure that explains the risks of software piracy.

Send this coupon or your business card for more information. Or call us at (703) 522-5055 and ask for Marilyn. ADAPSO, 1300 North Seventeenth Street, Arlington, Virginia 22209

NAME _____ TITLE _____
COMPANY _____
ADDRESS _____
CITY _____ STATE ___ ZIP ___

 *Software Piracy is a Federal Crime*

Poster from ADAPSO's antipiracy campaign. The two paragraphs on the bottom left read, "Some people think they're saving their companies a few dollars by knocking off copies of software and giving them to fellow employees. However, that's a Federal crime. And lawsuits and negative publicity can cost companies far more than any savings. That's why companies everywhere are cracking down on pirates. At ADAPSO, the computer software and services industry association, we're working to keep you informed. Before you do your company any 'favors,' do yourself one. Return the coupon for a free brochure that explains the risk of software piracy." Image courtesy of the Charles Babbage Institute, University of Minnesota Libraries, Minneapolis.

working as a deterrent to piracy.[55] Users could simply use programs like Locksmith, which allowed them to bypass anticopy protections. Protected by the CSCA's provisions for backup copies, the creators of these so-called lock-picking programs were at once loved by users and hated by firms.[56] Perhaps the most famous of these figures was Michael Brown, a twenty-seven-year-old whose Oregon company, Central Point Software, produced a $40 lock-picker called Copy II. This program had generated $2 million in sales in 1985 and was expected to sell up to $6 million the following year. According to one manager, software firms were "waging a war" against Brown, to the point that some of them would "want to get a gun and shoot him." Continually in the industry's crosshairs, Brown had some legal protection from the CSCA and a small fortune that enabled him to hire good legal representation. One reporter claimed that Brown had set aside $180,000 for legal fees early in his career and added about $20,000 more to this legal defense pot every month.

Facing seemingly unstoppable entrepreneurs like Brown, software publishers and their lawyers started to think that ADAPSO's traditional strengths in lobbying, advocacy, and education were not enough. This motivated an attorney named Kenneth A. Wasch to create a new trade association called the Software Publishers Association (SPA) in 1984. Wasch was very familiar with government politics and technological change; he had a background in economics and international relations and had spent eight years working as a senior attorney at the Department of Energy.[57] The SPA's original twenty-five-member roster included gaming firms such as Atari and Datamost and business application publishers such as CBS Software. In a matter of months, more than a hundred firms had joined, including Apple, Broderbund, and Scholastic. Yearly membership dues were charged on a sliding scale from $400 to $19,900, depending on the prospective member's software sales.[58]

Wasch planned to attack software piracy head-on.[59] His experience with government agencies and industrial pressure suited him well on this front. A charismatic and well-connected leader, he turned the SPA into an antipiracy powerhouse, albeit a young one with a limited budget for litigation.[60] Walsh spoke at the Department of Justice, discussed the SPA with major newspapers, and delivered testimony at congressional hearings, condemning software piracy in all its forms. Under his leadership, and in cooperation with federal authorities, the SPA helped shut down a BBS in Upstate New York and secured a cash settlement from a bootlegger on the West Coast. Speaking to the *Chicago Tribune* in 1986, Wasch explained that the SPA was interested, not in "scaring people," but in achieving convictions for the piracy of copyrighted software.

Working separately, the SPA and ADAPSO gave the computing industry two sources of antipiracy initiatives at a time when computer users—from individual home users and educational institutions to the largest government agencies and corporations—were becoming very hostile to technical antipiracy measures such as copy locks. The seemingly unstoppable popularity of lock-picking programs and users' overwhelming complaints over copy-protected programs had motivated most top software firms to drop their antipiracy locks altogether.[61] Even Microsoft had removed copy protections from all its applications.[62] Continued use of technical protection was becoming a liability; large corporations and government agencies were refusing to deal with some of the most powerful software firms because their computer users considered copy protections either too burdensome or irreparably impractical. The Department of Defense, for example, had dropped the Lotus Corporation as the provider of spreadsheet software for 150,000 new PCs that Zenith Data Systems was scheduled to deliver. Copy-locked software could preclude Defense Department staff from creating backups quickly and frequently, which meant that a single system crash could be catastrophic.

The increasing unpopularity of copy locks finally put an end to lock-picking programs such as Brown's, but it also left software publishers more vulnerable than ever. Over the next few years, ADAPSO and the SPA continued to fight piracy in every available venue. When Congress held hearings on incorporating the United States into the Berne Convention, the two associations wrote enthusiastic letters that presented software piracy almost as an emergency in the American computing industry.[63] In the late 1980s, as lawsuits over proprietary GUIs started to make the industry periodicals' headlines again, the trade associations filed amicus briefs and delivered press statements deeming any effort to weaken IP protection as an attack on computing innovation itself. The SPA even created a toll-free number that users could call to report pirated software and developed a procedure to carry out what they called "audits": raids of organizations suspected of piracy that could end in large fines and criminal prosecution.[64] It comes as no surprise, then, that users would soon organize against the computing industry's effort to establish legal and commercial control over the programs they developed.

PROGRAMMING FREEDOM

United by Richard Stallman, users combined in opposition to measures such as the ones that the SPA proposed. A Harvard graduate and former programmer at MIT's Artificial Intelligence Laboratory, Stallman had risen to prominence in the software world thanks to the development of his Unix-compatible operating system, GNU, starting in 1983.[65] As programmers across the country adopted GNU, Stallman had received sizable donations from firms at home and abroad in support of both his vision for a version of Unix not controlled by AT&T and his strong stance against software IP. Under the banner of Stallman's Free Software Foundation, these groups promoted the production, modification, and dissemination of software free from the usage and reproduction restraints that software firms normally imposed.[66]

Stallman and his allies were not alone in opposing the copyright protection of user interfaces, though their views were stronger than those held by other computing professionals. In fact, a widespread opposition to look and feel copyrights was becoming especially clear to Pamela Samuelson, a legal scholar who would soon become a leading figure in the study of software IP. In May 1989, Samuelson hosted a debate at the annual meeting of the ACM's Conference on Computer-Human Interaction.[67] The event served simultaneously as an educational venue for computer professionals who might may be unfamiliar with legal doctrine and a research opportunity for Samuelson and her collaborator, a cognitive psychologist named Robert Glushko. The debate featured Jack Brown, Apple's chief lawyer in the conflict with Microsoft and HP, and Thomas Hemnes, a former defense lawyer for Lotus. Brown argued that strong copyright protections were necessary to assure companies that their investments in research and development would generate returns.[68] He explained that the design of user interfaces involved a significant amount of creative work and intellectual labor, so firms required some defense from people who would find it easier to duplicate their work than to create something for themselves. Hemnes countered that copyrights should not protect certain kinds of technologies, especially if they would deter further development. In his view, this was especially true in user interface development.

At the end of the debate, Samuelson and Glushko distributed a survey among the audience members and collected more than six hundred responses.[69] Seventy-seven percent of respondents with an opinion thought that the look and feel of an interface should not be protected by copyrights or patents, and only 18 percent identified copyrights as an appropriate form of protection. Eighty-eight percent opposed the protection of user commands through patents or copyrights, and 73 percent opposed the copyright protection of screen layouts. These numbers were high, but they did not suggest that respondents wholly rejected software IP, as Stallman did. On the contrary, 93 percent of survey respondents with an opinion supported either patent or copyright protection for source code, and 85 percent supported the protection of object code.

In Stallman's hands, however, look and feel copyright was not a doctrinal matter but a social one. Also in 1989, he released the GNU General Public License (GPL), the cornerstone of his vision for free software. His aim was to guarantee programmers' "freedom to share and change free software—to make sure the software is free for all its users," that anyone could receive and modify source code, and that no one attempted to take away people's ability to do these things.[70] The GPL formalized the mode of communal software ownership that the readers of *Dr. Dobb's* had adopted in the 1970s, and it was not entirely averse to copyright law. Users were free to claim copyright over their work, but they were required to license, free of charge, any programs they developed based on the GPL-protected work. In short, the GPL reduced copyright to an acknowledgment of a work's creator that provided no financial incentives.

Stallman's followers considered look and feel lawsuits to be an affront to their values, and in fact many of them boycotted Apple products. Stallman himself took a stand against these lawsuits in early 1989, when the Lotus Corporation launched a lawsuit from its headquarters in Cambridge, Massachusetts. Lotus targeted Paperback and Mosaic, two firms that made and sold spreadsheet programs that looked strikingly similar to the more popular predecessor Lotus 1-2-3.[71] In response to Lotus's complaint, Paperback (whose suit had been consolidated with Mosaic's) contended that Lotus's copyrighted menus and interfaces were functional elements that did not fall under the purview of copyright law in the first place.[72] Outside the courts, Paperback's lawyers and managers argued that they were forced to duplicate the 1-2-3 interface because their clients demanded strict compatibility with it and that this should not be a copyright infringement case because "a command sequence is analogous to the microprocessor instruction set."[73]

From his office at MIT, Stallman condemned this suit and others like it as examples of how corporations "threaten to kill the growth of the software industry by trying to create a new kind of legal monopoly" over how interfaces look and how they can be used.[74] To oppose them, he joined forces with John Gilmore, a programmer and activist best known for his work on the assignment of Internet protocol addresses. Together they designed a pin they called the "fanged Apple," a cartoon snake with the rainbow Apple logo as its head.[75] Protruding from the logo on its right-hand side, where the fruit's distinctive "bite" should have been, was the snake's monstrous mouth, with a pointed tongue and more than twenty fangs. Surrounding the snake were the words "Keep Your Lawyers Off My Computer."

Early in 1989, Stallman published an announcement in *The Tech*, the student newspaper at MIT. He invited all programmers to a protest rally

A mug, a pin, and a postcard made by the League for Programming Freedom. Note how the LPF modified the Apple logo on the pin so that a monstrous snake is protruding from its distinctive bite. The Statue of Liberty on the postcard holds a magnetic tape in her left hand and a floppy disk where the torch would normally be. Photograph by the author.

against Lotus.[76] Professing an anti-litigation sentiment, he rallied support from several prominent programmers and managers. They included Marvin Minsky and Patrick Winston, respectively the founder and the director of the MIT Artificial Intelligence Laboratory, as well as Gerald Sussman, a professor of electrical engineering at MIT. Even ACM president Bryan Kocher agreed to join the protest. Armed with this support from well-known figures, Stallman made the event highly visible among members of computing communities at MIT and beyond.

In response to Stallman's call, on May 24, 1989, nearly two hundred programmers gathered on the MIT campus.[77] These men and women marched for two miles to the Lotus headquarters. Many wore the fanged Apple pin and distributed leaflets urging people to boycott products from companies such as Lotus and Apple and to refuse working for them. They also carried signs protesting corporate control of software through intellectual property. One sign read

"Creative companies don't need to sue," and another featured a picture of a straitjacket and the exclamation, "Don't make me wear a suit!" A particularly striking sign featured a reproduction of Edvard Munch's painting *The Scream* and the words "Oh no! Look and Feel Copyright!"[78]

At the Lotus headquarters, the protesters marched and chanted anti-litigation slogans. Some of these were short and simple, along the lines of "Put your lawyers in their place; no one owns the interface," and "Hey, hey, ho, ho, software tyranny has got to go."[79] Other chants were significantly more complex, blending the counting that often accompanies protesting chants with specific references to packaged programs and programming syntax. Consider, for instance,

> 1-2-3-4, toss the lawyers out the door;
> 5-6-7-8, innovate don't litigate;
> 9-A-B-C, 1-2-3 is not for me;
> D-E-F-O, look and feel have got to go.[80]

The chant's author is unknown, so it is impossible to determine with certainty the references that he or she intended to make. However, there are three programming references that the protesters could have understood. First, the opening letters of the third verse are probably a reference to ABC, a simple and popular programming language for personal computers that *IEEE Software* had featured two years before.[81] Second, the numbers "1-2-3" in the same verse could serve as a reference to Lotus 1-2-3.[82] Third, the letters "D-E-F-O" are probably a nod to #DEF0 (Define Output), a command used to denote output ports in the programming of the Akai MPC. This was a popular electronic musical instrument, so the reference to #DEF0 is likely a humorous way of noting that the final verse is ready to be output—that is, chanted.[83]

Programmers were willing to do more than rally. In June 1989, software entrepreneur and Lotus cofounder Mitch Kapor, scientists at MIT's Artificial Intelligence Lab, and the staff at *MacWeek, Computer Currents,* and *InfoWorld* received unmarked floppy disks.[84] Accompanying the disks was a letter signed by an unknown group called "The NuPrometheus League (Software Artists for Information Dissemination)."[85] The letter explained that NuPrometheus's objective was to "distribute everything that prevents other manufacturers from creating legal copies of the Macintosh" and that future mailings would include code for the Macintosh's ROM, device drivers, and hierarchical filing system. It also noted that the group's only ambition was to see "the genius of a few Apple employees benefit the entire world, not just dissipated by Apple Corporate through litigation ill-will."

NuPrometheus invited anyone interested in receiving copies of the disk to place a classified ad in *MacWeek* or *Computer Currents* with nothing more than the word "NuPrometheus" and the address where they wished the copy to be sent.[86] In response, Apple representative Carleen LeVasseur told *MacWeek* that the firm would investigate the incident very aggressively and was prepared to prosecute NuPrometheus to the full extent of the law. Moreover, the president of Apple's products division, Jean-Louis Gassée, warned users that anyone who received a copy of the disk "may be in receipt of stolen property" that was "still covered by copyright law."

The identity of NuPrometheus was never revealed, and the disks—which contained only the code for the Quick Draw program that generated the Macintosh's color displays—proved to be far less damaging to Apple than NuPrometheus had promised.[87] Soon after media outlets reported having received the disks, Apple collaborated with the FBI to launch an investigation of NuPrometheus's actions as potential interstate theft. For the next few months, FBI agents visited the homes of prominent programmers and journalists in search of the group's members. Aggressively pursuing their leads, the agents demonstrated their lack of understanding of what the disks contained. According to one journalist, an agent named Joe Fallon seemed to think that if spies came across the disks, they might be able to break into the Macintosh and steal all its secrets.[88]

The NuPrometheus investigation quickly fizzled out, but it reinforced what Stallman and his followers thought all along—that corporations would protect their intellectual property at all costs. Stallman, another person of interest in the case, told *InfoWorld* that he didn't think what NuPrometheus did was wrong because "having a trade secret is a negative sum act."[89] In his view, the group's actions were the software industry's equivalent to the leak of the Pentagon Papers in 1971. Like these papers, which revealed that the Johnson administration had systematically lied to the public regarding the scope of its operations in the Vietnam War, the NuPrometheus disk had exposed an organization's willingness to keep secrets from its followers.[90]

After NuPrometheus disappeared from the hacker scene, Stallman transformed his alliance of Cambridge-based programmers into an organization called the League for Programming Freedom (LPF).[91] He became its president, and Chris Hofstader and Denis Filipetti served, respectively, as secretary and treasurer. The group's official launch announcement in the GNU email list presented the LPF as an organization "of people who oppose monopolistic practices in the computer industry" and who had recently become particularly concerned with look and feel lawsuits.[92] Stallman condemned those suits as government-sanctioned monopolies that would "enforce gratuitous incompat-ibility, stifle innovation, reduce productivity, and make computation more difficult and expensive for everyone."[93]

The announcement explained that the league might also fight against other monopolistic practices in the future. In particular, the league's leadership worried that software patents were potentially even more dangerous than look and feel copyright, especially because the proliferation of patents could "threaten to make every design decision in software development a risky one."[94] However, the cases still pending at the courts made software copyright a more pressing problem, and it would ultimately be up to the league's members to decide when and how they would campaign against software patenting.

The LPF was a classic example of what scholars term a recursive public—a public that is concerned, above all, with the maintenance and modification of the legal, practical, and technical conditions that enable it to exist.[95] It was a nonprofit corporation and a lobbying organization with a three-part charter.[96] First, it sought to identify and publicize any legal "restrictions and monopolies on classes of computer programs" that were likely to preclude the public from developing their own programs. Second, it aimed to "develop countermeasures and initiatives" through education, research, public assembly, and direct inter-vention in legal proceedings. Third, it sought to engage in the necessary busi-ness or any other activities necessary to advance the first two goals. Any money collected from membership dues or through the sale of merchandise would be used to file briefs at the courts, print materials for rallies, and make any other materials needed to effect change in the courts and Congress. "You won't get anything personally for your dues," the announcement added, "except for the freedom to write programs."

In June 1990, the Massachusetts district court gave the LPF a reason to launch its first official effort as a lobbying organization. The court ruled that the structure and word choices in Lotus 1-2-3's menus were protected by copy-right and that Paperback had committed infringement.[97] By August, Lotus had sued two more firms (Borland and Santa Cruz Operation) on similar grounds, and Stallman worried that additional firms would continue to file look and feel lawsuits. He was especially concerned with the possibility that the court handling Apple's suit against Microsoft would follow the lead of the Lotus court, thereby creating "a monopoly on window systems."[98]

In response to this potential long-term threat, the LPF organized a second rally against Lotus.[99] Perhaps in an effort to distance the LPF from any connota-tions of unlawful behavior, the announcement of the upcoming rally instructed participants to "behave as responsible citizens of a democratic society" by refusing to litter, staying out of the street, and making sure not to block any pedestrians.[100] Once again armed with slogans that favored users over corporations—including "PROGRAMMERS ARE ANGRY" and "USERS WANT COMPATIBLE SOFTWARE"—about three hundred protesters gathered at the MIT campus to march toward Lotus.[101] Some wore the fanged Apple pin that Stallman had distributed at the previous rally, but a new logo was circulating among them. This logo was called "Liberty Empowering the Programmer." It featured the Statue of Liberty raising a floppy disk in lieu of her torch and holding a roll of computer tape instead of her stone tablet. Their work had just begun.

Chapter 11 Patent Enforcement and Software Embodiment, 1986–1995

By the early 1990s, firms were securing more software patents than ever.[1] The number of issued patents of this kind rose steadily from at least 2,657 in 1986 (3.7 percent of all issued patents) to at least 8,031 (7.9 percent) in 1994. Most of these patents belonged to a handful of firms; by one estimate, in the first half of the 1990s, just 5 percent of assignees owned 63 percent of software patents. As before, software patenting was attracting firms in a wide range of industries wherein software development could provide a competitive edge. Manufacturers of all kinds were securing them far more frequently than were software publishers. It was among the publishers and users, however, that widespread skepticism over the value and uses of software patenting became most prominent.

This chapter documents how many programmers, managers, and lawyers across the country started to question whether software patenting was, indeed, beneficial to American computing. They worried that some patent holders were obtaining overly broad patents—that is, patents phrased to encompass more than just one variation of an invention—and enforcing their patent rights too

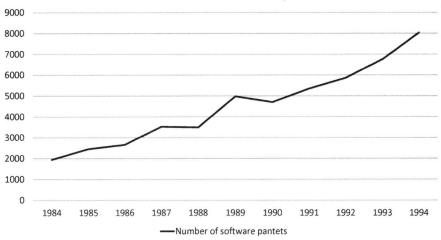

Software patents issued every year from 1984 to 1994. Table crafted by the author based on data collected by James Bessen and Robert Hunt. Bessen and Hunt, "An Empirical Look at Software Patents."

aggressively. The League for Programming Freedom, which already included some of the country's most vocal opponents of software IP in all its forms, mobilized against software patents once firms threatened to sue its members and allies for patent infringement. Corporate managers who oversaw patent portfolios started to realize that even just one very litigious software patent holder could cause an industrywide uproar. This growing skepticism encouraged a new commissioner of patents, Bruce Lehman, to hold hearings to determine how the Patent and Trademark Office could and should handle software patents. However, Lehman (who had once represented the Software Publishers Association and generally favored strong IP protections) ultimately concluded that software and patents were far too intertwined for the PTO ever to sever the connections between them.

GIFGATE

The Unisys Corporation was born in 1986 when the Burroughs Corporation (led by former Treasury secretary Michael Blumenthal) acquired the Sperry Corporation.[2] This merger was such an extraordinary development in the mainframe computing industry that it prompted business commentators to claim that the market had not been restructured in such a dramatic way since the early 1970s, when RCA and GE had left the industry. Blumenthal's managers agreed that this acquisition, priced at $4.8 billion and approved by the Justice Department's Antitrust Division, would finally create a company powerful enough to compete with IBM. Blumenthal himself argued that increasing in size was the only effective way of competing with it. "We are trying to get over the fear factor," he told the *New York Times*, "the fear that no one has the staying power against I.B.M. . . . . Once you get to a certain size—and no one has reached it yet—that fear tends to lessen."[3]

Unisys owned its two constituent firms' lines of mainframe computers and their extensive patent portfolios. Most notable among the patents was one issued in 1985 for a high-performance image compression method invented two years earlier by Terry A. Welch, an electrical engineer and former computer scientist at the Sperry Research Center who had recently become a senior manager at the Digital Equipment Corporation.[4] This patent would soon become an example of what scholars know as a standard essential patent: one necessary to engage with an industry standard, in this case the image format called Graphics Interchange Format. Also known as GIF, this format was developed by the online service provider CompuServe, and it is still in use today.[5] At the core of Welch's patent was the so-called Lempel-Ziv-Welch (LZV) algorithm, which he had developed in collaboration with two of his colleagues, Abraham Lempel and Jacob Ziv. Welch's patent covered a program that enabled a user to compress and decompress an image or a block of text without losing data. It was especially useful whenever users wished to send an image from one computer to another through a network because it reduced the size of the file being sent.[6]

In 1987, one of Unisys's lawyers sent a letter to James A. Woods, a PC user at the NASA Ames Research Center who had developed image compression software of his own called Compress.[7] The lawyer, John B. Sowell, informed Woods that his firm held a patent over the LZW algorithm and that Compress—which AT&T distributed as part of Unix 5.4—could potentially infringe on Welch's patent.[8] In response, Woods explained that the Compress algorithms were not identical to the LZW algorithm and that his program had been "designed, developed, and distributed before the ink on the patent was dry." Woods was skeptical of the possibility that an algorithm could in fact be patented, as Unisys claimed, but he and Sowell had several telephone conversations to discuss the matter. Eventually, Sowell told him that Unisys would not seek damages or fees from Compress because the firm was interested in doing so only from people and firms who created "hardware implementations of LZW."

After this encounter, Woods used the LPF and FSF online message boards to emphasize what he considered to be the absurdity of software patenting, namely that a few lines of code would be enough to infringe on complex-sounding patents.[9] He even started using the LPF to distribute what he called the essences of software patents—copylefted snippets of code he had written and which, in his view, accomplished the same things as the patented invention. He shared twenty-eight lines of code that comprised the essence of Welch's patent, along with the essences of patents assigned to firms ranging from small software developers to AT&T. Other LPF members followed his lead by distributing partial texts of patents that they considered to be potential causes of damaging monopolies. Patents for gaming, graphic display systems, and portable computing technologies were especially popular choices.[10] At times, these messages included either a personal note from someone affected by the patent or threatening letters that a patent's assignee had allegedly sent out. Regardless of the legitimacy of these documents, which cannot be independently verified, the point they made was simple: programmers felt under attack from a range of software patent holders—from small firms protecting their sole asset to what one programmer described as a "multimillion-dollar company [that] can easily crush their competition" (most likely IBM).[11]

At the LPF, writing source code was an act of protest. One of the group's first moves against software patenting, in the early 1990s, was to demonstrate how a single patent could keep programmers from creating even a simple program. For instance, the LPF distributed flyers critiquing a 1980 patent for the display of overlapping images on a computer screen. Assigned to a firm called Nugraphics, the twenty-six-page-long patent had twelve images and sixteen claims.[12] In contrast, the LPF's flyer showed an arrow overlapping the image of a chess piece and read,

```
for (x = 0; x < height; x++)
    for (y = 0; y < width; y++)
        screen [x + xpos] [y + ypos] ^ = arrow [x] [y];
```

This simple program is all it takes to get **sued**!
So enjoy your programming.[13]

The league complemented materials like this one with its own position papers against software patents. Its key document, likely written by Stallman, was titled "Against Software Patents."[14] It stated that software patents "threaten to devastate America's computer industry" and that it was only a matter of time before patent licensing costs became so high that new companies would be unable to survive. This situation would likely benefit the wealthiest firms, but the paper did not frame the issues regarding software patents in terms of how small and large firms competed with one another. Instead, the LPF posited that software patents affected everyone, from individuals who created programs in their own time to big firms such as the Lotus Corporation. They were dangerous because they would enable greedy firms and individuals to file lawsuits against others who had developed their programs independently.

The document presented a sketch of the history of software patenting that positioned software as an intangible invention fundamentally incompatible with the materiality implicit in American patent law.[15] Software patenting was a recent phenomenon in this sketch, the result of changes in the Patent Office's policy immediate following the Supreme Court's decision in *Diamond v. Diehr*. Until then, the only kinds of processes eligible for patents were those that involved the transformations of matter such as the one that occurs when iron becomes steel. In contrast, a lot of computer programs were directed at actions such as scrolling down on a document in a graphic user interface, creating and manipulating digital images, or moving a mouse cursor from one corner of the screen to another. Thus, unlike the patents that the writers of the Constitution had in mind, the ones that computing firms were obtaining had nothing to do with the transformation of matter.

Ironically, in an effort to protest corporate control over software, the LPF was inadvertently repeating arguments that mainframe hardware manufacturers had developed in defense of their market dominance. First, there was a familiar one: software patents were grounded on a "legally questionable" interpretation of the case law. The Patent Office had interpreted the Supreme Court's allowance of a computerized rubber-curing system in *Diamond v. Diehr* so broadly that it had overlooked the transformation of rubber at the core of Diehr's invention. Second was a bureaucratic argument: the Patent Office's examiners were not nearly as experienced with software technologies as programmers at firms and universities, and they were therefore ill-suited to assess whether a program deserved a patent. In any case, even if examiners did develop greater expertise in computer programming, their investigations would be unreliable because the office lacked the robust classification system necessary to make sense of software as a field of invention.

The third argument was that the nature of software as a technology and the characteristics of the labor involved in producing it rendered it an improper and undesirable subject matter for patents. According to the LPF, software was "built from ideal infallible mathematical objects" defined by abstract rules. Unlike hardware, software was easy to design because it required attention to the relations among algorithms, not electrical currents. To illustrate this point, the LPF explained: "When an if-statement follows a while-statement, there is no need to study whether the if-statement will draw power from the while-statement and thereby distort its output, nor whether it could overstress the while-statement and make it fail."[16] In contrast, hardware systems were "designed using real components."[17] They had varying costs, physical limits to their operation, and sensitivity to environmental factors such as temperature and humidity. Unlike the pure mathematical objects that make up software, hardware components must be "physically assembled in their proper places, and they must be accessible for replacement in case they fail." Tied to this difference in nature is the fact that the labor required to invent software was very different from its hardware counterpart. Software involved the creation of mathematical objects to be expressed as lines of code, and even the smallest subroutine that a programmer writes and rejects constituted an invention. In short, programmers "throw away more 'inventions' each week than other people develop in a year."

Stallman and his colleagues disseminated these views in an academic article published in the 1991 issue of *Issues in Science and Technology* titled "Why Patents Are Bad for Software."[18] This essay sketched the arguments from "Against Software Patents" and added that the Patent Office's granting of software patents amounted to "carving up the intellectual property domain of computer science and handing little pieces to virtually any company that files an application."[19] It also claimed that the "best argument against the wisdom of software patents may be history itself"—that is, the fact that firms ranging from Lotus and WordPerfect to Microsoft all became global leaders of the software industry "before the current explosion of software patents began."[20]

The strong opposition to software patenting that Stallman advocated was not an anomaly among computing professionals. Also in 1991, Pamela Samuelson and Robert Glushko, the scholars who had investigated attitudes toward look and feel copyright two years earlier, conducted a follow-up study at the annual meeting of the ACM's Special Interest Group on Computer Graphics (SIGGRAPH).[21] Three hundred and forty-five members filled out surveys similar to the ones that Samuelson and Glushko had used in 1989. Their responses revealed an extraordinarily low level of support for the patent protection of computer programs: only 12 percent of respondents with an opinion considered patents to be appropriate protections for algorithms, and 79 percent thought that algorithms should not be protected by patents or copyrights.

Opposition to software patenting was so strong at the LPF that Stallman and his colleagues even advocated for copyrights and trade secrets as the more desirable forms of IP protection. This was not an affront to the group's origins in opposition to look and feel copyright but instead an affirmation of its stance against software monopolies. Their article in *Issues in Science and Technology* argued that while patents provided absolute control over the very ability to solve an abstract problem using lines of code, copyrights and trade secrets protected the specific ways in which programmers had solved those problems. The LPF considered the latter to be akin to the central assumption that authors own their own writings, a proposition that programmers could restate as "if you write a program, you own it."[22]

The LPF's online message boards soon became a prime forum for members to air out their grievances against software patents. Members sometimes wrote about the patents they considered most egregious, drawing on their expertise in mathematics and statistics to argue that the patents fenced off well-known or obvious algorithms.[23] Others reported on scholarly work and resolutions by professional associations compatible with the LPF's views. These included, for example, a statement from a subcommittee at the Mathematical Programming Society condemning software patents as "harmful to the progress of research and teaching."[24] Still other contributors kept track of issued patents. For instance, Dave Farber, a computer scientist at the University of Pennsylvania, forwarded a message titled "[INFO] 55 software patents in one week!!!!"[25] It contained a list of fifty-five patents issued to IBM in July 1992 and noted that "IBM is building up a tremendous body of software patents that they intend to exploit quite aggressively." Similarly, Michael Ernst, at MIT's Theory of Computation Lab, maintained a database of issued software patents and their disclosures. His extensive database even included Richard Hamming and Bernard Holbrook's *Error Detecting and Correcting System* patent from 1951.[26]

Unlike programmers and developers such as the ones who followed Stallman or attended SIGGRAPH, managers at large computing firms were eager to secure and enforce patent rights. As the pressure to protest software patents increased at the LPF, Unisys intensified its efforts to license out Welch's patent. Its newest target was CompuServe, GIF's developer. For a flat hourly fee, CompuServe's clients could download business software, games, and newspapers through their telephone lines.[27] They could book airline tickets, check their stock portfolio, and even timeshare on one of CompuServe's twenty-six mainframe computers. These services had started to become more popular than ever in the mid-1980s, as major firms such as IBM, Control Data Corporation, Sears, and even the Reader's Digest Association started to compete with CompuServe by creating their own networks. In service of its own international expansion, CompuServe's research and development staff had become especially interested in developing file formats that would enable them to transmit smaller files. That's one of the reasons they had developed the GIF format in the first place.[28]

To attract developers and perhaps create an industry standard, CompuServe had placed the GIF specification and its associated software in the public domain. The firm celebrated GIF as the ideal image format for computer networks, because it allowed users to exchange images even if their PCs were incompatible with one another. Casual users could get to know the format by downloading GIF images directly from CompuServe and sending them to each other through electronic mail.[29] Over the next few years, users did in fact gravitate toward GIF images: their small size made them much easier to transmit through slow dial-up connections than their alternatives. GIF became CompuServe's alternative to formats such as AT&T's TGA, Microsoft's MSP, and the popular PostScript (PS) format on which desktop publishers often relied.[30] It became, as one industry commentator put it in the mid-1990s, "the Web's de facto graphics standard."[31]

However, Unisys's lawyers considered Welch's patent to cover, broadly, any computerized implementation of the LZW algorithm, including those that CompuServe had incorporated into their GIF software. After all, Welch's patent contained 181 claims, most of them for embodied software that the patent called a "compression apparatus" in a "data compression and data decompression system," and it included code written in the FORTRAN language "for implementing in software [the] data compressor" that the claims described.[32] For this reason, as the demand for online services grew, smaller firms eager to incorporate GIFs into their online services approached Unisys in hopes of licensing the patent. In the process, Unisys's lawyers learned about CompuServe's use of LZW algorithms, and they considered suing for patent infringement.[33]

No records survive of the communications between Unisys and CompuServe, but two things are clear. First, either CompuServe or some other firm interested in the LZW algorithm requested a "reexamination" of Welch's patent. This term refers to a procedure wherein the Patent and Trademark Office reexamines the validity of a patent when information not available during the examination process suggests that there is a problem with it. As far as Unisys was concerned, the reexamination was a smashing success, since the PTO affirmed the validity of the firm's original 181 claims and approved 55 new claims for Unisys's "compression apparatus," bringing the total to 236.[34] Second, after a series of closed-door meetings, CompuServe agreed to pay $125,000 and 1 percent of any of its GIF-related royalties and to craft a license agreement for commercial GIF developers.[35] The agreement mandated collection of a $1 initial fee and either 1.5 percent or $0.15 for every copy of GIF software that developers sold.[36] Noncommercial developers or those based at nonprofit firms would be exempt from this arrangement, as would anyone developing their programs with the intent of distributing them for free.[37]

Unisys then announced that it would probably sue all commercial developers who did not secure the appropriate licensing rights. One of its spokespeople even warned that people "writing their own stuff using C code" should arrange to have a proper license because "we have a patent on [the] technology and we mean to protect it."[38] In turn, managers and programmers often considered Unisys's patent to cover both a computerized implementation of LZW algorithms and the GIF format itself. One writer speculated that perhaps this "GIFgate" was a sign that Unisys was desperate enough to rely on lawsuits to make its profits.[39] Web browser development firms such as Netscape and America Online (AOL) condemned the patent and launched internal investigations to determine whether they could be liable for an infringement suit. Smaller firms even put their entire GIF-related projects on hold. Only a handful of writers for industry periodicals voiced their support for Unisys's decision to protect its IP by any means necessary. For instance, one high-ranking executive for a Tennessee-based software firm noted that opposing Unisys's actions amounted to what he deemed a "liberal attitude . . . that people should not be entitled to their property but should share it freely."[40] Asking Unisys to forego its patent rights over GIF, in his view, amounted to asking a farm owner to give away his farm just because a squatter claimed possession of it.

Stallman and his colleagues at the helm of the LPF used GIFgate as an opportunity to show their followers how a single patent can "show its teeth."[41] Their website announced that Unisys had done the LPF a favor by reminding everyone that the problem with software patents was "too serious to ignore." They presented the story of GIF's dissemination as one of corporate greed, wherein Unisys enforced the Welch patent "with private threats" and left most of its targets either afraid of or legally barred from discussing the situation. Even if programmers thought that they would never be the target of a patent infringement lawsuit, they could learn one key lesson from Unisys's legal efforts, namely that "software patents may not seem like an urgent problem until you find one aimed at you."

LPF members called on their peers to protest Unisys's legal maneuvering. One way was to write to Unisys to express their anger. A post on the LPF website invited members to use only snail mail because "a physical pile of letters is more impressive, psychologically, than a big file of email."[42] A more long-term form of protest came in the form of a boycott. The LPF, FSF, and GNU all banned GIF images from their servers.[43] In fact, even after the LZW patent expired in 2003, the official GNU website retained a notice explaining that GNU would continue to ban GIFs to remind users about the long-lasting damage that a patent can cause.[44] By then, programmers had even developed their own open-source alternative, the PING format. With extension ".png," this format was named after the phrase "Ping is not GIF," and it is still in use today.[45]

THE SOFTWARE PATENT HEARINGS

While Stallman and his colleagues fueled grassroots opposition to software patenting, firms in the multimedia industry were becoming acquainted with the impact that a single patent over an essential technology could have on their daily operations. Back in November 1993, the Las Vegas Convention Center hosted COMDEX, the Computer Dealers' Exhibition.[46] Labeled a "Nerd's Paradise" by a local newspaper, COMDEX was an opportunity for firms of all sizes to show off and advertise their latest technologies.[47] Representatives from Apple Computer stood by their booth inviting visitors to try out their new handheld wireless digital assistant, the Newton. In one of the convention center's rooms, Intel had created a motherboard-themed walk-in maze featuring a human-sized mock-up of an Intel Pentium processor at its core. Motorola, IBM, and Apple—which had teamed up to create the PowerPC microprocessor and aimed to compete with Intel—all had booths. Even manufacturers of small peripherals were eager to show off their goods; a firm called MotorMouse invited visitors to try out its Corvette-shaped mouse, which honked every time users clicked its middle button.

The 1993 installment of COMDEX featured, above all else, digital media.[48] One of the attendees noted that "the biggest theme is multimedia," which was "transforming computers into an information tool that can communicate."[49] CD-ROMs lined the convention hall's aisles, each one able to hold over 600 megabytes of material.[50] COMDEX attendees were marketing all kinds of multimedia CD-ROMs, from business applications such as WordPerfect to X-rated games such as Interotica's multimedia pornographic adventure *The Dream Machine*.[51] Each of these CD-ROMs represented an enormous investment; producing high-end multimedia software cost anywhere between $500,000 and $2 million, and each CD-ROM could sell somewhere between fifty thousand and sixty thousand copies per year.[52]

The array of multimedia choices available on CD-ROM at the time was staggering. Someone with a passion for the news, for example, could purchase a disk from *Time* magazine containing more than twenty thousand articles, along with photographs, maps, and historical videos, for $99.95.[53] For $40 less, people with a penchant for historical events could purchase a disk such as *JFK Assassination: A Visual Investigation*, in which they could analyze, frame by frame, four home movies related to the assassination of John F. Kennedy. Home computer users could even invest in digital encyclopedias made by firms such as Microsoft, Grolier, and Encyclopaedia Britannica. A few hundred dollars were enough to purchase a set of disks that had both the thousands of pages' worth of text that they could expect from a print encyclopedia, and materials such as audio excerpts of historical speeches.

The technologies at COMDEX made headlines almost immediately, but no firm at the convention became as controversial as Compton's New Media. This was a subsidiary of Encyclopaedia Britannica that was outperforming its competitors by distributing more than a hundred CD-ROM titles for twenty-two software publishers.[54] Founded in the 1980s, Compton's was the division that allowed Encyclopaedia Britannica to add interactive multimedia encyclopedias to its product lines.[55] It had also enabled the company to expand its portfolio of copyright registrations beyond traditional print. Best-selling items such as Compton's Multimedia Encyclopedia—arguably the first fully interactive multimedia encyclopedia—were protected by copyright registrations that the firm had obtained by submitting compact disks, a magnetic disk in a box, and printouts of all the text to the Copyright Office.[56] Alongside Compton's, Encyclopaedia Britannica had registered copyrights for its CD-ROMs that encompassed text, illustrations, and the software at their core.[57]

Compton's representatives at COMDEX announced that they had recently obtained a patent for a "database search system that retrieves multimedia information in a flexible, user-friendly manner."[58] Issued two and a half months before the conference, the patent covered a specific means of searching through a database and a system to enable a user to retrieve multimedia content from a database contained in a CD-ROM. The images showed the encyclopedia's interface, but the patent claimed as the invention a "computer search system for retrieving information" comprising things such as means to interrelate text and graphics, a textual "search entry path," and output means to provide search results to the user. Indeed, the patent explained that the invention "can be used with any information that can be stored in a database."[59]

One of Compton's executives flaunted that the patent covered "the entire concept of linking text, sound and image," and the firm's representatives at COMDEX urged people to obtain a license as soon as possible because royalties would increase from 1 percent to 3 percent of sales in June 1994.[60] The

U.S. Patent   Aug. 31, 1993   Sheet 13 of 20   **5,241,671**

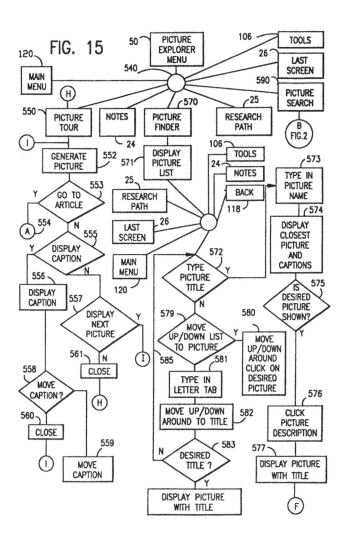

Flowchart for "Picture Explorer," one of the features in the broad database patent that Compton's advertised at COMDEX. US Patent 5,241,671 (1993).

scope of the patent was indeed broad—the ability to link databases of different media types was essential to the display of multimedia material. In theory, anyone who created a program that stored and retrieved sounds, graphics, texts, and videos could infringe on Compton's patent, regardless of what specific hardware or software they used.[61] Even this patent's issuance had made

FIG. 23

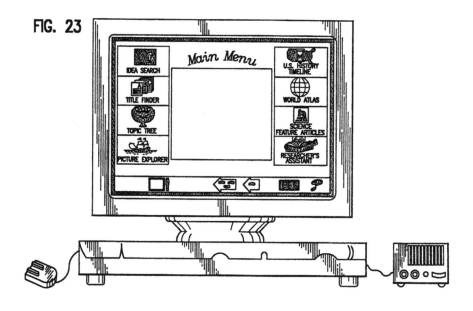

U.S. Patent   Aug. 31, 1993   Sheet 20 of 20   5,241,671

Encyclopedia interface from the patent that Compton's New Media obtained in 1993. The patent was aimed at the search functions that would enable users to navigate a database. US Patent 5,241,671 (1993).

Compton's a very desirable firm to own; Encyclopaedia Britannica would soon sell Compton's to the Tribune Publishing Company for $57 million.[62]

The granting of very broadly phrased patents was no news in the multimedia industry. Since the 1980s, gaming firms like Atari and Nintendo had come into conflict with the Magnavox Corporation, a firm that owned the patents for some of the most fundamental technologies that allowed the display of games on television screens.[63] Created primarily by the American gaming pioneer Ralph Baer, these inventions had come under legal scrutiny at least half a dozen times; firms new and old often found that they needed to license things such as a system for the "generation, display and manipulation of symbols upon the screen of the television receivers for the purpose of playing games."[64] More recently, in 1992, a firm called the Optical Data Corporation had obtained several patents aimed at interactive multimedia educational systems. One covered a teacher's use of a remote-controlled CD player in order to alternate between traditional classroom activities and the content on the CD.[65] The other covered a computer system that allowed the teacher to preselect the CD's content in order to match a lesson plan's goals.[66]

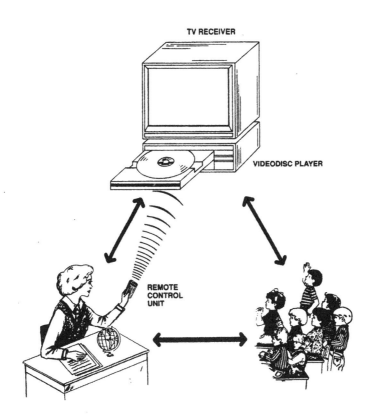

FIG. 1

Illustration from *Interactive Method for the Effective Conveyance of Information in the Form of Visual Images*. In this case, a teacher is employing the patented invention by using a remote control to show students images that match her lesson plan. US Patent 5,120,230 (1992).

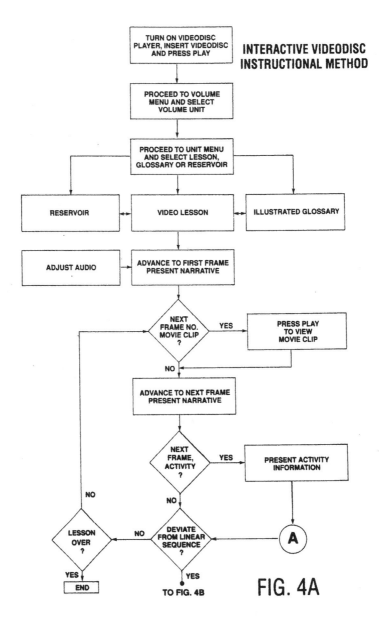

INTERACTIVE VIDEODISC
INSTRUCTIONAL METHOD

FIG. 4A

Flowchart for the program at the core of *Interactive Method for the Effective Conveyance of Information in the Form of Visual Images.* US Patent 5,120,230 (1993).

Unlike Magnavox or Optical Data, Compton's aggressively advertised its patent. It generated widespread contempt by handing out copies of the patent at COMDEX and warning onlookers about an upcoming hike in royalties. For their part, managers and executives viewed the patent as an affront to the industry. Rod Turner, the president of an educational multimedia firm, condemned the granting of the patent as a mistaken and government-sanctioned suggestion that Compton's had "singlehandedly built the multimedia industry."[67] Stan Cornyn, one of the founding members of Time Warner's multimedia group, reacted by saying that the "entire industry should rise up and throw fruit in the direction of Compton's."[68] Journalists criticized the patent as an illustration of the federal government's inability to handle new information technologies. One writer for the *New York Times* reported that the patent "may simply be the latest example of a patent system that is overwhelmed by the pace and complexity of today's high-technology industry."[69] Another, for the *Los Angeles Times*, wrote that the Patent and Trademark Office found it difficult to identify the novelty of this kind of invention because the impulse to secure software copyrights the decade before had caused the examiners to fall behind the state of the art in computer programming.[70]

The number of software patents issued every year had been increasing slowly and steadily for nearly a decade. The Patent and Trademark Office had issued at least 1,402 in 1982 (2.4 percent of all patents issued), and by 1991 the number had risen at least to 5,347 (5.5 percent).[71] Many of these patents were very broad, and the media companies' outcry against Compton's suggested that many firms were on edge about their scope. In an unusual development, the PTO responded to this outcry by announcing that it would reexamine Compton's patent.[72] The new patent commissioner, Bruce Lehman, had worked previously with the Software Publishers Association, and he shared with that trade group a very positive view of software patenting (see chapter 12). Still, he explained, the original examination had been hampered by the office's lack of data on software inventions, and he now asked interested parties to submit books, software manuals, and even advertisements for products that might demonstrate the patent's invalidity.[73] He probably considered the reexamination to be both a matter of quality control and a key example of how the eight-month-old administration of President Bill Clinton would seek to correct the previous administration's poor management of the PTO. "The Bush people said that there was no problem," Lehman told the *Los Angeles Times*, "but there is clearly a problem."[74]

Lawyers and managers in the media industry celebrated Lehman's decision to reexamine the patent, but they worried that the process would be a private affair. It would involve an overly aggressive firm and an examiner whom Lehman had handpicked and who might not know just how important the patent could be.[75] In support of the reexamination, one manager noted, "When somebody sends out a news release saying they have a patent that covers everything in the whole world, it's right to have a great deal of skepticism. I don't think the patent was that broad, but Compton's made a big deal out of it, and it's biting them."[76]

Compton's did, indeed, suffer at the hands of the PTO and the multimedia industry. Just three months after the reexamination started, the office rejected the patent and concluded that the inventions in each of its forty-one claims were obvious by the time Compton's filed its application in 1989.[77] The firm responded by arguing that the breadth of its patent had been artificially magnified by media reports, that the original claims were valid but poorly phrased, and that its invention would surely appear obvious to a contemporary user of multimedia software. The government disagreed, and in October 1994 the office issued a final rejection. Along the way, Compton's sales had plummeted. By November, just a year after announcing the patent, the firm had suffered a loss of $11 million, its CEO and vice president had resigned, and commentators viewed the company as an industry pariah. Compton's would continue producing multimedia CDs, but its patent and reputation were gone.

The PTO's reexamination of Compton's patent drew so much attention from firms in many industries that in 1994 Lehman decided to hold public hearings on "patent protection for software-related inventions."[78] Unlike previous hearings on this matter, these would not focus on whether computer programs were eligible for patent protection. On the contrary, Lehman understood the Supreme Court's opinions on *Diamond v. Chakrabarty* and *Diamond v. Diehr* as implying that statutory subject matter included "anything under the sun that is made by man" and that an invention is not rendered ineligible for protection just because it includes a "computer-software-implemented mathematical algorithm."[79]

The first round of hearings took place in San Jose, California, in January 1994. The main topic of discussion was the "use of the patent system to protect software-related inventions."[80] The office's guidelines for the day instructed participants to address such issues as whether software patenting had made any noticeable impact on their firm's finances, the difficulties that witnesses foresaw in "maintaining or altering the standards for patent-eligibility," and the relation between patent law and software innovation. The office also sought guidance on the kinds of patent claims that should be considered allowable—a question that it phrased in terms of the kinds of software-related inventions that should be "protectable." The goal was to determine whether inventors should be required to embody their software and, if so, what kinds of software embodiment were admissible.

The San Jose hearings suggested to Lehman that although lawyers believed software patents to be desirable, programmers generally didn't, and managers were divided on the matter.[81] The one point on which most managers and lawyers seemed to agree was that it would be impossible to put an end to software patents because software and hardware were functional equivalents. Timothy Casey, the senior patent counsel at a firm called Silicon Graphics, explained that "in practical terms, software is not really different from hardware," and that the Patent and Trademark Office would do well to realize that just as hardware patents had not impeded the progress of hardware development, so software patents would not stand in the way of software innovation.[82] Michael Lachuck, a partner at the IP law firm Poms, Smith, Lande & Rose, reinforced this point in his testimony by noting that regardless of the office's policies, "clever patent drafters will always [find] a way to disguise a mathematical algorithm or some other form of software-related invention either as a piece of hardware" or as a step central to an otherwise patentable method.[83]

Companies like IBM, Intel, Apple, and Microsoft—the major firms in the PC industry—were avid supporters of the idea that the interchangeability of hardware and software made software patenting a perennial feature of the information technology industry. Victor Siber, IBM's senior corporate counsel, insisted that the PTO "can't divorce computer program-related inventions from computer hardware and other microprocessor inventions" and that curtailing patent protection on either one would therefore automatically curtail patents on the other.[84] Computer-related inventions could be "implemented in hardware or software," so it was futile for the PTO or the courts to focus on altering the standards for patent-eligibility that they would apply to software inventions. In the worst-case scenario, applicants would "simply cast their patent claims in terms of electrical circuitry," and the office would be unable to curtail this effort without turning all "electrical patents into nullities."

Firms that made or sold application programs or multimedia packages were noticeably less supportive of software patenting. Douglas Brotz, the principal scientist at Adobe Systems, told an origin story about his company aimed at showing how software patents could only hurt innovative firms. Two pioneering inventors, John Warnock and Charles Geschke, had set out to work on printing technologies without any hope that their software would be patented. Their lack of patents did not deter any venture capitalists from investing in their firm, nor did it keep Warnock and Geschke from creating the most innovative programs they could. However, Adobe was at risk of having to pay what Brotz called a "patent litigation tax," because firms and programmers who had witnessed its growth over the past decade were sure to start securing patents in order to derive licensing revenue from Adobe.[85] For this reason, Brotz concluded, "software per se should not be allowed patent protection," regardless of whether it was eligible for it or not.[86]

Individual programmers also spoke at the hearings, but primarily as representatives of organizations that opposed software patenting altogether. On behalf of the LPF, Gordon Irlam argued that copyright should continue to be the norm for software protection. Addressing the merits of copyright, he said, "It basically means if you copy code, you know, you can't do that, but if you wrote the code yourself, that's all you need to know. You can then go out and sell it, and you're safe in the knowledge that you can, and you won't be sued later on. You know you owned it."[87] Underpinning Irlam's testimony was the notion that software is a product that combines code and ideas.[88] The code is a vehicle for the ideas; it is what results from a programmer's creative efforts, and it is therefore the proper subject matter for copyright. Different programmers were likely to produce different code in order to solve the same problems, create the same structures, or express the same ideas. As long as these problems, structures, and ideas remained available to everyone—that is, free of patent protection—programmers would be able to create code that they could own without impeding competition in the industry.

The LPF's position paper for the commission, which Irlam delivered, drew on a videogame called *Colossal Cave Adventure* for metaphors that illustrate both the improperly broad scope of software patents and how difficult it would be to compete in a software industry wherein patenting was rampant. *Colossal Cave Adventure* was a text-based game. It allowed players to navigate a virtual world by entering simple commands such as "drink water," "open chest," "west" (to move westward), and so on. The game could become very repetitive, because it could require players to input the same instruction several times until a task was completed or to guess what kind of instruction would advance the plot.[89] Successful players could find a treasure chest or a beautiful setting; unsuccessful ones would read descriptions of their character's death.

The LPF's position paper opened with a printout of a fictional conversation between a player and a parody of *Colossal Cave Adventure* called *Patent Adventure*.[90] In lieu of being dropped in a cave, the player had become the CEO of a software company called AcmeSoft. The text adventure began:

Suddenly the fax machine rumbles.

[Player Command] READ FAX

It's from SharkTech! They're claiming that your company's product "Acme Professional" violates their software patent "Distinguishing Nested Structures by Color." They want 1% of your wholesale price in royalties.

[Player Command] GIVE ROYALTIES

Now they want 5%.

[Player Command] GIVE ROYALTIES

That satisfied them. Hmm, the fax machine is humming again. It's from ParaTech! They're claiming that your "Acme Professional" assigns clients to whichever server process is least busy, and as a result want 3% of your wholesale price.

[Player Command] IGNORE THEM

ParaTech have decided to take you to court. Do you want to settle for 10%, pay $800,000 in legal fees, or circumvent their patent?

[Player Command] CIRCUMVENT

Your programmers say they can't circumvent the patent without hurting performance—causing you to lose 30% of your customer base. Do you want to circumvent?

. . .

[Player Command] GO TO COURT

Legal fees are $600,000. Current funds are $400,000. You've gone broke![91]

Patent Adventure was a humorous and unusual submission to a PTO hearing, but the patents that the scenario mocked were real. SharkTech's patent, *Distinguishing Nested Structures by Color*, was in fact a nod to IBM's own patent of the same name.[92] Similarly, ParaTech's patent for the assignment of clients to available servers alluded to AT&T's recent patent, *Method of and Apparatus for Operating a Client/Server Computer Network*.[93] Finally, the choice of percentages (1 percent or 5 percent) was based on IBM's alleged practice of charging those percentages in royalties to license, respectively, a single software patent or a full portfolio.[94]

Stallman himself spoke at the hearings, not in his official capacity as a member of the FSF or LPF but as a prominent programmer. His testimony echoed the arguments that hardware manufacturers had made at the courts since the 1960s, advancing conceptions of the nature of software as an invention that would render the technology ineligible for protection. Unlike inventions in other fields of engineering, computer programs "are built out of ideal mathematical objects"; programming is the one field wherein a person can "build a castle in the air supported by a line of zero mathematical thickness."[95] Moreover, whereas firms such as pharmaceutical companies could allocate one patent for each of its products, software firms could not. A single program could combine many different techniques and features, mixing new and old inventions in what could be thousands of pages of code.

To impress these points on Lehman and his colleagues, Stallman brought with him a printout of ten thousand pages of source code for a compiler, likely the GNU compiler for the Ada language.[96] He explained that the source code was the result of an intensive collaboration and that organizations such as Intel, Motorola, and the U.S. Air Force were funding projects to extend and adapt it. The program was so long and its elements were so tightly woven together that it was impossible to tell whether it infringed on any patents, so its widespread adoption showed how private firms and government agencies were not at all concerned with verifying the licensing status of the programs they used. In any case, he told the commissioners, the program was freely available on the Internet on an FTP (File Transfer Protocol) server, and it was distributed widely by individuals and organizations alike. Without discussing the free software movement—which he described as a digression irrelevant to the discussion at hand—Stallman therefore argued that patents were impractical protections for computer programs such as his.

The commissioners, however, were not interested in debating whether software was patent-eligible. They wanted to discuss instead how the patent system could best serve the software industry. For this reason, even if the dramatic testimony that Stallman and the LPF delivered had shown that patents harmed users, the argument that software patents should not be allowed carried no weight during the hearings. It was abundantly clear that software patenting was already taking place, and Lehman believed that it was not the PTO's role to decide whether the thousands of software patents that had already been issued should remain valid. That was a problem for the courts, and there was no indication that judges would start invalidating patents like they once did in the aftermath of the *Benson* decision.

This reasoning continued to trouble both free software advocates such as Stallman and mathematically minded computer scientists. Earlier that year, Donald Knuth had written to Lehman asking him to reconsider the PTO's "policy of giving patents for computational processes."[97] The letter implied that software patenting was a rather recent phenomenon, as before 1980 "it was generally believed that patent law did not pertain to software." Without acknowledging the traditions of software embodiment from which software patenting had emerged, Knuth encouraged the PTO to embrace an absolute duality between hardware and software that would render software ineligible for patent protection. He posited that the "computer revolution" had been made possible by the absence of patent protection for computational processes and warned that such patents could mean the end of American software development.

Conceptually driven arguments like Knuth's, however passionate, no longer carried the legal significance that they did in the 1960s and 1970s. Back then, assessments of software's patent-eligibility hinged on contests among competing conceptions of its nature. However, by the mid-1990s, the notion that inventors could obtain patents for computer-controlled systems such as the one at stake in *Diamond v. Diehr* had led judges to assure that software embodiment (as software firms had understood it in the 1970s) could be done implicitly, without the need to disclose specific components.[98] The Court of Appeals for the Federal Circuit had repeatedly noted that these systems could have another kind of special purpose, which could range from performing secondary computational processes required for the original program to work to serving as a mediator between the program and a broader computer system. This meant that if inventors could disclose some special purpose machine on which a program could be loaded—perhaps a ROM, a special computer peripheral, or even the embodiment of another program—then they could potentially secure this kind of implementation-based patent protection.[99]

While Lehman reflected on the San Jose hearings, the Federal Circuit decided five new cases on software patenting affirming the validity of this line of thought.[100] To any legal scholars and commentators who assumed software patenting to be just a little older than PCs, these decisions appeared to be sudden expansions of previous rationales. In fact, one such author deemed 1994 the "Year of the Algorithm" and noted that the Federal Circuit now had a dire need of a "radical algorithmectomy."[101] Certainly, the most recent decisions by the court appeared radically permissive when compared to landmark cases such as *Benson* or even *Diehr*, but in practice they only affirmed something that people such as Morton Jacobs, Howard Markey, and even Richard Stallman already knew: even if algorithms and programs are ineligible for patent protection on their own, an inventor could secure patent protection for them by spelling out their effect on, or implementation through, a machine.

The most influential 1994 Federal Circuit decision along these lines was *In re Alappat*, which marked the end of a six-year-long battle over the patent-eligibility of an invention developed at a firm called Tektronix. Founded in 1946, Tektronix was the country's leading manufacturer of oscilloscopes (devices that create graphs depicting an electrical signal's variation in voltage over time).[102] The two-dimensional graphs that oscilloscopes produced enabled users to analyze a wave signal's properties, and they were especially useful in the design and production of electronics equipment. By the mid-1980s, the engineers at Tektronix had become especially interested in oscilloscopes that used cathode ray tubes to display the wave's voltage changes over time. In particular, three of its engineers, Kuriappan Alappat, Edward Ayerill, and James Larsen, had developed a computerized device called a rasterizer, which transformed discrete measurements into pixelated images for display on a cathode ray tube oscilloscope. Previous rasterizers often depicted discrete voltage measurements as jagged or discontinuous graphs, but Alappat and his colleagues had developed a program that created and displayed smooth graphs based on those measurements.

The PTO's Board of Appeals had deemed that the invention's fifteenth claim was ineligible for patent protection because it fell within a "mathematical algorithm" exception to patent-eligibility.[103] The claim read,

> 15. A rasterizer for converting vector list data representing sample magnitudes of an input waveform into anti-aliased pixel illumination intensity data to be displayed on a display means comprising:
>
> (a) means for determining the vertical distance between the endpoints of each of the vectors in the data list;
> (b) means for determining the elevation of a row of pixels that is spanned by the vector;
> (c) means for normalizing the vertical distance and elevation; and
> (d) means for outputting illumination intensity data as a predetermined function of the normalized vertical distance and elevation.[104]

On appeal, the majority of the court's judges construed the phrase "means for" as a shorthand to signal the presence of electronic components. The majority opinion used bracketed and underlined text to disclose those components on the inventors' behalf and noted that the claim "unquestionably recites a machine, or apparatus, made up of a combination of known electronic circuitry components." Their rewriting of the claim read,

> 15. A rasterizer [a "machine"] for converting vector list data representing sample magnitudes of an input waveform into anti-aliased pixel illumination intensity data to be displayed on a display means comprising:
>
> (a) [an arithmetic logic circuit configured to perform an absolute value function, or an equivalent thereof] for determining the vertical distance between the endpoints of each of the vectors in the data list;
> (b) [an arithmetic logic circuit configured to perform an absolute value function, or an equivalent thereof] for determining the elevation of a row of pixels that is spanned by the vector;
> (c) [a pair of barrel shifters, or equivalents thereof] for normalizing the vertical distance and elevation; and

(d) [a read only memory (ROM) containing illumination intensity data, or an equivalent thereof] for outputting illumination intensity data as a predetermined functioned of the normalized vertical distance and elevation.[105]

This rephrasing allowed the court to affirm the validity of software embodiment as a patent-drafting technique and to signal its willingness to consider the phrase "means for" as a placeholder for the tangible systems on which a program could be implemented. Citing *Diamond v. Chakrabarty* and *Diamond v. Diehr*, the judges affirmed that patent law is intended to protect "anything under the sun that is made by man," and they recognized that things such as laws of nature, natural phenomena, and abstract ideas were ineligible for patent protection because they are not man-made.[106]

The *Alappat* ruling was grounded on the notion that any digital electronic circuits are, in fact, "circuitry elements that perform mathematical calculations."[107] This meant that the presence of mathematical algorithms in a claim did not render it ineligible for patent protection. As a result, a ban on the patent-eligibility of mathematical algorithms exists only to the extent that "certain types of mathematical subject matter" are abstract ideas until they are "reduced to some type of practical application."[108] Grounded on the *Diehr* rationale, the court therefore concluded that claims such as the ones in Tektronix's application were "directed to a combination of interrelated elements which combine to form a machine," albeit one that happens to process numerical data through mathematical algorithms.[109] In short, the court found that the invention is not an abstract idea but a "specific machine to produce a useful, concrete, and tangible result."[110]

Ultimately, decisions such as *Alappat* carried much more weight at the PTO than whatever activists had to say. Indeed, in 1995, Lehman announced that the office's job was not to decide on the merits of software patenting but to develop the guidelines and procedures that would enable inventors to secure patents for "anything under the sun that is made by man."[111] The 1994 hearings had made clear that some inventors and firms wished to secure software patents and that the PTO had failed to give them a thorough and efficient examination process. To this end, on April 1, 1995, Lehman announced that the PTO would develop new guidelines to "govern the examination of patent applications on computer software inventions," which he described as "the first step in our efforts to make the patent system more receptive to software innovation."[112]

Lehman's guidelines were the most lenient that the PTO had ever published officially, but they were not a radical break from the patenting practices that the office had seen since the 1950s. The guidelines simply recognized the practice of software embodiment as a viable means to secure patent protection and provided a framework with which examiners could assess the kinds of embodiment that inventors could employ in their patent applications. They were directed not at the software itself but at what they called "computer-implemented" inventions. This term encompassed everything from the multimedia systems that Compton's had once patented to the computerized rubber-curing mechanisms at the heart of *Diamond v. Diehr*.[113]

The guidelines and their accompanying documentation were almost forty pages long.[114] They affirmed that things like data structures and mathematical algorithms were ineligible for patent protection, and they explained that computer programs, on their own, were neither physical "things" nor "acts" being performed. Software became eligible for patent protection only in relation to tangible components such as memory circuits and electronic computers. This reasoning enabled the PTO to reconcile its history of issuing software patents with what they considered to be the only three kinds of subject matter that courts had deemed ineligible for patent protection: natural phenomena, laws of nature, and abstract ideas.

Just as inventors would need to create a practical application of a law of nature (perhaps the harnessing of steam to move an engine or the storage of electricity to denote quantities), so too did they need to create practical applications for their abstract ideas. This meant that there would be no patents over the process of addition, but inventors would be allowed to patent the specific machines and processes that enabled them to add, even if the core of their invention was a generic programmed computer that would do so. When patent applications for such inventions arrived at the PTO, it would be the examiner's job to characterize the relations between the computer program and the tangible components of the invention.

Once again, this characterization was based not so much on the way that the invention worked but in the way that the claim described machines and algorithms. According to the guidelines,

> If it is clear that the claim uses the computer program elements to define actions to be performed by a computer, Office personnel should treat the claim as a process claim. If the computer program elements are recited in conjunction with a physical structure, such as a computer memory, the claim should be treated as a product claim. If the claimed subject matter cannot be treated as a process and does not have any physical structure, then it is non-statutory *information*.[115]

This three-part criterion would allow examiners to determine whether a claim used a program to "*describe*" the physical structure of a manufacture or

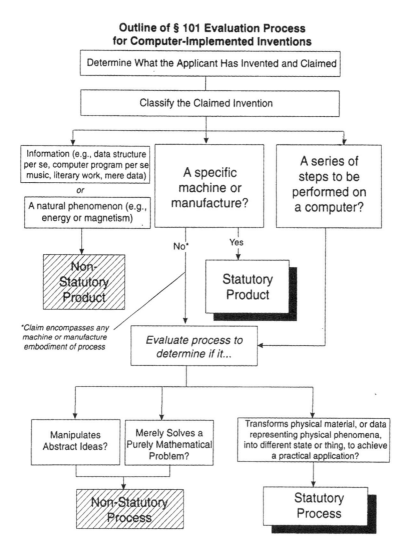

Flowchart for the Patent and Trademark Office's 1995 Guidelines for the Examination of Computer Processes. Note that the condition for a process to be statutory is that it transform physical material or data representing physical phenomena into a "different state of thing." *Official Gazette of the Patent and Trademark Office,* November 7, 1995, 29.

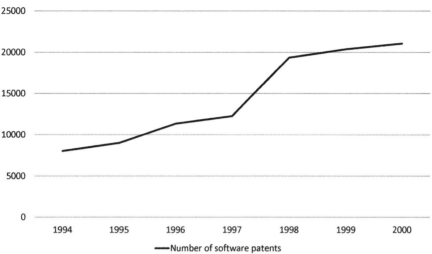

Number of software patents issued every year from 1994 to 2000. Table crafted by the author based on data collected by James Bessen and Robert Hunt. Bessen and Hunt, "An Empirical Look at Software Patents."

machine, or steps to be performed by a computer" or if instead it made the program "the object of the patent" and was therefore unallowable.[116]

However, not all machine and process claims in this scheme would be patent-eligible. Following the *Diehr* rationale, and in alignment with the *Abrams* and *Yuan* cases of the 1950s, computerized processes were required to manipulate physical matter in some way.[117] The office affirmed this requirement, though it also noted (likely based on the telegraphy patents of the nineteenth century) that the thing being manipulated could also be energy, such as electricity. Since electronic computers could store data as electrical impulses, this meant that a process claim involving a computer program would be patent-eligible if it either manipulated data or caused some physical change in the world.[118]

Over the coming years, these guidelines and the Federal Circuit opinions on which they stood enabled firms to secure thousands of Internet-related software patents. Some of these patents were even aimed at HTML (Hypertext Markup Language), the standard language that allowed people to create websites and link them with one another. They protected inventions ranging from web browsers to visualization tools for interlinked websites. At the same

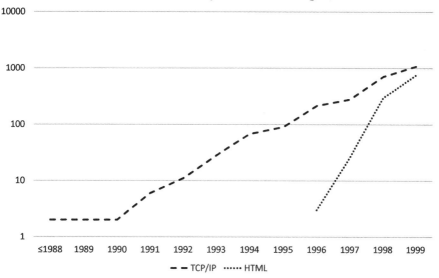

Number of patents issued per year that mention the terms TCP/IP or HTML. Graph in logarithmic scale (base 10), crafted by the author based on data collected by Gregory Stobbs. Stobbs, *Software Patents*, 347.

time, however, software makers intensified their effort to strengthen the copyright protections available to them. After all, no amount of patent protection over the technologies that enabled connection to and usage of the Internet would be enough to control what users could send to one another at the click of a button. This problem concerned almost everyone in the computing and telecommunications industries—from the firms that manufactured computers and modems to application developers and Internet service providers (ISPs).

Chapter 12 Software Rights for a New Millennium, 1993–2000

In 1996, during a public event at the Library of Congress, Vice President Al Gore picked up a white telephone and pretended to make a call.[1] A loud ring cut through the auditorium, and Lily Tomlin, the award-winning comedian, appeared on a small television screen in character as Ernestine, a nosy telephone operator she had portrayed since the late 1960s. With a smile on his face, Gore put the telephone down and enjoyed a video conversation with Ernestine:

> ERNESTINE: One gigabitty? Two gigabbies? A gracious hello! Have I reached the party to whom I am speaking?
>
> GORE: Yes, yes. Thank you, Ernestine. Would you please help the President and me place a call to some young people from Calvin Coolidge High School, please?
>
> ERNESTINE: Who is this?
>
> GORE: It's me, Ernestine: Al Gore!
>
> ERNESTINE: Oh, Mr. VEEP! Surfing the net! Downloading images of global climate change again? You crazy guy! It's true what I've been telling my friends. You're not stiff; you're just a techno-nerd!
>
> GORE: Thank you! Thank you, Ernestine.

ERNESTINE: When's the last time I saw you? Was it Los Angeles, two or three years ago? You were talking some mumbo jumbo about this super-duper info-mercial freeway, right?

Tomlin and Gore continued their exchange until he announced that Bill Clinton, who could barely contain his laughter, was ready to sign the Telecommunications Act of 1996. This was a comprehensive overhaul of American telecommunications that Gore presented as the legislation needed to complete the information superhighway (despite Ernestine's misnomer for it). The act was intended to deregulate American telecommunications and to take down government-imposed barriers to entry into the industry. It would draw intense criticism over the coming years, especially for its efforts to regulate content transmitted online, but at the time it was the pinnacle of the Clinton administration's efforts to fashion itself as the gateway into the twenty-first century.[2]

Aligned with Gore's long-standing commitment to technological development, the administration supported aggressive efforts to meet the needs of the country's information and telecommunications industries. Deregulating telecommunications was a central component of this project, but it was not the only one. This final chapter shows how, by the start of the new millennium, software IP rights became stronger than they had ever been. It narrates two interrelated stories that unfolded simultaneously. First is the story of how the Clinton administration's efforts to strengthen the nation's computing and telecommunications industries culminated with the passage of the Digital Millennium Copyright Act (DMCA), a law aimed at curbing the new kinds of software and media piracy that had been developing since the 1980s. Second is the story of how the Court of Appeals for the Federal Circuit ultimately endorsed many of the legal rationales and patent-drafting standards that lawyers at software firms had worked so hard to articulate and establish back in the mainframe era.

INTERNET COPYRIGHTS

On February 22, 1993, less than a month after his inauguration as president of the United States, Bill Clinton announced his plan to build a National Information Infrastructure.[3] The NII, as this project was known, was a web of networks, computers, databases, and consumer electronics that would work seamlessly to put information at users' fingertips.[4] Along with his vice president, Al Gore, Clinton celebrated his administration's vision of unleashing "an information revolution that will change forever the way people live, work, and interact with each other."[5] Perhaps one day people would be able to live anywhere they wanted and telecommute to their offices "though an electronic highway," or the country's best schools and teachers would be "available to all students, without regard to geography." Even the country's health-care system could benefit from this interconnection, because services could eventually be "available on-line, without waiting in line, when and where you needed them."

The NII was at once a vision for what the Internet could become and a politically charged call to craft new relations between innovation and governance for the twenty-first century.[6] It is an example of what scholars call a sociotechnical imaginary—a shared vision for a technological future.[7] This imagined future was strikingly similar to what we now know as the Internet of Things.[8] As the administration put it,

> The National Information Infrastructure will consist of (1) thousands of interconnected, interoperable networks, (2) computer systems, televisions, fax machines, telephones, and other "information appliances," (3) software information services and information databases (e.g., "digital libraries"), and (4) trained people who can build, maintain, and operate these systems. In the future, the NII will enable all Americans to get the information they need, when they need it and where they need it for an affordable price.[9]

This vision came as no surprise to industry leaders and political commentators. Gore (D-Tennessee) had spent so much of his congressional career advocating for stronger investments in science and technology that critics and supporters alike dubbed him "Senator Science."[10] He had been calling for the creation of "data highways" since 1970, and he had introduced several bills aimed at developing government-sponsored high-performance computing technologies. Clinton shared Gore's commitment to government sponsorship of cutting-edge innovation, and during his presidential campaign he had pledged to make the development of a "national information network" a priority.[11] Computing innovation was, in their view, the key to economic prosperity.

At a meeting of the International Telecommunication Union (ITU), an agency of the United Nations specializing in information and telecommunications technology, Gore presented the five interrelated principles that the administration supported: encouraging private investment, promoting competition, creating a flexible regulatory framework, providing access to the Internet without discriminatory pricing, and ensuring universal service. This meant that countries would need to cooperate with one another in the development of a strong and competitive global market for information and communication technologies. They would also need to take seriously the governance of technology and innovation within their borders, implementing whatever top-down measures were necessary to foster healthy competition and access-driven information infrastructures of their own.[12]

Clinton and Gore's domestic program for the creation of this competitive environment included an aggressive program of antitrust enforcement. Leading this front was Anne Bingaman, a former professor at the University of New Mexico School of Law who had spent more than twenty-five years practicing antitrust litigation.[13] Bingaman believed that one of the most important roles of government in the development of the NII was to promote an environment in which firms of all sizes had the "maximum incentive to innovate" and "develop the best products at the lowest cost."[14] This would be possible only through "intelligent antitrust enforcement and procompetitive legislation and regulation," a true commitment to encouraging competition "wherever technologically and economically feasible." In her view, no case illustrated this goal better than the past break-up of AT&T, which had caused the competitive pressure necessary for AT&T to update its physical infrastructure, allowed innovative newcomers to enter the industry, and triggered the "telecommunications revolution" that the NII would bring into the new millennium.

In addition to leading several investigations on the work and market power of the regional Bells, Bingaman launched a high-stakes investigation into Microsoft's power in the markets for operating systems and, later, Internet browsers.[15] The lawsuit that followed caused Bingaman to be known in the press as "Microsoft Corp.'s chief antagonist."[16] Inheriting an investigation initiated by the Federal Trade Commission, the Antitrust Division targeted two key aspects of Microsoft's licensing practices. First, the firm normally charged "per processor" fees in their licensing deals for Windows. This meant, for example, that Compaq paid fees based on the total number of processors they sold, regardless of how many of those used the Windows system. Bingaman believed that "per copy" licenses, which Microsoft eventually agreed to use almost exclusively, would encourage manufacturers to consider alternative operating systems. Second, the division targeted Microsoft's ability to tie in one product as a condition to license another, as IBM had done with software and services before its unbundling.[17] This had happened in Microsoft's incorporation of Internet Explorer into its Windows operating system. As competing browsers such as Netscape and Mosaic struggled to make and retain some market dominance, Bingaman's targeting of Microsoft's tie-ins involved the Antitrust Division in the first so-called Browser War—the struggle to establish usage dominance of one proprietary browser over all others.

US v. Microsoft, as the suit was formally known, is perhaps the best-known battle in the legal history of the PC.[18] Dramatic testimony, high-stakes appeals, and dozens of related suits entangled the Justice Department and Microsoft in ways unseen in the computing industry since IBM's antitrust battles during the mainframe era. Microsoft would ultimately agree, in a 2001 settlement, to share its application programming interfaces (the routines that would allow others to create compatible software with Windows and Internet Explorer). Along the way, this suit continually reminded scholars and commentators alike that the Clinton administration was willing to use strong government interventions to ensure that IP generated multilateral competition, and not competition-stifling market dynamics reinforced through proprietary technological systems.

While Bingaman performed these interventions through antitrust law, Bruce Lehman carried them out through IP. Soon before the start of *US v. Microsoft*, Lehman had become assistant secretary of commerce and commissioner of patents and trademarks, bringing Clinton and Gore's commitment to fostering technological change through directed government action into the Patent and Trademark Office.[19] In his capacity as commissioner, Lehman agreed to write an in-depth report on IP rights in service of the creation of the NII. This work would allow him to reflect on the needs of copyright holders while managing the country's patent system.

In the course of his research, Lehman found considerable global pressure to create stronger protections against software piracy through copyrights, not patents. Users were sharing computer programs with one another by transmitting full copies of a program's code from one computer to the next. Patents gave inventors the right to exclude others from making, selling, or using their creations, but they afforded little relief when users were copying one program and sharing it online. If the NII was ever to become a Global Information Infrastructure, as the Clinton administration hoped, then the United States would need to find a way of making up for the fact that patents were ineffective in the face of everyday piracy.[20] Market forces and technological innovation alone were not enough; international multilateral agreements would be necessary.

This need became a central theme at a World Intellectual Property Organization (WIPO) conference hosted by Harvard University in 1993 and a follow-up event at the Louvre Museum in Paris a year later.[21] Attendees included business leaders, industry representatives, and high-ranking government officials from around the globe. They agreed that the problems with everyday piracy in the computing industry resembled those the audio recording industry was facing in its dealings with music piracy and that the global patent system was not designed to handle either of them. At WIPO and its member countries, this meant that few things were more pressing in the global regulation of IP than updating the "existing copyright system in the face of the challenges of digital technology."[22] This would involve reconsideration of the scope of creators' rights and a direct response to new technical measures for the protection and unauthorized distribution of copyrighted works.

Soon after these conferences, the Clinton administration committed even further to taking whatever means would be necessary to align the United States with the international IP system. Worldwide concerns over the enforceability of WIPO's long list of treatises and guidelines had prompted all members of the World Trade Organization (which the United States had joined in 1994) to sign a document called TRIPS, the Agreement on Trade-Related Aspects of Intellectual Property Rights.[23] Using somewhat vague language on matters relating to information technology, TRIPS required signatories to comply with the Berne Convention, and in practice it prompted member countries to treat computer programs as machines constructed through copyrightable texts.[24] On the one hand, it required member countries to protect computer programs, "whether in source or object code," as literary works eligible for copyright protection.[25] On the other hand, it affirmed that patents should be available "for any inventions, whether products or processes, in all fields of technology, provided that they are new, involve an inventive step and are capable of industrial application." This meant that programmers could obtain a combination of patent and copyright protections for their work.

Lehman believed that the American patent system was already on track to provide the protections required by TRIPS.[26] His 1995 NII report affirmed that patents could provide inventors of new information technologies the protection they would need.[27] He wrote that inventions involving computer software had "enjoyed some degree of protection under the patent system since the beginning of the computer industry," even though courts since then had found it difficult to distinguish which aspects of a program can be protected. In his view, the Federal Circuit's recent opinions amounted to recognizing that software—through the computers on which it runs and the media that contains it—becomes an invention as patent-eligible as any computer system or electronic component.[28]

The report spent more than 130 pages discussing copyright law and about 20 pages discussing patents, trademarks, and trade secrets combined. It implied that the availability of patent protection for software was so evident that the energy spent in clarifying the matter would be better spent in strengthening the broader frameworks that would regulate software ownership as the NII became denser and more global in nature. The most important step in this regard was a major revision of copyright law intended to establish, at a statutory level, that users of online technologies were not exempt from copyright infringement. A situation that had worried the CONTU commissioners in the 1970s had finally become a widespread reality: programs, music, books, and almost any other kind of copyrighted work could be transmitted electronically on demand, and sometimes this transmission left no discernible trace. Without a copyright overhaul, Lehman concluded, unabated piracy could endanger the NII's development in ways that patent law would be unable to correct.

Congress was very receptive to Lehman's views and, more broadly, to the idea that strengthening IP protection across all fields of work was essential to the country's long-term economic well-being. Lobbying from several industries, along with the pro-IP momentum that the formation of the NII was building, encouraged lawmakers to favor acts that strengthened IP rights one industry at a time. In 1995 both chambers passed the Digital Performance Right in Sound Recordings Act, granting copyright owners in sound recordings the right to exclude others from performing their work "publicly by means of a digital audio transmission."[29] They also passed the Biotechnology Process Patent Act, which exempted creators of a new biotechnology process from the non-obvious requirement if their process resulted in a new and non-obvious composition of matter.[30] President Clinton promptly signed off on these two new laws, which at the time were received very positively by the industries they targeted.

Starting in 1995, momentum grew for a more general revision of the IP system thanks to the convergence of Lehman's work, the administration's focus on the NII, lobbying from information and telecommunications firms, and WIPO's recent flurry of activity. For the next two years, lawmakers faced once again the thorny copyright problems that their predecessors had left to CONTU two decades earlier. At first, they tried to pass a bill called the NII Copyright Protection Act, which would have granted copyright holders the right to exclude others from transmitting their creations and given libraries and visually impaired people the right to make up to three copies of digital copyrighted works.

This bill would have implemented much of Lehman's and WIPO's recommendations. It defined the transmission of a work as its distribution "by any device or process whereby a copy [or] phonorecord of the work is fixed beyond the place from which it was sent."[31] Unsurprisingly, software publishers were eager to see this bill become a law. The Software Publishers Association submitted several statements celebrating the bill and its successors as a way of giving software developers incentives to continue creating the programs at the NII's core.[32] However, the bill's focus on transmission also meant that ISPs could be held liable for copyright infringement if a customer shared a copyrighted work through the Internet or that a phone company could be charged if users posted a copyrighted program on a BBS. This had the potential to cause significant financial losses or generate waves of litigation; the SPA was already planning to file several lawsuits charging ISPs with copyright infringement.[33]

The Internet had added telecommunications firms to the landscape of copyright infringement in ways that lawmakers had yet to acknowledge and that the NII Copyright Protection Act failed to address. This made ISPs, online service providers, and their trade associations the most vocal opponents of the NII Copyright Protection Act. For instance, Stephen Heaton, the general counsel and secretary at CompuServe, testified that the bill's scope should "be expanded to address issues and uncertainty" that ISPs faced regarding copyright liability. He insisted that it was simply impossible for ISPs to monitor every single bit of data contained in the millions of messages and packets that traveled around the world every day. To illustrate this point, he compared ISPs to transportation companies: just like a trucking firm or an airline, ISPs cannot be held responsible for "originating, managing, or reviewing" the content it delivers. Requiring providers to check for copyright infringement would be so technically and logistically complex that it "would result in no less than bringing their business to a halt, almost immediately cutting off the flow of information and communications to millions of people."[34]

ISPs appeared ready to end the Internet if they did not receive protection from liability. Edward Black, president of the Computer and Communications Industry Association (CCIA), delivered highly critical testimony that depicted the bill as the opposite of what innovators needed to make the NII a reality. He told Congress that if ISPs became potentially liable for users' copyright infringement, they might find themselves pressured to transform the nature of the Internet. This could result in an NII "that only allows users to view data, not to engage in two-way interactive communication that allows the uploading and manipulation of data."[35] Even worse, ISPs might be forced to restrict access only to companies and individuals with the financial resources necessary to indemnify themselves. William Burrington, assistant general counsel at AOL, expressed similar views on behalf of a group called the Ad Hoc Copyright Coalition—a group of regional Bell operating companies, long-distance telephony providers, online service companies, and ISPs.[36] In his view, the bill had "the potential to cripple this great new communications medium of the twenty-first century," thereby depriving Americans access to the "next great leveler in our evolution to a fairer and more open society."[37]

Views like these put the NII Copyright Act to rest, but developments on the international stage kept the momentum building. In 1996, WIPO approved what some commentators at the time called the two "Internet Treaties," though neither actually used the word "Internet."[38] The two treaties were part of WIPO's long-standing efforts to update the Berne Convention. The first concerned performances and phonographs; it reaffirmed performers' and producers' rights to authorize and make available to the public any original recordings and copies of them.[39] The second was a broad copyright treaty intended to affirm member countries' rights and responsibilities regarding creative works. It also indicated that computer programs are protected as literary works among WIPO member countries.[40] Like the first one, it required countries to "provide adequate legal protection and effective legal remedies against the circumvention of effective technological measures" incorporated into copyrighted works.[41] The treatises did not carry the provisions that ISPs wished to see, but the effort to align the country with WIPO's newest mandates would ultimately yield the protection from liability that they sought.

In an extraordinary and unusual demonstration of bipartisan cooperation, Congress took less than two years to pass a bill (unanimously in the Senate) that incorporated WIPO's treatises and gave ISPs the protections they demanded.[42] Later known as the Digital Millennium Copyright Act, this bill criminalized the production and dissemination of lock-picking technologies, criminalized lock-picking itself, and increased penalties for copyright infringement. It also granted ISPs a release of liability if their users committed copyright infringement through their networks. The hearings preceding the DMCA's passage demonstrated that Congress favored the demands of ISPs over those of software and media publishers. Once again, the CCIA and the SPA had submitted mutually incompatible testimony: the CCIA argued that Congress was not providing enough protection to ISPs, while the SPA condemned the ISP's release of liability as a low blow to software publishers.[43]

Clinton signed the Digital Millennium Copyright Act into law on October 28, 1998.[44] However, just like the Computer Software Copyright Act in the 1980s, the DMCA was but the start of a debate on copyright law that would carry on for decades. Legal scholars and scientists worried that the anticircumvention rules would have a chilling effect on innovation—precluding scientists and developers from reverse engineering the software that they studied.[45] This was especially pressing in encryption research, which grew in complexity and importance as the spread of e-commerce technologies generated significant demand for network security. The passage of the DMCA also caused the most pressing problems in software copyright to shift in character and content. Gone were the days when determining copyright-eligibility or distinguishing between useful and creative elements were the focus of scholars and litigants alike. In their place was a pressing need to delineate what didn't count as copyright infringement—determining what safe harbors users had when engaging with digital technologies now that copyright laws were stronger than ever before.

BUSINESS METHODS AND SOFTWARE PATENTS

In the mid-1990s, while Congress debated copyright bills, software patenting flourished. The Federal Circuit judges issued more opinions confirming that it was not necessary to disclose specific machine components in software patent applications. In the process, they enabled yet one more way of drafting patents for software—one in which claims no longer needed to be restricted to specific arrangements of tangible machinery. Indeed, *Alappat* showed lawyers and patent agents that the Federal Circuit was willing to rephrase the claims' language to examine their validity, and the guidelines affirmed inventors' ability to disclose their inventions in such general terms that simply mentioning a computer was enough to meet the tangibility requirement that had once forced firms to embody their software. This also made it more difficult to argue against the validity of a patent on patent-eligibility grounds: it was no longer enough to point out that the invention failed to process tangible substances.

The number of issued software patents was increasing rapidly, from at least 5,862 (6 percent of issued patents) in 1992 to 11,359 (10.4 percent) in 1996.[46] From 1994 to 1997, three-fourths of issued software patents had originated from manufacturing industries of various kinds—from chemicals and electronics to instrumentation and assorted machinery. Five percent had been issued to software publishers, and a stunning 6 percent had been issued to one firm: IBM. As commissioners in the 1994 hearings had realized, software patenting had become a pervasive feature of the country's patent system, reaching far beyond the technological and commercial reach of the computing industry. At IBM, however, these software patents were more valuable than ever, as the firm and the Department of Justice reached a settlement in 1996 that would phase out, over the next five years, the restrictions imposed by the Consent Decree of 1956.

Firms that offered computer services benefited especially from the simpli-
fied patent-drafting standards of the mid-1990s. The spread of the World
Wide Web was enabling companies to operate remotely, even across national
boundaries.[47] This was especially true for financial services such as portfolio
management, credit card transactions, and the batch processing required for
e-commerce firms to tally their online sales. As a result, managers and lawyers
had developed an increased interest in so-called business method patents—
that is, those aimed at some aspect of a business transaction, from the intake
of consumer debts at an online store to the forecasting of stock prices and
interest rates.[48] Applications for this kind of patent were far from a new development; Thomas R. Johnston's 1967 application (the patent at stake in *Dann
v. Johnston*) was for an automation of a check-balancing algorithm, as were a
few other patents issued that decade.[49]

The credit card industry's reliance on software patents illustrates this trend.
Firms in this industry had been securing patent protections for their proprietary programs for about a decade, often by embedding them in broader
computer systems at which they could aim their applications. This was an
important practice at the Visa Corporation, which had secured at least eleven
patents since the 1980s. Some of these patents covered the credit cards themselves and the methods of making them.[50] Other patents were aimed at the
computer systems that enabled the transmission and processing of encrypted
information, the sorting of an account holder's card transactions, the processing of digital signatures, and the online communication between sales terminals and Visa's servers.[51] The latter patents protected software as the control
system for a device or as the means that enabled a tangible object such as a
transaction terminal to process certain data.

One example is *Automatic Purchasing Control System,* a patent filed early in
1994 most likely in expectation of a ruling in Alappat's favor.[52] The sole independent claim, which protected the programs at the patent's core, disclosed a
"method for authorizing transactions for distributing currency or purchasing
goods and services." Several steps in this patent involved the transmission of
numerical or textual data. They included, for example, "receiving, from a
remote terminal, a transmitted card number and debit amount."[53] The application also included a flowchart of what the patent called "the authorization
software of the present invention."[54] This patent would be issued two years
after submission, with few changes to the original application.

Unlike Visa, Mastercard started developing its software patent portfolio in
the 1990s. Software had been a feature of Mastercard's patents from the very
beginning, not as the sole invention being protected, but as the control system

for the card processing terminals that businesses could use to process travelers' checks.[55] Nearly all of the patents that Mastercard had received were, in fact, software patents aimed at processing electronic transactions in one way or another—from the ones triggered when a person used a credit card at a vending machine to those involving the use of personal computers to make a payment to an online store.[56] Consider *System and Method for Conducting Cashless Transactions*, filed early in 1994, again likely in expectation of a ruling for Alappat.[57] One of its independent claims was a "method for conducting a cashless transaction with a user card apparatus."[58] This method involved steps such as increasing the amount of funds in an electronic account and conducting cashless transactions at small programmed terminals such as the ones installed in systems like vending machines.

Much like IBM in the 1960s, Visa and Mastercard soon started to oppose the very same kinds of patents that they were already obtaining. In 1994, a small firm called Meridian Enterprises filed a patent infringement lawsuit against both credit card firms.[59] Meridian likely alleged that Visa and Mastercard had infringed on a patent it had obtained in 1991 for a computer system that automatically administered a credit card reward program; this appears to be the firm's only patented invention at the time.[60] The suit lasted for six years, and although the documentation is no longer available for research, PTO and District Court of New Jersey records suggest that it may have ended in 2000 with a settlement.[61]

Along the way, Mastercard's and Visa's attorneys sought out opportunities to have the Federal Circuit invalidate patents for business methods involving software. Their most important chance came in 1996, when an infringement suit brought one such patent to the court. The patent at stake had been filed in 1991 and issued two years later to R. Todd Boes, from an investment advisory firm called the Signature Financial Group.[62] It was aimed at a system for managing a mutual fund investment structure called the hub and spoke model, wherein several individual mutual funds (spokes) pooled their assets in a single portfolio (hub).[63] The hub could potentially create economies of scale, lower administrative costs, and reduce the tax rate, making the funds more profitable.

Boes's invention was especially helpful when handling the transactions required by tax law.[64] The hub was required to transfer any gains and losses to the spokes daily. If the number of spokes was very high, then this transfer could involve thousands of calculations that a single computer could perform almost instantly at the end of each day. The patent claimed this invention as a "data processing system for managing a financial services configuration of a

U.S. Patent   Mar. 9, 1993   Sheet 1 of 18   5,193,056

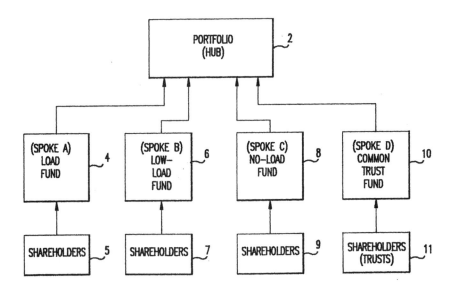

FIG.1

Schematic representation of the hub and spoke arrangement in R. Todd Boes's invention. Reading from the bottom up: First, shareholders come together through mutual funds of varying yields. These funds are pooled together in a single portfolio, potentially creating economies of scale and lower taxes. US Patent 5,193,056 (1993).

portfolio established as a partnership, each partner being one of a plurality of funds."[65] This system comprised such things as "computer processor means for processing data" and several "means for processing data" related to each spoke's gains and losses. This was, at its core, a simple program—one that could perform the basic accounting functions required to keep track of the spokes' performance.

The patent's validity was soon contested in an infringement suit brought by the State Street Bank and Trust Company. State Street serves institutional investors, and at the time it controlled just over 40 percent of the country's mutual funds market.[66] Signature's lawyers had conveyed to State Street's that any data processing system that handled funds arranged through a hub and spokes would likely infringe on their patent.[67] In response, State Street attempted to negotiate a licensing agreement with Signature, but negotiations broke down for reasons that remain undisclosed. Faced with a potential infringement suit, the District Court of Massachusetts granted State Street a declaratory judgment invalidating Signature's patent. Based on the PTO's guidelines, the FWA test, and the *Alappat* decision, the court had found that the patent was not directed at statutory subject matter.

In 1996, after Signature filed an appeal at the Federal Circuit, Visa and Mastercard filed a joint amicus brief urging the patent's invalidation and citing their pending suit with Meridian as a justification for their interest in the matter.[68] Their brief warned that the "standard for patentability" that the court adopted would have "far-reaching implications in the financial services industry."[69] The brief took no issue with the district court's rationale, and in fact it affirmed the patent's invalidity on the grounds that it combined two abstract ideas (a mathematical algorithm and a business method). Its purpose was, instead, to encourage the Federal Circuit to affirm that methods of doing business were ineligible for patent protection, even when computerized. Such an affirmation would likely rid the two firms of their suit with Meridian and grant them a go-to defense should more suits like it arise in the future.

Visa and Mastercard's brief did not rehearse old arguments on tangibility, implementation, or the nature of computer programs.[70] It warned that it was becoming very common for patents to involve abstract ideas—in this case, "business methods, bookkeeping techniques, and marketing schemes"—that would normally fall outside of the scope of patent protection. These patents had been approved because the use of a computer allowed inventors to claim "unpatentable business concepts" as computer programs, systems, or devices. "This approach lends to the claims a superficial air of technology," the brief explained, "but often the only 'art' involved in the purported invention is that of business."[71] In other words, these patents were a modern counterpart to embodied software: embodied business methods.

In contrast, firms such as IBM, Apple, Intel, NCR, and AT&T all supported the issuance patents like Signature's.[72] Their trade association was CBEMA's successor, the Information Technology Industry Council. ITI, as this trade association was known, submitted a brief applying to business method patents the same arguments that ADAPSO and ADR had applied to software patents decades earlier—that even if there was a computer program at the patent's core, the invention was in fact a machine. ADAPSO had become a new trade association called the Information Technology Association of America (ITAA), and for a few years ADR had been integrated into a larger firm (Computer Associates) that did not normally participate in other firms'

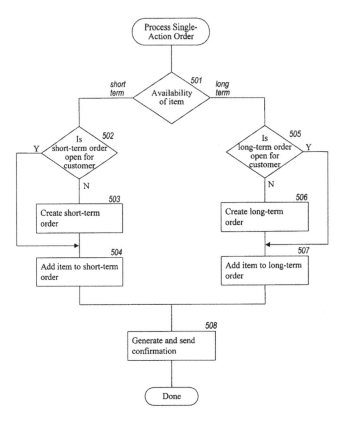

Fig. 5

Flow diagram for the routine that enables Amazon's 1-click order system. It allows customers to order items from the website with a single click of the mouse, without having to add them to a purchasing list or entering all their information. US Patent 5,960,411 (1999).

legal battles. Still, the arguments that they had advanced lived on, this time supported by many of the firms that had worked so hard to defeat them two decades earlier. Indeed, ITI's brief implied that the presence of computing machinery in the claims' disclosures was not a coincidence but in fact evidence that the invention was not reducible to disembodied abstractions.

Firms that were still too small to submit briefs of their own to the Federal Circuit were very invested in a ruling in favor of Signature. Among them was Amazon.com, a fledgling online book store created by Jeff Bezos, an electrical engineer and computer scientist.[73] The store's online debut occurred in 1995, the same year that Bezos started obtaining patents in several countries for the cornerstone invention that enabled the store to exist—a method for the secure transmission of credit card information through nonsecure networks such as those that people have in their homes.[74] In 1997, Bezos and his associates had submitted several more software patents. They were aimed at the systems that allowed other websites to market Amazon products, the search engine at Amazon.com, and the store's 1-Click ordering system.[75] It is unlikely that the success of these applications hinged exclusively on the outcome of the pending case at the Federal Circuit, but their submission on the eve of the court's decision does suggest that Amazon's lawyers and patent agents expected a ruling in Signature's favor.

Finally, in 1998, the Federal Circuit handed down its decision on *State Street v. Signature*.[76] The court cast aside the arguments that State Street, Visa, and Mastercard had advanced and affirmed the validity of Signature's patent under the *Alappat* rationale, namely that the transformation of data by a machine was patent-eligible because it produced a "useful, concrete and tangible result."[77] Once again adding words to the claims in their interpretation, the Federal Circuit now affirmed that the word "means" in a claim could be a stand-in for the electronic components that grant the claim the tangibility necessary to affirm its validity. Explicit embodiment through claim language would not be necessary under the *State Street* ruling: a claim for a computerized algorithm, like the one for its underlying computer program, was now understood to imply its own embodiment.

State Street was the last major decision on software patenting that courts issued in the twentieth century. It provided legal grounding for arguments that software firms three decades earlier could have only dreamed of. The days when mathematicians, lawyers, and engineers needed to collaborate to disclose a computer's programming in terms of a machine's circuitry were long gone. Disputing a software patent's validity became more difficult because the courts' track record made it harder to argue that software was an intangible, and therefore unpatentable, invention.[78] Firms like ADR no longer existed, and their lawyers had retired, but their arguments and ideals had lived on, of all places, at some of the same organizations that once opposed software patenting at all costs. These former opponents had learned, over the 1980s and 1990s, that protecting software was akin to protecting what made computer systems valuable and profitable: their uses. In the process, software patents had become key strategic weapons in the range of industries wherein computing technologies could provide a competitive edge. Like the new copyright laws designed to curb piracy in the online world, this patent-based regime for software ownership was the strongest that the world had ever seen.

Conclusion

In 2014, in *Alice v. CLS*, the Supreme Court invalidated a software patent on the grounds that its claims "merely require generic computer implementation" of an algorithm and that they "fail to transform that abstract idea into a patent-eligible invention."[1] Soon thereafter, at the Court of Appeals for the Federal Circuit, Judge William Bryson (Howard Markey's successor, appointed by President Bill Clinton) took this ruling one step further. In his estimation, software patents were often "dressed up in the argot of invention," but they had no inventive characteristics whatsoever. Instead, they merely "describe a problem, announce purely functional steps that purport to solve the problem, and recite standard computer operations to perform some of those steps."[2] Inserting a computer into a familiar process, Bryson argued, did not render the process itself patent-eligible.

Industry and legal commentators sometimes thought, as one author for the American Bar Association put it, that it was now "open season on these patents."[3] Many writers speculated on the future of software patenting in the United States after *Alice*. Perhaps software firms would now turn to copyright law and trade secrecy more eagerly than ever before, or they might abandon traditional IP protections altogether. Patent agents might need to develop entirely new ways of drafting patent applications, at least until courts and the Patent and Trademark Office ceased to interpret *Alice* as an indictment of what software patenting had become. Or perhaps license agreements would become longer than ever. Even if the industry continued to thrive, writers disagreed on what it would mean to own a program in this new legal environment.

These discussions are reminiscent of those after *Gottschalk v. Benson*, wherein legal scholars and commentators debated whether an end had come for software patents despite the Supreme Court's assurance that ending them was not its intention. By then, the problem of determining whether software was patent-eligible had become an alluring and yet somewhat misleading problem on which scholars and practitioners could focus. It was misleading because the main problem patent lawyers and agents in the trenches had been grappling with for years was not *if* software was patent-eligible but instead *how* to disclose it in a patent application. Software patenting to them was a matter of patent-drafting—a discursive exercise that transformed algorithms into machines to bypass long-standing doctrinal issues.

The same is true today. Major IP firms are giving advice similar to the guidance that Morton Jacobs would have given his clients back in the 1960s.[4] These firms' publicly available guidelines suggest that patent drafters should include plentiful references to specific hardware in their applications for software patents. This hardware could be computer electronics or well-known technologies such as antennas, radios, or neural chips. Regardless, the drafter should carefully note how the invention improves upon something tangible. The guidelines sometimes explain that including source code can be helpful, especially because its presence may demonstrate that the invention is not a trivial program that happens to be implemented in a computer. In other words, the main issues continue to be patent-eligibility and the modes of discursive embodiment that patent drafters can employ.

Court opinions have not been the only determinants of the legal frameworks for software ownership. Changes in legal doctrine can certainly cause these frameworks to change, but so can the host of broader commercial, technological, and sociopolitical forces that shape the country's legal infrastructures. In particular, the conceptual and legal grounding of software patenting has developed in response to the slowly changing relations among four things: firms' use of law and legislation to develop a competitive edge and protect their technology; transformations of legal practice tied to changes in legal doctrine and business strategy; popular and professional conceptions of the computing industry's needs and the nature of its technologies; and the challenges that arise when incorporating new technologies into well-established legal systems and bureaucratic infrastructures.

Since the early 1950s, firms have used software patents to gain or maintain a competitive advantage, carve out a place for themselves in the industry, and fence off emerging technologies. IBM's turn against software patents in the 1960s was fueled not so much by the patents themselves as by the firm's effort to reduce the risks of having its research and development costs skyrocket and of being locked out of important emerging areas of technological development. At small firms such as ADR, managers and lawyers considered patents to be crucial weapons to make inroads against IBM's market dominance, second only, perhaps, to antitrust suits. Twenty years later, Unisys tried using its LZV patent to profit from an industry for online services in which it was not yet a leading player, and its aggressive enforcement of this patent prompted League for Programming Freedom members to create their own free alternatives to the GIF format.

The emergence of personal computing made software IP a personal matter. Starting in the mid-1970s, many computer users became personally involved with patents and copyrights.[5] A handful of anonymous users distributed proprietary source code to clubs and magazines, while more visible ones started small businesses selling cloned software or launched periodicals to protest and subvert software IP protections. Historians and commentators writing about free and open-source software have recognized Richard Stallman as one of the most influential proponents of the need to bypass corporate control over information technologies.[6] Accordingly, the work of the LPF epitomizes user groups' efforts to shape the frameworks that govern software ownership. Its members took to the streets, incorporated computer code into their chants and leaflets, and used message boards to distribute source code in protest of issued patents. Like many of the members of the People's Computer Company the decade before, they considered IP protections to be the most significant obstacle standing in the way of users' ability to interact freely with computing technologies.

By the 1980s, everyday users were accusing large firms of patenting and copyrighting far too much and of asserting their ownership rights against individuals and organizations that couldn't afford to defend themselves. Concerns over firms dedicated to the aggressive enforcement of patent rights, however, have been a recurring feature in the computing industry for more than half a century. In the 1960s, IBM's managers feared that smaller companies would make their firm's production costs skyrocket by demanding licensing fees for patented programs. This concern intensified for the next two decades, as software firms patented programs they did not necessarily bring into the end-user market themselves and home users started to notice webs of IP protections over their devices. These tactics became especially visible by the century's end, as established firms such as Compton's New Media used them in an effort to control new online services and digital media technologies.

The rise of non-practicing entities, or NPEs—firms that secure patent rights for inventions they do not intend to commercialize, sometimes derogatively known as patent trolls—is not a recent development in the computing industry. Other historians have demonstrated that firms dedicated to selling and litigating their patent rights have existed since the late nineteenth century and that such firms back then were far more litigious than their counterparts today.[7] Similarly, since the 1950s, American computing firms have been securing patent protections for programs that they did not necessarily aim to produce. However, what changed in the 1990s was not firms' willingness to litigate but instead the ease with which they could obtain software patents. By then, the assumption that a computer's presence guaranteed the kinds of embodiment required for patent-eligibility made patent drafting for software the simplest it had ever been.

Discussions about NPEs in recent years have rekindled discussions on whether software patenting is harmful to innovation in computing. Quantitatively and empirically inclined scholars have developed powerful tools to examine this problem.[8] A focus on historical contingency and change, however, reveals that nothing inherent to software patents as legal objects necessarily hinders or promotes innovation. The main problem since the 1990s has been that software patent holders have been able to secure overly broad patents and litigate them very aggressively. This situation was made possible by changes in the patent-drafting standards for software inventions that have been accumulating since the 1960s, but these changes were not necessary and unavoidable consequences of doctrinal developments. Nowadays, in response to doctrinal developments since *Alice*, the Patent and Trademark Office has changed its examination guidelines for software inventions once again. It now requires patent applicants to recite additional elements that demonstrate the existence of an inventive concept beyond whichever algorithms constitute a given program.[9] How this new rule will work out remains to be seen, but one thing is clear: a new version of the requirement to perform some kind of discursive embodiment, which examiners and the courts had been shedding slowly since the 1970s, is in place once again.

More generally, making sense of the long-term relations between computer programs and IP law requires close attention to the circumstances that have yielded competing conceptions of the nature of software. It was not unusual in the 1950s for people to construe the making of a computer program as an activity that could involve the creation of electrical circuits. Even after programming languages made it possible to create programs by stringing words and symbols together, the distinct physicality of computer programming continued to be in the minds of engineers and lawyers at hardware and software firms alike. At this time, the patent protection for computer programs was rather similar to those that special purpose computers could receive. In the late 1970s, as computing started to infiltrate people's homes, this sense of programming as a distinctly physical task began to take a back seat to the conception of software as a textual invention. This made it more intuitive for people to consider programs as objects that could be copyrighted, not patented, and yet software patenting persisted through the coming decades in the form of automated computing systems and computer implementations of specific processes.

In this sense, what has distinguished software from other technologies that the American IP system has faced is its capacity to be continually reconceptualized—compared to creations ranging from nineteenth-century looms to books and algorithms. There have been enough of these comparisons to generate many conceptions of its nature that are at once robust in their own terms and incompatible with one another. Some of these conceptions have been so commercially and strategically valuable that firms advanced them for decades in high-stakes legal conflicts. In short, software has had a permanently unstable place in the country's IP system because every conception of its nature has failed to advance the commercial and personal needs of all the stakeholders involved.

TECHNOLOGY, LAW, AND BUSINESS: A VIEW FROM THE HISTORY OF AMERICAN COMPUTING

This book's overarching methodological aim has been to connect the history of the computing industry with the legal history of science and technology.[10] Scholars in the latter field have demonstrated that law and legislation have continually served as both testing grounds for technoscientific knowledge and sources of authority for specific conceptions of the world around us.[11] The history of software IP, ripe with its own examples of legal testing and validation, is no exception. Starting in the 1960s, a deceptively simple-sounding question—what is software?—generated complex legal and commercial problems with which programmers, managers, and attorneys would grapple for nearly three decades. No preconception of what software is or of how it should be characterized as a technology has served as a general organizing principle in the history of software patenting: software's changing conceptualizations have been inseparable from the long-term strategies of its developers and users. The doctrinal dissonance that these competing conceptualizations generated started slowly to fade away as courts and lawmakers turned their gaze from the problem of characterizing software as a technology toward that of understanding its place in broader sociotechnical systems.

The study of law in the history of computing is made possible by something that many scholars are starting to notice: technology, law, and business have developed jointly, each field facilitating changes in the relations between the other two. For this reason, rather than just asking how any two of these affect each other, scholars can investigate the long-term interplay among the three in their broader historical contexts. This approach enables the systematic introduction of patent law into the business history of technology without having to accept the internalism and ahistoricity often present in doctrinal legal scholarship.[12] The list of industries for which this approach has been fruitful includes railroads, electrification, pharmaceuticals, biotechnology, manufacturing, telephony, and now computing.[13]

This hybrid method emphasizes that legal systems (much like science and technology) comprise infrastructures for knowledge- and decision-making, and it opens up two methodological opportunities. First is the use of archives traditionally reserved for legal and regulatory history—court and congressional records, bureaucratic archives for federal agencies, and legal scholarship itself—to investigate technological and industrial change. For instance, court records and the PTO archives contain a wealth of internal correspondence, technical documentation, minutes for meetings, presentation slides, and special executive reports that might otherwise remain tucked away at IBM's corporate archives.[14] This archival expansion enables the use of law to historicize American computing.[15] Indeed, as computing technologies traveled among firms, industries, and homes, so did ways of understanding the law and envisioning its roles in the country's commercial and technoscientific development.[16]

The second opportunity is the study of discursive change to understand the close relations between competing commercial and technological priorities on the one hand and complex legal problems on the other. Until the 1980s, debates over what software is and how patents can and should be drafted were not merely occasions for lawyers and federal agents to test out their rhetorical flare and doctrinal prowess. They were efforts to establish conceptual underpinnings for the doctrines and policies that framed software rights—a matter that concerned all firms that developed computer programs, regardless of whether they commercialized them. Each conception of the nature of software had the potential to transform the legal frameworks that governed its ownership and to determine which kinds of legal obstacles stood between a firm and its ability to enter the computing industry or retain its market share.

The efforts to govern the country's computing industry and its IP system have provided vital spaces for the emergence of software as a distinct entity. In recent years, scholars have shown that law and politics can trigger transformations in the design and uses of computing technologies and that these technologies can be central to the creation and maintenance of a region's political and technological identity.[17] This mutual influence can unfold at the local and global scales. Even the Internet, despite its stateless appearance, is governed by a complex web of laws and regulations that often vary from one location to the next.[18] A focus on software patenting shows that the political economy of the American computing industry has developed jointly with the long-term relations between the technologies at its core and the country's formal and informal systems for the governance of ownership. The effort to secure software patents has triggered high-stakes negotiations on the nature of computing technologies, the kinds of proprietary rights that firms and users would find acceptable, and the place of law on computing firms' short- and long-term business strategies. These negotiations caused transformations of users' and developers' understanding of what it takes to use and monetize software and of the legal doctrines that sustain the country's IP infrastructure.

This book is an invitation to keep using the study of law as a means of gaining insight into the history of computing. Scholars are continually revising and enriching this history by analyzing the making of expertise and authority at and across computing firms, revealing the long-term impact of the industry's increasingly oppressive gender politics, and uncovering the rich traditions of computer usage, governance, and services at the industry's core.[19] A focus on the long-term interplay among legal and industrial change promises both new ways of inquiring into these familiar themes and entirely new avenues of research. More work on antitrust law is crucial to make sense of the industry's dynamics, especially given Microsoft's history of antitrust entanglements and the parallels between IBM's and AT&T's relationships with the Antitrust Division of the Justice Department.[20] Labor and discrimination law are also very pressing subjects of study, as new research on the gender and race politics of computing has demonstrated the need to scrutinize the systematic inequalities that have developed at the industry's core.[21] In addition, work on environmental history and anthropology suggests that research in global environmental law would be particularly useful to the historiography of information technology.[22]

The histories of computing, law, and business in America are inseparable from one another. Crucial processes in the computing industry's development—from the rise of IBM as the dominant firm among mainframe makers to the commodification of software and the spread of home Internet—were tied to new ways of using IP to carve out markets for new firms and their technologies. These processes involved a very broad range of people who repeatedly negotiated the law of software to advance their own commercial, legal, personal, or bureaucratic interests. This range became even broader when users at homes and universities protested IP protections as unwarranted efforts to establish corporate control and new industries became involved in the legal and legislative efforts that computing firms and industrial research laboratories had normally led. Along the way, all these stakeholders slowly expanded our conceptions of what software is and what it means to make, own, and sell it. They also crystallized, sometimes inadvertently, the deep connections between computer programs and American patent law that have been developing since the end of the Second World War.

Notes

All URLs listed below were active at the time of writing.

INTRODUCTION

1. In the United States today, patents are granted by the Patent and Trademark Office. They are intended to grant these exclusive rights in exchange for a public disclosure of the invention that would allow a person ordinarily skilled in the art to understand and construct the invention. See Steven Haber, "Patents and the Wealth of Nations," *George Mason Law Review* 23:4 (2016): 811–835.

2. Peri Hartman, Jeffrey Bezos, Shel Kaphan, and Joel Spiegel, Method and system for placing a purchase order via a communications network, US Patent 5,960,411, filed September 12, 1997, and issued September 28, 1999.

3. Apple Computers, "Apple Licenses Amazon.com 1-Click Patent and Trademark," press release, September 18, 2000, https://www.apple.com/newsroom/2000/09/18Apple-Licenses-Amazon-com-1-Click-Patent-and-Trademark/; Amazon.com, Inc. v. Barnesandnoble.com, Inc., 1999 U.S. Dist. LEXIS 18660 (W.D. Wash. 1999).

4. Cover, *Time*, December 27, 1999.

5. Jeff Bezos, Secure method for communicating credit card data when placing an order on a non-secure network, US Patent 5,727,163, filed March 39, 1995, and issued March 10, 1998.

6. 35 U.S.C. § 101.

7. Tim O'Reilly to Richard Caley, undated (ca. 2000), http://archive.oreilly.com/pub/a/oreilly/ask_tim/2000/amazon_patent.html.

8. Jeff Bezos, "An Open Letter from Jeff Bezos on the Subject of Patents," March 9, 2000, http://archive.oreilly.com/pub/a/oreilly//news/amazon_patents.html; Free Software Foundation, "Why We Boycott Amazon," ca. 2001, https://www.gnu.org/philosophy/amazon.html.

9. Free Software Foundation, "Why We Boycott Amazon."

10. Tim O'Reilly, "My Conversation with Jeff Bezos," March 2, 2000, http://archive.oreilly.com/pub/a/oreilly/ask_tim/2000/bezos_0300.html.

11. Intellectual property is the field of law that provides legal protection for things such as inventions, creative works, and brands. It includes patents, copyrights, trademarks, trade secrets, and special protections such as those afforded to plants and industrial designs.

12. Fred R. Shapiro, "Origin of the Term Software: Evidence from the JSTOR Electronic Archive," *IEEE Annals of the History of Computing* 22:2 (2000): 69–71.

13. Thomas Haigh, "Software in the 1960s as Concept, Service, and Product," *IEEE Annals of the History of Computing* 24:1 (2002): 5–13.

14. Michael Mahoney, "The History of Computing in the History of Technology," *IEEE Annals of the History of Computing* 10:2 (1988): 121.

15. See Wendy Chun, *Programmed Visions: Software and Memory* (Cambridge, MA: MIT Press, 2014).

16. See Matthew Fuller, ed., *Software Studies: A Lexicon* (Cambridge, MA: MIT Press, 2008).

CHAPTER 1. CODE MADE TANGIBLE, 1945–1954

1. See Richard Hamming, "Mathematics on a Distant Planet," *American Mathematical Monthly* 105:7 (1998): 640–650; Samuel Morgan, "Richard Wesley Hamming (1915–1998)," *Notices of the AMS* 45:8 (1998): 972–977; J. A. N. Lee, "Richard Wesley Hamming," *Computer Pioneers*, https://history.computer.org/pioneers/hamming.html; and "Richard W. Hamming," *Association for Computing Machinery*, http://amturing.acm.org/award_winners/hamming_1000652.cfm. For more on the design of the bomb, see Daniel J. Kevles, *The Physicists: The History of a Scientific Community* (New York: Knopf, 1997); and Richard Rhodes, *The Making of the Atomic Bomb* (New York: Simon and Schuster, 1997).

2. Nicholas Metropolis and E. C. Nelson, "Early Computing at Los Alamos," *IEEE Annals of the History of Computing* 4:4 (1992): 384–357; Hamming, "Mathematics on a Distant Planet," 640. See also Richard Hamming, "You and Your Research," transcript of speech delivered in Morristown, New Jersey, March 7, 1986, archived by the Institutional Archive of the Naval Postgraduate School and available online at http://hdl.handle.net/10945/37504.

3. Metropolis and Nelson, "Early Computing at Los Alamos," 349; Alan B. Carr, "The History of Computing from Punched Cards to Petaflops," *National Security Science*

(Los Alamos, NM, Los Alamos National Laboratory), April 2013, 36. For more on the women who worked as human computers during the Second World War, see Janet Abbate, *Recoding Gender: Women's Participation in Computing* (Cambridge, MA: MIT Press, 2012); David Alan Grier, *When Computers Were Human* (Princeton, NJ: Princeton University Press, 2007); and Jennifer Light, "When Computers Were Women," *Technology and Culture* 40:3 (1999): 455–483. For more on Wanda Hamming, see "Richard W. Hamming," *Association for Computing Machinery*; and "Obituary: Wanda L. Hamming," http://www.legacy.com/obituaries/montereyherald/obituary.aspx?n=wanda-l-hamming&pid=145156509.

4. Carr, "History of Computing," 35–36; Rhodes, *Atomic Bomb*; Kevles, *Physicists*.

5. Metropolis and Nelson, "Early Computing at Los Alamos."

6. Ibid.; Tekla Perry, "Richard W. Feynman," *IEEE Spectrum* 30:5 (1993): 80–82. For Feynman's work at Los Alamos, see Peter Galison, "Feynman's War: Modelling Weapons, Modelling Nature," *Studies in the History and Philosophy of Modern Physics* 29:3 (1998): 391–434; and Perry, "Feynman."

7. Richard Hamming, quoted in Samuel Morgan, "Richard Wesley Hamming," http://www.ams.org/notices/199808/mem-morgan.pdf; "Richard Wesley Hamming," *IEEE Annals of the History of Computing* 20:2 (1998): 60–62.

8. Perry, "Feynman," 80.

9. Richard Hamming, cited in ibid.

10. Ibid.; Morgan, "Hamming"; "Hamming," *Association for Computing Machinery*.

11. Morgan, "Hamming"; "Hamming," *Association for Computing Machinery*.

12. For the M-9, see S. Millman, ed., *A History of Engineering and Science in the Bell System: Communications Sciences (1925–1980)* (Indianapolis, IN: Bell Telephone Laboratories, 1984), 354. This book is part of a series of internal histories that AT&T published in an effort to fend off antitrust prosecution by the federal government. For more on AT&T, see Richard John, *Network Nation: Inventing American Telecommunications* (Cambridge, MA: Harvard University Press, 2015); and John Gertner, *The Idea Factory: Bell Labs and the Age of American Innovation* (New York: Penguin, 2013).

13. J. A. N. Lee, "George Stibitz," *Computer Pioneers,* http://history.computer.org/pioneers/stibitz.html; Paul Ceruzzi, *Reckoners: The Prehistory of the Digital Computer, from Relays to the Stored Program Concept* (Westport, CT: Greenwood Press, 1984).

14. The construction of the Model I required Stibitz to perform some additional theoretical work on the translation into relays of operations in Boolean algebra, a field of mathematical logic in which variables can have only the values "true" or "false." Lee, "George Stibitz"; Ceruzzi, *Reckoners.*

15. Lee, "George Stibitz"; Millman, *History of Engineering and Science in the Bell System: Communications Sciences,* 356–359. See also M. Fagen, ed., *A History of Engineering and Science in the Bell System: National Service in War and Peace (1925–1975)* (Indianapolis, IN: Bell Telephone Laboratories, 1978); S. Millman, ed., *A History of Engineering and Science in the Bell System: Physical Sciences (1925–1980)* (Indianapolis, IN: Bell Telephone Laboratories, 1983); and F. M. Smits, *A History of Engineering and Science in the Bell System: Electronics Technology (1925–1975)* (Indianapolis, IN: Bell Telephone Laboratories, 1985). I am grateful to Sheldon Hochheiser, the archivist at Bell Telephone Laboratories, for helping me grasp the interpretive issues that arise when drawing from these works.

16. George Stibitz, Automatic calculator, US Patent 2,666,579, filed December 26, 1944, and issued January 19, 1954. The Model V was patented in 1954, after an examination procedure that lasted nearly ten years. For more on the Model V, see E. G. Andrews, "Telephone Switching and the Early Bell Laboratories Computers," *Bell Systems Technical Journal* 42:2 (1963): 341–353.

17. Errors could be caused by common physical problems such as faulty relay contacts, open circuitry, or even outside disturbances. Stibitz, Automatic calculator, 1–3. See also "Hamming's Technique of Error Correction Marks 30th Birthday," *Computerworld*, September 8, 1980; and Millman, *History of Engineering and Science in the Bell System: Communications Sciences*, 361–362.

18. Millman, *History of Engineering and Science in the Bell System: Communications Sciences*, 353.

19. The term "Young Turks" was a reference to the Turkish revolutionaries who sought to end the Ottoman Empire's absolute monarchy in the early twentieth century. Hamming quoted in Biographies, "Richard Wesley Hamming," *IEEE Annals of the History of Computing* 20:2 (1998): 61. See also Lee, "Hamming."

20. Hamming quoted in Biographies, "Richard Wesley Hamming"; Richard Hamming, "The Unreasonable Effectiveness of Mathematics," *American Mathematical Monthly* 87:2 (1980): 81–90.

21. Thomas M. Thompson, *From Error-Correcting Codes through Sphere Packings to Simple Groups* (New York: Carus, 1984).

22. These codes are now known as Hamming Codes, and they are probably his best-known contribution to computing after the Second World War. See "Richard W. Hamming: Additional Materials," *Association for Computing Machinery*, http://amturing.acm.org/info/hamming_1000652.cfm

23. Quotations in Thompson, *Error-Correcting Codes*, 25.

24. This interpretation is grounded on Adam Mossoff, "*O'Reilly v. Morse*" (Hoover IP² Working Paper No. 14010, May 2014).

25. As Mossoff notes, the original patent was Samuel Morse, Telegraph signs, US Patent 1,647, issued June 29, 1840, 1. However, the suit focused on a revised and reissued patent: Samuel Morse, Improvement in electro-magnetic telegraphs, US Patent RE117, issued June 13, 1848.

26. Morse, Improvement in electro-magnetic telegraphs, 3.

27. For more on conceptions of invention, see Matthew Jones, *Reckoning with Matter: Calculating Machines, Innovation, and Thinking about Thinking from Pascal to Babbage* (Chicago: University of Chicago Press, 2016); Brad Sherman and Alain Pottage, *Figures of Invention: A History of Modern Patent Law* (New York: Oxford University Press, 2010); Mario Biagioli, "Between Knowledge and Technology: Patenting Methods, Rethinking Materiality," *Anthropological Forum* 22:3 (2012): 285–299; and Catherine Fisk, *Working Knowledge: Employee Innovation and the Rise of Corporate Intellectual Property, 1800–1930* (Chapel Hill: University of North Carolina Press, 2009).

28. Alois Rack, Decoder for pulse code modulation, US Patent 2,514,671, filed September 23, 1947, and issued July 11, 1950; Samuel Saint, Means for airplane approach control, filed December 22, 1944, and issued January 17, 1950; Walter Bacon, Enciphering and deciphering device for secret telegraph systems, US Patent 2,504,621, filed December 3, 1946, and issued April 18, 1950; Frederick Laberty, Combined telephone and paging system, US Patent 2,496,629, filed December 16, 1947, and issued February 7, 1950;

29. Louis Potts, Error detecting code system, US Patent 2,512,038, filed June 7, 1947, and issued June 20, 1950.

30. Thomas Haigh, Mark Priestley, and Crispin Rope, *ENIAC in Action: Making and Remaking the Modern Computing* (Cambridge, MA: MIT Press, 2016); Abbate, *Recoding Gender*; and Light, "When Computers Were Women."

31. Halliburton v. Walker, 146 F.2d 817 (1944); Gerardo Con Díaz, "Computation and Materiality in American Patent Law: The Story of *Halliburton v. Walker*," in preparation.

32. Transcript of Record, Halliburton v. Walker, 329 U.S. 1, 29 (1946).

33. *Halliburton*, 146 F.2d at 821.

34. This paragraph is based on "Application," in Richard Hamming and Bernard Holbrook, Error detecting and correcting system, US Patent 2,552,629, filed January 11, 1950, and issued May 15, 1951, Records of the US Patent and Trademark Office, National Archives, Kansas City.

35. For Holbrook's relationship with Hamming, see Thompson, *Error-Correcting Codes*, 28. For his patents, see Bernard Holbrook, Telephone system, US Patent 2,317,191, filed January 24, 1941, and issued April 20, 1943; Bernard Holbrook and Logan Mason, Call distributing system, US Patent 2,405,214, filed April 10, 1945, and issued August 6, 1946; Bernard Holbrook, Alexis Lundstrom, and William Malthaner, Wind and spot computer, US Patent 2,658,680, filed February 13, 1945, and issued November 10, 1953; and Bernard Holbrook and Alexis Lundstrom, Sight order computer, US Patent 2,658,678, filed February 13, 1945, and issued November 10, 1953.

36. Hamming and Holbrook, Error detecting and correcting system, 13.

37. Ibid.

38. Hamming and Holbrook to Commissioner of Patents, January 10, 1951, US Patent 2,552,629, National Archives, Kansas City.

39. Quotations in Hamming and Holbrook, Error detecting and correcting system, 1, 23.

40. James Patterson, *Grand Expectations: The United States, 1945–1974* (New York: Oxford University Press, 1996), 61–81.

41. Kevles, *Physicists*.

42. Robert Bud, *Penicillin: Triumph and Tragedy* (New York: Oxford University Press, 2009).

43. These numerical estimates are based on the historical and extended-year statistics kept by the US Patent and Trademark Office. Calendar Year Patent Statistics, https://www.PTO.gov/web/offices/ac/ido/oeip/taf/reports.htm#by_hist.

44. This application is found in Appeal 5726, Court of Customs and Patent Appeals, National Archives, Kansas City. For more on Socony-Vacuum, see National Research Council, *Industrial Research Laboratories of the United States, including Consulting Research Laboratories* (Washington, DC: National Academies Press, 1946), 179.

45. "Examiner's Statement," November 17, 1947, in Appeal 5726.

46. Ibid., 34–35.

47. In re Abrams, 188 F.2d 165, 166 (C.C.P.A. 1951).

48. In re Yuan, 188 F.2d 377 (C.C.P.A. 1951).

49. Quoted in Brief for Appellant, 3, Appeal 5776, Court of Customs and Patent Appeals, National Archives, Kansas City; and Application of Shao Wen Yuan, 49, in Appeal 5776.

50. *Yuan*, 188 F.2d.

51. What remains of this chapter is methodologically grounded on the work of historians of science and technology who have shown that patent drafting has its own history. See Kara W. Swanson, "The Emergence of the Professional Patent Practitioner," *Technology and Culture* 50:30 (2009): 519–548; and Kara W. Swanson, "Authoring an Invention: Patent Production in the Nineteenth-Century United States," and William J. Rankin, "The 'Person Skilled in the Art' Is Really Quite Conventional: U.S. Patent Drawings and the Persona of the Inventor, 1870–2005," both in *Making and Unmaking Intellectual Property: Creative Production in Legal and Cultural Perspective*, ed. Mario Biagioli, Peter Jaszi, and Martha Woodmansee (Chicago: University of Chicago Press, 2001).

52. For more on the Bessen-Hunt technique, see James Bessen and Robert Hunt, "An Empirical Look at Software Patents," *Journal of Economics and Management Strategy* 16:1 (2007): 157–189. See also James Bessen and Michael J. Meurer, *Patent Failure: How Judges, Bureaucrats, and Lawyers Put Innovators at Risk* (Princeton, NJ: Princeton University Press, 2008).

53. O'Reilly v. Morse, 56 U.S. 62 (1856).

54. Thomas Swafford, Correlation of seismic signals, US Patent 2,907,400, filed May 12, 1954, and issued October 6, 1959, 6.

55. Ibid., 3.

56. See, e.g., Frank Motte, Matrix translator, US Patent 2,856,597, filed July 26, 1956, and issued October 14, 1958; David Hagelbarger, Continuous digital error correcting system, US Patent 2,956,124, filed May 1, 1958, and issued October 11, 1960; Robert Taylor and James Volgenson, Error-checking circuit for data transmission system, US Patent 3,140,463, filed November 22, 1960, and issued July 7, 1960. For the computerization of telephony systems, see Millman, *History of Engineering and Science in the Bell System: Communications Sciences.*

57. James Woodbury, Binary decoder, US Patent 2,814,437, filed July 30, 1956, and issued November 26, 1957.

58. "Patent Application," 1, File Wrapper for Patent 2,814,437, Records of the Patent and Trademark Office, RG 241, National Archives, Kansas City.

59. Patents of this kind assigned to major firms like IBM, RCA, and GE include Andrew Reynolds, Error detection and correction system, US Patent 3,024,992, filed March 16, 1959, and issued March 13, 1962; James McDonnell, Data processing system memory controls, US Patent 2,968,027, filed August 29, 1958, and issued January 10, 1961; Constantin Melas, Error correcting system, US Patent 3,213,426, filed September 25, 1959, and issued October 19, 1965; Joseph Brustman, Data translating system, US Patent 2,702,380, filed December 24, 1953, and issued February 15, 1955; Roger Greenhalgh, Data transfer and translating system, US Patent 2,872,666, filed December 21, 1955, and issued February 3, 1959; and Andrew Reynolds, Decimal to binary translators, US Patent 3,021,065, filed March 16, 1959, and issued February 13, 1962.

60. Frederick Brooks and Dura Sweeney, Program interrupt system, US Patent 3,048,332, filed December 9, 1957, and issued August 7, 1962.

61. Brustman, Data translating system; Greenhalgh, Data transfer and translating system; Reynolds, Decimal to binary translators.

62. Brustman, Data translating system, 2.

63. Martin Campbell-Kelly and Daniel D. Garcia-Swartz, *From Mainframes to Smartphones: A History of the International Computer Industry* (Cambridge, MA: Harvard University Press, 2015); Lars Heide, *Punched Card Systems and the Early Information Explosion, 1880–1945* (Baltimore: Johns Hopkins University Press, 2009).

64. Campbell-Kelly and Garcia-Swartz, *From Mainframes to Smartphones*, 42–44. For the global reach of BTM's competitive efforts, see Marie Hicks, *Programmed Inequality: How Britain Discarded Women Technologists and Lost Its Edge in Computing* (Cambridge, MA: MIT Press, 2017), 231–233.

65. Oral History of Raymond Bird, performed by Thomas Lean, British Library, on January 25, 2010, http://sounds.bl.uk/Oral-history/Science/021M-C1379X0004XX-0001V0.

66. Ibid.; "Britain's First Mass-Produced Business Computer," The National Museum of Computing, http://www.tnmoc.org/news/news-releases/britains-first-mass-produced-business-computer; Raymond Bird, "BTM's First Steps into Computing," *Resurrection: The Bulletin of the Computer Conservation Society* 22 (1999), http://www.computercon servationsociety.org/resurrection/res22.htm#c.

67. See, e.g., Harold Keen, Interlocking electromagnetic relay, US Patent 2,694,758, filed March 29, 1951, and issued November 16, 1954; Vivian Ivor, Electrical contact device, US Patent 2,688,665, filed February 21, 1952, and issued September 7, 1954; William Hill, Electrical impulse generator, US Patent 2,782,304, filed January 13, 1953, and issued February 19, 1957.

68. Raymond Bird, Binary adder, US Patent 2,861,741, filed October 8, 1953, and issued November 25, 1958; Raymond Bird, Data translating apparatus, US Patent 2,970,765, filed November 4, 1952, and issued February 7, 1961.

69. Bird, Data translating apparatus, 1.

70. Examiner's Letter from L. M. Andrews to Frederick Hane, September 22, 1954, File Wrapper for Patent 2,970,765, Records of the Patent and Trademark Office, RG 241, National Archives, Kansas City.

71. "Application of Raymond Bird," File Wrapper for Patent 2,970,765. This claim is a classic example of what lawyers sometimes call functional claiming—a form of claiming an invention allowed by section 112 of the Patent Act. This section allows inventors to claim "a means or step for performing a specified function." In other words, it allows inventors to claim an invention, not by what it is, but by what it does. 35 U.S.C. § 112(f).

72. For patents of this kind filed in the 1960s and assigned to IBM, RCA, and Texas Instruments, see, respectively, William McDermid, Harold Petersen, and Shelton Glenmore, Unambiguous identification systems, US Patent 3,167,743, filed December 19, 1960, and issued January 26, 1965; Morton Lewin, Ordered retrieval of information stored in a tag-addressed memory, US Patent 3,329,937, filed March 28, 1962, and issued July 4, 1967; and John Burg and William Schneider, Multi-point, multi-channel linear processing of seismic data, US Patent 3,284,763, filed October 30, 1962, and issued November 8, 1966. See Gerardo Con Díaz, "The Long History of Software Patenting in the United States" (Hoover IP² Working Paper presented at "What Patents Really Do: Historical Perspectives on Current Debates," Stanford University, May 17, 2018).

73. See, e.g., Lucas Pun, Fire control systems, US Patent 3,339,457, filed August 18, 1964, and issued September 5, 1967.

CHAPTER 2. FROM ANTITRUST TO PATENT LAW AT IBM, 1950–1966

1. Emerson Pugh, *Building IBM: Shaping an Industry and Its Technology* (Cambridge, MA: MIT Press, 2009). For more on the business history of IBM, see James Cortada, *IBM: The Rise and Fall and Reinvention of a Global Icon* (Cambridge, MA: MIT Press, 2019). *Software Rights* was in production by the time *IBM* was published.

2. Steven W. Usselman, "Public Policies, Private Platforms: Antitrust and America Computing," in *Information Technology Policy: An International History*, ed. Richard Coopey (New York: Oxford University Press, 2008), 97–120; Steven W. Usselman, "Unbundling IBM: Antitrust and the Incentives to Innovation in American Computing," in *The Challenge of Remaining Innovative: Insights from Twentieth-Century American Business*, ed. Sally H. Clarke, Naomi R. Lamoreaux, and Steven W. Usselman (Stanford, CA: Stanford University Press, 2009), 249–279.

3. IBM Corp. v. United States, 298 U.S. 131 (1936).

4. Usselman, "Public Policies, Private Platforms."

5. This relation is a good example of what STS scholars know as coproduction. See Sheila Jasanoff, ed., *States of Knowledge: The Co-Production of Science and the Social Order* (New York: Routledge, 2004).

6. Written Deposition of Cuthbert Hurd, *U.S. v. IBM*, Tr. 86338, box 17, folder "Page 86272–86765, 3–5 January 1979," Computer & Communications Industry Association IBM antitrust trial records (Accession 1912), Hagley Museum and Library, Wilmington, Delaware. See Pugh, *Building IBM*, 166–168; "Mancke Testimony," DX 14971, *U.S. v. IBM*, Computer and Communications Industry Association, Antitrust Records (CBI 13), Charles Babbage Institute, University of Minnesota, Minneapolis (further references to the transcript of record of *U.S. v. IBM* are to this archive); and Franklin M. Fisher, James W. McKie, and Richard B. Mancke, *IBM and the U.S. Data Processing Industry: An Economic History* (New York: Praeger, 1983), 12–15.

7. Written Deposition of Hurd, Tr. 86338–86339.

8. Thomas J. Watson and Peter Petre, *Father, Son and Co.: My Life at IBM and Beyond* (New York: Bantam Books: 2000); J. A. N. Lee, "James Birkenstock," *Computer Pioneers,* http://history.computer.org/pioneers/birkenstock.html.

9. Written Deposition of Hurd, Tr. 86309–86315. See also Oral history interview with Cuthbert Corwin Hurd (1995), Charles Babbage Institute, https://conservancy.umn.edu/handle/11299/107371; Oral history interview with Cuthbert Corwin Hurd (1994), Charles Babbage Institute, https://conservancy.umn.edu/handle/11299/107370; and Oral history interview with Cuthbert Corwin Hurd (1981), Charles Babbage Institute, https://conservancy.umn.edu/handle/11299/107368.

10. Written Deposition of Hurd, Tr. 86339; Pugh, *Building IBM*, 166.

11. Written Deposition of Hurd, Tr. 86340–86345; Cross Examination of Hurd, Tr. 87670–87672.

12. Direct Examination of Hurd, Tr. 86345–86346; Cross Examination of Hurd, Tr. 87672–87674; "Mancke Testimony," 34–35.

13. Pugh, *Building IBM*.

14. Ibid.; Usselman, "Unbundling IBM"; Written Deposition of Hurd, Tr. 86416–86418; "Mancke Testimony," 63–65.

15. Jeffrey R. Yost, *Making IT Work: A History of the Computer Services Industry* (Cambridge, MA: MIT Press, 2017).

16. "U.S. Files Anti-Trust Suit against I.B.M.; Company Denies Charge," *Wall Street Journal*, June 22, 1952.

17. These data are found in Jonathan Barnett, "The Great Patent Grab" (Hoover IP² Working Paper presented at "What Patents Really Do: Historical Perspectives on Current Debates," Stanford University, May 17, 2018).

18. Thurman Arnold, *Fair Fights and Foul: A Dissenting Lawyer's Life* (New York: Harcourt Brace, 1951); Wyatt Wells, *Antitrust and the Formation of the Postwar World* (New York: Columbia University Press, 2003).

19. Barnett, "Great Patent Grab."

20. Paul E. Ceruzzi, *A History of Modern Computing*, 2nd ed. (Cambridge, MA: MIT Press, 2003), 54–57. See also "Mancke Testimony," 262.

21. Arthur Norberg, *Computers and Commerce: A Study of Technology and Management at Eckert-Mauchly Computer Company, Engineering Research Associates, and Remington Rand, 1946–1957* (Cambridge, MA: MIT Press, 2005).

22. Ibid.; A. W. Fisher and J. L. McKenney, "The Development of the ERMA Banking System: Lessons from History," *IEEE Annals of the History of Computing* 15:1 (1993): 44–57.

23. Martin Campbell-Kelly, *From Airline Reservations to Sonic the Hedgehog: A History of the Software Industry* (Cambridge, MA: MIT Press, 2003), 49.

24. Ibid.

25. Atsushi Akera, "Voluntarism and the Fruits of Collaboration: The IBM User Group, SHARE," *Technology and Culture* 42:4 (2001): 710–736.

26. Deposition of Martin Goetz, DX 1096, quoted in "Mancke Testimony," 67.

27. Ibid.

28. Deposition of Larry Welke, Tr. 19225, quoted in "Mancke Testimony," 64–65.

29. Usselman, "Unbundling IBM," 256–257.

30. United States v. Shoe Machinery Corp., 110 F. Supp. 295 (1953).

31. Ibid., 297.

32. Anthony Lewis, "AT&T Settles Antitrust Case; Shares Patents," *New York Times*, January 25, 1956.

33. Usselman, "Unbundling IBM," 252–253.

34. Usselman, "Public Policies, Private Platforms."

35. Consent Decree, Sections I–VIII; Department of Justice, "Justice Department Agrees to Terminate Last Provisions of IBM Consent Decree in Stages Ending 5 Years from Today," press release, July 2, 1996.

36. Ibid. For more on the SBC, see Yost, *Making IT Work*.

37. Usselman, "Unbundling IBM"; Usselman, "Public Policies, Private Platforms"; Yost, *Making IT Work*.

38. Consent Decree, Section XI.

39. Ibid.

40. Ibid.

41. Oral history of James Birkenstock (1980), 18, Charles Babbage Institute, https://conservancy.umn.edu/handle/11299/107118.

42. Ibid.

43. Ibid.

44. Thomas Watson to K. N. Davis, "Pricing and Profit," memorandum, November 11, 1963, as disclosed in Tr. 16286. See also Martin Campbell-Kelly et al., *Computer: A History of the Information Machine*, 3rd ed. (Boulder, CO: Westview Press, 2013), 124–130.

45. Tr. 16288.

46. Campbell-Kelly et al., *Computer*.

47. T. A. Wise, "IBM's $5,000,000,000 Gamble," *Fortune*, September 1966, 118.

48. Ibid.

49. T. V. Learson, quoted in "Mancke Testimony," 279.

50. P. W. Knaplund to D. R. Futh, April 18, 1965, PX1439.

51. "DP Advertising Plans—1965," Memorandum from C. J. Jenks to C. C. Hollister, December 10, 1964, Tr. 16292.

52. Tr. 16293.

53. Ibid.

54. "Memorandum," November 29, 1965, PX5254, Richard DeLamarter Collection of Antitrust Records, Hagley Museum and Library.

55. Ibid.

56. Galambos and Pratt, *Rise of the Corporate Commonwealth*, 199.

57. Ceruzzi, *History of Modern Computing*, 175–206.

58. Executive Order, April 9, 1965, 1, Accession Number 241-83-44, box 1, folder PCPS, National Archives, College Park, MD.

59. Ibid., 2.

60. "President Announces Commission Membership," *Patent Office Employee Bulletin* 121 (August 1965): 1, 5.

61. Harry Ransom to the Members of the Commission, July 8, 1966, Accession Number 241-83-44, box 1, folder PCPS, National Archives, College Park, MD.

62. The other members were the patent attorney Sidney Neuman; Hewlett-Packard's vice president of research and development, Bernard Oliver; the president of the Carnegie Institute of Technology, Horton Guyford Stever; and the president of Litton Industries, Charles Thornton. The secretary of state (Dean Rusk) and the director of the Office of Science and Technology (Donald Hornig) would sit with the commission as observers.

63. "The Report of the President's Commission," *Bulletin of the New York Patent Law Association* 6:4 (1967): 1–5.

64. Letter from Frank Cacciapaglia, June 29, 1966, Accession Number 241-83-44, box 5, National Archives, College Park, MD.

65. Carl Ruoff, Magnetic checking device, US Patent 3,177,468, filed December 21, 1960, and issued April 6, 1965; Mensahe Teitelbaum and William Henn, Carrier signal attenuation, US Patent 3,192,374, filed September 30, 1960, and issued June 29, 1965; Chester Stern, Automatic price computation, US Patent 3,235,713, filed April 2, 1959, and issued February 15, 1966; James Moore, Electrical signal modifying circuits, US Patent 3,235,719, filed December 15, 1959, and issued February 15, 1966.

66. Malcolm A. Morrison to Harry Huntt Ransom, June 3, 1966, Accession Number 241-83-44, box 5, National Archives, College Park, MD.

67. Ibid., 3.

68. Ibid., 5.

69. Ibid., 5, 6.
70. Ibid., 6.
71. Ibid., 11.
72. Ibid.
73. Ibid., 12.
74. Presentation by Malcolm A. Morrison, Supervisory Patent Examiner for Group 230, August 12, 1966, Accession Number 241-83-44, box 5, National Archives, College Park, MD.
75. The former echoed the British Patent Office's practice, which was predicated on the view that a process carried out by a computer is either a new process altogether or a new use of a known machine.
76. Presentation by Morrison, August 12, 1966.
77. British Board of Trade, "Patentability of Computer Programs," December 14, 1965, Accession Number 241-83-44, box 2, folder "#35-Computer Programming," National Archives, College Park, MD.
78. For Bird's British patents, see Raymond Bird, Improvements in or relating to electronic apparatus for translating a number from a first to a second radix of notation, GB Patent 745,907, issued October 2, 1953; Raymond Bird, Improvements in or relating to electronic calculating machines, GB Patent 734,253, issued October 8, 1953; Raymond Bird, Improvements in or relating to electronic digital calculating equipment, GB Patent 839,242, issued August 17, 1956; and Raymond Bird, Improvements in or relating to data storage equipment, GP Patent 839,243, issued August 17, 1956.
79. See note 78, above.
80. A. Donald Messenheimer, "Analysis of Certain Provisions of the Atomic Energy Act of 1954 Pertaining to Problems of Businessmen Attempting to Enter the Nucleonics Field," *American University Law Review* 6 (1957): 91–104.
81. A. Donald Messenheimer, Statement to the President's Commission on the Patent System Regarding Computer Programs, August 12, 1966, Accession Number 241-83-44, box 5, National Archives, College Park, MD.
82. Ibid., 3.
83. Ibid., 4. See also Nathan Ensmenger, *The Computer Boys Take Over: Computers, Programmers, and the Politics of Technical Expertise* (Cambridge, MA: MIT Press, 2010).
84. Norman Zachary, Presentation to the President's Commission on Patents, August 12, 1966, Accession Number 241-83-44, box 5, National Archives, College Park, MD.
85. "Zachary, Norman," in *American Men and Women of Science: A Biographical Directory of Today's Leaders in Physical, Biological, and Related Sciences*, ed. Andrea Kovacs Henderson, 29th ed., vol. 7 (Detroit, MI: Gale, 2011), 1032.
86. Zachary, Presentation, August 12, 1966.
87. Ibid., 3.
88. Ibid., 1.
89. Ibid.
90. Ibid.
91. Ibid., 4.
92. Ibid., 2.
93. Ibid., 3.
94. Ibid.

95. This was, of course, an introduction of novelty into matters of patent-eligibility. Normally, patent-eligibility has been a matter that examiners considered before moving on to the three other criteria for eligibility (novelty, usefulness, and nonobviousness). However, from the 1960s onward, people such as Zachary would propose introductions of the three criteria into the assessment of patent-eligibility. Even courts would perform this unusual blend of patent-eligibility requirements, most often in conjunction with their effort to determine whether the use of a computer to automate a mental process constituted a bar of eligibility.

96. Zachary, Presentation, August 12, 1966, 4.

97. Ibid., 5.

98. The main counterargument he had heard against this point was that patents for programs were needed in order to encourage investment in programming development. He wholeheartedly rejected this argument, since he found it difficult to believe that having more patents would have enabled the "field of programming" to grow any more rapidly than it did in their absence.

99. Zachary, Presentation, August 12, 1966, 5.

100. "Edward Brenner," in *The Law of Software: 1968 Proceedings*, ed. Irving Kayton (Washington, DC: Computers-in-Law Institute, 1968), E-8.

101. Martin Goetz, Sorting system, US Patent 3,380,029, filed April 9, 1965, and issued April 23, 1968; Martin Goetz, Automatic system for constructing and recording display charts, US Patent 3,533,086, filed December 24, 1968, continuing application 512,113, filed December 7, 1965, and issued October 6, 1970.

102. US Patent Office, "Guidelines to Examination of Programs," *Official Gazette of the United States Patent Office* 829:3 (1966): 866.

103. Ibid.

104. Ibid., 865.

105. James Essinger, *Jacquard's Web: How a Hand-Loom Led to the Birth of the Information Age* (Oxford: Oxford University Press, 2004).

106. US Patent Office, "Guidelines to Examination of Programs," 865.

107. T. V. Learson, address at the Patent Attorney's Conference, August 2, 1966, PX 1847, Richard DeLamarter Collection of Antitrust Records, Hagley Museum and Library.

108. Ibid.

109. This paragraph is based on Dewey J. Cunningham to Simon H. Rifkind, September 14, 1966, Accession Number 241-83-44, National Archives, College Park, MD.

110. Attachment in ibid.

111. Ibid.

112. Ibid.

113. Commission on the Patent System, *To Promote the Progress of Useful Arts: Report of the President's Commission on the Patent System* (Washington, DC: GPO, 1967), 1.

114. Ibid., 62–65.

115. Paris Convention for the Protection of Industrial Property (amended on September 28, 1979), World Intellectual Property Organization, http://www.wipo.int/wipolex/en/treaties/text.jsp?file_id=288514.

116. This paragraph is based on Commission on the Patent System, *To Promote the Progress of Useful Arts*, 20.

CHAPTER 3. THE MYTH OF THE NON-MACHINE, 1964–1968

1. See Jeffrey R. Yost, *Making IT Work: A History of the Computer Services Industry* (Cambridge, MA: MIT Press, 2017).

2. This categorization is based on Martin Campbell-Kelly et al., *Computer: A History of the Information Machine*, 3rd ed. (Boulder, CO: Westview Press, 2013), 176–178.

3. Ibid., 176, 50–53; Franklin M. Fisher, James W. McKie, and Richard B. Mancke, *IBM and the U.S. Data Processing Industry: An Economic History* (New York: Praeger, 1983), 322.

4. Direct Examination of Larry Welke, Tr. 17083, cited in Fisher, McKie, and Mancke, *IBM and the U.S. Data Processing Industry*, 322.

5. Larry Welke, cited in Martin Campbell-Kelly, *From Airline Reservations to Sonic the Hedgehog: A History of the Software Industry* (Cambridge, MA: MIT Press, 2003), 50. See also Campbell-Kelly et al., *Computer*, 177.

6. Martin Goetz, "Memoirs of a Software Pioneer: Part 1," *IEEE Annals of the History of Computing* 24:1 (2002): 43–56; Oral history of Martin A. Goetz (1996), Computer History Museum, http://archive.computerhistory.org/resources/text/Oral_History/Goetz_Martin/Goetz_Martin_2.oral_history.1996.102658240.pdf; Oral history of Martin A. Goetz (1985), Computer History Museum, http://archive.computerhistory.org/resources/text/Oral_History/Goetz_Martin/Goetz_Martin_1.oral_history.1985.102658239.pdf; Oral history interview with Martin Goetz (2002), Charles Babbage Institute, University of Minnesota, Minneapolis, https://conservancy.umn.edu/handle/11299/107328.

7. Information in this paragraph draws on sources in the previous note.

8. Herbert R. Koller, "Preface," in *AFIPS Conference Proceedings,* Volume 25, *1964 Spring Joint Computer Conference* (Baltimore: Spartan Books, 1964).

9. Goetz, "Memoirs of a Software Pioneer, Part 1," 50.

10. Biographical information from Software Protection Workshop 1968, E-7.

11. Conference Program, 1964 Spring Joint Computer Conference, partially provided in electronic format to me by Marty Goetz.

12. Morton C. Jacobs, "Patent Protection of Computer Programs," *Journal of the Patent and Trademark Office Society* 47 (1965): 7.

13. Ibid., 8.

14. Goetz, "Memoirs of a Software Pioneer, Part 1."

15. Campbell-Kelly, *From Airline Reservations to Sonic the Hedgehog*, 71–72.

16. Oral history interview with Walter Bauer (1983), Charles Babbage Institute, https://conservancy.umn.edu/handle/11299/107108.

17. Ibid., 16.

18. Frederick Booth, High speed printer, US Patent 3,087,421, filed May 1, 1961, and issued April 30, 1963; Gale Jallen, Linear motors, US Patent 3,130,331, filed June 26, 1961, and issued April 21, 1964; Wallace Koskie, Transducer, US Patent 3,170,149; Ralph Pulka-break, Transducer, US Patent 3,158,847, filed March 14, 1962, and issued November 24, 1964.

19. Oral history interview with Walter Bauer (1983), 48; interview of Martin Goetz by Gerardo Con Díaz, October 23, 2017, Teaneck, NJ, audio recording in my possession.

20. Oral history interview with Bauer; interview of Goetz.

21. Oral history interview with Bauer; interview of Goetz.

22. Martin Goetz, Sorting system, US Patent Application 3,380,029, filed April 9, 1965, and issued April 23, 1968.

23. J. A. N. Lee, "Isaac L. Auerbach," *Computer Pioneers*, https://history.computer.org/pioneers/auerbach.html.

24. International Federation for Information Processing, *Information Processing, 1965: Proceedings of IFIP Congress 65* (Washington, DC: Spartan Books, 1965), iv–v.

25. Ibid., 532.

26. Martin Campbell-Kelly and Daniel D. Garcia-Swartz, *From Mainframes to Smartphones: A History of the International Computer Industry* (Cambridge, MA: Harvard University Press, 2015), 42–44; Martin Campbell-Kelly, *ICL: A Business and Technical History* (Oxford: Oxford University Press, 1990).

27. Marie Hicks, *Programmed Inequality: How Britain Discarded Women Technologists and Lost Its Edge in Computing* (Cambridge, MA: MIT Press, 2017), 100.

28. Rene D. Tegtmeyer, "The Patent Cooperation Treaty," *Mississippi Law Journal* 42:2 (1971): 160–164.

29. International Federation for Information Processing, *Information Processing, 1965*, 532.

30. Ibid., 533.

31. Ibid., 533–534.

32. "Computer Program Copyrighted for First Time," *New York Times*, May 8, 1964.

33. International Federation for Information Processing, *Information Processing, 1965*, 51.

34. Office of Technology Assessment, *Finding a Balance: Computer Software, Intellectual Property and the Challenge of Technological Change* (Washington, DC: GPO, 1992), 66.

35. The programs were named "Recomp II program" and "SCOPAC, PROG. 63." Banzhaf was not the first person to try securing copyright protection for a computer program; North American Aviation had submitted two programs in 1961, and the company was awaiting a response when Banzhaf submitted his two programs. What distinguished Banzhaf's programs from these predecessors was not just that his were the first two programs to be registered, but also that they were born out of his desire to test the limits of the law. Announced in *Catalog of Copyright Entries,* 3rd Ser., vol. 18, pt. 1, no. 1, *Books and Pamphlets: Including Serials and Contributions to Periodicals, January–June 1964* (Washington, DC: Library of Congress, Copyright Office, 1964), 634.

36. "Computer Program Copyrighted for First Time."

37. Ibid.

38. Berne Convention for the Protection of Literary and Artistic Works (amended September 28, 1979), World Intellectual Property Organization, http://www.wipo.int/wipolex/en/treaties/text.jsp?file_id=283698.

39. International Federation for Information Processing, *Information Processing, 1965*, 534–535.

40. Ibid.

41. Applied Data Research, "Summary of Autoflow COMPUTER DOCUMENTATION SYSTEM," box 1, folder 13, Applied Data Research, Software Products Division Records (CBI 154), Charles Babbage Institute (hereafter cited as CBI 154).

42. John Boothe to Applied Data Research, July 7, 1967, box 1, folder 14, CBI 154.

43. Applied Data Research, "Summary of Autoflow COMPUTER DOCUMENTATION SYSTEM."

44. Morton Jacobs, In the United States Patent Office, Application for Letters Patent, 1, box 28, folder 3, CBI 154.

45. Ibid., 2.

46. Ibid., 18.

47. Ibid., 6.

48. Martin Goetz, Automatic system for constructing and recording display charts, US Patent 3,533,086, filed December 24, 1968, continuing application 512,113, filed December 7, 1965, and issued October 6, 1970.

49. Patents sometimes describe a means of obtaining the invention being protected. For instance, a patent for a chemical invention may show how to synthesize the specific substance that a chemist had invented. Three years later, at the 1968 Software Protection Workshop, Jacobs would suggest that attorneys in the software industry would benefit from adopting this strategy. Morton C. Jacobs, "Patentable Machines—Systems Embodiable Either in Software or Hardware," in *The Law of Software: 1968 Proceedings*, ed. Irvin Kayton (Washington, DC: Computers-in-Law Institute, 1968), B-77–B-93.

50. Morton Jacobs to Burke Marshall, August 16, 1967, box 1, folder 14, CBI 154.

51. Ibid.; interview of Goetz.

52. Jacobs to Marshall, August 16, 1967.

53. Ibid.

54. Ibid.

55. Marshall to Jacobs, September 21, 1967, box 1, folder 14, CBI 154.

56. Jacobs to Martin Goetz, September 22, 1967, in ibid.

57. Jacobs to Burke, October 4, 1967, in ibid.

58. Jacobs to Goetz, January 11, 1968, in ibid.

59. Donald Turner to Jacobs, October 9, 1967, in ibid.

60. Donald Turner, DX 9110, quoted in Fisher, McKie, and Mancke, *IBM and the U.S. Data Processing Industry*, 323–324.

61. "Statement by the President on Release of the Report of the Commission on the Patent System," Accession Number 241-83-44, Carton 7, National Archives, College Park, MD.

62. The White House Message on the Patent System, February 3, 1967, 7, in ibid.

63. Ibid., 8.

64. Ibid., 10.

65. Ibid., 8.

66. Patent Law Revision, S.2, S.1042, S.1377, S.1691, Hearings Before the Subcommittee on Patents, Trademarks, and Copyrights of the Committee on the Judiciary, U.S. Senate, 9th Cong., 1st Sess., May 17 and 18, 1967.

67. Ibid., 9.

68. Ibid., 137.

69. Ibid., 394.

70. Ibid., 743.

71. Ibid., 454.

72. Ibid., 461.

73. Ibid.

74. Ibid., 616.

75. Ibid., 181.

76. Ibid., 259, 262. The Cleveland Patent Law Association aligned with this view; ibid., 699.

77. Ibid., 307.

78. Ibid., 516.

79. Ibid., 533.

80. Ibid.

81. Ibid., 751.

82. Ibid.

83. Ibid., 753.

84. Ibid., 6.

85. Goetz, Sorting system.

86. "First Patent Is Issued for Software, Full Implications Are Not Yet Known," *Computerworld*, June 19, 1968, 1, 2.

87. Richard E. Kurtz, "Examples of Inventions Embodying Software, Types of Disclosures and Claims," in *Software Protection by Trade Secret, Contract, Patent: Law, Practice, and Forms* (Washington, DC: Patent Resources Group, 1969), 160–191.

88. Ibid.

89. Obtaining reliable historical data on the hundreds of software contracting firms that developed in the late 1960s is nearly impossible, especially because most of those firms left no historical records on which we can rely. See Campbell-Kelly, *From Airline Reservations to Sonic the Hedgehog*.

90. Ibid., 103.

91. John A. Postley, "Mark IV: Evolution of the Software Product, A Memoir," *IEEE Annals of the History of Computing* 20:1 (1998): 43–50.

92. Richard Forman and Francis Wagner, *Fulfilling the Computer's Promise: The History of Informatics, 1962–1982,* vol. 1 (N.p.: Informatics General Corporation, 1985), chapter 9, copy in Computer History Museum, Mountain View, CA, Lot Number X5964.2011.

93. Ibid.

94. John Postley, Herb Jacobson, and Fred Braddock, Data processing system and process, CA Patent 937,331, issued November 20, 1973; John Postley, Herb Jacobson, and Fred Braddock, Data processing system and process, CA Patent 937,331, issued November 20, 1973; John Postley, Herb Jacobson, and Fred Braddock, Digital computers, GB Patent 1,290,889, filed May 23, 1969, and issued November 10, 1969.

95. Kayton, *Law of Software: 1968 Proceedings.*

96. Ibid.

97. John H. Banzhaf III, "Copyright Protection for Computer Programs," in Kayton, *Law of Software: 1968 Proceedings*, C-33–C-34.

98. George D. Cary, "Registrability of Computer Programs," in Kayton, *Law of Software: 1968 Proceedings*, C-18.

99. Ibid., 22.

100. Jacobs, "Patentable Machines."

101. Ibid., B-77.

102. Ibid., B-84.
103. Ibid., B-78.
104. Edward Brenner, "The Future of Computer Programs in the United States," in Kayton, *Law of Software: 1968 Proceedings*, B2.
105. Ibid.
106. Ibid.
107. Ibid., B-3.
108. Ibid., B-2.
109. Ibid., B-4.
110. David Bender, "Single Pricing for Hardware and Software," in Kayton, *Law of Software: 1968 Proceedings*, D-1–D-23.

CHAPTER 4. ANTITRUST LAW AND SOFTWARE SALES, 1965–1971

1. Lawrence Welke, "Founding the ICP Directories," *IEEE Annals of the History of Computing* 24:1 (2002): 85–89.
2. Oral history interview with Lawrence Welke (2002), Charles Babbage Institute, University of Minnesota, Minneapolis, https://conservancy.umn.edu/handle/11299/107708.
3. Jeffery R. Yost, *Making IT Work: A History of the Computer Services Industry* (Cambridge, MA: MIT Press, 2017), 126.
4. Ibid.; Devin Kennedy, "The Machine in the Market: Computers and the Infrastructure of Price at the New York Stock Exchange, 1965–1975," *Social Studies of Science* 47:6 (2017): 888–917.
5. Welke, "Founding the ICP Directories."
6. Larry Welke, "How the ICP Directory Began," 1998, Corporate Histories Collection, Computer History Museum, Mountain View, CA, http://corphist.computerhistory.org/corphist/view.php?s=stories&id=376.
7. Ibid.
8. See, e.g., Oral History of Lawrence A. Welke (1986), Computer History Museum, http://archive.computerhistory.org/resources/text/Oral_History/Welke_Lawrence/Welke_Lawrence_1.oral_history.1986.102658249.pdf; Oral History of Lawrence A. Welke (1995, 1996), Computer History Museum, http://archive.computerhistory.org/resources/text/Oral_History/Welke_Lawrence/Welke_Lawrence_2.oral_history.1995-96.102658258.pdf; and Luanne Johnson, "Obituary of Lawrence A. Welke," *IEEE Annals of the History of Computing* 34:4 (2012): 83–85.
9. This paragraph is based on Steven W. Usselman, "Public Policies, Private Platforms: Antitrust and America Computing," in *Information Technology Policy: An International History*, ed. Richard Coopey (New York: Oxford University Press, 2008), 108–109. See also Steven W. Usselman, "Unbundling IBM: Antitrust and the Incentives to Innovation in American Computing," in *The Challenge of Remaining Innovative: Insights from Twentieth-Century American Business*, ed. Sally H. Clarke, Naomi R. Lamoreaux, and Steven W. Usselman (Stanford, CA: Stanford University Press, 2009), 249–279; and Franklin M. Fisher, James W. McKie, and Richard B. Mancke, *IBM and the U.S. Data Processing Industry: An Economic History* (New York: Praeger, 1983). Usselman's analysis of unbundling is further enriched and expanded in James Cortada, *IBM: The Rise and Fall and Reinvention of a Global Icon* (Cambridge, MA: MIT Press, 2019).

10. See, e.g., Nathan Ensmenger, *The Computer Boys Take Over: Computers, Programmers, and the Politics of Technical Expertise* (Cambridge, MA: MIT Press, 2010). See also Fred Brooks, *The Mythical Man-Month: Essays in Software Engineering* (New York: Addison-Wesley, 1975).

11. Introduction of Contributed Program Library, A. E. Brown to F. T. Cary, memorandum, January 15, 1965, *U.S. v. IBM*, Tr. 16216–16220. In this and all other references to the transcript of record of *U.S. v. IBM*, the references are directed at the Computer and Communications Industry Association, Antitrust Records (CBI 13), Charles Babbage Institute.

12. Ibid.

13. This paragraph is based on Introduction of Sale of Programs as Individual Packages, R. A. Reichart to R. S. Jackson, memorandum, February 16, 1966, *U.S. v. IBM*, Tr. 16228.

14. Yost, *Making IT Work*.

15. T. C. Papes to Frank Cary and John Opel, August 16, 1966, PX1683. In this and all references to exhibits for *U.S. v. IBM*, all references are directed at Richard Thomas deLamarter collection of IBM antitrust suit records (Accession 1980), Hagley Museum and Library, Wilmington, Delaware.

16. A. J. McGill to T. V. Learson, memorandum, October 18, 1966, *U.S. v. IBM*, Tr. 16270.

17. Harry Anderson, "One Staff, One Software Package," *Computerworld*, July 21, 1972, 5; Morris Collen and Marion J. Ball, eds., *The History of Medical Informatics in the United States* (New York: Springer, 2015).

18. McGill to Learson, October 18, 1966.

19. D. M. Sturges to H. L. Kavetas, memorandum, November 21, 1966, *U.S. v. IBM*, Tr. 16268.

20. Data Processing Group, "1967–1968 Operating Budget," PX4286.

21. Watts Humphrey, "Software Unbundling: A Personal Perspective," in *The IBM Century: Creating the IT Revolution*, ed. Jeffrey R. Yost (Piscataway, NJ: IEEE Computer Society, 2011), 202.

22. Sturges to R. L. Degnan, "Sale of Type II Programs—Test Case," memorandum, December 16, 1966, PX1964, transcribed at Tr. 16275.

23. A. W. Jensen to Degnan, "Sale of Type II Programming Systems," memorandum, January 6, 1967, PX197.

24. H. Bartow Farr to P. W. Knaplund, March 29, 1967, PX5272, transcribed and reproduced in full at Tr. 62919.

25. Richard Whalen to W. P. Graham, memorandum, May 2, 1968, PX2232.

26. "Session 4," reproduced in its entirety in ibid.

27. R. S. McKewan to Sturges, memorandum, May 8, 1968, PX2236.

28. Press Release, Spring Joint Computer Program, reproduced in its entirety in Edward Nanas to W. P. Graham, memorandum, May 2, 1968, PX2230.

29. Whalen to Graham, May 2, 1968; McKewan to Sturges, May 8, 1968.

30. Whalen to Graham, May 2, 1968; McKewan to Sturges, May 8, 1968; R. A. Pfeiffer to G. B. Betzel, F. T. Cary, and F. G. Rogers, memorandum, May 13, 1968, PX2241.

31. McKewan to Sturges, May 8, 1968.

32. Ibid.

33. "Alternatives Regarding Tie-in Problem," PX5260-B.

34. DPD Scientific Marketing Newsletter, March 1968, PX5274A, Tr. 62936.

35. J. W. S. Davis, memorandum, June 14, 1968, PX5274, Tr. 62935.

36. Memorandum, November 25, 1968, PX5154, Tr. 62755.

37. PX5296, 7.

38. Martin Campbell-Kelly, *From Airline Reservations to Sonic the Hedgehog: A History of the Software Industry* (Cambridge, MA: MIT Press, 2003), 110.

39. United States v. IBM Corp., 69 Civ. 200 (S.D.N.Y. 1969).

40. Introduction of Pricing Policy, Jacques Maisonrouge to C. A. Northrop, memorandum, stamped March 11, 1969, produced sometime in 1968, Tr. 16342.

41. Ibid., Tr. 16346.

42. Ibid., Tr. 16350.

43. Ibid., Tr. 16349.

44. Ibid., Tr. 16351.

45. "Communications Response Planning Agenda," May 5, 1969, PX5296, 2.

46. PX5296, 4.

47. Ibid., 5.

48. Ibid., 12.

49. Ibid., 17.

50. "To Our Customers," Open letter from F. G. Rodgers, June 23, 1969, digital reproduction in my possession.

51. "Alternatives Regarding Tie-in Problem," PX5260-B.

52. JoAnne Yates, "Application Software for Insurance in the 1960s and Early 1970s," *Business and Economic History* 24:1 (1995): 123–134.

53. Yost, *Making IT Work*; Campbell-Kelly, *From Airline Reservations to Sonic the Hedgehog*.

54. Introduction of "New World Marketing," J. W. Hinchcliffe, memorandum, October 2, 1969, Tr. 16555.

55. Martin Goetz, Automatic system for constructing and recording display charts, US Patent 3,533,086, filed December 24, 1968, continuing application 512,113, filed December 7, 1965, and issued October 6, 1970.

56. Goetz to P. Borkowitz, October 29, 1971, box 1, folder 14, Applied Data Research, Software Products Division Records (CBI 154), Charles Babbage Institute (hereafter cited as CBI 154).

57. Quoted in Robert Caughey to Martin Goetz, January 26, 1970, box 25, folder 11, CBI 154.

58. Jerry Braverman to Goetz, April 29, 1978, Richard Moll to Goetz, May 21, 1970, and Don Tittle to Goetz, March 16, 1970, all in box 25, folder 11, CBI 154.

59. Applied Data Research, Inc. v. IBM Corp., 3-69 Civ. 158 (S.D.N.Y. 69 Civ. 1682), 4.

60. Roscoe Sales Contact Summary for Archison, received June 19, 1970, box 27, folder 4, CBI 154, emphasis in the original.

61. "Costs and Revenue," box 11, folder 3, CBI 154.

62. *Applied Data Research*, 3-69 Civ. 158.

63. Treble damages are a form of augmented financial compensation that a plaintiff may seek. They are normally three times the amount in actual financial losses (damages) that the plaintiff claims to have incurred. Douglas Cray, "ADR Trust Suit Settled by IBM," *New York Times*, August 21, 1970.

64. Ibid., 3, citing section 1 of the Sherman Act, 15 U.S.C. § 1 (1964) and section 3 of the Clayton Act, 15 U.S.C. § 14 (1964).

65. Appendix to open letter by Applied Data Research, August 14, 1970, box 1, folder 12, CBI 154.

66. Memorandum in Support of Motion of Plaintiff, *Applied Data Research*, 3-69 Civ 158.

67. On behalf of the plaintiffs were Lauress Ackman and Maclay Hyde for ADR; John Robertson and Leon Goodrich for the Control Data Corporation; and Allen Saeke for the Data Processing Financial and General Corporation. Representing IBM were Norman Carpenter, Thomas Barr, David Boies, Arnold Messing, and Duane Krohnke. Ibid., 2.

68. Hearing transcript, June 26, 1970, Control Data Corporation, Data Processing Financial and General Corporation, Applied Data Research, and Programmatics, Inc. v. IBM Corp., 3-68 Civ. 312, 3-69 Civ. 157, 3-69 Civ. 158, 3-69 Civ. 159, U.S. District Court, District of Columbia, Third Division, box 1, folder 9, CBI 154.

69. Ibid., 5.

70. Ibid., 7.

71. Ibid., 9.

72. Ibid., 4–5.

73. Ibid., 10.

74. Ibid.

75. Ibid., 11.

76. Ibid.

77. Ibid.

78. Memorandum in Support of Motion of Plaintiff, Applied Data Research v. International Business Machines, Civil Action No. 69-1682, United States District Court, Southern District of New York, box 1, folder 9, CBI 154.

79. Ibid., 46.

80. Ibid.

81. Ibid., 47–48.

82. Ibid., 49.

83. Ibid., 50.

84. Rule 33 of the Federal Rules of Civil Procedure.

85. Interrogatories Addressed to Plaintiff, Applied Data Research v. International Business Machines, Civil Action No. 69-1682, United States District Court, Southern District of New York, box 1, folder 9, CBI 154.

86. Ibid., 3.

87. Ibid.

88. For Immediate Release, HSBO Public Relations to Applied Data Research, undated, box 1, folder 12, CBI 154.

89. Ibid.

90. John Bennett, An Open Letter, July 14, 1970, box 1, folder 12, CBI 154.

91. Cray, "ADR Trust Suit Settled by IBM."

92. "NCR to Sell Software for *Rivals'* Hardware," *Computerworld*, July 24, 1968, 1.

93. Don Leavitt, "ADR Claims 'Roscoe' Superior to CRJE," *Computerworld*, July 14, 1971, 11.

94. Roscoe: Costs and Revenue, 1968–1971, box 11, folder 2, CBI 154.

95. For ADR's sales, see Campbell-Kelly, *From Airline Reservations to Sonic the Hedgehog*, 114.

96. ADR's Advertising Campaign and Background Information, box 11, folder 2, CBI 154.

97. Ibid., section II.

98. Ibid.

99. Ibid.

100. "Applied Data Research, Advertising Campaign, Did You Know? ADR Has Installed . . . ," box 11, folder 4, CBI 154.

101. Ibid.

102. Ibid.

CHAPTER 5. SOFTWARE PATENTS AT THE COURTS, 1961–1973

1. Nathan Ensmenger, *The Computer Boys Take Over: Computers, Programmers, and the Politics of Technical Expertise* (Cambridge, MA: MIT Press, 2010), 111–136; William Aspray, "Was Early Entry a Competitive Advantage?," *IEEE Annals of the History of Computing* 22:3 (2000): 42–87; Ceruzzi, "Electronics Technology and Computer Science," *IEEE Annals of the History of Computing* 10:4 (1988): 257–275; Michael S. Mahoney, "Computer Science: The Search for a Mathematical Theory," in *Science in the Twentieth Century*, ed. John Krige (New York: Harwood Academic, 1997), 617–634.

2. Richard Hamming, "One Man's View of Computer Science," *Journal of the Association for Computing Machinery* 16:1 (1969): 8, also cited in Ensmenger, *Computer Boys Take Over*.

3. Bennett Wall, *Growth in a Changing Environment: A History of Standard Oil Company (New Jersey), Exxon Corporation, 1950–1975* (New York: McGraw-Hill, 1988).

4. Charles Prater and James Wei, Application, Patent Number 3,294,859, National Archives, Kansas City, Missouri.

5. In mathematical terms, this can be phrased in the following way: Let p denote the number of peaks and c the number of constituents. Then, in most cases, p will be greater than c. Each of the peaks has associated with it a linear equation in c variables, so the collection of peaks generates a system of p equations in c variables, where each variable denotes the percentage of the corresponding constituent. In order to find the solution to this system, the scientist needs to select a collection of c equations. The difficult part of this selection was deciding which equations would yield the most accurate values for the constituents.

6. This number would be 30,045,015; this is the number of collections of ten objects taken from a total of thirty objects, or "thirty choose ten."

7. Each system of linear equations has associated with it a value called the determinant. For each of the possible systems of equations, the determinant can be computed by using only elementary arithmetic. Prater and Wei had discovered that the optimum collection of equations was the one with the lowest determinant. Their invention calculated these determinants, compared them to one another, and selected the system of equations to be solved.

8. Amendment, August 7, 1963, Patent Number 3,294,859, National Archives, Kansas City. See, e.g., Alfred Lorenzo, "Insufficient Disclosure, Obviousness, and the Reasonable Man," *Journal of the Patent and Trademark Office Society* 49 (1967): 387.

9. Ibid.

10. Communication from the Examiner, January 7, 1963, Patent Number 3,294,859, National Archives, Kansas City. This was grounded on Morrison's understanding of Halliburton v. Walker, 146 F.2d 817 (1944), and In re Abrams, 188 F.2d 165 (C.C.P.A. 1951).

11. Transcript of Record, Patent Appeal No. 7987, 128, National Archives, Kansas City.

12. He cited Middleton, 77 U.S.P.Q. 615; Nicholas, 80 USPQ 143; Ashbaugh, 81 U.S.P.Q. 129; Washburn, 86 U.S.P.Q. 108; Hastings, 88 U.S.P.Q. 431; Abrams, 89 U.S.P.Q. 266; Hitchins, 99 U.S.P.Q. 288; and Mienhardt, 1907 C.D. 238.

13. Transcript of Record, Patent Appeal No. 7987, 129.

14. Abrams, in ibid., 4.

15. Ibid.

16. "In the United States Patent Office," June 28, 1966, Patent Number 3,294,859, National Archives, Kansas City.

17. William Robinson, *The Law of Patents for Useful Inventions* (Boston: Little, Brown, 1890), 230–231.

18. Richards made this claim to make the decision in Hotel Security Checking Co. v. Lorraine Co., 160 F. 467 (2nd Cir. 1908), inapplicable to Prater and Wei's invention. Transcript of Record, Patent Appeal No. 7987, 138.

19. Ibid.

20. Ibid.

21. Ibid., 139.

22. Ibid., 145–179.

23. Examiner's Answer, January 6, 1966, ibid., 197, emphasis in the original.

24. Ibid.

25. Ibid., 200–201.

26. Letter of Examiner, January 13, 1965, ibid., citing Novocol Chemical Mfg. Co. v. Powers & Anderson Dental Co., 128 F.2d 904 (4th Cir. 1942), and Anderson, 54 U.S.P.Q. 40, at 43.

27. Transcript of Record, Patent Appeal No. 7987, 142.

28. Ibid., 143.

29. Ibid.

30. Ibid.

31. Ibid., 200–201.

32. Decision of Board of Appeals, May 24, 1966, ibid., 205.

33. Quoted in ibid., 207.

34. Notice of Appeal, June 16, 1966, ibid.

35. "Brief for Appellants," ibid.

36. Ibid.

37. "Brief for the Commissioner of Patents," ibid.

38. Ibid., 6.

39. Ibid.

40. Ibid., 7.

41. Ibid.

42. H. R. 3760 before Subcommittee No. 3 of the House Committee on the Judiciary, 82d Cong., 1st Sess., 37 (1951); S. Rep. No. 1979, 82d Cong., 2d Sess., 5 (1952); H. R. Rep. No. 1923, 82d Cong., 2d Sess., 6 (1952). See also Diamond v. Chakrabarty, 407 U.S. 303 (1980).

43. In re Prater I, 415 F.2d 1378 (C.C.P.A. 1968), 1389.

44. Ibid., 1386.

45. Ibid., 1389.

46. Ibid., 1390.

47. Petition for Rehearing, Patent Appeal No. 7987.

48. Quoted in Morton Jacobs, "Brief Amici Curiae in Opposition to Petition for Rehearing," Patent Appeal No. 7987.

49. Quoted in ibid.

50. Quoted in ibid., 3.

51. Ibid.

52. Quoted in ibid., 6.

53. Virgil E. Woodcock, "Appellant's Reply to IBM's Motion for Leave to File a Brief Amicus Curiae," Patent Appeal No. 7987.

54. Morton Jacobs, "Brief Amicus Curiae on Rehearing in Support of Prater and Wei Opinion," Patent Appeal No. 7987.

55. Ibid., 11–12.

56. Ibid. in reference to patents 3,167,743; 3,333,243; 3,339,182; and 3,400,371.

57. Quotations in ibid., 13.

58. D. D. Allegretti, "Brief of Honeywell Inc. Amicus Curiae," Patent Appeal No. 7987.

59. Ibid., 2.

60. Citing IBM Motion to Leave to File Brief Amicus Curiae, Appendix, 7–8, Patent Appeal No. 7987.

61. Quoted in ibid., 4.

62. Quoted in ibid., 5.

63. Ibid.

64. Ibid., 5–6.

65. Ibid., 6–7.

66. Ibid., 3.

67. Ibid., 4.

68. Ibid.

69. Ibid.

70. Ibid., 5.

71. Ibid., 12.

72. Ibid., 16.

73. Ibid.

74. Ibid.

75. Quoted in ibid.

76. Programming: Words That Move Machines, 3, Patent Appeal No. 7987.

77. Ibid.

78. Ibid., 10.

79. "Examination of Patent Applications on Computer Programs," *Federal Register* 33:206 (October 22, 1968), 15610.

80. "Patent Office Is Set for Reorganization to Aid Processing," *New York Times*, November 29, 1969.

81. "Examination of Patent Applications on Computer Programs," 15610.

82. In re Prater 2, 415 F.2d 1393 (C.C.P.A. 1969), 1402 n.22.

83. Ibid.

84. *Prater 2*, 415 F.2d at 1404 n.29.

85. Gottschalk v. Benson, 409 U.S. 63 (1972).

86. Brief for Respondents, Gottschalk v. Benson, No. 71-485 (1972), 2.

87. The Binary Coded Decimal (BCD) consists of writing down the binary form of each digit in a decimal expression. A literal digit-by-digit translation, BCD notation creates very long sequences of zeroes and ones.

88. Brief for Respondents, *Gottschalk*, No. 71-485 at 8.

89. Gary Benson and Arthur Tabbot, "Application," Patent Appeal Docket No. 8376, Transcript of Record, In the Matter of the Application of Gary R. Benson and Arthur C. Tabbot (C.C.P.A. 1969), 10.

90. Daryl W. Cook, "Examiner's Answer," in ibid., 122.

91. Ibid.

92. Ibid.

93. Quotations in Cook, "Examiner's Answer," 122.

94. Donald Knuth, "What Is an Algorithm?," *Datamation*, October 1967, 31.

95. Ibid.

96. Quotations in Robert O. Nimtz, "Brief for Appellants," Patent Appeal Docket No. 8376, 12.

97. Ibid. See also Christopher Beauchamp, "Who Invented the Telephone? Lawyers, Patents, and the Judgments of History," *Technology and Culture* 51:4 (2010): 854–878.

98. Nimtz, "Brief for Appellants," 28.

99. Ibid.

100. Ibid.

101. Ibid., 13.

102. Application of Benson, 441 F.2d 682 (C.C.P.A. 1971).

103. Ibid., 688.

104. Ibid.

105. Ibid.

106. "Patent Chief Sees an End to Woes," *New York Times*, January 29, 1972.

107. Respondent's Brief, *Gottschalk*, No. 71-485 at 23.

108. Ibid., 20.

109. Ibid., 19.

110. Martin Campbell-Kelly, *From Airline Reservations to Sonic the Hedgehog: A History of the Software Industry* (Cambridge, MA: MIT Press, 2003).

111. John S. Voorhees, "Brief Amicus Curiae on Behalf of the Business Equipment Manufacturers Association," *Gottschalk*, No. 71-485; Henry Hanson and D. D. Allegretti, "Brief Amicus Curiae for Honeywell Inc.," ibid.; Lloyd Cutler, "Brief for Amicus Curiae International Business Machines Corporation," ibid.

112. See, e.g., Morton C. Jacobs, "Brief Amicus Curiae for the Association of Data Processing Service Organizations, Software Products and Service Section (ADAPSO/ AISC)," *Gottschalk*, No. 71-485.

113. Ibid.

114. Morton C. Jacobs, "Brief Amicus Curiae for Applied Data Research, Inc. (ADR)," *Gottschalk,* No. 71-485.

115. Jeffrey R. Yost, *Making IT Work: A History of the Computer Services Industry* (Cambridge, MA: MIT Press, 2017), 117–123; Thomas Haigh, "ADAPSO, Time-Sharing Firms, and Software Companies: 1968–1975," *IEEE Annals of the History of Computing* 27:1 (2005): 67–73.

116. Interview of Martin Goetz by Gerardo Con Díaz, October 23, 2017, Teaneck, NJ, audio recording in my possession.

117. Ibid., 1.

118. Voorhees, "Brief Amicus Curiae on Behalf of the Business Equipment Manufacturers Association."

119. Ibid., 6.

120. Ibid.

121. Hanson and Allegretti, "Brief Amicus Curiae for Honeywell Inc."; Cutler, "Brief for Amicus Curiae International Business Machines Corporation."

122. James Clabault and Edward Fiorito, "Brief Amicus Curiae for Burroughs Corporation," *Gottschalk*, No. 71-485 at 13.

123. Ibid., 14.

124. Ibid.

125. Ibid., 16.

126. *Gottschalk*, 409 U.S. at 65.

127. Louis Kohlmer, "Computer Work Isn't Patentable, High Court Says," *Wall Street Journal*, November 21, 1972.

128. Ibid.

129. "COMPUTERS: Hard Ruling for Software Victory for Hardware," *Time*, December 4, 1972.

130. "U.S. Supreme Court Rules Bell Labs Program 'Idea'; Therefore Not Patentable," *Electronic News*, November 27, 1972, 1.

131. Morton Jacobs, "Patents for Software Inventions in the Supreme Court's Decision," *Jurimetrics* 13:3 (1973): 132–134.

132. Ibid., 132.

133. Ibid., 133.

134. Ibid., 134.

135. Martin Goetz, "A Different Viewpoint on the Benson-Tabbot Decision," *Communications of the ACM* 16:5 (1973): 334.

136. Ibid.

137. Michael Duggan, "Patents and Programs: The ACM's Position," *Communications of the ACM* 14:4 (1971): 278–279.

138. Michael Duggan, "Patents on Programs? The Supreme Court Says No," *Jurimetrics* 13:3 (1973): 136.

139. Ibid., 137.

140. This phrasing originated in the decision In re Christensen (478 F.2d 1392, C.C.P.A. 1973). Even Judge Rich held that this synthesis was applicable to classes of inventions that could sometimes fall outside the scope of his interpretation of the Benson decision. Giles Rich, dissent to In re Christensen, 478 F.2d 1392 (C.C.P.A. 1973).

141. As seen in In re Abrams, 188 F.2d 165 (C.C.P.A. 1951). See also In re Bernhart, 417 F.2d 1395 (C.C.P.A. 1969); and *Christensen*, 478 F.2d.

142. Though the test's key precedent is *Christensen*, the rationale behind it is based on *Bernhart*, 417 F.2d; In re Yuan, 188 F.2d 377 (C.C.P.A. 1951); and *Abrams*, 188 F.2d.

CHAPTER 6. REMAKING SOFTWARE COPYRIGHT, 1974–1981

1. Ringer, "Copyright Law Revision: History and Prospects," in *Technology and Copyright: Annotated Bibliography and Source Materials*, ed. George P. Bush (Mount Airy, MD: Lomond Systems, 1972), 288–289.

2. See, e.g., Robert D. Hadl, "Toward International Copyright Revision: Report on the Meetings in Paris and Geneva, September, 1970," *Bulletin of the Copyright Society of the U.S.A.* 18:3 (February 1971): 183–228; Morton David Goldberg, "Report of the President of the Copyright Society of the U.S.A. 1973–1974," *Bulletin of the Copyright Society of the U.S.A.* 21:5 (June 1974): 289–302; and Heinz Dawid, "Basic Principles of International Copyright," *Bulletin of the Copyright Society of the U.S.A.* 21:1 (October 1973): 1–24.

3. Goldberg, "Report of the President"; Smith, "The Emergence of CATV: A Look at the Evolution of a Revolution," in Bush, *Technology and Copyright*, 344–370.

4. Martin Campbell-Kelly et al., *Computer: A History of the Information Machine*, 3rd ed. (Boulder, CO: Westview Press, 2013), 216–219.

5. Ross Bassett, *To the Digital Age: Research Labs, Start-Up Companies, and the Rise of MOS Technology* (Baltimore: Johns Hopkins University Press, 2002); Paul E. Ceruzzi, "Moore's Law and Technology Determinism: Reflections on the History of Technology," *Technology and Culture* 46:3 (2005): 584–593.

6. See, e.g., Joseph Thomas West, Error detection and correction in data processing systems, US Patent 4,005,405, filed May 7, 1975, and issued January 25, 1977; Joseph Thomas West, Automatic data priority technique, filed January 23, 1974, and issued April 6, 1976; and William Philip Churchill, Memory access technique, US Patent 3,949,369, filed January 23, 1974, and issued April 6, 1976.

7. Joy Lisi Rankin, *A People's History of Computing in the United States* (Cambridge, MA: Harvard University Press, 2018).

8. Barbara Ringer, "Our Copyright Law—Present Status and Proposals for Change," in *Copyright: The Librarian and the Law*, ed. George J. Lukac (New Brunswick, NJ: Rutgers University Press, 1972).

9. See, e.g., ibid.

10. Harvey S. Perlman and Laurens H. Rhinelander, "Williams & Wilkins Co. v. United States: Photocopying, Copyright, and the Judicial Process," *Supreme Court Review* (1975): 355–417.

11. Campbell-Kelly et al., *Computer*.

12. National Commission on New Technological Uses of Copyrighted Works, *Meetings 1 through 5* (Washington, DC: US Department of Commerce, 1975), n.p.

13. The three executives were Dan Lacy, senior vice president of McGraw-Hill; E. Gabriel Perle, vice president of Time, Inc.; and Hershel Sarbin, president of Ziff-Davis Publishing. National Commission on New Technological Uses of Copyrighted Works, *Final Report of the National Commission on New Technological Uses of Copyrighted Works* (Washington, DC: Library of Congress, 1979), 4.

14. These were Alice Wilcox, the director of the first library teletype network to cross state lines; William Dix, the librarian emeritus of Princeton University; and Robert Wedgeworth, the executive director of the American Library Association. Ibid.

15. Ibid., 43.

16. Ibid., 33.

17. Ibid., 43.

18. Ibid., 43–46.

19. Ibid., 43.

20. Quoted in ibid., 43–62.

21. Ibid., 50.

22. Ibid., 49–51.

23. Testimony of Daniel McCracken, in National Commission on New Technological Uses of Copyrighted Works, *Transcript, CONTU Meeting No. 10* (Washington, DC: US Department of Commerce, 1976), 2.

24. Marcian Edward Hoff, Stanley Mazor, and Federico Faggin, Memory system for a multi-chip digital computer, US Patent 3,821,715, filed January 22, 1973, and issued June 28, 1974; Federico Faggin, Masatoshi Shima, and Stanley Mazor, MOS computer employing a plurality of separate chips, US Patent 4,101,449, filed December 31, 1974, and issued March 1, 1977.

25. Testimony of Daniel McCracken, 20.

26. Hearings before the Subcommittee on Courts, Civil Liberties, and the Administration of Justice of the Committee on the Judiciary, H. Representatives, 98th Cong., 1st Sess., on H.R. 1028, August 3 and December 1, 1983, 22–23.

27. Ibid., 22–27.

28. Testimony of Daniel McCracken, 20.

29. Ibid., 6.

30. Ibid., 7.

31. Ibid., 6–7.

32. Ibid., 24–25.

33. Ibid., 31–32.

34. Ibid., 32.

35. Ibid., 38–39.

36. Ibid., 41–42.

37. Quoted in CONTU, "Report of the Software Subcommittee to the National Commission on New Technological Uses of Copyrighted Works," in "Computer Software," box 58, John Hersey Papers, Yale Collection of American Literature, Beinecke Rare Book and Manuscript Library, Yale University (hereafter cited as Hersey Papers).

38. The biographical remarks about Licklider here are based on M. Mitchell Waldrop, *The Dream Machine: JCR Licklider and the Revolution That Made Computing Personal* (New York: Penguin Books, 2002).

39. Rankin, *People's History of Computing*.

40. Quoted in Oral testimony of JCR Licklider, November 17, 1977, in "Computer Software," box 58, Hersey Papers.

41. Quoted in ibid.

42. John Hersey is now best known for his 1946 book *Hiroshima*, on six of the survivors of the atomic bombing of Hiroshima in August 1945.

43. Biographical information in Nancy Huse, *John Hersey and James Agee: A Reference Guide* (Boston: G. K. Hall, 1978).

44. "JLS Draft," in "Computer Software," box 58, Hersey Papers.

45. Quoted in Robert O. Nimtz to Arthur Levine, August 30, 1978, in "Computer Software," box 58, Hersey Papers.

46. Ibid.

47. National Commission for New Technological Uses of Copyrighted Works, *Transcript, CONTU Meeting No. 16* (Washington, DC: US Department of Commerce, 1977). See also Edith Holmes, "Program Copyright Gains Support," *Computerworld*, October 10, 1977, in "Computer Software 1," box 59, Hersey Papers.

48. National Commission for New Technological Uses of Copyrighted Works, *Transcript, CONTU Meeting No. 16*, 58. For more on AUTOFLOW, see Con Díaz, "Embodied Software"; and Nathan Ensmenger, "The Multiple Meanings of a Flowchart," *Information and Culture* 51:3 (2016): 321–351.

49. National Commission for New Technological Uses of Copyrighted Works, *Transcript, CONTU Meeting No. 16*, 62.

50. Ibid., 61.

51. For a view of this matter in the popular press, see Holmes, "Program Copyright Gains Support."

52. This paragraph is based on Harbridge House, "Legal Protections of Computer Software: An Industrial Survey" (Springfield, VA: National Technical Information Service, 1978), in *Copyright, Congress, and Technology: The Public Record*, vol. 4, ed. Nicholas Henry (Phoenix, AZ: Oryx Press, 1980), 370.

53. Statement of ADAPSO to National Commission on New Technological Uses of Copyrighted Works, Software Protection Committee, January 1976–August 1977, box 6, Martin A. Goetz Papers (CBI 159), Charles Babbage Institute, University of Minnesota, Minneapolis.

54. Ibid., 3.

55. Ibid., 5.

56. National Commission on New Technological Uses of Copyrighted Works, *Final Report*, 1.

57. Ibid., 10.

58. Music systems, especially Pianola rolls, have been a recurring source of metaphors for the American copyright system. This use is often grounded on the Supreme Court's decision in White-Smith Music Publishing Co. v. Apollo Co., 209 U.S. 1 (1908). See Capitol Records, Inc. v. Naxos of America, Inc., 4 N.Y.3d 540 (N.Y. 2005).

59. National Commission on New Technological Uses of Copyrighted Works, *Final Report*, 1.

60. Quoted in John Hersey, "Software: A Dissent," draft dated January 27, 1978, and annotated February 6, 1978, in "Computer and Software 2," box 59, Hersey Papers.

61. Quoted in ibid., 28.

62. Hersey was not concerned with whether programmers were creating original texts. Instead, his focus was on the idea that the texts that programmers created should not be considered to be the kind of works that copyright law was designed to protect. William H. Honan, "Hersey Apologizes to a Writer over an Article on Agee," *New York Times*, July 22, 1988; Anne Fadiman, *Ex Libris: Confessions of a Common Reader* (New York: Farrar, Straus and Giroux, 2011).

63. John Hersey to Arthur Levine, undated correspondence, in "Copyright and Software 4," box 59, Hersey Papers.

64. John Hersey, "Additional Views on Computer Software," box 58, Hersey Papers.

65. Ibid.

66. John Hersey, "Memorandum," February 3, 1978, box 58, Hersey Papers.

67. Quoted in "Software Subcommittee Report and Additional Views," undated, in "Computer Software," box 58, Hersey Papers.

68. H.R. 6933, 46.

69. [Attorney for ADAPSO?], "Discussion of Proposed Amendments," October 23, 1981, box 58, Hersey Papers; Office of Technology Assessment, *Finding a Balance: Computer Software, Intellectual Property and the Challenge of Technological Change* (Washington, DC: GPO, 1992), 65.

70. Office of Technology Assessment, *Finding a Balance*.

CHAPTER 7. MAKING SENSE OF *BENSON*, 1976–1982

1. Appendix, Patent Appeal No. 9088, National Archives, Kansas City, MO.

2. Ibid.

3. Ibid.

4. See, e.g., John F. Duffy, "Why Business Method Patents?," *Stanford Law Review* 63:6 (June 2011): 1247–1288; and Gregory A. Stobbs, *Business Method Patents* (New York: Aspen, 2008).

5. See, e.g., Richard Snook, Credit card verifier apparatus, US Patent 3,601,805, filed December 22, 1967, and issued August 24, 1971; Charles Adams, Herbert Behrens, Jerome Pustilnik, and John Gilmore, Instinet communication system for effectuating the sale or exchange of fungible properties between subscribers, US Patent 3,573,747, filed February 24, 1969, and issued April 6, 1971.

6. Gerhard Dirks, Data handling system, US Patent 3,343,133, filed August 9, 1963, and issued September 19, 1967.

7. See also Robert Tink, Robert Meinick, and Frank Andrews, On-line system, US Patent 3,308,429, filed January 2, 1964, and issued March 7, 1967.

8. Appendix, Transcript of Record, 5, Dann v. Johnston, 425 U.S. 219 (1976).

9. Ibid., 88.

10. Patent Appeal No. 9088, National Archives, Kansas City.

11. Application of Johnston, 205 F.2d 765 (C.C.P.A. 1974), 773.

12. Ibid.

13. Ibid., 774.

14. Rusty Pray, "C. Marshall Dann, 87," *Philadelphia Inquirer*, May 5, 2002.

15. Oral Argument of Morton Jacobs, *Dann*, 425 U.S.

16. *Dann*, 425 U.S. at 224, in Application of Noll, 545 F.2d 141 (C.C.P.A. 1976), at 151.

17. *Noll*, 545 F.2d at 150.

18. Ibid., 152.

19. Ibid., 159.

20. Ibid., 152.

21. Encyclopaedia Britannica Online, s.v. "Atlantic Richfield Company (ARCO)," http://www.britannica.com/topic/Atlantic-Richfield-Company.

22. Transcript of Record, No. 77-512, In the matter of the Application of Dale R. Flook, National Archives, Kansas City.

23. Ibid., 7–9.

24. Ibid.

25. Ibid., 42–43.

26. Ibid., 64–67.

27. Ibid., 77.

28. Appeal from the Board of Patent Appeals, No. 77-512, 4, Records of the Patent and Trademark Office, National Archives, Kansas City.

29. Ibid.

30. Application of Flook, 559 F.2d 21 (C.C.P.A. 1977).

31. Ibid., 22.

32. Ibid.

33. This statement was grounded on In re Christensen, 478 F.2d 1392 (C.C.P.A. 1973).

34. Richard Freeman, Computer typesetting, US Patent 4,195,338, filed May 6, 1970, and issued March 25, 1980.

35. Ibid., 1.

36. In re Freeman, 573 F.2d 1237 (C.C.P.A. 1978), 1245.

37. Ibid.

38. Gottschalk v. Benson, 409 U.S. 63 (1972), 71.

39. *Freeman*, 573 F.2d at 1245.

40. Brief of the Business Equipment Manufacturers' Association, Parker v. Flook, 437 U.S. 584 (1978), 4.

41. Ibid.

42. Ibid., 5.

43. Ibid., 18.

44. Ibid., 19.

45. Ibid.

46. Ibid., 27.

47. Interview of Martin Goetz by Gerardo Con Díaz, October 23, 2017, Teaneck, NJ, audio recording in my possession.

48. Amicus Brief for Applied Data Research, *Parker*, 437 U.S. at 6.

49. Ibid.

50. Ibid., 27.

51. David Waks and Adolf Futterweit, Telephone circuit monitoring system, US Patent 4,066,843, filed January 28, 1975, and issued January 3, 1978.

52. Amicus Brief for Applied Data Research, *Parker*, 437 U.S. at 2–3.

53. Lawrence Horwitz and Richard Karp, Optimum result computer, US Patent 3,339,182, filed June 30, 1964, and issued August 29, 1967.

54. Amicus Brief for Applied Data Research, *Parker*, 437 U.S. at 2.

55. Ibid., 3.

56. *Parker*, 437 U.S. at 591.

57. Ibid., 592.

58. Application of Walter, 618 F.2d 758 (C.C.P.A. 1980).

59. Ibid., 767.

60. Maureen O'Rourke, "The Story of *Diamond v. Diehr: Toward Patenting Software*," in *Intellectual Property Stories*, ed. Jane Ginsburg and Rochelle Dreyfuss (New York: Foundation Press, 2006), 194–219.

61. Ibid.

62. "Application of James R. Diehr," in Transcript of Record, Appeal No. 79-527, Records of the Patent and Trademark Office, National Archives, Kansas City.

63. Brief for the Respondents, Diamond v. Diehr, 450 U.S. 175 (1981).

64. "Obituary, Helen W. Nies, 71, Former US Judge," *New York Times*, August 11, 1996.

65. In re Diehr and Lutton, 602 F.2d 982 (C.C.P.A. 1979), 988.

66. In re Chakrabarty, 571 F.2d 40 (C.C.P.A. 1978).

67. Application of Bergy, 563 F.2d 1031 (C.C.P.A. 1977).

68. Ibid., 1037.

69. Ibid.

70. Ibid., 1038.

71. Daniel J. Kevles, "Ananda Chakrabarty Wins a Patent: Biotechnology, Law, and Society," *Historical Studies of the Physical and Biological Sciences* 25:1 (1994): 111–135, at 123.

72. Application of Bergy, 975.

73. Kevles, "Ananda Chakrabarty Wins a Patent," 132.

74. *Diamond*, 447 U.S. at 316.

75. Hearings Before Subcommittee No. 3 of the Committee on the Judiciary, House of Representatives, 82d Cong., 1st Sess., on H.R. 3760 (1951), 37, cited in *Diamond*, 447 U.S. at 318.

76. Ibid.

77. *Chakrabarty*, 571 F.2d.

78. *Diamond*, 450 U.S.

79. Petition for certiorari, *Diamond*, 450 U.S.

80. Ibid.

81. Brief for petitioner, *Diamond*, 450 U.S.

82. Ibid.

83. Quoted in ibid., 6.

84. This opening account is based on Wickersham's oral argument in *Diamond*, 450 U.S., available at the Oyez Project at IIT Chicago–Kent College of Law, http://www.oyez.org/cases/1980-1989/1980/1980_79_1112.

85. Ibid., at 45:13.

86. By "patentable," Wickersham meant "eligible for patent protection." However, the term "patentable" is commonly used in reference to an invention that meets all the

requirements established by section 35 of the United States Code. I use the term "patentable" only in this more common sense. Ibid., at 47:19.

87. Ibid., at 27:06.

88. Amicus Brief, Chevron Corporation, *Diamond*, 450 U.S. at 5.

89. Ibid., 6, 7.

90. *Diamond*, 450 U.S.

91. Ibid. See Robert Merges, Peter Menell, and Mark Lemley, *Intellectual Property in the New Technological Age* (New York: Aspen, 2012).

92. James Bessen and Robert Hunt, "An Empirical Look at Software Patents" (FRB of Philadelphia Working Paper No. 3-17, March 2004), reported partially in James Bessen and Robert Hunt, "An Empirical Look at Software Patents," *Journal of Economic and Management Strategy* 16:1 (2007): 157–189. I consider Bessen and Hunt's search algorithm for software patents to provide reliable minimum values for the number of issued software patents and of the overall trends of patenting, though the actual numbers may be much higher than what they found. This is because (as this book has shown) a key strategy to secure a software patent has been to disclose inventions in patent applications that appear to be something other than software—computer systems, special purpose computers, and so on.

93. *Manual of Patent Examining Procedure*, 4th ed., 8th rev. (October 1981), https://www.uspto.gov/web/offices/pac/mpep/old/mpep_E4R8.htm.

94. Ibid., Section 2110, 538.1.

95. Ibid., 538.2.

96. James T. Patterson, *Restless Giant: The United States from Watergate to Bush v. Gore* (New York: Oxford University Press, 2005), 60–65.

97. Richard H. K. Vietor, *Contrived Competition: Regulation and Deregulation in America* (Cambridge, MA: Harvard University Press, 1994).

98. David Mowery, Richard Nelson, Bhaven Sampat, and Arvids Ziedonis, "The Growth of Patenting and Licensing by U.S. Universities: An Assessment of the Effects of the Bayh-Dole Act of 1980," *Research Policy* 30 (2001): 99–119.

99. Ellen Sward and Rodney Page, "The Federal Courts Improvement Act: A Practitioner's Perspective," *American University Law Review* 33 (1984): 355–416.

100. William M. Landes and Richard A. Posner, *The Economic Structure of Intellectual Property Law* (Cambridge, MA: Harvard University Press, 2003), 334–340, 410–415.

101. Ibid., based on Rochelle Dreyfuss, "The Federal Circuit: A Case Study in Specialized Courts, *New York Law Review* 64 (April 1989): 1–77.

102. David Mowery, ed., *The International Computer Industry: A Comparative Study of the Industry Evolution and Structure* (New York: Oxford University Press, 1996).

103. In re Abele, 684 F.2d 902 (C.A.F.C. 1982).

104. Ibid., 907.

105. Ibid.

CHAPTER 8. HOBBYISTS AND INTELLECTUAL PROPERTY FROM ALTAIR TO APPLE, 1975–1981

1. Paul E. Ceruzzi, *A History of Modern Computing*, 2nd ed. (Cambridge, MA: MIT Press, 2003), 226–231; Martin Campbell-Kelly et al., *Computer: A History of the Information Machine*, 3rd ed. (Boulder, CO: Westview Press, 2013), 235–238.

2. "The MITS 1200 Series," *Radio Electronics*, March 1973, 27.

3. Cover, *Popular Electronics*, January 1975.

4. MITS advertisement, *Popular Electronics*, May 1975, 25.

5. Ceruzzi, *History of Modern Computing*, 221–228.

6. There is no clean break between the mainframe and minicomputer industries, on the one hand, and personal computers, on the other. Instead, the three industries coexisted in the 1970s, and in fact some of IBM's lines of mainframes thrived during the 1980s. This chapter's focus on PCs is informed, not by the assumption that PCs suddenly replaced their predecessors, but instead by the fact that software IP battles started to shift into the PC arena in the late 1970s. See Michael Sean Mahoney, *Histories of Computing*, ed. Thomas Haigh (Cambridge, MA: Harvard University Press, 2011); Jeffrey R. Yost, *Making IT Work: A History of the Computer Services Industry* (Cambridge, MA: MIT Press, 2017); and Ceruzzi, *History of Modern Computing*.

7. "Altair Software Library Update," uncataloged collection in the care of Peggy Kidwell, Smithsonian National Museum of American History.

8. See Martin Campbell-Kelly et al., *Computer: A History of the Information Machine*, 3rd ed. (Boulder, CO: Westview Press, 2013); and Ceruzzi, *History of Modern Computing*. Popular accounts of this story are found in Paul Freiberger and Michael Swaine, *Fire in the Valley: The Making of the Personal Computer*, 2nd ed. (New York: McGraw-Hill, 2000); and Walter Isaacson, *The Innovators: How a Group of Hackers, Geniuses, and Geeks Created the Digital Revolution* (New York: Simon and Schuster: 2015).

9. "MITS Dear Customer," uncataloged collection in the care of Peggy Kidwell, Smithsonian National Museum of American History.

10. Biographical information in Fred Turner, *From Counterculture to Cyberculture: Stewart Brand, the Whole Earth Network, and the Rise of Digital Utopianism* (Chicago: University of Chicago Press, 2006), 113.

11. See Joy Lisi Rankin, *A People's History of Computing in the United States* (Cambridge, MA: Harvard University Press, 2018).

12. *People's Computer Company* 1:1 (1972): 5.

13. Ibid., 2.

14. Biographical information in John Markoff, *What the Dormouse Said: How the Sixties Counterculture Shaped the Personal Computer Industry* (New York: Penguin, 2006).

15. Ibid.; Swaine and Freiberger, *Fire in the Valley*.

16. Biographical Sketch, box 31, folder V-330, Calvin Mooers Papers (CBI 81), Charles Babbage Institute, University of Minnesota, Minneapolis (hereafter cited as Mooers Papers).

17. Presentation at Association for Computing Machinery, 1964, box 14, folder 65, Mooers Papers.

18. See, e.g., box 18, folder 34, Mooers Papers.

19. Calvin Mooers, "Submission to CONTU," August 25, 1977, box 36, folder "Copyright Information & CONTU," Mooers Papers.

20. Calvin Mooers, "Submission to the: National Commission on New Technological Uses of Copyrighted Works," November 5, 1976, 3, box 36, folder "Copyright Information & CONTU," Mooers Papers.

21. Robert Albrecht to Calvin Mooers, March 10, 1975, folder 53, box 20, Mooers Papers.

22. Mooers to Albrecht, May 29, 1975, folder 53, box 20, Mooers Papers.

23. Ibid.

24. Quoted in ibid.

25. The story of Gates's conflict with the hobbyists, which I recount briefly in this paragraph and the next one, is well known in the historiography of computing. See, e.g., Stephen Manes and Paul Andrews, *Gates: How Microsoft's Mogul Reinvented an Industry—and Made Himself the Richest Man in America* (New York: Doubleday, 1993); and Freiberger and Swaine, *Fire in the Valley.* For an analysis focused on the Homebrew Computer Club, see Elizabeth Petrick, "Imagining the Personal Computer: Conceptualizations of the Homebrew Computer Club," *IEEE Annals of the History of Computing* 29:4 (2017): 37–39.

26. Manes and Andrews, *Gates;* Petrick, "Imagining the Personal Computer."

27. Computer Notes, August 1975, uncataloged collection in the care of Peggy Kidwell, Smithsonian National Museum of American History.

28. Ibid.

29. Quoted in Bill Gates, "Open Letter to Hobbyists," *Homebrew Computer Club Newsletter,* January 31, 1976, 2.

30. Unlike previous works on hobbyists and Gates's letter, this chapter focuses on how the hobbyists conceived the nature of computer programs and embraced new ways of distributing them. See Kevin Driscoll, "Professional Work for Nothing: Software Commercialization and 'An Open Letter to Hobbyists,' " *Information and Culture* 50:2 (2015): 257–283. See also Turner, *From Counterculture to Cyberculture;* Markoff, *What the Dormouse Said;* and Freiberger and Swayne, *Fire in the Valley.*

31. Robert Reiling, "This Month," *Homebrew Computer Club Newsletter,* January 31, 1976, 1.

32. Michael Hayes to Bill Gates, February 20, 1976, *Homebrew Computer Club Newsletter,* February 29, 1976, 2.

33. Ibid.

34. Quoted in ibid.

35. Quoted in Charles Pack to Bill Gates, February 20, 1976, *Homebrew Computer Club Newsletter,* February 29, 1976, 3.

36. Markoff, *What the Dormouse Said.*

37. Jim C. Warren, "Copyright Mania: It's Mine; It's Mine, and You Can't Play with It!," *Dr. Dobb's Journal of Computer Calisthenics and Orthodontics,* May 1976, 3.

38. Ibid.

39. Ibid.

40. Ibid.

41. Quoted in ibid.

42. Quoted in ibid.

43. Quoted in ibid.

44. Quoted in Dennis Allison, "Design Notes for Tiny BASIC," *People's Computer Company* 4:2 (1975).

45. Dennis Allison, "Implementation Strat[e]gies and Onions," *Dr. Dobb's Journal of Tiny BASIC Calisthenics and Orthodontics,* January 1976, 6.

46. Ibid.

47. Historians and media theorists have gravitated towards the onion metaphor as a starting point for software studies. See Ceruzzi, *History of Modern Computing*, 80, as cited in Wendy Chun, *Programmed Visions: Software and Memory* (Cambridge, MA: MIT Press, 2014), 4.

48. Ibid.

49. Ibid.

50. Jim Warren, "Correspondence," *SIGPLAN Notices* 11:7 (1976): 1.

51. Li-Chen Wang, "Palo Alto Tiny BASIC," *Dr. Dobb's Journal of Computer Calisthenics and Orthodontia*, May 1976, 13.

52. Ibid., 25. I have modified this quotation by extracting from Wang's original text the source code directed toward the display of this text on the printed paper. The elements extracted were just character instructions and additional line breaks in between the paragraphs. No text has been added.

53. For more on copyleft, see Christopher Kelty, "Inventing Copyleft," in *Making and Unmaking Intellectual Property: Creative Production in Legal and Cultural Perspective*, ed. Mario Biagioli, Peter Jaszi, and Martha Woodmansee (Chicago: University of Chicago Press, 2001).

54. Roger Rauskolb, "Dr. Wang's Palo Alto Tiny Basic," *Interface Age*, December 1976, 2.

55. Bill Gates, "A Second and Final Letter," *Computer Notes,* April 1976, 5.

56. Ibid.

57. Ibid.

58. Quoted in Calvin Mooers, "How Can Hobby Software Be Protected?," box 31, folder V-332, Mooers Papers.

59. Quoted in ibid.

60. Quoted in ibid.

61. Quoted in ibid.

62. Computer Community Center, "Public Repository and Tape Duplication Facility," *Dr. Dobb's Journal of Computer Calisthenics and Orthodontics*, March 1976, 8.

63. Ibid.

64. Ibid.

65. Quoted in Jim Warren, "What's DDJCC&O All About?," *Dr. Dobb's Journal of Computer Calisthenics and Orthodontics*, February 1976, 2.

66. Martin Campbell Kelly et al., *Computer: A History of the Information Machine* (Boulder, CO: Westview Press, 2014), 238–245.

67. Charles Ingerham Peddle, Wilbur Mathys, William Mensch, and Rodney Orghill, Integrated circuit microprocessor with parallel binary adder having on-the-fly correction to provide decimal results, US Patent 3,991,307, filed September 16, 1975, and issued November 9, 1976; Gregg Williams and Rob Moore, "The Apple Story, Part 1: Early History," *Byte*, December 1984, A67–A70, at A67. See also Ross Bassett, *To the Digital Age: Research Labs, Start-Up Companies, and the Rise of MOS Technology* (Baltimore: Johns Hopkins University Press, 2002).

68. Ceruzzi, *History of Modern Computing*; Campbell-Kelly et al., *Computer*.

69. See *Patents at Apple: Apple's Future Depends on You*, VHS (Cupertino, CA: Apple Computers, 1992), box 80, videotape 10, Apple Computers, Inc. Records, M1007, Department of Special Collections, Stanford University Libraries, Stanford, CA.

70. Ibid., at 0:08.

71. Ibid., at 0:10.

72. Steven Wozniak, quoted in Williams and Moore, "Apple Story, Part 1," A68.

73. Ibid., A69.

74. Ibid.

75. Ibid.

76. Ibid.

77. Ibid.

78. Paul Terrell, quoted in Harry McCracken, "The Man Who Jump-Started Apple," *PC World's Techlog*, August 23, 2007, http://web.archive.org/web/20110511184229/http://blogs.pcworld.com/techlog/archives/005240.html.

79. Ibid.

80. Paul Terrell, quoted in McCracken, "The Man Who Jump-Started Apple."

81. Steven Wozniak, quoted in Gregg Williams and Rob Moore, "The Apple Story, Part 1," A70.

82. Ibid.

83. *Patents at Apple*, at 0:08-0:34; Campbell-Kelly et al., *Computer*, 242.

84. *Patents at Apple*, at 0:08-0:34; Campbell-Kelly et al., *Computer*, 242.

85. Blakely, Sokoloff, Taylor & Zafman, "Who We Are," https://web.archive.org/web/20160215123224/http://www.bstz.com/who-we-are/history/.

86. Stephen Wozniak, Microcomputer for use with video display, US Patent 4,136,359, filed April 11, 1977, and issued January 23, 1979, 1.

87. Apple Computer, Floating point routines, US Copyright Registration TX0000809448, published May 28, 1977, and issued October 11, 1979; Apple Computer, Integer basic, US Copyright Registration TX0000809447, published May 28, 1977, and issued October 11, 1979; Apple Computer, Applesoft, US Copyright Registration TX0001084422, filed January 2, 1978, and issued March 3, 1983; Apple Computer, Applesoft, US Copyright Registration TX0000886569, filed January 2, 1978, and issued May 4, 1982; Apple Computer, Apple Soft by Apple Computer, Inc., US Copyright Registration TXu000090674, created 1978 and issued April 14, 1982. For more on the interrelations among these programs, see Apple Computer, *Applesoft Extended Precision Floating Point Basing Language Reference Manual* (Cupertino, CA: Apple Computer, Microsoft, 1977), available online at https://archive.org/details/Apple_II_Extended_Precision_Floating_Point_BASIC_Language_Reference_Manual.

88. Apple Computer, Autostart ROM, US Copyright Registration TX0000873203, published January 1, 1979, and issued April 14, 1982; Apple Computer, Chain, US Copyright Registration TX0000886563, published January 2, 1978, and issued May 4, 1982; Apple Computer, Copy OBJO, US Copyright Registration TX0000886568, published January 2, 1978, and issued May 4, 1982; Apple Computer, Apple 13-sector boot ROM, US Copyright Registration TX0000886567, published January 2, 1978, and issued May 4, 1982.

89. Apple Computer, DOS 3.3, US Copyright Registration TX0000793845, filed April 15, 1980, and issued October 8, 1981.

90. "Censorship in Computer Magazines," *Hardcore Computing* 1:1 (1981): 8–9.

91. See, e.g., ibid., 8.

92. Interview of Margot Comstock by Jason Scott, June 20, 2015, https://archive.org/details/2015_06_Margot_Comstock_Interview.

93. Margot Comstock and Allan Tommervick, "Pirate, Thief. Who Dares to Catch Him?" *Softalk,* October 1980, 14.

94. Ibid., 15–16.

95. Ibid., 16.

96. Ibid., 15.

97. Ibid.

98. Chuck Haight, "A Few Words from the Publisher," *Hardcore Computing* 1:1 (1981): 2.

99. Ibid.

100. *Hardcore Computing* 1:1 (1981).

101. "Hardcore Alert," *Hardcore Computing* 1:1 (1981): 4–5.

102. This paragraph is based on Beverly Haight, "CENSORSHIP in Computer Magazines," *Hardcore Computing* 1:1 (1981): 4–5.

103. Ibid., 4.

104. Ibid.

105. "IBM PC Users," advertisement for Lockssmith, in box 8, folder 34, ADAPSO Records (CBI 172), Charles Babbage Institute; "IBM Personal Computers Users!," advertisement for Nagy Systems, in ibid.

106. "13 Ways to Beat the Software Piracy Problem," *Micro Software Marketing,* 1982, in box 8, folder 34, ADAPSO Records (CBI 172), Charles Babbage Institute (hereafter cited as CBI 172).

107. I am grateful to Peggy Kidwell, Curator of Mathematics at the Smithsonian Museum of American History, for enabling me to investigate the printed aids for video games in the 1970s.

108. "Avantgarde 64 Software & BBS," box 8, folder 34, CBI 172.

CHAPTER 9. CLONED COMPUTERS AND MICROCHIP PROTECTION, 1981–1984

1. Martin Campbell-Kelly et al., *Computer: A History of the Information Machine,* 3rd ed. (Boulder, CO: Westview Press, 2013), 245. See also James Cortada, *IBM: The Rise and Fall and Reinvention of a Global Icon* (Cambridge, MA: MIT Press, 2019).

2. Ibid.; Paul Carroll, *Big Blues: The Unmaking of IBM* (New York: Crown, 1993); and Steven W. Usselman, "Unbundling IBM: Antitrust and the Incentives to Innovation in American Computing," in *The Challenge of Remaining Innovative: Insights from Twentieth-Century American Business,* ed. Sally H. Clarke, Naomi R. Lamoreaux, and Steven W. Usselman (Stanford, CA: Stanford University Press, 2009), 249–279.

3. Campbell-Kelly et al., *Computer,* 246–247.

4. Ibid., 247.

5. Ibid., 247–248.

6. Lewis Eggebrecht, David Kummer, and Jesus Saenz, Synchronization of CRT controller chips, US Patent 4,495,594, filed July 1, 1981, and issued January 22, 1985; David Bradley, Dennis Gibbs, Donald Kostuch, and James Martin, Method for using page addressing mechanism, US Patent 4,374,417, filed February 5, 1981, and issued February 15, 1983; Lewis Eggebrecht and Jesus Saenz, Self-pacing serial keyboard interface for data

processing system, US Patent 4,460,957, filed August 12, 1981, and issued July 17, 1984; Lewis Eggebrecht and David Kummer, Extended addressing apparatus and method for direct storage and access devices, US Patent 4,658,350, filed August 12, 1981, and issued April 14, 1987; James Brewer, Lewis Eggebrecht, David Kummer, and Patricial McHough, Refresh circuit for dynamic memory of a data processor employing a direct memory access controller, US Patent 4,556,952, filed August 12, 1981, and issued December 3, 1985; David Bradley, Lewis Eggebrecht, Dennis Gibbs, and Donald Kostuch, Page addressing mechanism, US Patent 4,443,847, filed April 17, 1984, filed February 5, 1981, and issued April 17, 1984; Mark Dean, David Kummer, and Jesus Saenz, Composite video color signal generation from digital color signals, US Patent 4,442,428, filed August 12, 1981, and issued April 10, 1984; Mark Dean, Lewis Eggebrecht, David Kummer, and Jesus Saenz, color video display system having programmable border color, US Patent 4,437,092, filed August 12, 1981, and issued March 13, 1984.

7. I performed this estimation using the Copyright Office's Public Catalog by searching for computer file registrations for which IBM is the claimant.

8. I performed this estimation using the Copyright Office's Public Catalog by searching for computer file registrations for which IBM is the claimant.

9. International Business Machines, [The I B M personal computer DOS: version 1.0], US Copyright Registration TX0001029418, published September 25, 1981, and issued August 19, 1982; International Business Machines, The IBM personal computer BASIC: version C1.00], US Copyright Registration TX0001029419, published September 25, 1981, and issued August 19, 1982.

10. Jeffrey R. Yost, *Making IT Work: A History of the Computer Services Industry* (Cambridge, MA: MIT Press, 2017), 233.

11. Thomas K. McCraw and William R. Childs, *American Business since 1920: How It Worked,* 3rd ed. (Hoboken, NJ: John Wiley and Sons, 2018), 229–240.

12. Department of Justice, press release 96-324, July 2, 1996, electronic copy in my possession.

13. Richard H. K. Vietor, *Contrived Competition: Regulation and Deregulation in America* (Cambridge, MA: Harvard University Press, 1994).

14. Ibid., 211–214.

15. James Bessen and Robert Hunt, "An Empirical Look at Software Patents" (FRB of Philadelphia Working Paper No. 3-17, March 2004), 47.

16. See, e.g., Henry Kucera, Graphic word spelling correction using automated dictionary comparisons with phonetic skeletons, US Patent 4,580,241, filed February 18, 1983, and issued April 1, 1986; Hanana Potash and Howard Green, Method of transforming high level language statements into multiple lower level language instructions sets, US Patent 4,462,423, filed July 14, 1982, and issued July 31, 1984.

17. See, e.g., James Letwin, Method and operating system for executing programs in a multi-mode microprocessor, US Patent 4,779,187, filed April 10, 1985, and issued October 18, 1988.

18. Charlie Montague et al., "Technical Aspects of IBM PC Compatibility," *Byte,* November 1983, 247–252; Susan Chace, "Firms Allege Approach by Ex-IBM Aide Who Is Accused of Trying to Sell Secrets," *New York Times,* September 17, 1982.

19. Advertisement, *Byte,* October 1982, 83.

20. James McCoy, "The Top Six Compatibles," *Popular Computing*, April 1984, 132–136.

21. "Price Cut Pressure on Compatible Makers," *InfoWorld*, July 16, 1984, 4; Nancy Pocock, "Succeeding in the IBM-Compatible Market," *Data Processing* 28:5 (1986): 247–250.

22. McCoy, "Top Six Compatibles," 133.

23. Mark Dahmke, "The Compa Computer," *Byte*, January 1983, 30–36.

24. Marguerite Zientara, "Q&A: H.L. Sparks," *InfoWorld*, April 2, 1984, 84–85.

25. For more on employee mobility, see AnnaLee Saxenian, *Regional Advantage: Culture and Competition in Silicon Valley and Route 128* (Cambridge, MA: Harvard University Press, 1996).

26. "IBM Accuses 3 of Conspiracy with Secrets," *Washington Post*, September 15, 1982.

27. Chace, "Firms Allege Approach by Ex-IBM Aide Who Is Accused of Trying to Sell Secrets"; Andrew Pollack, "IBM Accuses 3 Executives of Stealing Computer Secrets," *New York Times*, September 15, 1982.

28. Pollack, "IBM Accuses 3 Executives."

29. "IBM Accuses 3 of Conspiracy with Secrets."

30. Ibid.

31. Michael Alpert, quoted in ibid.

32. Chace, "Firms Allege Approach by Ex-IBM Aide."

33. Ibid.; "IBM Accuses 3 of Conspiracy with Secrets."

34. "IBM vs. Bridge Tech Suit Put on Hold until Oct. 20," *Computerworld*, September 27, 1982; Deborah Wise, "Trade-Secret Trial Set for Former IBM Employees," *InfoWorld*, October 11, 1982, 11; "Judge Extends I.B.M. Order," *New York Times*, October 28, 1982; "IBM Trade-Secrets Suit against 3 Ex-Employees Is Speeded Up by Judge," *Wall Street Journal*, October 28, 1982, 23. Of course, the lawyers representing Bridge argued that the information disclosed was not, indeed, a secret. "IBM Data Involved in Suit Wasn't Secret, Opposing Lawyer Says," *Wall Street Journal*, October 29, 1982.

35. Deborah Wise, "IBM Wins in Court, Ex-Employees Put under Injunction," *InfoWorld*, December 27, 1982, 8; "IBM Secrets Lawsuit Is Amended to Include Tie to New Jersey Firm," *Wall Street Journal*, November 23, 1982; Andrew Pollack, "I.B.M. Suit on Secrets Is Widened," *New York Times*, November 23, 1982; William Carley, "No Title," *Wall Street Journal*, December 1, 1982; "IBM Concluded a Case Involving Trade Secrets," *Los Angeles Times*, December 1, 1982; "Editorial," *Computerworld*, January 17, 1983, 36.

36. Pollack, "IBM Accuses 3 Executives." See also Andrew Pollack, "I.B.M. Suit on Secrets Is Settled," *New York Times*, December 1, 1982.

37. Jeffrey Young, "Lewis Eggebrecht," *Forbes*, July 7, 1997, 334; Martin Porter, "Ostracized PC1 Designer Still Ruminates 'Why?,'" *PC Magazine*, September 18, 1984, 33, 39, 41.

38. Porter, "Ostracized PC1 Designer," 39; Lewis Eggebrecht, *Interfacing to the IBM Personal Computer* (Indianapolis, IN: H. W. Sams, 1983).

39. See Marie Ancordoguy, *Reprogramming Japan: The High-Tech Crisis under Communitarian Capitalism* (Ithaca, NY: Cornell University Press, 2005); and James Cortada, *The Digital Flood: The Diffusion of Information Technology across the U.S., Europe, and Asia* (New York: Oxford University Press, 2012).

40. Ancordoguy, *Reprogramming Japan*, 158–159.

41. Ibid. Newspaper accounts include Andrew Pollack, "The Publicity Effect of IBM Sting," *New York Times*, November 5, 1983; "Hitachi Guilty in IBM Case," *New York*

Times, November 9, 1983; and "2 Hitachi Aides Plead Guilty in IBM Case," *New York Times*, December 22, 1983.

42. Assistant Secretary for Trade Development, *A Competitive Assessment of the US Software Industry* (Washington, DC: US Department of Commerce, International Trade Administration, [1984?]); Danesh Sharma, *The Outsourcer: The Story of India's IT Revolution* (Cambridge, MA: MIT Press, 2015); Arora Ashish and Alfonso Gambardella, eds., *From Underdogs to Tigers: The Rise and Growth of the Software Industry in Brazil, China, India, Ireland, and Israel* (New York: Oxford University Press, 2005).

43. AnnaLee Saxenian, *The New Argonauts: Regional Advantage in a Global Economy* (Cambridge, MA: Harvard University Press, 2007).

44. Werner Frank, "Fake Apples in Hong Kong: Rotten to the Core," *Computerworld*, February 28, 1983, box 8, folder 34, ADAPSO Records (CBI 172), Charles Babbage Institute, University of Minnesota, Minneapolis.

45. Ibid.

46. Dick Cooper, "Counterfeit Computers Are Seized," box 8, folder 34, ADAPSO Records (CBI 172), Charles Babbage Institute.

47. Tracy Deliman, "TRS-80 Copy from Hong Kong," *InfoWorld*, August 18, 1980, 1, 7; Sol Libes, "Bytelines: News and Speculation about Personal Computing," *Byte*, December 1980, 218.

48. Deliman, "TRS-80 Copy from Hong Kong"; Libes, "Bytelines."

49. Deliman, "TRS-80 Copy from Hong Kong"; Libes, "Bytelines."

50. Deliman, "TRS-80 Copy from Hong Kong," 7.

51. See, e.g., Robert Ringland, Frequency modulated signal pre-amplifier with amplitude modulated signal bypass, US Patent 3,965,426, filed January 10, 1974, and issued June 22, 1976; Bernard Grae, Computer housing, US Patent D271101, filed December 15, 1980, and issued October 25, 1983; Steven Leininger, Apparatus for alpha-numeric/graphic display, US Patent 4,228,599, filed April 18, 1980, and issued July 6, 1982.

52. Tandy Corporation, Blackjack: Backgammon, US Copyright Registration TX0000376277, published January 11, 1978, and issued April 16, 1979; Tandy Corporation, Quick, Watson!, US Copyright Registration TX0000376278, published October 18, 1978, and issued April 16, 1979.

53. See, e.g., Tandy Corporation, Real Estate Analysis, Volume 1, US Copyright Registration TX0001318776, published December 15, 1979, and issued March 28, 1984; Tandy Corporation, Accounts Payable System, US Copyright Registration TX0000477421, published February 14, 1980, and issued March 20, 1980; and Tandy Corporation, Business Finance, US Copyright Registration TX0000570052, published September 30, 1980, and issued October 21, 1980.

54. See, e.g., Tandy Corporation, Radio Shack TRS-80 Level II Basic Instruction Course, US Copyright Registration TX0000282024, published April 24, 1979, and issued June 6, 1979; and Tandy Corporation, Math Drill, US Copyright Registration TX0000570054, published September 30, 1980, and issued October 21, 1980.

55. I found these numbers by counting the registrations for which Tandy is a claimant, as listed in the online registration records of the US Copyright Office. The search interface is available online at http://cocatalog.loc.gov/cgi-bin/Pwebrecon.cgi?DB=local& PAGE=First.

56. Tandy Corporation, Input/Out Computer Program: Radio Shack Level II Basic for Model I TRS-80, US Copyright Registration TXu000083443, created 1978, and issued January 26, 1981.

57. Lester Lee, quoted in "Tandy Files against PMC," *InfoWorld*, May 25, 1985, 1.

58. Tandy Corp. v. Personal Micro Computers, Inc., 254 F. Supp. 171 (N.D. Cal. 1981).

59. Ibid., 173, 174.

60. Ibid., 175.

61. Stern Electronics, Inc. v. Kaufman, 523 F. Supp. 635 (E.D. N.Y. 1981); Stern Electronics, Inc. v. Kaufman, 669 F.2d 852 (2d Cir. 1982); Williams Electronics, Inc. v. Artic International, Inc., 685 F.2d 870 (3d Cir. 1982).

62. Perry Greenberg, "The Making of a Computer," *Easy Home Computer*, September 1983, 52–53.

63. Quoted in ibid., 52.

64. Joel Shusterman, quoted in Deborah Wise, "A New Apple Look-Alike," *InfoWorld*, March 1, 1982, 1.

65. Appellee's brief, Apple Computer, Inc. v. Franklin Computer Corp., Case File 82-1582, National Archives, Philadelphia, 7.

66. Greenberg, "Making of a Computer," 53.

67. Appellee's brief, Apple Computer, Inc. v. Franklin Computer Corp., 545 F. Supp. 812 (E.D. Pa. 1982), 8; Wise, "New Apple Look-Alike," 1.

68. Advertisement in *Personal Computing Magazine* 6 (1982): 650.

69. Gerry Elman, "Franklin Wins Round 1 in Courtroom Battle with Apple," *InfoWorld*, September 6, 1982, 3.

70. *Apple*, 545 F. Supp. at 817.

71. The records of Franklin's appeal do not survive. This summary is based on Elman, "Franklin Wins Round 1 in Courtroom Battle with Apple," 3–4.

72. *Apple*, 545 F. Supp. at 825.

73. Ibid.

74. Elman, "Franklin Wins Round 1," 3.

75. Ibid., 4.

76. *Franklin Ace 1000 User Reference Manual* (Pennsauken, NJ: Franklin Computer, 1982), 29.

77. Ibid.

78. Quoted in Brief of Microsoft Corporation, Apple v. Franklin, Appeal no. 82-1532, National Archives, Philadelphia, 6, P1160386.

79. Brief of Digital Research, Apple v. Franklin, Appeal no. 82-1532, 6.

80. Ibid.

81. Ibid., 7.

82. Brief of ADAPSO, Apple v. Franklin, Appeal no. 82-1532.

83. Ibid., 7.

84. Ibid.

85. Ibid.

86. Brief of Pro-Log Corporation, Apple v. Franklin, Appeal no. 82-1532.

87. Ibid., 2.

88. Original text in all capital letters, ibid., 2.

89. Ibid., 2–3.

90. Ibid., 3.

91. Ibid.

92. Ibid., 2.

93. Apple Computer, Inc. v. Franklin Computer Corp., 714 F.2d 1240 (3d Cir. 1983), 1249.

94. Ibid.

95. Ibid., 1251.

96. *Apple*, 714 F.2d at 1252.

97. CONTU, cited in ibid., 1251.

98. David Needle, "Franklin Responds to Apple Suit with Countersuit," *InfoWorld*, June 28, 1982, 7; Paul Freiberger, "Apple and Franklin Hurl Charges and Countersuit Threats," *InfoWorld*, August 30, 1982, 3.

99. Ibid.

100. Franklin Computer Corp. v. Apple Computer, Inc., 454 U.S. 1033 (1984).

101. Greenberg, "Making of a Computer," 52–53.

102. "The Economic Effects of Chip Piracy on the U.S. Semiconductor Industry," in Hearings before the Subcommittee on Courts, Civil Liberties, and the Administration of Justice of the Committee on the Judiciary, House of Representatives, 98th Cong., 1st Sess., on H.R. 1028, August 3 and December 1, 1983, 180.

103. Ibid.

104. 17 U.S.C. § 102(a), quoted in Dorothy Schrader, "Prepared Statement of Dorothy Schrader," Hearing Before the Subcommittee on Patents, Copyrights and Trademarks of the Committee on the Judiciary, U.S. Senate, 98th Cong., 1st Sess., on S. 1201, May 19, 1983, 29.

105. Barbara Ringer, H.R. Rep. No. 94-1476, 94th Cong., 2d Sess., 1976, 105, cited in Schrader, "Prepared Statement of Dorothy Schrader," 28.

106. Schrader, "Prepared Statement of Dorothy Schrader," 29, 30.

107. Zilog, Inc. v. Nippon Electronic Co. et al., Civ. 83-1241-WHO (N.D. Cal. 1983); Intersil v. Teledyne Corp, Civ. 82-4187-WHO (N.D. Cal. 1982).

108. "Zilog, NEC Resolve Differences in Chip Dispute," *Computerworld*, March 19, 1984, 108.

109. Ibid.; Masatoshi Shima, Federico Faggin, and Ralph Ungermann, Microprocessor apparatus and method, US Patent 4,332,008, filed November 9, 1979, and issued May 25, 1982; Masatoshi Shima, Federico Faggin, and Ralph Ungermann, Microprocessor apparatus and method, US Patent 4,486,827, filed January 18, 1982, and issued December 4, 1984.

110. "Zilog, NEC Resolve Differences in Chip Dispute"; Schrader, "Prepared Statement of Dorothy Schrader," 30.

111. H.R. 14293 (1978); H.R. 1007 (1979); H.R. 7207 (1092); S. 3117 (1982).

112. H.R. 1007, 96th Cong., 1st Sess., January 18, 1979.

113. Hearing before the Subcommittee on Courts, Civil Liberties, and the Administration of the Committee on the Judiciary, House of Representatives, 96th Cong., 1st Sess., on H.R. 1007, April 16, 1979.

114. Ibid., 32.

115. Ibid., 33.

116. Ibid., 52.

117. Ibid.

118. The Semiconductor Chip Protection Act of 1983, Hearing Before the Subcommittee on Patents, Copyrights and Trademarks of the Committee on the Judiciary, U.S. Senate, 98th Cong., 1st Sess., on S. 1201, May 19, 1983.

119. Ibid., 75.

120. Ibid.

121. Ibid.

122. Ibid.

123. Ibid., 77–82.

124. Ibid., 100.

125. Ibid., 101.

126. Copyright Protection for Semiconductor Chips, Hearings before the Subcommittee on Courts, Civil Liberties, and the Administration of Justice of the Committee on the Judiciary, House of Representatives, 98th Cong., 1st Sess., on H.R. 1028, August 3 and December 1, 1983, 66.

127. Ibid.

128. Ibid.

129. "Obituary, Dorothy M. Schrader," http://www.legacy.com/obituaries/schuylkill/obit uary.aspx?pid=172037495.

130. Berne Convention for the Protection of Literary and Artistic Works (amended September 28, 1979), World Intellectual Property Organization, http://www.wipo.int/ treaties/en/text.jsp?file_id=283698.

131. Copyright Protection for Semiconductor Chips, 98th Cong., 1st Sess., H.R. 1028, August 3 and December 1, 1983, 82.

132. H.R. 2985, 98th Cong., 1st Sess., 1983, 1, 3.

133. Ibid., 1, 5.

134. Statement of Dorothy Schrader, in Copyright Protection for Semiconductor Chips, H.R. 1028, August 3 and December 1, 1983, 143.

135. Ibid., 125.

136. Ibid.

137. Pub. L. No. 98-620, 98 Stat. 3335 (1984), 3347, 3349.

138. Ibid., 3349.

139. Richard Stern, *Semiconductor Chip Protection* (Washington, DC: Harcourt Brace, 1986), xxx.

140. US Copyright Office, *Circular R100* (Washington, DC: GPO, 1984), reproduced in Stern, *Semiconductor Chip Protection*, 590–595.

141. Ibid.

142. Ibid.

143. Ibid.

144. Brooktree Corp. v. Advanced Micro Devices, Inc., 705 F. Supp. 491 (S.D. Cal. 1988); Altera Corp. v. Clear Logic, Inc., 424 F.3d 1079 (9th Cir., 2005).

145. Alexander Galetovic, "Intellectual Property and the History of the Semiconductor Industry" (Hoover IP[2] Working Paper presented at "What Patents Really Do: Historical Perspectives on Current Debates," Stanford University, May 17, 2018. See, e.g.,

Steven P. Kasch, "The Semiconductor Chip Protection Act: Past, Present, and Future," *Berkeley Technology and Law Journal* 7 (1992): 71–105.

146. Leon Randomsky, "Sixteen Years after the Passage of the Semiconductor Chip Protection Act: Is International Protection Working?," *Berkeley Technology Law Journal* 15 (2000): 1049–1098.

CHAPTER 10. LOOK, FEEL, AND PROGRAMMING FREEDOM, 1984–1995

1. Martin Campbell-Kelly et al., *Computer: A History of the Information Machine*, 3rd ed. (Boulder, CO: Westview Press, 2013), 247–258.

2. Ibid., as well as my experience operating a Macintosh computer loaded with the original MAC OS.

3. Ibid., 248.

4. For more on PARC, see Campbell-Kelly et al., *Computer*, 260–261.

5. Xerox Corp. v. Apple Computer, Inc., 734 F. Supp. 1542 (N.D. Cal. 1990).

6. See "Brief of Appellee Microsoft," Apple Computer, Inc. v. Microsoft Corp., Nos. 93-161867, 93-16869, 93-16883 (9th Cir. February 23, 1994); and *Xerox*, 734 F. Supp.

7. Bruce Daniels, cited in "Brief of Appellee Microsoft."

8. *Xerox*, 734 F. Supp.

9. Smalltalk license, quoted in ibid., 1543.

10. Xerox Corporation, Star User Interface for Xerox 8010 Professional Workstation, US Copyright Registration TX0002428306, filed April 27, 1981, and issued April 28, 1986.

11. Ibid., 261; Martin Campbell-Kelly, *From Airline Reservations to Sonic the Hedgehog: A History of the Software Industry* (Cambridge, MA: MIT Press, 2003), 246–251.

12. For the hiring of Tesler, see Campbell-Kelly et al., *Computer*, 261; and Campbell-Kelly, *From Airline Reservations to Sonic the Hedgehog*, 246–247.

13. Jerrold Manock and James Steward, Dual disk drive, US Design Patent 271,102, filed August 24, 1981, and issued October 25, 1983; William Lapson and William Atkinson, Cursor device for use with display system, US Patent 4,464,652, filed July 19, 1982, and issued August 7, 1984; Jerrold C. Manock, Terrel Oyama, and Steven Jobs, Computer housing, US Design Patent 285,687, filed October 13, 1983, and issued September 16, 1986.

14. Three sequentially issued registrations covered this suite of programs. See Apple Computer, Lisa Office System Release 1.0, US Copyright Registration PA0000336104, published June 1, 1983, and issued May 1, 1987; Apple Computer, Lisa Office System Release 1.0, US Copyright Registration PA0000336103, published June 1, 1983, and issued May 1, 1987; and Debra Willret, Apple Computer, Lisa Office System Release 1.0, US Copyright Registration PA0000336106, published June 1, 1983, and issued May 1, 1987.

15. Bruce Horn, Apple Computer, Finder, US Copyright Registration TX0002130713, published January 24, 1984, and issued August 25, 1987; Bruce Horn, Steve Capps, Apple Computer, The Macintosh Finder, US Copyright Registration TX0002970418, published May 2, 1984, and issued December 4, 1990; Apple Computer, The Macintosh Finder: version 1.0, US Copyright Registration PA0000336105, published January 24, 1984, and issued May 1, 1987.

16. Apple Computer, Macintosh ROM, US Copyright Registration TX0001640052, published January 24, 1984, and issued April 14, 1987; Apple Computer, MacPaint, US Copyright Registration TX0002130711, published January 24, 1984, and issued August 25, 1987; K. R. Wigginton, Apple Computer, and Encore Systems, MacWrite, US Copyright Registration TX0002132477, published January 24, 1984, and issued August 25, 1987.

17. Peggy Watt, "The 'Look and Feel' Debate," *InfoWorld*, March 21, 1988.

18. Agreement between John Sculley and William Gates, November 22, 1985, copy in my possession and available online at tech-insider.org/windows/research/1985/1122.html.

19. "Brief of Appellee Microsoft," *Apple v. Microsoft*; Campbell-Kelly et al., *Computer*, 265.

20. Ibid.; Apple Computer, Inc. v. Microsoft Corp., 717 F. Supp. 1428 (N.D. Cal. 1989).

21. "Brief of Appellee Microsoft," *Apple*, 717 F. Supp.

22. Ibid.

23. Ibid.; Agreement between Sculley and Gates.

24. Agreement between Sculley and Gates. See also Lawrence Fisher, "Apple and Microsoft Disclose a 1985 Pact," *New York Times*, March 24, 1988.

25. Campbell-Kelly et al., *Computer*, 265.

26. For more on the comparative benefits of these systems, see, e.g., Jim Forbes, "Micro Execs Holding Off on Windows," *InfoWorld*, December 18, 1985, 1.

27. Campbell-Kelly et al., *Computer,* 265.

28. Steven Burke, "Speculation about Topview Persists," *InfoWorld*, October 7, 1985, 34–35; Edward Foster, "Windows Spells Trouble for Topview," *InfoWorld*, September 23, 1985, 14.

29. "Brief for Appellant Apple Computer," Apple Computer, Inc. v. Microsoft Corp., Nos. 93-161867, 93-16869, 93-16883 (9th Cir. February 11, 1994).

30. *Apple*, 717 F. Supp. 1428 at 1431.

31. Apple Computer, Inc. v. Microsoft Corp. and Hewlett-Packard Co., 25 F.3d 1435 (9th Cir. 1994).

32. Broderbund Software, Inc. v. Unison World, Inc., 648 F. Supp. 1127 (N.D. Cal. 1986). For more on *The Print Shop* and samples of the kinds of documents that it enabled users to produce, Deborah Kovacs, "The Print Shop and the Newsroom," *II Computing*, October–November 1985, 48–57; Tom Shea, "Graphics Program Lets Users Design, Print Greeting Cards," *InfoWorld*, April 23, 1984, 42; Cheryl Peterson, "Editorial," *Ahoy!*, August 1985, 5, 114.

33. *Broderbund*, 1648 F. Supp. at 133; Eric Loch, "Court Backs 'Look & Feel' Copyright," *InfoWorld*, October 20, 1986; Watt, " 'Look and Feel' Debate," 85. See also Ashton Tate Corp. v. Fox Software, Inc., 760 F. Supp. 831 (C.D. Cal. 1991).

34. See Lawrence Fisher, "Xerox Sues Apple Computer over Macintosh Copyright," *New York Times*, December 15, 1989.

35. *Xerox*, 734 F. Supp. at 1544.

36. Ibid., 1545–1546.

37. David Kearns, quoted in Fisher, "Xerox Sues Apple Computer over Macintosh Copyright."

38. Apple Computer, Inc. v. Microsoft Corp., 799 F. Supp. 1006 (N.D. Cal. 1992), 1024.

39. Ibid.

40. Apple Computer, Inc. v. Microsoft Corp., 35 F.3d 1435 (9th Cir. 1994), 1443.

41. Steve Jobs, cited in "Brief of Appellee Microsoft," Apple v. Microsoft, Nos. 93-161867, 93-16869, 93-16883 (9th Cir. February 23, 1994).

42. Andrew Pollack, "Most of Xerox's Suit against Apple Barred," *New York Times*, March 24, 1990.

43. Kevin Driscoll, "Hobbyist Inter-Networking and the Popular Internet Imaginary: Forgotten Histories of Networked Personal Computing, 1978–1998" (Ph.D. diss., University of Southern California, 2014).

44. See, e.g., Martin Lasden, "Of Bytes and Bulletin Boards," *New York Times*, August 4, 1985.

45. Ibid.

46. "Complete Pirated Apple/IBM Pirated 'Pursuitable' BBS List 01/08/88," cited in Driscoll, "Hobbyist Inter-Networking," 263n463.

47. Lasden, "Of Bytes and Bulletin Boards"; Bruce Sterling, *The Hacker Crackdown: Law and Disorder on the Electronic Frontier* (New York: Bantam Books, 1993).

48. Ric Manning, "Software Industry's on the Trail of Video 'Robin Hoods,'" *Chicago Tribune*, July 26, 1985.

49. Ibid.; Lasden, "Of Bytes and Bulletin Boards."

50. Lasden, "Of Bytes and Bulletin Boards."

51. ADAPSO, press release, November 12, 1984, box 7, folder 11, CBI 172.

52. ADAPSO, "Thou Shalt Not Dupe," pamphlet, 1985, box 10, folder 20, CBI 172.

53. ADAPSO poster, "I got in big trouble," box 7, folder 10, CBI 172.

54. ADAPSO poster, "No one told me," ibid.

55. Paul Carroll, "On Your Honor: Software Firms Remove Copy-Protection Devices," *Wall Street Journal*, September 25, 1986.

56. Patricia Gray, "A Software-Lock Breaker Becomes a Hero to Some, a Villain to Others," *Wall Street Journal*, February 7, 1986.

57. "Kenneth Wasch," U.S. Information Technology Office, http://www.usito.org/about-us/leadership/kenneth-wasch.

58. "Group Formed for Publishers of Software," *Washington Post*, April 23, 1984.

59. Lasden, "Of Bytes and Bulletin Boards."

60. See Manning, "Software Industry's on the Trail of Video 'Robin Hoods.'"

61. "Uncle Sam's Marching Orders," *PC Magazine*, May 27, 1986, 42.

62. Stewart Alsop and Charles Bermant, "Copy Protection Losing Its Favor," *PC Magazine*, May 27, 1986, 33.

63. U.S. Adherence to the Berne Convention, 95th Cong., 1st and 2d Sess., May 16, 1985, and April 15, 1986, 716–718.

64. Pamela Samuelson, "Fair Use for Computer Programs and Other Copyrightable Works in Digital Form: The Implications of Sony, Galoob, and Sega," *Journal of Intellectual Property Law* 49 (1993–1994): 49–118; Joel Gilman, "When the SPA Comes A-Knockin'," *Computerworld*, December 7, 1992, 108.

65. These biographical notes on Stallman are based on Christopher J. Tozzi, *For Fun and Profit: A History of the Free and Open Source Software Revolution* (Cambridge, MA: MIT Press, 2017), 23–50.

66. For more on the free software movement's history, see Christopher M. Kelty, *Two Bits: Cultural Meaning of Free Software* (Durham, NC: Duke University Press, 2008); and Tozzi, *For Fun and Profit*.

67. Pamela Samuelson and Robert Glushko, "Comparing the Views of Lawyers and User Interface Designers on the Software Copyright 'Look and Feel' Lawsuits," *Jurimetrics* 30:1 (1989): 121–140. See also Pamela Samuelson, "Protecting User Interfaces through Copyright: The Debate," *CHI Proceedings of the SIGCHI Conference on Human Factors in Computing Systems* (New York: ACM, 1989), 97–104.

68. Samuelson and Glushko, "Comparing the Views of Lawyers and User Interface Designers," 124; Peter Lewis, "Legal Constraints on Sharing Ideas," *New York Times,* May 7, 1989.

69. Samuelson and Glushko, "Comparing the Views of Lawyers and User Interface Designers." See also Pamela Samuelson and Robert Glushko, "Survey on the Look and Feel Lawsuits," *Communications of the ACM* 33:5 (1990): 483–487.

70. GNU General Public License, February 1989, https://www.gnu.org/licenses/old-licenses/gpl-1.0.en.html.

71. Lotus Development Corp. v. Paperback Software Int'l, 740 F. Supp. 37 (D. Mass. 1990). This case was consolidated with Lotus Development Corp. v. Mosaic Software, Civ. Action No. 87-74-K. See *Lotus,* 740 F. Supp. at 87 n.1.

72. *Lotus,* 740 F. Supp. at 55.

73. Rachel Parker, "NEX/Intel Decision May Influence Other Copyright Rulings," *Info-World,* February 20, 1989, 6.

74. League for Programming Freedom (LPF), "Programmers and Users Picket Lotus, Protesting User-Interface Copyright Litigation," http://groups.csail.mit.edu/mac/projects/lpf/Links/prep.ai.mit.edu/demo.final.release.

75. My description of the pin is based on my examination of a personal copy of the pin (reissued in the mid-1990s). LPF, "History of the LPF . . . ," http://groups.csail.mit.edu/mac/projects/lpf/History/history.html.

76. Ibid.; Alan Cooperman, "Scientists Challenge Companies' Lock on Software Programs," http://groups.csail.mit.edu/mac/projects/lpf/Links/prep.ai.mit.edu/demo.ap-wire.

77. LPF, "Programmers and Users Picket Lotus, Protesting User-Interface Copyright Litigation," http://groups.csail.mit.edu/mac/projects/lpf/Links/prep.ai.mit.edu/demo.final.release.

78. These signs are described in ibid.

79. Ibid.

80. Ibid.

81. Steven Pemberton, "An Alternative Simple Language and Environment for PCs," *IEEE Software* 4:1 (1987): 56–64.

82. See, e.g., Oral history interview with Jonathan Sachs (2004), Charles Babbage Institute, https://conservancy.umn.edu/handle/11299/107619.

83. This analysis of the phrase "D-E-F-O" draws on a programming manual for the Akai MPC 2000. See "Chapter 3 Programming Examples," http://www.accelmpc.co.jp/eng_site/manual/816-3.pdf.

84. Connie Guglielmo, "Nu Prometheus Unbound," *MacWeek,* June 13, 1989, 1, 8. See also "Hackers Leak Mac OS Source Code," *InfoWorld,* June 12, 1989, 1, 3; Laurie Flynn, "FBI Searches for 'Nu Prometheus' Mac Source-Code Leak," *InfoWorld,* November 27, 1989, 6; Steven Levy, "Code and Dagger," *Macworld,* September 1990, 69–80. See also

Bruce Sterling, *The Hacker Crackdown: Law and Disorder on the Electronic Frontier* (New York: Bantam Books, 1992), 232–233.

85. Quoted in Guglielmo, "Nu Prometheus Unbound," 1.

86. Quoted in ibid., 8.

87. Levy, "Code and Dagger."

88. Ibid.

89. Richard Stallman, quoted in Flynn, "FBI Searches for 'Nu Prometheus' Mac Source-Code Leak."

90. The National Archives maintains an online database on the Pentagon Papers. "Pentagon Papers," https://www.archives.gov/research/pentagon-papers.

91. "Fight 'Look and Feel' Lawsuits," undated, printout in my possession and available online at http://groups.csail.mit.edu/mac/projects/lpf/Links/prep.ai.mit.edu/. See also LPF, "History of the LPF."

92. Richard Stallman to GNU.emacs, "Announcing the League for Programming Freedom," email, November 10, 1989, http://tech-insider.org/free-software/research/1989/1110.html.

93. Ibid.

94. Ibid.

95. Kelty, *Two Bits*, 3.

96. Stallman, "Announcing the League for Programming Freedom."

97. *Lotus v. Paperback*, 65–71.

98. "Fight 'Look and Feel' Lawsuits."

99. Michael Alexander, "Lotus Litigation Draws Protest," *Computerworld*, August 6, 1990, 6.

100. "Fight 'Look and Feel' Lawsuits."

101. Quotations in ibid.

CHAPTER 11. PATENT ENFORCEMENT AND SOFTWARE EMBODIMENT, 1986–1995

1. James Bessen and Robert Hunt, "An Empirical Look at Software Patents," *Journal of Economic and Management Strategy* 16:1 (2007): 157–189. See also James Bessen and Michael J. Meurer, *Patent Failure: How Judges, Bureaucrats, and Lawyers Put Innovators at Risk* (Princeton, NJ: Princeton University Press, 2008). As before, I consider these numbers to be minimum values.

2. David Sanger, "Burroughs, in Challenge to I.B.M., to Acquire Sperry for $4.8 Billion," *New York Times*, May 28, 1986; Calvin Sims, "Burroughs Announces New Company Name," *New York Times*, November 11, 1986; David Sanger, "Burroughs Is Seeking to Overhaul Its Image," *New York Times*, May 9, 1986; and David Sanger, "Corporate America in Turmoil," *New York Times*, December 29, 1986.

3. Michael Blumenthal, cited in Sanger, "Burroughs, in Challenge to I.B.M., to Acquire Sperry for $4.8 Billion."

4. Terry A. Welch, High speed data compression and decompression apparatus and method, US Patent 4,558,302, filed June 20, 1983, and issued December 10, 1985. See also Terry Welch, "A Technique for High-Performance Data Compression," *Computer*, June 1984, 9–19.

5. Carl Shapiro, "Navigating the Patent Thicket: Cross Licenses, Patent Pools, and Standard Setting," in *Innovation Policy and the Economy*, ed. Adam B. Jaffe, Josh Lerner, and Scott Stern (Cambridge, MA: MIT Press, 2001), 119–150.

6. See also Willard Eastman, Abraham Lempel, Jacob Ziv, and Martin Cohn, Apparatus and method for compressing data signals and restoring the compressed data signals, US Patent 4,464,650, filed August 10, 1981, and issued August 7, 1984.

7. James Woods, "Sperry Patent #4,558,302 Does *Not* Affect Compress," email list communication, July 31, 1990, http://www.perlmonks.org/?displaytype=displaycode; node_id=270034.

8. See Alistair Moffat and Andrew Turpin, *Compression and Coding Algorithms* (New York: Springer, 2012), 220.

9. James Woods, "Patent Essence," http://groups.csail.mit.edu/mac/projects/lpf/Links/prep.ai.mit.edu/patent.essence.

10. "Patent Number 4,856,787," http://groups.csail.mit.edu/mac/projects/lpf/Links/prep.ai.mit.edu/patent.games; "US Patent # 4,916,610," http://groups.csail.mit.edu/mac/projects/lpf/Links/prep.ai.mit.edu/patent.4916610; Untitled, http://groups.csail.mit.edu/mac/projects/lpf/Links/prep.ai.mit.edu/patent.4956809; "5,083,262," http://groups.csail.mit.edu/mac/projects/lpf/Links/prep.ai.mit.edu/patent.5083262.

11. "Patent Number 4,856,787."

12. Josef Sukonik and Greg Tilden, Method for dynamically viewing image elements stored in a random access memory array, US Patent 4,197,590, filed January 19, 1978, and issued April 8, 1980.

13. Undated flyer, reproduction in my possession.

14. LPF, "Against Software Patents," http://groups.csail.mit.edu/mac/classes/6.805/articles/int-prop/lpf-against-software-patents.html.

15. Ibid.

16. Ibid.

17. Ibid.

18. Simon Garfinkel, Richard Stallman, and Mitchell Kapor, "Why Patents Are Bad for Software," *Issues in Science and Technology*, Fall 1991, 50–55.

19. Ibid., 51.

20. Ibid., 54.

21. Pamela Samuelson, Michel Denber, and Robert Glushko, "Developments on the Intellectual Property Front," *Communications of the ACM* 35:6 (1992): 33–39.

22. Ibid.

23. See, e.g., Edmund L. Andrews, "BC Patents," July 26, 1991, http://groups.csail.mit.edu/mac/projects/lpf/Links/prep.ai.mit.edu/integration.patent.

24. "Report of the Committee on Algorithms and the Law," http://groups.csail.mit.edu/mac/projects/lpf/Links/prep.ai.mit.edu/mps-patents.tex.

25. Dave Farber, "[INFO] 55 Software Patents in One Week !!!!," http://groups.csail.mit.edu/mac/projects/lpf/Links/prep.ai.mit.edu/ibm-patents-1week.

26. Michael Ernst, "Partial List of Software Patents," http://groups.csail.mit.edu/mac/projects/lpf/Links/prep.ai.mit.edu/patent-list.

27. This information on CompuServe is based on Martin Campbell-Kelly et al., *Computer: A History of the Information Machine*, 3rd ed. (Boulder, CO: Westview Press, 2013), 271–274.

28. CompuServe, "G I F (tm)," June 15, 1987, https://www.w3.org/Graphics/GIF/spec-gif87.txt. See also David Salomon, *Data Compression: The Complete Reference* (New York: Springer, 2012), 216.

29. "CompuServe Supports Graphic File Format," *InfoWorld*, June 15, 1987, 25; Stott Mace, "Screen Capture Utility Enhanced for OS/2, VGA," *InfoWorld*, February 20, 1989, 16.

30. Karen Rodriguez, "Unisys Seeks Royalties from GIF Developers," *InfoWorld*, January 9, 1995, 3.

31. Adam Gaffin, "Confusion Reigns on the Web over GIF Patent Claims," *Network World*, January 9, 1995, 4.

32. Welch, High speed data compression and decompression apparatus and method, 12, 36.

33. Ibid.; Julia King, "Users Outraged over Fees for GIF Format," *Computerworld*, January 9, 1995, 6; Tim Oren, "GIF, UNISYS, and CompuServe," email, January 4, 1995, http://web.archive.org/web/19981202215207/http://lpf.ai.mit.edu:80/Patents/Gif/orig-CompuServe.html.

34. Reexamination Certificate, in Welch, High speed data compression and decompression apparatus and method.

35. Ibid.; King, "Users Outraged over Fees for GIF Format."

36. "Agreement for Use of Graphics Interchange Format (SM)," http://web.archive.org/web/19981203040751/http://lpf.ai.mit.edu:80/Patents/Gif/gif_lic.html.

37. Ibid.; "Unisys Clarifies Policy Regarding Patent Use of On-Line Service Offerings," http://web.archive.org/web/19981203000955/htto://lpf.ai.mit.edu:80/Patents/Gif/unisys.html.

38. Oliver Picher, quoted in Karen Rodriguez, "Unisys Seeks Royalties from GIF Developers," *InfoWorld*, January 9, 1995, 3.

39. Ibid.; Mark Gibbs, "GIFgate—Nothing Is Sacred," *Network World*, January 16, 1995, 16.

40. Brad Gran, "Owner Has Rights," *Network World*, February 20, 1995, 33.

41. Quoted in "LPF Position on the GIF Controversy," undated, http://web.archive.org/web/19981203000948/http://lpf.ai.mir.edu:80/Patents/Gif/lpf_position.html.

42. Ibid.

43. Ibid.; "Unisys/CompuServe GIF Controversy," undated, http://web.archive.org/web/19981203054919/http://lpf.ai.mir.edu:80/Patents/Gif/Gif.html. See also "Why There Are No GIF Files on GNU Web Pages," undated, https://www.gnu.org/philosophy/gif.en.html.

44. "Why There Are No GIF Files on GNU Web Pages."

45. See "Thoughts on a GIF-Replacement Format," January 5, 1995, https://groups.google.com/forum/#!msg/comp.graphics/tylpVt2y9s8/eHWKNVLYMREJ.

46. *Computer Chronicles*, "COMDEX Fall 93," produced by Sara O'Brien, WTF-TV, 1993, digital copy in my possession.

47. "Comdex A Nerd's Paradise, Logistical Nightmare," *Sun Sentinel*, November 22, 1993.

48. Martha Groves, "Computer Industry Descends on Vegas for Comdex Crunch," *Los Angeles Times*, November 16, 1993; Peter Lewis, "The Executive Computer," *New York Times*, November 21, 1993.

49. Tim Bajarin, quoted in *The Computer Chronicles: COMDEX (1993)*, https://www.youtube.com/watch?v=nMqc_oZK3UA, at 1:30.

50. See Lawrence Magid, "An Extravaganza on Your Desktop," *Los Angeles Times*, November 25, 1994.

51. Ibid.; *Computer Chronicles*, "COMDEX Fall 93."

52. Amy Harmon, "Granting of Broad Patent Stuns Multimedia Industry," *Los Angeles Times*, November 17, 1993.

53. Magid, "Extravaganza on Your Desktop."

54. Harmon, "Granting of Broad Patent Stuns Multimedia Industry."

55. Michael Bednarek, "Compton's New Media's Patent Saga: Lessons for the Software Industry and Others in Emerging Technologies," *Patent World*, February 1995, 29–34.

56. Compton's Learning Company, Compton's Multimedia Encyclopedia, US Copyright Registration TX 0003402533, published January 15, 1990, and registered July 14, 1992.

57. See, e.g., Encyclopaedia Britannica, Britannica CD, US Copyright Registration TX0003977978, published August 25, 1994, and issued September 8, 1994.

58. Michael Reed et al., Multimedia search system using a plurality of entry path means which indicate interrelatedness of information, US Patent 5,241,671, filed October 26, 1989, and issued August 31, 1993, 2.

59. Ibid., 23.

60. Quoted in Bednarek, "Compton's New Media's Patent Saga," 32.

61. Ibid., 30.

62. Harmon, "Granting of Broad Patent Stuns Multimedia Industry."

63. I am grateful to Peggy Kidwell, Curator of Mathematics at the Smithsonian National Museum of American History, for enabling me to study many of these consoles.

64. Ralph Baer, Television gaming apparatus and method, US Patent 3,659,285, filed April 25, 1972, and issued August 21, 1969. See also Ralph Baer, Television gaming and training apparatus, US Patent 3,728,480, filed March 22, 1971, and issued April 17, 1973; Ralph Baer, Method of employing a television receiver for active participation, US Patent RE32,305, filed June 27, 1977, and issued December 16, 1986; and Nintendo of America, Inc. v. Magnavox Co., 707 F. Supp. 717 (S.D. N.Y. 1989).

65. William Clark and Elizabeth Paxto, Interactive method for the effective conveyance of information in the form of visual images, US Patent 5,120,230, filed June 3, 1991, and issued June 9, 1992.

66. Theodore May et al., Curriculum planning and publishing method, US Patent 5,173,051, filed October 15, 1991, and issued December 22, 1992.

67. Rod Turner, quoted in Peter Lewis, "The New Patent That Is Infuriating the Multimedia Industry," *New York Times*, November 28, 1993.

68. Stan Hornyn, quoted in Amy Harmon, "Granting of Broad Patent Stuns Multimedia Industry," *Los Angeles Times*, November 17, 1983.

69. Lewis, "New Patent."

70. Michael Schrage, "Too-Broad Patenting of High Tech Points Up Patent Flaws in System," *Los Angeles Times*, November 18, 1993, D1.

71. James Bessen and Robert Hunt, "An Empirical Look at Software Patents" (FRB of Philadelphia Working Paper No. 3-17, March 2004).

72. Jube Shiver, "Government to Re-Examine Patent Award to Compton's: About-Face Follows Complaints by Software Inventions," *Los Angeles Times*, December 17, 1993.

73. Bednarek, "Compton's New Media's Patent Saga," 30.

74. John Markoff, "Patent Office to Review a Controversial Award," *Los Angeles Times*, December 17, 1993.

75. Ibid.; Bednarek, "Compton's New Media's Patent Saga," 31.

76. Paul Heckel, cited in Markoff, "Patent Office to Review a Controversial Award."

77. Bednarek, "Compton's New Media's Patent Saga."

78. "Patent Barred for Compton's," *New York Times*, October 23, 1994; "Notice of Public Hearings and Request for Comments on Patent Protection for Software-Related Inventions," US Patent and Trademark Office, Docket # 931222-3322, https://www.PTO.gov/web/offices/com/hearings/software/notices/notice94.html.

79. "Notice of Public Hearings and Request for Comments on Patent Protection for Software-Related Inventions."

80. Ibid.

81. "Public Hearing on Patent Protection for Software-Related Inventions," Transcript of Public Hearings, January 26 and 27, 1994, San Jose, CA, US Patent and Trademark Office, 1994.

82. Ibid., 74.

83. Ibid., 81.

84. Quoted in ibid., 78.

85. Ibid., 17.

86. Ibid., 16.

87. Ibid., 40.

88. Ibid.

89. This description is based on my experience playing *Colossal Cave Adventure*.

90. Gordon Irlam and Ross Williams, "Software Patents: An Industry at Risk," January 25, 1994, http://tech-insider.org/free-software/research/acrobat/9401.pdf.

91. Ibid.

92. Mark Brown, Distinguishing nested structures by color, US Patent 4,965,765, filed May 16, 1986, and issued October 23, 1990.

93. Isaac Heizer, Method of and apparatus for operating a client/server computer network, US Patent 5,249,290, filed February 22, 1991, and issued September 28, 1993.

94. Irlam and Williams, "Software Patents."

95. "Public Hearing on Patent Protection for Software-Related Inventions," 72.

96. Ibid.; Richard Stallman, *Free Software, Free Society: Selected Essays of Richard M. Stallman* (Boston: GNU Press, 2006), 40.

97. Donald Knuth to Bruce Lehman, February 23, 1993, https://ia801902.us.archive.org/13/items/DonaldKnuthLetterAgainstSoftwarePatents/donaldKnuthLetterAgainstSoftwarePatents.pdf.

98. In re Grams, 888 F.2d 835 (Fed. Cir. 1989); In re Iwahashi, 888 F.2d 1370 (Fed. Cir. 1989); Arrhythmia Research Technology, Inc. v. Corazonix Corp., 958 F.2d 1053 (Fed. Cir. 1992).

99. In re Abele, 684 F.2d 902 (C.C.P.A. 1982); Manlio Abele and Christopher Marshall, Tomographic scanner, US Patent 4,433,380, filed November 15, 1977, and issued February 21, 1984. See also In re Grams, 888 F.2d 835 (Fed. Cir. 1989).

100. The cases are In re Schrader, 22 F.3d 290 (Fed. Cir. 1994); In re Alappat, 33 F.3d 1526 (Fed. Cir. 1994); In re Warmedam, 33 F.3d 1354 (Fed. Cir. 1994); In re Lowry, 33 F.3d 1579 (Fed. Cir. 1994); and In re Trovato, 42 F.3d 1376 (Fed. Cir. 1994).

101. Richard Stern, "Solving the Algorithm Conundrum: After 1994 in the Federal Circuit Patent Law Needs a Radical Algorithmectomy," *AIPLA Quarterly Journal* 22:2 (Spring 1994): 169.

102. For more on Tektronix, see William Hewlett, "Charles Howard Vollum," in *Memorial Tributes,* vol. 3 (Washington, DC: National Academies Press, 1989), 347–350.

103. *Alappat,* 33 F.3d.

104. Ibid., 1538–1539.

105. Ibid., 1541, emphasis added.

106. Ibid., 1542.

107. Ibid., 1544.

108. Ibid., 1543.

109. Ibid., 1544.

110. Ibid.

111. Diamond v. Chakrabarty, 407 U.S. 303 (1980), cited in Patent and Trademark Office, *Legal Analysis to Support Proposed Examination Guidelines for Computer-Implemented Inventions* (Washington, DC: US Department of Commerce, 1995), 4.

112. "USPTO to Develop Guidelines to Protect Software Inventions," press release PTO 95-18, April 1, 1995, https://www.uspto.gov/about-us/news-updates/uspto-develop-guidelines-protect-software-inventions; Bruce Lehman, cited in "Software Patent Guidelines Released Today," press release PAT 95-21, June 1, 1995, https://www.uspto.gov/about-us/news-updates/software-patent-guidelines-released-today.

113. Patent and Trademark Office, *Legal Analysis,* 1.

114. Ibid.

115. Ibid., 7.

116. Ibid.

117. Ibid., 12.

118. In some cases, examiners could encounter machine claims that involve programs but which are phrased in such broad terms that they encompass any computer or computerized system that can carry out a given process. In such cases, the patent eligibility of the claim would hinge on that of the process. Ibid., 9.

CHAPTER 12. SOFTWARE RIGHTS FOR A NEW MILLENNIUM, 1993–2000

1. Bill Clinton, "Remarks on the Signing the Telecommunications Act of 1996," February 8, 1996, Master Tape #04848–04850, William J. Clinton Presidential Library.

2. For content regulation, see Laura DeNardis, *The Global War for Internet Governance* (New Haven: Yale University Press, 2014).

3. Fred Cate, "The National Information Infrastructure: Policymaking and Policymakers," *Stanford Law and Policy Review* 6:1 (1994): 43–59.

4. Information Infrastructure Task Force, *The National Information Infrastructure: Agenda for Action,* September 15, 1993.

5. Ibid., 3.

6. Ibid., 3–4.

7. Sheila Jasanoff and Sang-Hyun Kim, eds., *Dreamscapes of Modernity: Sociotechnical Imaginaries and the Fabrication of Power* (Chicago: University of Chicago Press, 2015).

8. Samuel Greengard, *The Internet of Things* (Cambridge, MA: MIT Press, 2015).

9. Cate, "National Information Infrastructure," 25.

10. Lois Romano, "The Reliable Source," *Washington Post,* October 2, 1992.

11. Cate, "National Information Infrastructure," 44.

12. Al Gore, "Inauguration of the First World Telecommunication Development Conference," March 21, 1994, http://search.itu.int/history/HistoryDigitalCollectionDocLi brary/4.144.57.en.104.pdf.

13. "Anne K. Bingaman," https://www1.villanova.edu/content/dam/villanova/law/docu ments/forms/academics/Anne_K_Bingaman.pdf.

14. Anne K. Bingaman, "Competition Policy and the Telecommunications Revolution," address before the Networked Economy Conference USA, September 26, 1994, Washington, DC, https://www.justice.gov/atr/file/519416/download.

15. See Andrew I. Gavil and Harry First, *The Microsoft Antitrust Cases: Competition Policy for the Twenty-First Century* (Cambridge, MA: MIT Press, 2014).

16. Mike Mills, "The Competitive Nature of Anne K. Bingaman," *Washington Post*, November 17, 1997.

17. See US v. Microsoft Corp., https://web.archive.org/web/19981201174413/http://www. webcom.com/software/issues/docs-htm/microjud.html.

18. Gavil and First, *Microsoft Antitrust Cases*.

19. Nomination of Bruce Lehman to Be Commissioner of the U.S. Patent and Trademark Office, 100th Cong., 1st Sess., July 28, 1993, 26.

20. Information Infrastructure Task Force, *National Information Infrastructure: Progress Report, 1993–1994* (Washington, DC: GPO, 1994); Information Infrastructure Task Force, *Global Information Infrastructure: Agenda for Cooperation* (Washington, DC: GPO, 1995).

21. *WIPO Worldwide Symposium on the Impact of Digital Technology on Copyright and Neighboring Rights* (Geneva: WIPO, 1993).

22. Ibid., 19.

23. "Overview: The TRIPS Agreement," World Trade Organization, https://www.wto.org/ english/tratop_e/trips_e/intel2_e.htm.

24. Julie Sheinblatt, "The WIPO Copyright Treaty," *Berkeley Technology Law Journal* 13:1 (1998): 535–550.

25. "TRIPS Agreement," World Trade Organization, https://www.wto.org/english/docs_e/ legal_e/27-trips.pdf.

26. "WIPO Worldwide Symposium on the Future of Copyright and Neighboring Rights," *Copyright*, July–August 1994, 153.

27. Bruce A. Lehman, *Intellectual Property and the National Information Infrastructure: The Report of the Working Group on Intellectual Property Rights* (Washington, DC: Information Infrastructure Task Force, 1995), 166–167.

28. Ibid.

29. Digital Performance Right in Sound Recordings Act of 1995, 104th Cong., 1st Sess., November 1, 1995.

30. 35 U.S.C. § 103. See Becca Alley, "The Biotechnology Process Patent Act of 1995: Providing Unresolved and Unrecognized Dilemmas in U.S. Patent Law," *Journal of Intellectual Property Law* 12 (2004): 229–254.

31. NII Copyright Protection Act of 1995, 104th Cong., 1st Sess., November 15, 1995, 2.

32. National Information Infrastructure Copyright Protection Act of 1995, 104th Cong., 2d Sess., May 7, 1996, 49, 109.

33. WIPO Copyright Treaties Implementation Act, 105th Cong., 1st Sess., September 16 and 17, 1997, 84.

34. NII Copyright Protection Act of 1995 Part 2, 104th Cong., 2nd Sess., February 7 and 8, 1996, 234–235.

35. Ibid., 64.

36. National Information Infrastructure Copyright Protection Act of 1995.

37. Ibid., 35.

38. Mihály Ficsor, "Copyright for the Digital Era: The WIPO Internet Treaties," *Columbia Journal of Law and Arts* 21 (1997): 197–223.

39. WIPO Performances and Phonographs Treaty, December 20, 1996, http://www.wipo.int/wipolex/en/treaties/text.jsp?file_id=295578.

40. WIPO Copyright Treaty, December 20, 1996, http://www.wipo.int/treaties/en/text.jsp?file_id=295166.

41. Ibid., Article 18.

42. Digital Millennium Copyright Act, 105th Cong., 2d Sess., October 28, 1998.

43. WIPO Copyright Treaties Implementation Act.

44. See Jessica Litman, *Digital Copyright* (New York: Prometheus Books, 2006).

45. Pamela Samuelson, "Anticircumvention Rules: Threat to Science," *Science* 293:5537 (2001): 2028–2031.

46. This is based on James Bessen and Robert Hunt, "An Empirical Look at Software Patents" (FRB of Philadelphia Working Paper No. 3-17, March 2004), reported in James Bessen and Robert Hunt, "An Empirical Look at Software Patents," *Journal of Economic and Management Strategy* 16:1 (2007): 157–189. See also James Bessen and Michael J. Maurer, *Patent Failure: How Judges, Bureaucrats, and Lawyers Put Innovators at Risk* (Princeton, NJ: Princeton University Press, 2008). For IBM's consent decree, see Peter Passell, "I.B.M and the Limits of a Consent Decree," *New York Times,* June 9, 1994; Bart Ziegler, "IBM Reaches Settlement to End Consent Decree," *Wall Street Journal,* July 3, 1996; and David Lazarus, "Judge to IBM: It's Not 1956 Anymore," *Wired,* May 2, 1997.

47. Jeffrey R. Yost, *Making IT Work: A History of the Computer Services Industry* (Cambridge, MA: MIT Press, 2017), 231–272.

48. Gregory A. Stobbs, *Business Method Patents* (New York: Aspen, 2008), 137–231.

49. See, e.g., Gerhard Dirks, Data handling system, US Patent 3,343,133, filed August 9, 1963, and issued September 19, 1967.

50. Joseph Francini, Transaction card with magnetic stripe emulator, US Patent 4,701,601, filed April 26, 1985, and issued October 20, 1987; Catherine Michels, Transaction card, US Design Patent 310,386, filed August 7, 1987, and issued September 4, 1990; Victor Monia, Method for making a magnetic transducer head cleaning card, US Patent 4,734,145, filed September 22, 1986, and issued March 29, 1988.

51. See, e.g., Carl Campbell, Key management system for on-line communication, US Patent 4,605,820, filed November 10, 1983, and issued August 12, 1986; Roger Peirce, Loss control system, US Patent 4,485,300, filed March 18, 1982, and issued November 27, 1984; Howard Zeidler, End-to-end encryption system and method of operation, US Patent 4,578,530, filed December 7, 1983, and issued March 25, 1986; Einar Asbo, Method and apparatus for dynamic signature verification, US Patent 4,646,351, filed October 4, 1985, and issued February 24, 1987; and Wyner Spencer, Usage promotion method for payment card transaction system, US Patent 4,906,826, filed September 19, 1988, and issued March 6, 1990.

52. Stephen Langhans, Lawrence Goodman, and Sigman Shapiro, Automatic purchasing control system, US Patent 5,550,513, filed May 11, 1994, and issued March 19, 1996. See also Stobbs, *Business Method Patents*, 37.

53. Lawrence et al., Automatic purchasing control system, 17.

54. Ibid., 3.

55. William Lutz, John Wright, Noel Moss, and Richard Delia, Travelers cheque transaction terminal, US Patent 5,023,782, filed March 26, 1990, and issued June 11, 1991.

56. See, e.g., Edward Hogan, System and method for conducting cashless transactions, US Patent 5,557,516, filed February 4, 1994, and issued September 17, 1996; Constance Kling, System and method for processing multiple electronic transaction requests, US Patent 5,878,215, filed May 23, 1994, and issued March 2, 1999; Edward Hogan, System and method for conducting cashless transactions on a computer network, US Patent 5,692,132, filed June 7, 1995, and issued November 25, 1997; and Edward Hogan, System and method for bill delivery and payment over a communications network, US Patent 5,699,528, filed October 31, 1995, and issued December 16, 1997.

57. Hogan, System and method for conducting cashless transactions.

58. Ibid., 15.

59. MasterCard v. Meridian Enterprises Corp., No. C94-4105 DRD (D.N.J., filed August 24, 1994).

60. James Burton and Daniel Henke, System and method for administration of incentive award program through the use of credit, US Patent 5,025,372, filed September 25, 1989, and issued June 18, 1991.

61. This is based on my analysis of the information available through PACER and PAIR.

62. R. Todd Boes, Data processing system for hub and spoke financial services configuration, US Patent 5,193,056, filed March 11, 1991, and issued March 9, 1993.

63. This description of the investment structure's benefits and drawbacks is based on Stobbs, *Business Method Patents*, 11.

64. Ibid.

65. Quoted in Boes, Data processing system for hub and spoke financial services configuration, 13.

66. This identifying information about State Street is drawn from Stobbs, *Business Method Patents*, 10.

67. State Street Bank & Trust Co. v. Signature Financial Group, Inc., 927 F. Supp. 502 (D. Mass. 1996), 506.

68. Brief Amicus Curiae Visa International Service Association and Mastercard International Incorporated, State Street Bank & Trust Co. v. Signature Financial Group, Inc., 94-CV-10625, October 7, 1996.

69. Ibid., 1.

70. Ibid., 2.

71. Ibid.

72. Brief Amicus Curiae Information Industry Council, State Street Bank & Trust Co. v. Signature Financial Group, Inc., 94-CV-10625, 1.

73. Brad Stone, *The Everything Store: Jeff Bezos and the Age of Amazon* (New York: Little, Brown, 2013).

74. Jeff Bezos, Secure method for communicating credit card data when placing an order on a non-secure network, US Patent 5,727,163, filed March 30, 1995, and issued March 10, 1998.

75. See, e.g., Jeffrey Bezos, Internet-based customer referral system, US Patent 6,029,141, filed June 27, 1997, and issued February 22, 2000; John Bair, Method and apparatus for producing sequenced queries, US Patent 5,999,924, filed July 25, 1997, and issued December 7, 1999; and Peri Hartman and Joel Spiegel, Method and system for placing a purchase order via a communications network, US Patent 5,960,411, filed September 12, 1997, and issued September 28, 1999.

76. State Street Bank & Trust Co. v. Signature Financial Group, Inc., 149 F.3d 1368 (Fed. Cir. 1998).

77. Ibid., 1373.

78. AT&T Corp. v. Excel Communications, Inc., 172 F.3d 1352 (Fed. Cir. 1999).

CONCLUSION

1. Alice Corp. v. CLS Bank Int'l., No. 13-298 (S. Ct. 2014).

2. Loyalty Conversion Sys. Corp. v. American Airlines, Inc., No. 2:13-cv-655 (E.D. Tex. 2015).

3. Steven Seidenberg, "Business-Method and Software May Go through the Looking Glass after Alice Decision," February 1, 2015, http://www.abajournal.com/magazine/article/business_method_and_software_patents_may_go_through_the_looking_glass_after/.

4. Rather than quoting law firms' pages directly, I offer here a summary of the viewpoints that I have encountered online. I do this to avoid disseminating what they may consider to be legal advice specific to their firms. I accessed the sites by browsing through several pages of Google search results for the phrase "drafting patents after Alice."

5. In this sense, this work adds a legal dimension to the argument found in Joy Lisi Rankin, *A People's History of Computing in the United States* (Cambridge, MA: Harvard University Press, 2018).

6. A recent treatment of this subject is found in Christopher J. Tozzi, *For Fun and Profit: A History of the Free and Open Source Software Revolution* (Cambridge, MA: MIT Press, 2017). See also Christopher M. Kelty, *Two Bits: The Cultural Meaning of Free Software* (Durham, NC: Duke University Press, 2008).

7. Naomi Lamoreaux, Kenneth Sokoloff, and Dhanoos Sutthiphisal, "Patent Alchemy: The Market for Technology in US History," *Business History Review* 87 (2013): 3–38; Christopher Beauchamp, "The First Patent Litigation Explosion," *Yale Law Journal* 125:4 (2016): 796–1149.

8. See, e.g., James Bessen and Michael J. Meurer, *Patent Failure: How Judges, Bureaucrats, and Lawyers Put Innovators at Risk* (Princeton, NJ: Princeton University Press, 2008); James Bessen and Robert Hunt, "An Empirical Look at Software Patents," *Journal of Economics and Management Strategy* 16:1 (2007): 157–189; Ben Klemens, *Math You Can't Use: Patents, Copyright, and Software* (Washington, DC: Brookings Institution Press,

2006); Robert Hahn and Scott Walls, "A Review of Bessen and Hunt's Analysis of Software, Patents" (November 2003), https://ssrn.com/abstract=467484; and Knut Blind, Jakob Edler, and Michael Friedewald, *Software Patents: Economic Impacts and Policy Implications* (Surrey, UK: Edward Elgar, 1995).

9. US Patent and Trademark Office, *Manual of Patent Examining Procedure*, "2106 Patent Subject Matter Eligibility [R-08.2017]," https://www.uspto.gov/web/offices/pac/mpep/s2106.html.

10. See Daniel J. Kevles, "Ananda Chakrabarty Wins a Patent: Biotechnology, Law, and Society," *Historical Studies of the Physical and Biological Sciences* 25:1 (1994): 111–135; Tal Golan, *Laws of Men and Laws of Nature: The History of Scientific Expert Testimony in England and America* (Cambridge, MA: Harvard University Press, 2004); Sheila Jasanoff, ed., *States of Knowledge: The Co-Production of Science and the Social Order* (New York: Routledge, 2004); and Adrian Johns, *Piracy: The Intellectual Property Wars from Gutenberg to Gates* (Chicago: University of Chicago Press, 2009).

11. See D. Graham Burnett, *Trying Leviathan: The Nineteenth-Century New York Court Case That Put the Whale on Trial and Challenged the Order of Nature* (Princeton, NJ: Princeton University Press, 2010); Paul Lombardo, *Three Generations, No Imbeciles: Eugenics, the Supreme Court, and Buck v. Bell* (Baltimore: Johns Hopkins University Press, 2010); Christopher Beauchamp, *Invented by Law: Alexander Graham Bell and the Patent That Changed America* (Cambridge, MA: Harvard University Press, 2015); Ian Burney, *Poison Detection and the Victorian Imagination* (Manchester, UK: Manchester University Press, 2012); Ian Burney, *Bodies of Evidence: Medicine and the Politics of the English Inquest, 1830–1926* (Baltimore: Johns Hopkins University Press, 2002); Daniel J. Kevles, *The Baltimore Case: A Trial of Politics, Science, and Character* (New York: W. W. Norton, 2000); Leslie J. Reagan, *When Abortion Was a Crime: Women, Medicine, and Law in the United States, 1867–1973* (Berkeley: University of California Press, 1997).

12. Scholars such as Kara Swanson, Joseph Gabriel, Naomi Lamoreaux, and Daniel Kevles have long embraced this legal-historical project, which continues to gain momentum in legal scholarship more broadly conceived. See Kali Murray, "A Welcome Conversation: Toward a New Historiography of Intellectual Property," *Law and Social Inquiry* 43:3 (2018): 1113–1129.

13. See, e.g., Shobita Parthasarathy, *Patent Politics: Life Forms, Markets, and the Public Interest in the United States and Europe* (Chicago: University of Chicago Press, 2017); Joseph M. Gabriel, *Medical Monopoly: Intellectual Property Rights and the Origins of the Modern Pharmaceutical Industry* (Chicago: University of Chicago Press, 2014); Catherine L. Fisk, *Working Knowledge: Employee Innovation and the Rise of Corporate Intellectual Property, 1800–1930*; Steven W. Usselman, *Regulating Railroad Innovation: Business, Technology, and Politics in America, 1840–1920* (New York: Cambridge University Press, 2002); Jeremy Greene, *Generic: The Unbranding of Modern Medicine* (Baltimore: Johns Hopkins University Press, 2014); Richard John, *Network Nation: Inventing American Telecommunications* (Cambridge, MA: Harvard University Press, 2010); Chris Beauchamp, *Invented by Law: Alexander Graham Bell and the Patent That Changed America* (Cambridge, MA: Harvard University Press, 2015); Stathis Araposthathis and Graeme Gooday, *Patently Contestable: Electrical Technologies and Inventor Identities on Trial in Britain* (Cambridge, MA: MIT Press, 2013); Adrian Johns, *Piracy: The Intellectual Property Wars from Gutenberg to Gates* (Chicago: University of Chicago Press, 2010).

14. These records are held at the National Archives in Kansas City, MO, College Park, MD, and Washington, DC; the Charles Babbage Institute, University of Minnesota, Minneapolis; the Hagley Museum and Library, Wilmington, Delaware; and federal repositories across the country. See Gerardo Con Díaz, "Antitrust at CBI: Engaging with the Archival Holdings on *US v. IBM*," *CBI Newsletter* 37:1 (2015): 19–20. A very useful volume for archival work on *U.S. v. IBM* is Franklin M. Fisher, James W. McKie, and Richard B. Mancke, *IBM and the U.S. Data Processing Industry: An Economic History* (New York: Praeger, 1983).

15. In this sense, the study of software IP offers a new way of answering Mike Mahoney's pioneering call for finding the place of computing in the history of technology. Michael S. Mahoney, "The History of Computing in the History of Technology," *IEEE Annals of the History of Computing* 10:2 (1998): 113–125.

16. Foundational business histories of computing focus primarily on technological and commercial change. See Martin Campbell-Kelly, *From Airline Reservations to Sonic the Hedgehog: A History of the Software Industry* (Cambridge, MA: MIT Press, 2003); Paul E. Ceruzzi, *A History of Modern Computing*, 2nd ed. (Cambridge, MA: MIT Press, 2003); Martin Campbell-Kelly et al., *Computer: A History of the Information Machine*, 3rd ed. (Boulder, CO: Westview Press, 2013); Jeffrey R. Yost, *The Computer Industry* (Westport, CT: Greenwood Press, 2005); and Emerson Pugh, *Building IBM: Shaping an Industry and Its Technology* (Cambridge, MA: MIT Press, 2009).

17. Eden Medina, *Cybernetic Revolutionaries: Technology and Politics in Allende's Chile* (Cambridge, MA: MIT Press, 2011); Rebecca Slayton, *Arguments That Count: Physics, Computing, and Missile Defense, 1949–2012* (Cambridge, MA: MIT Press, 2013); Elizabeth R. Petrick, *Making Computers Accessible: Disability Rights and Digital Technology* (Baltimore: Johns Hopkins University Press, 2015); Paul N. Edwards, *The Closed World: Computers and the Politics of Discourse in Cold War America* (Cambridge, MA: MIT Press, 1996); Paul N. Edwards, *A Vast Machine: Computer Models, Climate Data, and the Politics of Global Warming* (Cambridge, MA: MIT Press, 2010); Andrew L. Russell, *Open Standards and the Digital Age* (New York: Cambridge University Press, 2014).

18. Laura DeNardis, *The Global War for Internet Governance* (New Haven: Yale University Press, 2014); Shane Greenstein, *How the Internet Became Commercial: Innovation, Privatization, and the Birth of a New Network* (Princeton, NJ: Princeton University Press, 2015).

19. Rankin, *People's History of Computing;* Jeffrey R. Yost, *Making IT Work: A History of the Computer Services Industry* (Cambridge, MA: MIT Press, 2017); Marie Hicks, *Programmed Inequality: How Britain Discarded Women Technologists and Lost Its Edge in Computing* (Cambridge, MA: MIT Press, 2017); Janet Abbate, *Recoding Gender: Women's Participation in Computing* (Cambridge, MA: MIT Press, 2012); Nathan Ensmenger, *The Computer Boys Take Over: Computers, Programmers, and the Politics of Technical Expertise* (Cambridge, MA: MIT Press, 2010); Petrick, *Making Computers Accessible;* Russell, *Open Standards and the Digital Age.*

20. Andrew I. Gavil and Harry First, *The Microsoft Antitrust Cases: Competition for the Twenty-First Century* (Cambridge, MA: MIT Press, 2014).

21. Rankin, *People's History of Computing;* Hicks, *Programmed Inequality;* Margot Lee Shetterly, *Hidden Figures: The American Dream and the Untold Story of the Black Women Mathematicians Who Helped Win the Space Race* (New York: William Morrow, 2016);

Abbate, *Recoding Gender*; Safiya Umoja Noble, *Algorithms of Oppression: How Search Engines Reinforce Racism* (New York: NYU Press, 2018); Virginia Eubanks, *Automating Inequality: How High-Tech Tools Profile, Police, and Punish the Poor* (New York: St. Martin's Press, 2017).

22. Shannon Mattern, *Code and Clay, Data and Dirt: Five Thousand Years of Urban Media* (Minneapolis: University of Minnesota Press, 2015); Sean Cubbitt, *Finite Media: Environmental Implications of Digital Technologies* (Durham, NC: Duke University Press, 2017); Nathan Ensmenger and Rebecca Slayton, eds., *Computing and the Environment*, Special Issue of *Information and Culture* 52:3 (2017); Nathan Ensmenger, "Dirty Bits: Environmental History of the Computer" (work in progress).

Index

An italicized page number indicates a figure.

343